Studies in modern capitalism • Etudes sur le capitalisme moderne

Tunisian peasants in the eighteenth and nineteenth centuries

Studies in modern capitalism • Etudes sur le capitalisme moderne

This series is devoted to an attempt to comprehend capitalism as a world-system. It will include monographs, collections of essays and colloquia around specific themes, written by historians and social scientists united by a common concern for the study of large-scale, long-term social structure and social change.

The series is a joint enterprise of the Maison des Sciences de l'Homme in Paris and the Fernand Braudel Center for the Study of Economies, Historical Systems, and Civilizations at the State University of New York at Binghamton.

Other books in the series

Maurice Aymard (ed.): *Dutch capitalism and world capitalism/Capitalisme hollandais et capitalisme mondial*
Iván T. Berend, György Ránki: *The European periphery and industrialization, 1780–1914*
Pierre Bourdieu: *Algeria 1960*
Andre Gunder Frank: *Mexican agriculture 1521-1630: transformation of the mode of production*
Folker Fröbel, Jürgen Heinrichs, Otto Kreye: *The new international division of labour: structural unemployment in industrialised countries and industrialisation in developing countries*
Caglar Keyder: *The definition of a peripheral economy: Turkey 1923–1929*
Peter Kriedte, Hans Medick, Jürgen Schlumbohm: *Industrialization before industrialization: rural industry in the genesis of capitalism*
Bruce McGowan: *Economic life in Ottoman Europe: taxation, trade and the struggle for the land, 1660-1800*
Ernest Mandel: *Long waves of capitalist development: the Marxist interpretation*
Michel Morineau: *Incroyables gazettes et fabuleux métaux: les retours des trésors américains, d'après les gazettes hollandaises (XVIe–XVIIIe siècles)*
Henri H. Stahl: *Traditional Romanian village communities: the transition from the communal to the capitalist mode of production in the Danube region*
Immanuel Wallerstein: *The capitalist world-economy: essays*
Immanuel Wallerstein: *The politics of the world-economy: the states, the movements and the civilizations*

This book is published as part of the joint publishing agreement established in 1977 between the Fondation de la Maison des Sciences de l'Homme and the Press Syndicate of the University of Cambridge. Titles published under this arrangement may appear in any European language or, in the case of volumes of collected essays, in several languages.

New books will appear either as individual titles or in one of the series which the Maison des Sciences de l'Homme and the Cambridge University Press have jointly agreed to publish. All books published jointly by the Maison des Sciences de l'Homme and the Cambridge University Press will be distributed by the Press throughout the world.

Tunisian peasants in the eighteenth and nineteenth centuries

LUCETTE VALENSI
École des Hautes Études en Sciences Sociales, Paris

Translated by Beth Archer

The right of the University of Cambridge to print and sell all manner of books was granted by Henry VIII in 1534. The University has printed and published continuously since 1584.

Cambridge University Press

Cambridge
London New York New Rochelle Melbourne Sydney

& Editions de la Maison des Sciences de l'Homme
Paris

CAMBRIDGE UNIVERSITY PRESS
Cambridge, New York, Melbourne, Madrid, Cape Town, Singapore, São Paulo, Delhi

Cambridge University Press
The Edinburgh Building, Cambridge CB2 8RU, UK

With Editions de la Maison des Sciences de l'Homme
54 Boulevard Raspail, 75270 Paris Cedex 06, France

Published in the United States of America by Cambridge University Press, New York

www.cambridge.org
Information on this title: www.cambridge.org/9780521109017

Originally published in French as *Fellahs tunisiens: L'économie rurale et la vie des campagnes aux 18e et 19e siècles* by Mouton & Co. and École des Hautes Études en Science Sociales in 1977

English translation first published in 1985

This digitally printed version 2009

A catalogue record for this publication is available from the British Library

Library of Congress Cataloguing in Publication data

Valensi, Lucette.

Tunisian peasants in the eighteenth and nineteenth
centuries.

(Studies in modern capitalism = Etudes sur le
capitalisme moderne)

Translation of: Fellahs tunisiens.

Bibliography: p.

Includes index.

1. Peasantry – Tunisia – History. 2. Agriculture –
Economic aspects – Tunisia – History. 3. Tunisia – Rural
conditions. 4. Tunisia – Population – History. I. Title.
II. Series: Studies in modern capitalism.
HN784.A8V3513 1985 305.5′63 84-29206

ISBN 978-0-521-25558-5 hardback
ISBN 978-0-521-10901-7 paperback

Contents

Figures, maps and tables

Figures

Maps

Tables

Introduction

The origin of this study of Tunisian peasantry before colonization has to be placed within the context of an event, or a series of events. For when I began this work Tunisia and Morocco had just achieved their independence. War was raging in Algeria. Those years of *histoire chaude* revealed fundamental realities in all three countries that had long been disguised by the *pax gallica*: among these revelations were that the peasants, the people – until then ignored and despised – had been the silent guardians of their culture, "The National Library" of North Africa (in the felicitous expression of an Algerian writer) and that the interior, considered backward and ignorant, had kept alive more than anachronistic values. Once independence was obtained, the burdensome heritage of underdevelopment remained, along with the ever-present question of how to overcome it. Historians, as well as everyone else, asked, Why such poverty, why such dependency?

I had just come out of the Faculté des lettres et sciences humaines in Paris, where I had studied history. The notion of "kings and battles" was under constant attack. The concept of *l'événementiel*, denoting political and diplomatic history, was universally condemned, however one pronounced it. Economics and history took over its terrain. Ernest Labrousse introduced us to economic history, initiating us into the study of demographic and economic fluctuations, the history of prices, and the construction of a model for the economy of the ancien régime in France. As for social history, after Marc Bloch's death, historians remained faithful to him and his works became our gospel. Demography discreetly made its way into the Sorbonne with an optional and introductory course by Marcel Reinhardt. Thanks to junior faculty and to the "extracurricular" questions that cropped up in our oral examinations, we learned about the existence of pioneering reviews (*Annales*), important books (Braudel on the Mediterranean), and research in progress, particularly that of Pierre Goubert and Pierre Vilar.

Armed with the instruments of research and interpretation forged by these historians, we set out to conquer new lands in history, to plow new fields. For me, it was to be precolonial Tunisia, with the mid-nineteenth century as my ultimate destination. The later period had become known through the work of Jean Ganiage, Jean Poncet, and the geographers. Had there been archives, I would unhesitatingly have chosen the sixteenth century as my starting point and taken up where Robert Brunschvig left off – at the arrival of the Turks. But sources were lacking up to the very end of the seventeenth century. Chance thus determined my chronological framework and obliged me to begin in the eighteenth century. There were, in fact, other reasons for this choice. The seventeenth century, as related by Ibn Abi Dinār Al Qairawāni or Paul Lucas (1712), had witnessed a series of massacres and internecine struggles. By comparison, the eighteenth and nineteenth centuries enjoyed relative stability. To begin with, the Husaynite dynasty, founded in 1705 by Husayn Ibn Ali, remained in power until the twentieth century. It is true that there was no dearth of conflicts within the reigning family, the first among them having caused serious consequences for the entire country: From 1729 to 1740 a civil war bloodied the land. Ali Pāsha, nephew of Bey Husayn, thought he would succeed him to the throne. However, he was eliminated from the succession when the bey fathered his first son. Ali Pāsha's rebellion, supported by Algeria, completely divided the country. Bey Husayn, under long siege in Kairouan, was finally vanquished and replaced by Ali Pāsha. His reign (1740–56) was in turn agitated by the revolt of his son, Yūnis, in 1752. But the rest of the regency remained unaffected by it. In 1756 the Algerian army invaded Tunisia, devastated the capital, returned to power the sons of the first bey of the dynasty – Muhammad (1756–9) and Ali Bey (1759–82) – and forced them to pay a tribute. This episode, though very serious, was similarly localized and brief, as was the revolt of Yūnis's son Ismā'īl between 1759 and 1762.

As for foreign relations during this period, French naval demonstrations in 1728, 1731, and 1770, followed by a Venetian naval engagement in 1784, were limited to a few shellings without major damage. In 1741 Yūnis recaptured the island of Tabarka from the Genoese, who had been exploiting it since 1540. The war with Algeria, which lasted from 1807 to 1813, had no significant effect on Tunisia. On the whole, the eighteenth century seems to have been a period during which the country was spared both foreign and domestic upheavals, despite the dynastic struggles. The power of the bey took root and gained strength, reaching its apogee with the reign of Bey Hammūda, the son of Ali Bey, who governed from 1782 to 1814.

In contrast, the end of the Napoleonic Wars and the reestablishment of peace in Europe altered the balance of power between Western countries and the entire Muslim Mediterranean. Tunisia, like other parts of the Ottoman Empire, and later Morocco, was subjected to ever greater European domination. But at least within the country, the succession of sovereigns (unlike Algeria and Morocco) took place smoothly, and their control over the country remained unchallenged. Othman, the son of Hammūda Bey, reigned three months in 1814, followed by his brother Mahmūd Bey (1814–24). The throne then passed to Mahmūd's sons, Husayn Bey (1824–35) and Mustapha (1835–37). The next sovereign, Ahmad Bey (1837–55), tried in vain, under pressure from the outside, to strengthen his army and modernize the country. The effect of his failures on the country, the equally disastrous attempts of his successors to resist the European intrusion and to restore or reform the political and fiscal systems, the reactions of the population – all these factors were already present in the process of alienation that I propose to describe.

Since the only political regime during the entire period under study was undisputed by internal or external crises, I had before me a chronological framework ideally suited to examination. And since the geopolitical framework also remained unchanged during this time, the overall conditions were favorable to analysis.

Tunisia, with approximately 155,000 square kilometers, a large part of which is barren, is comparatively tiny. Morocco today is two and a half times as large, and Algeria, admittedly with its uninhabitable Sahara, is fourteen times larger. Tunisia is a particularly homogeneous territory. The Berber language and the institutions that prevail in Berber-speaking regions have receded to the outer limits of the country and are restricted to the jabals of the south and the island of Jerba, or to such inaccessible mountain reaches as Jabal Waslāt. This tiny kingdom is therefore relatively easy to encompass, though part of the much larger geographic, political, and cultural spheres of the Maghreb, the Ottoman Empire, and the Arabic-speaking and Muslim world color any interpretation of Tunisia.

There was no dearth of documentary material, and the voluminous archives of the Tunisian government looked very promising. Historical "fieldwork" was thus begun in the government archives, pursued in the Mediterranean ports with which Tunisia had commercial relations – Marseille, Leghorn, Venice, Valetta – and continued in Paris, where not only consular and commercial correspondence had been preserved, but above all, the first systematic investigations of the different regions and tribes of the country, undertaken by the French army at the beginning of the protectorate.

Elaboration of the empirical data required similar methodological displacements. I had first planned a decidedly serial and quantitative history. This soon appeared impossible. It is not enough to raise the right questions for a research project; one must also find the means to answer them. Thorough examination of hundreds of ledgers for the purpose of reconstructing price curves resulted in impure, heterogeneous, and largely unacceptable material. In the account books of the state, when prices were indicated, the volume of merchandise was missing. Or else, dissimilar commodities appeared together under a global figure. In the case of payments in kind, it was impossible to determine whether they were in toto, which made reconstruction of any system of accounting completely arbitrary. Scribes had the habit of mixing categories. Charitable contributions, funeral expenses, or the cost of clothing were listed in the same column as the purchase of foodstuffs for the Bardo. Data concerning primary commodities are buried in the mass of all the others. There is also a confusion of wholesale and retail, market prices, those paid by the bey, and so on. It was similarly impossible to reconstruct fluctuations in population or land rent, which accounts for the consistently fragmentary, often descriptive, character of the results obtained and the hypotheses that take the place of conclusions.

This direction consequently led to a dead end. Instruments of measurement provide a tool that is not adaptable to all societies. In an economy in which self-subsistence and nonmonetary exchange play an important role, market prices do not have the same meaning as in distinctly market economies. Salary scales make no sense where manpower is not a commodity, any more than measurements of productivity are applicable where a domestic organization of production prevails. In other words, figures allow one only to measure performance, and thus to compare it in time and space. But it is no more than a symptom, and like a fever curve, it says little about the anatomy or physiology of the subject under scrutiny.

Since those traces visible on the surface proved insufficient, it became necessary to take a comprehensive view of Tunisian society, to open up its structures and analyze the relationships between its constituent parts. This goal sent me back to the definition of a social and economic formation. The initial answer seemed to suggest that I was dealing with a pre- or noncapitalist system: in which case, a feudal society. Let us not blame – or at least not exclusively – the Marxism of the time and its paradigm of the unilinear development of societies for this simplistic view. Even outside that school little else was discussed, and recently the most well-informed historians who queried me on precolonial North Africa continued to ask the question that contained its own reply: "Was it not a feudal society?" I therefore looked for serfs, feudal landlords, a weak political power, fragmented for the benefit of the landlords, and so on. If one wished, such things could be found. *Khammās* could be disguised as serfs, caids as feudal barons, and the substance of the whole structure ultimately juggled away.

In the 1960s, discussions regarding the concept of modes of production turned the model of the 1930s upside down. The publication and introduction by Eric Hobsbawm, in 1964, of texts by Marx on precapitalist formations and their translation into French in 1967 and 1970, although not providing answers, at least made it possible to discard false solutions, allowed for a more rigorous and comprehensive definition of modes of production, and encouraged new interpretations. I was unaware at the time of the debates that were taking place among economic anthropologists over Karl Polanyi's propositions. My belated reading of those important works provided me with a confirmation of the analyses I had obtained.

This set of problems required the modification and multiplication of investigative methods and the use of various techniques that may seem somewhat syncretic to a historian of the Western world. It became necessary to go beyond the chronological limits originally set, adopting instead the regressive method dear to Marc Bloch, and when the past turned out to be too reticent, to question the present. For an understanding of the past, direct fieldwork was required, as well as the kind of information to be found in geographic and ethnological publications. It also became necessary to go beyond the boundaries of history, if history has any, and to study from within the functioning of that society. Instead of thinking *about fellahs*, I began thinking in their language. Such developments as the organization of the tribe, agrarian traditions, and food habits may fall under the rubric of ethnology. But if one wishes to concentrate on structures, permanent features, and endlessly repeated formulas, these procedures become indispensable. With regard to rural history, I still consider them legitimate.

Admittedly, the ultimate result is a phenomenological description rather than a formalized elaboration. What I am proposing is a factual history in which epidemics, plants, and tools have replaced the events of our history books. If a theory of underdevelopment is yet to be evolved, this picture of the Tunisian countryside should at least provide the rudiments for an explanation of the Maghreb's paralysis.

This presentation follows two paths. The first, the synchronic, stresses the inhabitants, then the economy and the material culture. The second, the diachronic, studies the Tunisian countryside in terms of its relations, on the one hand, with the central government and, on the other, with the other provinces of the Mediterranean basin.

Part I

"Families coming from the same stock..."

Peyssonnel, eighteenth century

1. Population: size, distribution, and migratory movements

The people, their number, their geographic distribution, and the relationship between them and the lands they occupy constitute the first symptom of the social conditions of production. As to their number, that is very hard to determine. Tunisia had no bureau of vital statistics until 1912, and no general census was conducted until 1921. The results of that first census were incomplete and questionable by virtue of its having been the first.

As of 1856, however, there was a systematic count of adult males when the head tax was restored. That survey provides a figure for the end of the period under present study: Around 1860 the population of Tunisia barely exceeded one million inhabitants. Although lower than estimates of contemporaries, this figure, established by Ganiage, is nonetheless perfectly acceptable.[1]

Earlier than that, we must make do with contemporary records, scanty for the eighteenth century, increasingly numerous for more recent periods, but always lacking a statistical basis and thus unreliable. Tunisia would appear to have had a population of two million during the first half of the nineteenth century, a higher number at the end of the eighteenth century and the early years of the nineteenth: between two and one-half and five million, according to MacGill, Frank, and Nyssen. While these figures are not acceptable as such, they do show, at the very least, that no demographic progress was seen by contemporaries during the nineteenth century; quite the contrary. In the same way, their estimations of the population of the capital – which like the preceding are products of suppositions and not of census takings – do not point to a vigorous development.

We shall return later to the subject of growth and the periodicity of demographic crises that Tunisia underwent (see chap. 6). For the moment, it is enough to remember that with a population of one million inhabitants, the average density was barely ten inhabitants per square kilometer; twice that number if, during a period of prosperity, the population increased to two million. This is a very low figure, if according to Fernand Braudel, between 1300 and 1800 the kilometric density of the favorable zones of the earth varied between 19 and 47.5.

Situating the groups

The urban population was small, nomadic groups were more numerous than sedentary ones, and the different regions were not equally populated.

There is considerable difficulty in trying to establish a list of the cities of precolonial Tunisia. How does one determine a city? Quantitative criteria are inadequate. There was no dearth of agglomerations numbering a few thousand inhabitants covering a vast area, but these were not cities. Kalaa Kebira, which numbered 7,000 inhabitants around the middle of the nineteenth century, Kalaa Serira, Ksour Essaf, and Ksar Hellal, whose population was around 3,000 or 4,000, and other agglomerations of the Sahel were purely and simply villages. Conversely, centers of lesser dimensions and sparser population were tantamount to cities. Along with quantitative criteria, morphological data must be taken into consideration (architectural whole, fortified walls, buildings for trade and manufacture) as well as functional criteria. A city, in short, was a place where administrative, religious, and commercial activities were concentrated at the same time as ethnic and social diversity converged.

In fact, a combination of these three factors is still not enough. A city was less distinguishable by its urban characteristics than by its position within a network. Each sector of activity was organized according to a hierarchy in which the city stood at the top – which is suggested by the term urban "center." Thus in the domain of religion, each sedentary group had its mosque, *masjid*, but the Friday mosque, *jāmi*ʿ, indicated a higher degree of social order. The elementary school, *kuttāb*, was found down to the level of the *dawār*, the tent village, but the *madrasa* (religious college) required an infrastructure and a staff that went beyond the needs and means of a primary social organism. As to the university, it existed only in Tunis. In the same way, in the economic sector, although cottage artisanry could be active in the city as well as in the country, only the city could support an entire body of trades grouped in particular quarters or streets. By thus breaking down each activity into its simplest elements, one can construct a table that on the one hand designates cities and on the other sanctions their classification (Table 1.1).

This table is insufficient for it does not take into account the likely changes that took place in the eighteenth and nineteenth centuries. It indicates only the broader characteristics and remains incomplete because information is lacking. It nonetheless makes possible certain affirmations: fifteen agglomerations were clearly urban – Tunis, Kairouan, Sousse, Sfax, Bizerte, Béja, Gabès, Nabeul, Monastir, Mahdia, Gafsa,

Table 1.1. *Hierarchy of Tunisian agglomerations*

	Designated a city	Presence of Turks	Presence of Jews	Male crafts	Administrative center	Walls	Fortress	Permanent bazaar	Jāmiʿ	Madrasa	Public baths	Caravanserai	University	Periodic market	Population in the 1860s (in thousands)
Tunis	+	+	+	+	+	+	+	+	+	+	+	+	+		80
Kairouan	+	+	+	+		+	+	+	+		+	+			15
Sfax	+	+	+	+	+	+	+	+	+	+	+	+			10
Sousse	+	+	+	+	+	+	+	+	+	+	+	+			8
Béja	+	+	+	+	+	+	+			+	+			+	2–3
Bizerte	+	+	+	+	+	+	+	+							5
Gabès (Menzel + Jara)	+	+	+	+		+	+	+	+	+					4.5
Mahdia	+	+	+	+	+	+	+		+		+	+			4
Monastir	+	+	+		+	+	+				+	+			4
Nabeul	+	+	+	+	+			+		+	+		+		4
Le Kef	+	+	+	+	+	+		+		+					3
Porto Farina	+	+	+	+	+		+								
Gafsa	+	+	+	+		+	+	+	+						3
Hammamet	+	+	+	+		+	+								2
El Hamma de Gabès	+	+	+				+								
Tozeur	+			+	+			+							8
Zaghouan	+	+	+	+	+			+	+		+				
Mateur	+		+		+			+			+			+	1.6
Testour	+	+	+	+					+					+	2–3
Tebourba	+		+	+										+	2–3
Soliman	+		+	+					+					+	
Téboursouk	+				+	+									2–3
Nefta	+			+		+									8

Tozeur, Porto Farina, Le Kef, and Zaghouan.* Beyond this, with Tebourba, Téboursouk, and El Hamma, a zone of uncertainty begins. Was Téboursouk really a city? It was indeed walled and was the seat of a fiscal district, but its population was homogeneous from an ethnic and religious viewpoint, as well as an economic one. Contemporaries called it a city. A number of similar centers were also lacking in certain urban characteristics. Other agglomerations were simply markets with no other urban qualifications. In the Sahel, Moknine, with 5,000 inhabitants, among them many Jews, a permanent market, and a specialized artisanry, had neither the other characteristics of a city nor the appearance of one.

*Convention followed in spelling of names: For place names the French and Tunisian names commonly seen on road signs and maps have been retained, whereas for personal and tribal names the transliterated Arab forms are used.

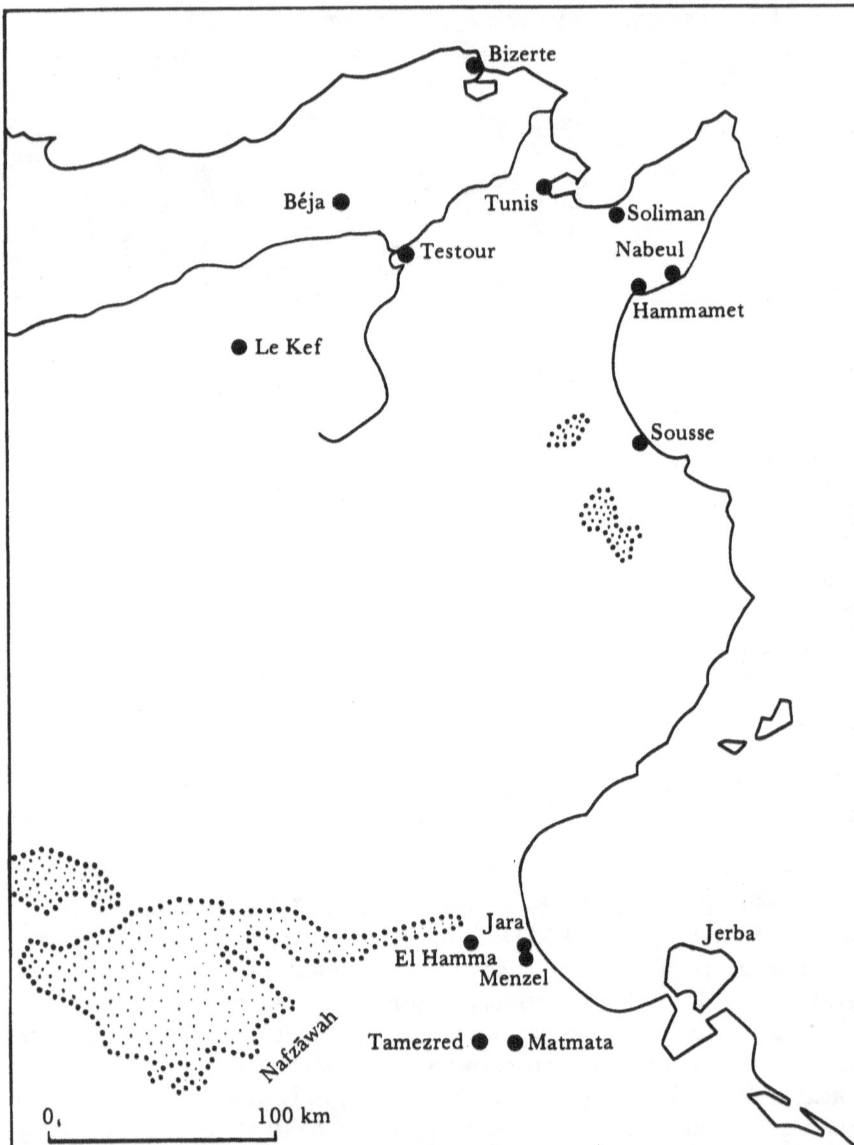

Map. 1.1. Concentrations of Jews in the eighteenth century according to fiscal records.

More populous than Sousse, Msaken, which held many *jāmiʿ*, had neither walls nor souk. Its activities included the cultivation of olives, religious studies, and wool weaving. "Dico città e dico male," said a nineteenth century author of Msaken.[2]

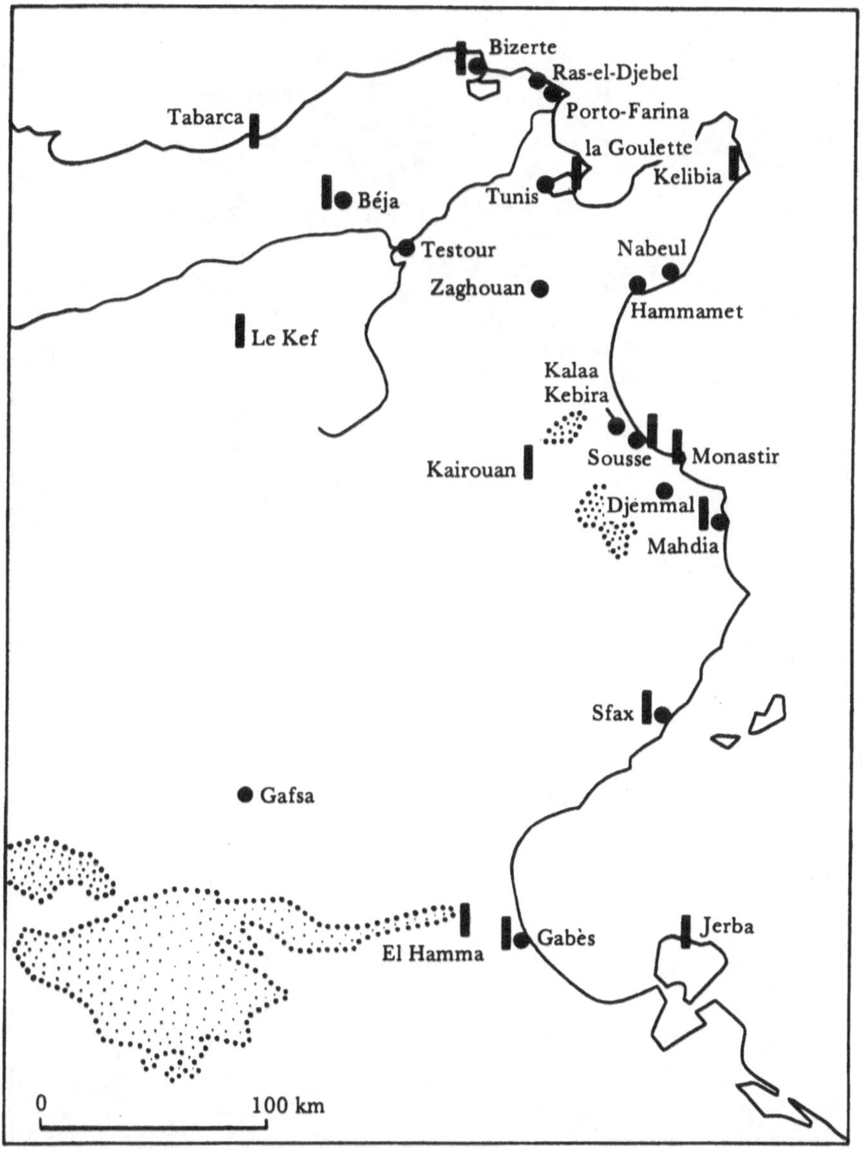

Map 1.2. Concentrations of Turks in the eighteenth and nineteenth centuries. Black blocks indicate presence of Turkish garrisons in the eighteenth century; black circles denote places where Turks and their descendants resided in the eighteenth and nineteenth centuries.

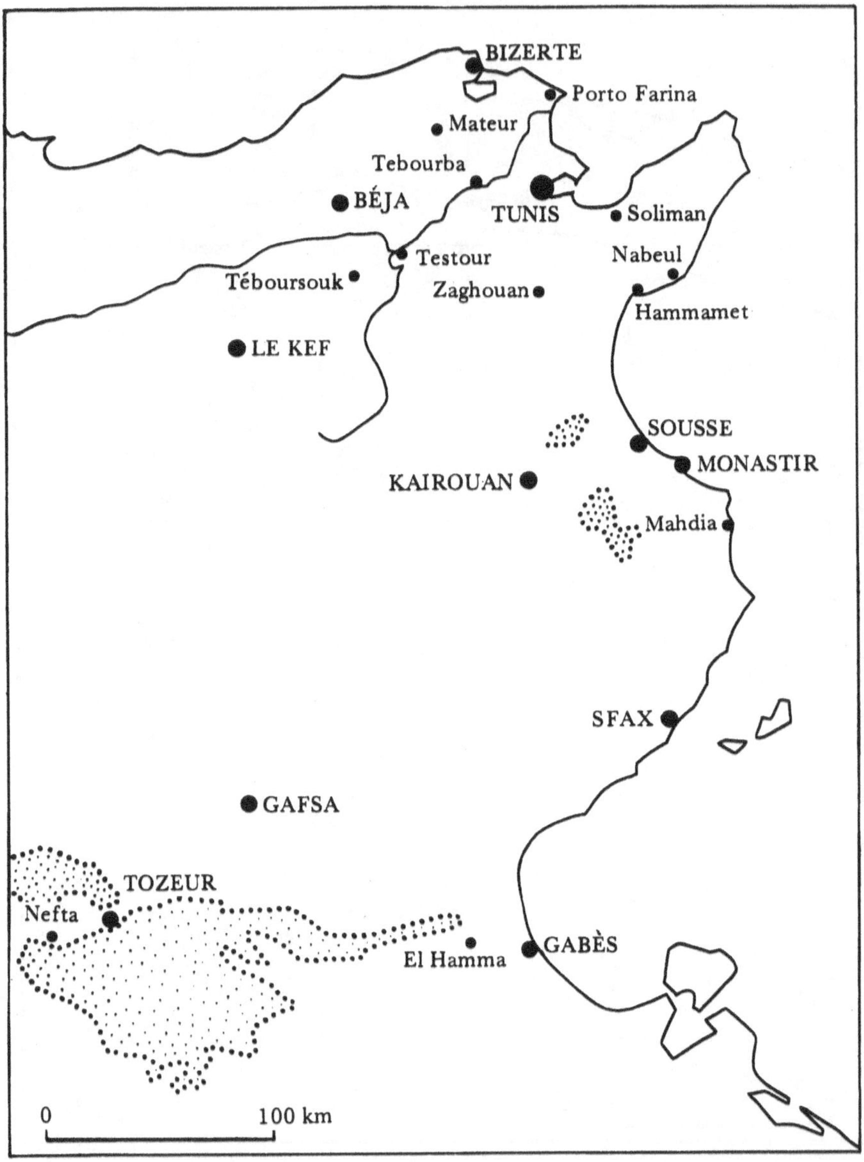

Map 1.3. Urban centers in the eighteenth and nineteenth centuries. (District seats are in capital letters.)

If we limit ourselves to those centers whose qualification as cities is incontestable, their number and quality of existence suffice to constitute an urban network. At the head, evidently, was the capital, followed by regional metropolises: on the coast, Bizerte, Nabeul, and Sousse, particularly important for its busy bazaars, its production of fine cloth (which declined in the nineteenth century), and the commerce of its port. Farther south there were Monastir, similar to Sousse, an active little port whose population spilled over the ramparts into the suburbs, and Sfax, "a very pretty town," surrounded by huge walls, an industrious center whose people, in the words of a French writer, "are assuredly the wickedest in the kingdom,"[3] but who, according to a local historian, were the most devout of Moslems. This can be interpreted to mean that the Sfaxians were shrewd profiteers; they were also merchants, fishermen, and weavers. Farther south was Gabès, a twin city and the outlet for the great province of the south.

Inland the chain of cities was not as closely linked. Tozeur was the capital of the Jarīd, the annual gathering place of nomadic and sedentary people, a reasonable resting place on the pilgrimage to Mecca, where Maghrebians stopped if they had taken the southern route. It was the center of the textile industry of the entire regency and the residence of the bey when his fiscal expedition set out to collect taxes in the south. From Gafsa, farther north, it took a number of days – in a region where shady spots were scarce and far apart – to reach Kairouan, the ancient capital, repeatedly devastated in the eighteenth century, living in slow motion during the nineteenth, but still pulsing, not only with devout believers, but also with artisans of all kinds: tanners, saddlers, blacksmiths, coppersmiths, weavers, and many others. Due north of Tozeur, Béja hosted the winter camp whose arrival coincided with a great fair held by merchants and artisans from the entire country. A fortified town, the ancient Vaga had remained the leading grain market.

> Si deux Beggies étoient
> Assises en deux plaines
> Les grains surmonterioient
> Le nombre des arènes

is what people said about Béja in the capital.[4] In addition to these cities were large towns with less diverse activities and populations, and centers that, although lilliputian, were nonetheless cities.

Whether one counts generously or not, the urban population probably did not exceed 160,000 to 170,000 inhabitants, or 15–16 percent of the total population, a small proportion, and even smaller if one bears in mind that many of the townspeople also engaged in agriculture or horticulture. This is hardly surprising in a traditional and predominantly agrarian population. The vast majority of the population consisted of country people, tent dwellers, and villagers.[5]

If we situate the nomads and settled rural inhabitants in the territory of seventeenth- and eighteenth-century Tunisia, we observe in the north, along the valley of the Medjerdah and its affluents, a string of villages along an axis running from Le Kef to Tunis.[6] There were some twenty sites, many of which were revived by the Moors driven from Spain: the centers of Testour and Tebourba, already mentioned; the villages of Slouguia, Grich el Oued, Djedeida, Medjez el Bab. North of Tunis was another cluster of villages, near the littoral, stretching as far as Bizerte. There too a number of Andalusian refugees settled. In the opposite direction was a third settled region, also populated with Iberians, at the beginning and along the coast of Cape Bon.

These settled pockets were doubtless less populous and fewer in number than nomadic groups, of which there were more than twenty in the region of Le Kef, some twenty-odd in the area of Béja, among whom were the Nafzah, the Amdūn, the Ushtata, from whom the agents of the Compagnie d'Afrique bought wheat; the same number in the region of Téboursouk, with the *ʿarūsh kebār,* the "great tribes," the Awlād Abu Sālem, the Jundūbah, the Wartān, the Awlād ʿAyār, and so on. To this can be added the five or so tribes near Mateur and those that occupied Cape Bon. In northern Tunisia we see an inextricable blend of nomads and sedentaries. In central Tunisia, on the other hand, a segregation took place: On the coast there were more villages, in the interior, more tent dwellers. In fact, in the Sahel, the heavy concentration of villages was around Sousse and Monastir: twenty-four villages in the first canton – from Zriba in the north to Djemmal in the south – and twenty-eight in the district of Monastir, which is more coastal and more southerly. In the vicinity of Mahdia – in the eighteenth-century part of the district of Monastir – and in the region of Sfax farther to the south, village settlements thinned out and gave way to pastoralist tribes: the 'Aqarība, the Lawāta, and the Methallīth. But once across the littoral, the plain became the domain of the great tribes: the Jlāss, Qoʿūb, and Quazīn near Kairouan; the Frashīsh, Mājer, and Hamāma deeper into the interior. From Kairouan to Gafsa there was not a single village. But there were a few sedentary groups perched in inaccessible villages scattered throughout the mountainous area; a few *dashras* around La Kessera, a handful in Jabal Bargu, and a few more in Jabal Waslāt.

Sedentary life took over again in the south where villages proliferated from the Algerian border to the island of Jerba: around Gafsa, in the Jarīd, in Nafzāwah, near Gabès, and finally, in Jabal Matmata. And there were as many archipelagos of oases, surrounded everywhere by shepherd tribes: ʿAkkārah, Fatnāssa, Warghamma, Hazem, and others.

From the eighteenth to the nineteenth century there was neither a great wave of nomads nor a proliferation of villages. Only minor changes occurred in this overall picture. The Mahādhba, who in the nineteenth century were settled in the region of Sfax, seem to have been in a more northerly position in the eighteenth; sedentary life lost more ground in central Tunisia with the dispersion of the Waslatiya in 1762. However, the other pieces on this checkerboard remained in place throughout the period, and even up to the beginning of the protectorate. As to earlier periods, one would like to be able to situate the groups and follow their movements, but history, less attentive than tax collectors, has kept track only of the most important ones, leaving undocumented most of the others.[7] It is nevertheless true, despite endless repetitions about the instability of nomadic tribes, that they maintained their location over a very long period of time.

And they maintained not only their location, but their strength as well. In the nineteenth century throughout the country, there was a higher percentage of nomads than settlers. It is true that pockets of settlements lay within the territory of certain tribes: these were *zāwiya*, settlements built up around the tomb of a marabout, inhabited by some members of the tribe, in some cases a number of families, which could attain the dimensions of large villages. During the nineteenth century, from the north to the south, there were more than sixty of them. Among the Wartān, which numbered 16,000 individuals, nearly a quarter of the tribe was settled in the nine *zāwiya* of the territory. Similarly, 5,000 members of the Awlād ʿAyār, of a total population of 25,000, were settled around the marabouts. However, the overall population of these settled groups did not exceed 25,000, which does not alter the proportion of nomads to settlers.

Do natural conditions account for the distribution of these two groups? In part, yes. The southern band occupied by settled group is at the boundary of the cultivation of date palms; only with the aid of irrigation can the olive tree be grown there. In the north, the last line of villages coincided with the zone of grain farming – practicable even without irrigation. Between the two is the zone given over to herding. In fact, irrigated farming would have been possible. In the north, where climate and terrain lend themselves to sedentary occupations, nomads were preponderant. The south, conversely, despite unfavorable natural conditions, harbored a much larger number of villages and settlers in the nineteenth century than did the north. Geographic determinism is thus misleading. History – the very long history of the settlements and migrations of these groups, which this present study cannot attempt to investigate – and sociology, to be discussed in later chapters, may well provide the key to this relationship.

Let us not, however, overestimate its rigidity. Tunisia was crossed by migratory currents that reinforced the regional contrasts already observed.

Geographic mobility

Let us proceed from the most to the least familiar. Around 1856, when the first census was taken, vast numbers of people were not in their place of origin. To begin with, the "Turks" came by sea – Levantines of many provenances – and were installed in garrisons until the beginning of the nineteenth century, remaining settled in the cities (see Map 1.2). Except for Tunis, and chiefly Mahdia where there were more than a thousand, they were few in number.

From the heart of Africa and against their will came the blacks, 6,000 to 7,000 scattered throughout the country, descendants of slaves long since freed, engaged in the most menial work as day laborers, servants, and field hands.

Also from the south came the Trabelsiya, of Libyan origin numbering around 20,000. These immigrants stayed in close groups that could amount to 2,000 individuals. Having emigrated in search of water even more than land, they were massed in the north. Stable though not settled, with the exception of a few who guarded marabouts, they continued to be tent dwellers. A few left the tribe and spread out in small groups or even, though rarely, attempted individual forays into the Sahel. The large province of Aʿrādh, also in the south, provided thousands of migrants. Both the oases and the nomadic tribes contributed their share of migrants who then scattered all along the routes in the vicinity of Sfax, in the Sahel, in Kairouan and its environs, in the peninsula of Cape Bon, Tunis, or the region of Bizerte. Some clung to villages and cities, others remained in herding zones among the Methallīth or the Sawāsi. Cape Bon was the region that received the greatest number of migrants from the Aʿrādh. There were some 800 of them in Tunis, as many around Porto Farina and Bizerte, and on the lands of the Sawāsi. All in all, however, they were fewer in number and more widely scattered than the Libyans.

The islands, in turn, emptied onto the continent. One Jerban in eleven and one Kerkennan in five lived off their island. For the first there were two favorite zones: the Sahel and Cape Bon. Some were also to be found in Le Kef, in Kairouan, Tunis, or the region of Bizerte. The Kerkennans, curiously, did not stop in Sfax. It was to the Sahel, first of all, and to Tunis next in order of preference, that they wended their way. Their concentration in the Sahel should not be misunderstood; they were scattered among many different towns: three in Ouardenine, two in El Djem, two in Boudher, and so on. The entire region of Sfax, like the Kerkenna Islands, operated like a negative pole, the tribes migrating to the north, the villagers preferring the Sahel.

Contrary to all expectation, the central part of the country was not a region of emigration. The powerful tribes of the Drid, the Jlāss, Frashīsh, or Mājer, though they may have welcomed strangers, did not send their men into the rest of the country. There is an exception: The Drid and their common cohort, the Arab Majour, were settled in the Jarīd, numbering 250 men, out of the 13,000 of the two tribes; this is a very small number. Mistake, or oversight of the census takers? Not at all. In the districts of the Sahel where strangers were carefully accounted for, only thirty-odd Jlāss could be found, a dozen Drid, and a few from other tribes of central Tunisia. Did the high plains support their inhabitants? In the low plains, the tribes of the Awlād Saʿīd, Sawāsi, and Naffāt also remained on their lands. Similarly stable were the tribes that shared the north. Neither the neighboring cities nor the Sahel attracted them.

The Sahel, on the other hand, was a region of great turbulence. Seemingly the most sedentary, its population was in a constant state of flux. Jerbans, Kerkennans, and Waslatiya all flocked there while the natives of the Sahel themselves, whom one would imagine rooted to their soil, were migratory. Each village sent its own to neighboring places and received others in turn. Thus Moknine exchanged its inhabitants with Djemmal, Msaken, and Kalaa Kebira; sent some to Sousse and Kalaa Serira; and received some from Menzel and Akouda. All told, these small-scale migrations finally amounted to thousands of individuals.

Does this mean that instability was generalized and that migrations were reversible? No. Regions of agglomeration stand out sharply: the north (the region of Tunis and Bizerte, the valley of the Medjerdah, Cape Bon) and the Sahel. The zone of dispersion, on the other hand, was the south and the southeast, reservoirs of men flowing into more favorable regions. The stationary groups were the tribes of the center, the north, and some groups in the lower plains. Generally speaking, the primary direction of migrations was from south to north; there was also another movement from the west that wound up in the north. North–south migrations were rare. There were no Waslatiya, Jerbans, or Kerkennans to be found south of Ksour Essaf, nor were there any Andalusians. There is another constant: Some nomadic migrants might have settled among sedentary groups or on the outskirts of towns, but townspeople never became nomads.

These movements may be summed up in a simple formula: The zones that attracted migrants are those most favored by natural conditions; the zones of emigration were the less privileged. But the plain, however barren it may be, held on to its people, thereby suggesting that the explanations are not merely geographic.

If all these migrants converged on the Sahel and the north, it is hardly surprising to find an extraordinary ethnic mix in those regions. This is particularly noticeable in the north where there were fewer sedentary

Table 1.2. *El Alia: geographic origin of nonnative landowners*

Geographic origin	North	Center	East	South
Villagers	45	8	8	4
Nomads	23	2	—	12

groups. It is there, where tribes were less compact and more diverse, that one finds those groups known as "the little tribes," *ʿarūsh rqāq*, originating from the splintering of once powerful tribes and the merger of smaller groups, or the *Taiyāch*, offshoots of more important tribes. In the Sahel, the strength of village life was such that it succeeded in fragmenting migrant groups and merely tolerated tent dwellers within the fabric of village life.

Last, the cities contributed greatly to this flux from the countryside. Tunis, Sousse, Sfax, Kairouan, and Béja all drew from the rural population a good portion of their inhabitants. In Béja, 38 percent of the population came from other parts of the country, or from bordering regencies.

Can these displacements be dated and measured in length of duration? The census was taken around 1860. Twenty years earlier, the proprietors of olive groves were registered in the Sahel and in the north, as were date growers in the south. Thus one finds among the growers in Msaken more than 300 "foreigners": Thirty-odd are from the south (Jerbans, people from the Aʿrādh, Libyans), others from Kairouan and members of the Waslatiya, more than fifty from the Sahel, and around twenty Andalusians. They were landowners: Their settlement there was thus neither recent nor temporary. The migrations observed in 1860 were the same as twenty years earlier; they were not motivated by the pressure of particular circumstances.

In El Alia, a village of produce growers near Porto Farina, a hundred or more landowners were not native to the region. Most of them came from the north, which confirms the regional exchanges noted in 1860 (See Table 1.2.) But other regions also provided their contingent, and Libyans and people from the Aʿrādh were also found here. On the other hand, the date growers in the Gabès oasis were entirely from the region. The only outsiders to be found were a few Sfaxians or Jerbans.[8]

If we go back to the eighteenth century, information is completely fragmentary but already sheds some light. Under Hammūda Pāsha, wrote Ibn Abi Dhiaf, the Libyans had no lands of their own and were scattered in different regions. By the middle of the century some of them were already settled in the region of Béja, providing portage between that city and Tunis. Others went to the peninsula of Cape Bon, where for seventy years they occupied one of the domains of the bey. Still others were registered in Sousse, along with Jerbans and a variety of immigrants from the Sahel.

These indications, scarce as they are, do not refute the observations made in the nineteenth century. Can one then speak of waves of migrations, whose regularity and continuity would be confirmed by these data? Can one rather speak of ancient displacements of groups that did not merge with their host region and continued to live as outsiders? The designation of origin would therefore indicate together with geographic mobility, a position in the social structure and would assign a place to the migrants thus designated.

2. Social organization: praxis and ideology

In the early days of the protectorate, the people recounted their history to the French officials who had come to interrogate them. These uniformed ethnologists conscientiously filled voluminous ledgers with the exploits of all the tribes, villages, and hamlets, thereby compiling something of a corpus of tales of origin.[1] Since they translated what they were told, their mediation warrants a few caveats before we look at those texts.

Two readings of the tales of origin

There are, in fact, two possible readings of this collection of histories. The first would be to find in them the elements of a broader history that could apply to the whole of Tunisia. This would involve gathering traditional oral accounts – in a land where writing existed but was little used – reading them literally, and compiling them so as to recreate a general history of the country. The officials who recorded these accounts did indeed try to place them within a precise chronological context, interpolating them between Roman and Byzantine Africa at one end, and the French occupation at the other. They were, however, well aware that these tales could not account for the entire interval.

Fortunately, these officials were not knowledgeable enough to fill in the gaps themselves. Though not without historical background, they were inadequately prepared to bridge the distance that separates the early Middle Ages from a more recent past. The writer of one of the reports concerning the Hamāma, for example, quotes among his sources Procopius, Al Qairawāni (a translation of this seventeenth-century historian was published in 1845, at the time of the scientific exploration of Algeria), and the *Kitab el adouani*. The report on the region of Monastir was based on the texts of El Bekri and Al Idrisi, and the writer appears to have been familiar with the translation of Al Qairawāni.

After the seventeenth century, however, sources became meager. At best, the sum total of information they yielded was fragmentary. Entire centuries and whole regions remained in darkness. In view of this, the only available method for establishing historical continuity was to arrange the different sequences of the collected oral traditions in chronological order. The official who documented the region of Gafsa thus presents us with an unbroken panorama stretching from antiquity – via Sallust – to the seventeenth century. Roman prosperity is followed by episodes of Vandal and Arab invasions, then by the resistance of the last remnants of the Byzantine Empire and the Berbers led by the Kahena, which ultimately led to a period of tranquility. Then, along came the Hillalian invasion, which demolished Gafsa and the neighboring villages but had the compensating virtue of providing the historian with a tabula rasa on which anything could be written. Consequently, it was now possible to introduce the current oral tradition and prevent the line of history from being interrupted. The first nucleus of repopulation was thus placed in the eleventh century; a second group joined it in the twelfth century; in the thirteenth century, the founders of the third group arrived. The fourteenth century saw the settlement of still other immigrants, followed shortly thereafter by the last component of Gafsa's inhabitants. In this way, the recording officer held the "thread" of history, taking care not to break it. He pulled the collected traditions in a diachronic direction so that no chronological space would remain empty.

That this deformation was introduced by the investigator is apparent in the regularity of the waves of immigration. Each century deposited a new population layer with the intervals lengthened somewhat toward the end in order to reach the nineteenth century without a break. In addition, a tradition concerning Gafsa's past compiled by another official confirms that the first account was reworked by the person who transcribed it. In the second version, the human "strata" are no longer dated precisely, and what is more, they are crudely synchronic, instead of spanning more than six centuries.

The collected accounts are moreover contradictory. The history of a single tribe varies from one clan to another. Or else, compared with the political history that has become known since those reports were compiled, the accounts reveal improbabilities, chronological errors, or even a complete inversion of data. The officials were well aware of this and, happily, did not try to lessen the contradictions by concealing them. When they noticed incoherencies in an account, or pieced together conflicting versions, they generally transcribed them as they were reported without correcting them. The history of the Awlād Mʿāmar, a branch of the Hamāma tribe, as told by its members in 1887, provides an illustration of such inconsistency. They recounted their version of a well-known episode in Tunisian history concerning a conflict between Husayn Ibn Ali, the founder of the Husaynite dynasty, and his nephew, Ali Pāsha. The facts can be briefly recalled: Once Husayn Ibn Ali had fathered two sons, Ali Pāsha was left with no hope of succeeding him to the throne. In 1728 Ali attempted an unsuccessful revolt against the bey and fled to Algeria. He returned in 1735 and, after a long civil war, won out over Bey Husayn in 1740.

How is this civil war related by the Awlād Mʿāmar? In one account, the two protagonists appear as cousins. Their roles are reversed, Ali presented as the ruling bey, while Husayn becomes the usurper. The beginning of the conflict is placed in 1680. The outcome is the very opposite of the truth: Husayn, the victor, has Ali decapitated and takes his place on the throne. In a second version, the belligerents are brothers, one of whom changes name: Ali becomes M'hamad Ibn Ali. In this version, it is indeed Husayn who is in power and who is rivaled for the throne, but the outcome of the struggle is as far from reality as is the first version: The usurper is defeated at Le Kef and submits to his brother. There are as many errors as there are events.[2]

Any hope of establishing a historical continuum on the basis of the oral tradition is thus completely illusory. The facts that this tradition records cannot possibly constitute a chronological series of actual events. It is nonetheless this kind of historicist reading that was made by most of the greatest specialists of North Africa. Jean Despois, for example, in his admirable book, *La Tunisie orientale, Sahel et Basse Steppe* – a classic among studies of the Maghreb – wonders about the geographic distribution and history of the tribes. "To what degree," he wrote, "can one know the origin of the various factions that constitute [the tribes]? Oral traditions, even doubtful ones, will help us answer this second question."[3]

It is symptomatic that this question was asked *after* the chapters devoted to ancient Byzantium, seventh to ninth century Ifriqīya, the invasions of the eleventh century, and their consequences. For it is in the empty spaces left by written history that the traditions were inserted. What Jean Despois did was to utilize two methods. For the major tribes and confederations, he searched in the written sources and in some cases, as for example the Awlād Saʿīd, he found their traces. When there were no texts and only an oral tradition, he categorically rejected it: "Let us disregard the legend," he wrote on the subject of the Jlāss, "that would make the sons of Jlās the begetters of the four clans of the tribe; there is nothing to that story." But what is considered inadmissible legend in the case of major groups is regarded as acceptable for those fractional groups that were separated from the main body of their tribes: "It was during the past two centuries that the foreign clans, still seen today, settled among the Awlād Saʿīd." And farther down: "The Awlād Nasir, the Methallith who settled in Zeghidan, and the Naffāt who live near the Jabal Fadlūn would seem to have arrived during the early years of the 19th century; they were fleeing famine and found a barren region, covered with brush, where they settled." As for the Libyans, "They left their lands roughly a century and a half ago. Their first sojourn would seem to have been near La Louza, north of Sfax, where they are said to have planted (?) 8,000 olive trees."

The use of the conditional, of indirect discourse, and question marks clearly indicates the author's doubts. However, when it suits his purpose, he appropriates the oral tradition. On the basis of these accounts, he speaks of "waves of immigrants who *poured* down from the northern steppes, a hundred and fifty to two hundred years ago." He applies this same selectivity when discussing the origin of any town about which written history has yielded no information, or maraboutic groups, whose traditions support the hypothesis of true migratory movements: "Most of the peoples of the Maghreb who settled in eastern Ifriqīya are Moroccan Berbers; though their role was great, their number was small. Almost all were marabouts."

In short, this method is somewhat random and uncertain. One cannot reject a tradition when it is contradicted by other sources and then accept it when such sources are lacking. Nor can one use every available means of expressing doubt while at the same time presenting as factual the migrations, settlements, and genealogies that such "legends" relate. And finally, there is no justification for excerpting passages presumed to be documentary while discounting others held to be legendary.

At the other end of the Maghreb, Moroccans tell stories about themselves that are similar to those told by Tunisians. Jacques Berque, who has quoted some of them, calls them legends and treats them as such. At the same time, he considers that some part of what is recounted may indeed have taken place, especially those passages dealing with the expansion and conquests of the group he studied. As a historian, he thus feels obliged to attach dates to the stages of such movements and the "phases" of the conquests, thereby separating the legendary from the historical in the oral tradition.[4]

That the history of the Maghreb is interwoven with migrations and conquests is undeniable. That the oral tradition documents any one of these aspects cannot be proved with any certainty. The oral tradition assuredly contains bits and pieces of true history, but it cannot be viewed as a chronicle of events.

Rather than take such tales literally, it would be more appropriate to read them differently, to seek out an implicit meaning beyond what is explicitly related – the second possible reading. Then, instead of being bothered by the errors of the tale and the mistakes of the investigator, one could make use of them. Just as a slip reveals a hidden truth, so discordances, improbabilities, and silences frequently tell more than stories that hold together. There is also reason to be grateful for the inadequacy of the historical knowledge of the time since it reduced the possibilities of manipulating the material collected by the writers of those reports. Originally, they intervened directly in the account, replacing the narrator in order to provide explanations. In some cases, the intrusions are so awkward that they can be caught on a first reading. Here, for example, is the account of the migrations of the Hamāma tribe as related in a report of 1887. The dating and the interpretation of the various moves clearly reveal the hand of the recorder.

It is likely that the Hamāma came from Sham (Syria) in the 11th century of the Christian era, spent some time in Tripolitania, and were slowly pushed by the resistance of the indigenous tribes on the one side, and by their migratory instinct on the other, as far as western Algeria.

When the Arab population in the west became too dense, and the invading groups began piling up one on the other, some of the groups, after careful consideration, and with the memory of the fertile plains they had crossed at the outset of their invasions, retraced their steps along the route they had traveled.[5]

The intervention of the compilers is not always as transparent as this, and we lack the criteria with which to isolate either their additions or the slivers of historical truth. One can at least limit the uncertainties by giving prior attention to those groups that bequeathed the largest body of oral traditions to us, thereby enabling a measure of comparison and interpretation. Such is the case with the powerful Hamāma tribe.

The powerful tribe of the Hamāma

The Awlād Ridwān and their account of the past: a structural time

This is the story of the Awlād Ridwān,[6] of the Hamāma tribe:

These people belong to the Arab race; they constitute one of the principal groups of the great family of Hamāma and represent approximately one-third of this important tribe of which the Awlād ʿAzīz and the Awlād Mʿāmar are the other two great branches.

Natives of the Hejaz (the Arabian desert), they emigrated at some time, unknown today, and settled in Algeria in the oasis of Ezzab (near Biskra). However, the arrival of the Turks in that reigion made them expatriate once more. They went east again and settled permanently in Tunisia never leaving it since that time.

Genealogy: Hamām, the founder of the tribe to which he gave his name, had two children, Rabīʿa and a daughter who married Drīss. The first branch produced ʿAzīz and Mʿāmår; the second, Ridwān. Still today, one calls the Ridwān, Ridwān ben Drīss. Generally speaking, they are called Hamāma.

The Ridwān are divided into a large number of groups, which are listed in Figure 2.1 This figure also indicates very clearly the varying degree of kinship between the Ridwān in particular and the Hamāma in general.

Outside groups: The Awlād Si Slimān, the Hawāmid, the Guemamdiya, and the

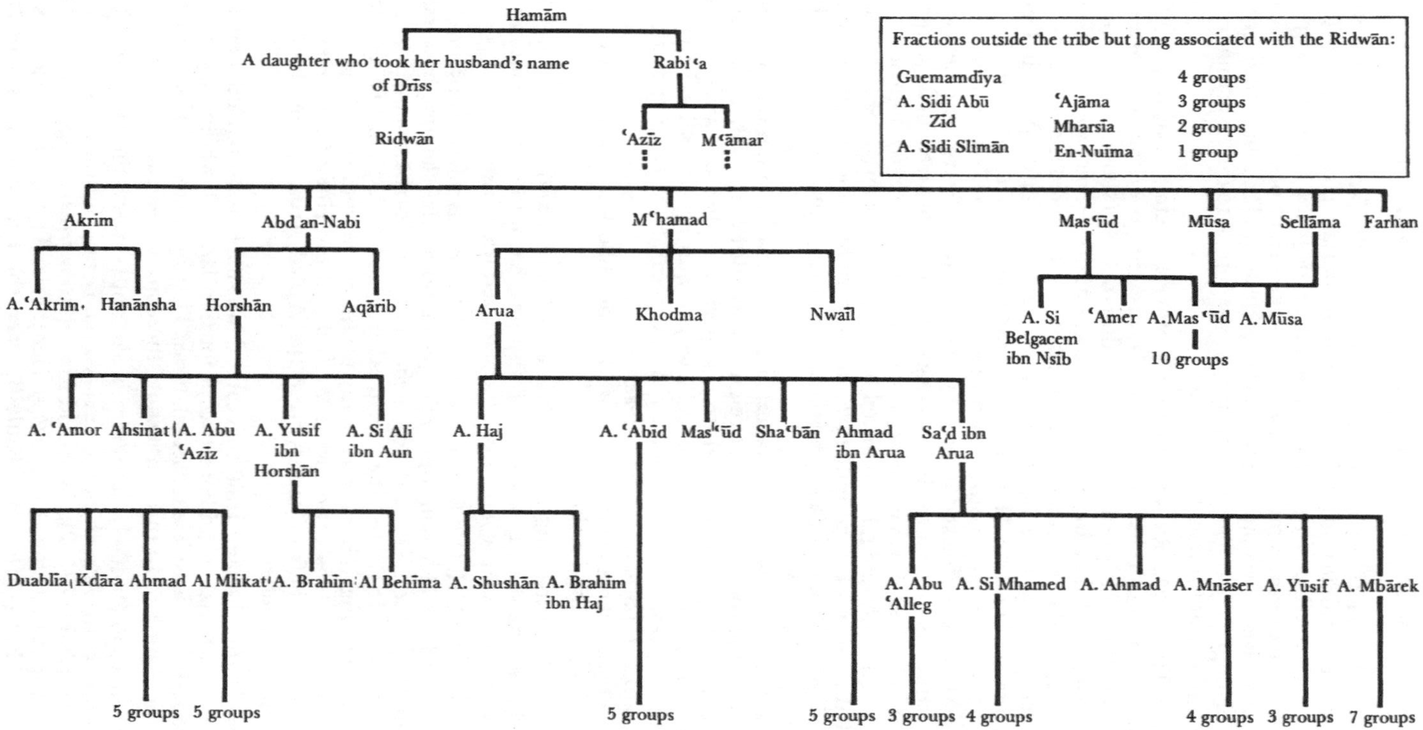

Fig. 2.1. Genealogy of the Hamāma provided by the Awlād Ridwān.

Awlād Sidi Abu Zīd do not appear to belong to the family of Awlād Ridwān by descent. The Guemamdiya, since time immemorial, have lived in the Guamūda, that is, at the edge of the *wadi* of that name, near the *zāwiya* Seddaguiya; their origin is unknown. Similarly unknown is the origin of the three other groups that have always lived among the Awlād Ridwān. In fact, these four groups have long belonged – from an administrative viewpoint – to the Hamāma tribe, whose habits and customs they have adopted.

Politics: The Awlād Ridwān, like their other Hamāma relatives, are from the Hasiniya soff and thus partisans of the present government on whose behalf they fought openly during the insurrection of 1281 (1864). The Arabs, crushed by taxation, had risen in revolt; many towns of the regency were attacked, taken, and pillaged; the continuation of this unrest precipitated the ruin of the country. The rebels had at their head Ali ben Ghedaun [*sic*], of the M'sāhil. Defeated at the gates of Tunis by Ahmad Zarruq, the commander of the bey's troops, the insurgents, after many other skirmishes, returned to the region of their origin where they were attacked in turn by the Hamāma. There were heavy losses on both sides. As a result of those defeats, the chief insurrectionist sought refuge in Tebessa, then in Constantine, where he was apparently imprisoned. Having succeeded in escaping, he returned to Tunisia and went to see Sidi Muhammad al-Abidi, a man of great influence, through whose intervention he was not executed on the spot. Si Sadoq Bey had him thrown into prison where he is said to have died of poison.

It was under these circumstances that the Awlād Ridwān demonstrated their fidelity to the dynasty that still reigns today. But despite their devotion to the bey, they lived just as well before this period as they did afterward, enjoying almost complete independence and always requiring armed force to make them pay their taxes. They seem somewhat less recalcitrant today than they used to be, thanks, apparently, to our presence.

This tribe shares many notions with its neighbors the Jlāss, and is inimical to the Mājer and the Frashīsh.

Internal soffs: Exceedingly quarrelsome, belligerent and thieving, they have engaged over the years in a variety of disputes that were not without importance. These are the major events that characterized their history:

1. In 1211 A.H. (1796–7 common era), there was a feud between the Awlād Masʿūd and the Horshān over Oglet Jedra, both sides claiming ownership. The Awlād Masʿūd left eleven dead on the field, the Horshān many fewer.

2. In 1233 (1817–18), the Awlād Mbārek and Awlād Yūsif fought as a result of some pillaging. There were many wounded on both sides.

3. In 1281 (1864), the Awlād Masʿūd and the Horshān quarreled with the Arua over the theft of camels from the Awlād Arua by the Horshān. There were many fatalities.

External soffs: The same traits that caused internal feuds often led them to serious disputes with their neighbors, except for the Jlāss with whom they seem to have had good, or at least less tense, relations. They are above all hostile to the Mājer and the Banī Zīd. In this connection, these are the events:

1. In 1050 (1640–1), hostilities broke out between the Hamāma, Jlāss, and the people of the Aʿrādh, at a place called Luiba, near Kairouan. Reason forgotten.

2. In 1206 (1791–2), the Awlād Ridwān took up arms against the Mājer who had brought their flocks to graze at Hensheria. This quarrel lasted six years.

3. In 1234 (1818–19), a battle between the Hamāma, Jlāss, and Naffāt on

the one side, and the Banī Zīd and Hawāya on the other; the motive is unknown but there were long-standing differences between the two sides.

4. In 1235 (1819–20), the Banī Zīd attacked the Hamāma at Hensheria for the purpose of pillage; they were beaten off and 200 of their horses were taken. A few dead and wounded on both sides.

5. In 1262 (1846), a dispute over land (Ain Rebaou) caused an outbreak between the Hamāma and Mājer. Order was not restored until the government sent troops to the area.

6. In 1280, (1863), the Hamāma pillaged the Hafīdh, who, with their allies the Mājer, attacked them to punish the thieves. Both sides suffered considerable losses.

7. In 1281 (1864), during the insurrection of that year, the Hamāma, who were supporters of the bey, defeated the rebels (Mājer and Frashīsh). The Mājer lost 150 men, the Hamāma somewhat fewer.

8. In 1281 (1864), the Awlād ʿAzīz attacked the Awlād Masʿūd for having stolen 200 of their camels. They lost ten men.

9. In 1284 (1867), the year of the great famine, Hamāma and Jlāss attacked the Mājer, whom they pillaged. There were severe losses on both sides.

10. In 1286 (1869–70), trouble broke out among the Banī Zīd, and the bey's troops led by Si Osman were sent to restore order, joined by the Hamāma. The Banī Zīd fled and were pillaged.

11. In 1291 (1874–75), the bey sent 100 cavalry commanded by Si Ahmad Juīni to restore order among the Awlād ʿAbdalkrīm (Awlād ʿAzīz) who had rebelled against their chiefs and had assassinated the cadi, Al Haj ʿAmāra. On the arrival of the troops, joined by the Hamāma and the Jlāss, the Awlād ʿAbdalkrīm fled. Reencountered near Gafsa, they were pillaged and taken back to their lands.

This account is first of all the history of a lineage, which is to say that the further back one goes in time, the fewer the protagonists. In the past, one does not find the totality of the present-day group, but rather ancestors in ever-decreasing numbers. The past is thus not just a projected image of the future.

Time here has a beginning that corresponds to the life span of the tribe's founder. But this time is not measured. Neither years nor reigns of sovereigns provide reference points. As Muslims, the Awlād Ridwān were of course aware of the Hegira calendar, but they referred to it only for the most recent events. Furthermore, numerical dating had only the appearance of accuracy; when one compares these dates to an established chronology they turn out to be incorrect. We have seen earlier how, in the account of the civil war between Husayn Bey and Ali Pāsha, the events were antedated by a good half century.

Time passes with variable speed, so that the most recent past is filled with events. There is a kind of acceleration during the decades that precede the account: Incidents followed one after the other between 1863 and 1875, but only six occurred during the preceding eighty years. As one moves back in time, the history becomes thinner; beyond a century, chronological dating is no longer operative and time ceases to be measurable. For the most remote past, one sees successive levels, as it were, marked by the different generations. But contrary to dated time, this portion of the past is richer the further back it goes; the closer to the founder, the more precise the account.

The past thus separates into three movements: a brisk tempo at the outset, with the life of the founder and his first descendants, followed by an andante, and then an allegro staccato for the final decades. Of these three movements, the last is the closest to historic time, not for its dating but for its content; the events it contains really could have taken place, even if their effects – the number of dead during a battle, or the herds rustled – are measured hyperbolically. The past taken as a whole, in any case, is the time that separates living men from their founding ancestor. In the history of the Awlād Ridwān, this distance covers eight generations (which corresponds to a period of two to three centuries). The temporal density is therefore meager, and nothing is left for the period preceding the appearance of the founder.

If we turn back to the first two movements, they seem similar insofar as they both describe the evolution of the lineage without a break. However, the first figures named – Hamām, Rebiʿā, Drīss, Maʿāmar, ʿAzīz – were founders of lineages whereas their descendants lacked this potential: A collective name (plural noun or Awlād so-and-so) replaces the individual name. Consequently, two or three generations after the founding ancestor, there was no new sublineage. In the genealogy presented in Figure 2.1, after the seven sons of Ridwān, there is no mention of the names of his grandchildren, merely collective names: Awlād Mūsa, Awlād Masʿūd, Khodmah, Hanānsha, to cite a few. The subdivisions of the line lose their significance. It is this change that explains the lack of temporal density in the traditional accounts that were gathered. From the moment that an Awlād so-and-so appears in the genealogy, it remains identical to itself with no need for separating the generations. Where the first period, that of the founders, is rigid, the subsequent one is more flexible, making it possible to condense certain generations. In this way the distance from the common ancestor is not altered with time.

The sequences of the past can be summed up in the following table:

	Unit of measure	Duration
0 Before the founders	None	Indefinite
1 Time of the founders	A generation	4–6 generations
2 Time of the lineages	Vague	4 generations
3 Historic time	Hegira year	About 100 years

The history of the Awlād Ridwān is no more than the reconstruction of a lineage, with no role assigned to the sacred or the supernatural, or to any outside actors. When persons or groups from without do figure in the account, the main roles are reserved for those within the tribe and outsiders are mentioned only in their relationship to the tribe. We have seen, in another version, how the chronicle of power struggles between Husayn and Ali Pāsha distorted actual events: The purpose of the sequence was not to establish "historic truth" but to determine the position of the Hamāma in relation to other tribes.

Finally, "the beginning of time," the starting point of the history, is in no way geared to Islamic history. Neither the revelation nor the propagation of the new faith has any place in the account. At no time does the group see itself as adopting or proselytizing Islam; it presents itself as Muslim from the very outset.

Thus the past is conceived of as an order of events in which the group, and the group alone, is involved. There is no reference other than that provided by its members, no texture except that of the lineage. What we are dealing with here is ancestral time. Or, to use the terminology introduced by Evans-Pritchard,[7] one might say that the time of the narrators is neither historical – as we understand it – nor ecological (i.e., the measure of time is not provided by agricultural or pastoral activities). Rather, it is structural in that it speaks of the social relations of members within a tribe as it does of their relations to other tribes.

The dimensions of the group: a segmentary society

The spread of the genealogical tree. The history of the Awlād Ridwān, of the Hamāma tribe – to limit our discussion to them – is diagrammed by the family tree presented in Figure 2.1. This configuration suggests first of all that the individual is defined by the chain of his ancestors, which ultimately takes him all the way back to the founder. But there is more to this backward progression, for in fact, the individual is immediately placed in a group – the descendants of X, the Awlād Mbārek, for example – which in turn is placed in a larger group. The individual is thus at the center of a series of concentric circles of which the last, the largest, is the tribe. In this way, the individual does not exist by himself; he is inseparable from the community. In the same way, the nuclear family has no status; it does not deserve consideration as the basis of a genealogy. Its initial stage is an extended family.

Filiation is clearly patrilinear. There is, however, an anomaly in Figure 2.1 that should be pointed out: One of the two children of the eponymous ancestor is a daughter. The Awlād Ridwān who descend from her do not bear the name of their paternal ancestor – the father of Drīss – but of their maternal grandfather. This fact is all the more remarkable in that it is the only infraction of the rule of symmetry to be observed here. The development of the lineage results from a fission that seems to be endlessly repeated. The tribe increases from the fertility of a single ancestor, each branch engendered by him and developing according to a process that remains the same at every chronological stage. By this process of division, the number of the subgroups would continue to grow from the founder (who in this case had only two children) all the way to present-day members of the tribe.

In point of fact, fission is not unlimited. On the one hand, in the three movements that delineate the tribe's past, the middle movement is a collective time – that of the lineages – in which the generations are no longer discrete. A group may retain the same name, the same position in the genealogical tree, the same dimensions, without proliferating: The process of fission is thus abbreviated by the elision of a certain number of generations, as it is by the extinction of a certain number of lines. The genealogical tree bears a few dead branches: Aqārib, Ridwān's grandson, seems to have been without issue; in the next generation, Shaʿbān and Masʿūd, the sons of Arua, died without offspring. All information gathered from other sources confirms this tradition.

A family tree may be subjected to a certain amount of pruning that limits its growth. But paradoxically, it may also undergo a certain amount of grafting. This is how the Awlād Ridwān distinguish groups "foreign to the tribe but living among the Awlād Ridwān for a very long time." This ambiguous explanation signifies that the Guemamdīya, Hawāmid, Awlād Sidi Abu Zīd, and Awlād Sidi Slimān attached themselves to the Awlād Ridwān by conglomeration without sharing a common ancestor.

To the question How do narrators see their society? one can reply that for them it is a group of extended families, related and defined by kinship ties. The degree of kinship is determined by the distance that separates two given groups from their common ancestor. Taken together, the agnates and descendants form a triangle whose base consists of living members with the founder of the line at the apex.

This diagram, however, is not sufficient to define a tribe. The lines of cleavage that cross it and those that separate it from other tribes have yet to be added.

Lines of fission. Fission, repeated with each generation and identical for each branch, gives the impression of a perfectly equilateral and symmetrical structure. In fact, it has already been pointed out that the basic unit is at the center of a number of concentric circles. Thus, if *A*, *B*, and *C* are equidistant from the common ancestor *O*, *A* and *B* are nevertheless

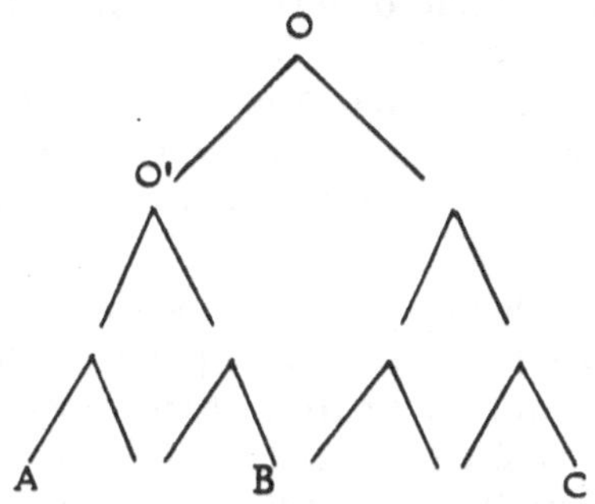

Fig. 2.2. Subdivision/fission of the family tree.

closer, since they stem from the same subdivision of the tribe, the same triangle *O'AB* enclosed within the larger *AOC* (Figure 2.2).

These subdivisions can be identified by the names they bear. The enormous ensemble of the Hamāma, which corresponds to the point *AOC* and comprised 50,000 individuals in 1880, consisted of two groups, the Awlād Drīss and the Awlād Rabīʿa. The former in turn consisted of the Awlād ʿAzīz and the Awlād Mʿāmar. Since the Mʿāmar alone numbered 4,000 members, it is not surprising that it was in turn broken down into smaller subdivisions with an eponymous ancestor marking each level of segmentation of the lineage. These subdivisions will not be described, first because of their large number and second because the contradictions between the different accounts made it impossible to reconstruct a family tree that covers *all* the traditions that were collected. For our purposes, it is enough to keep track of the principal branches (among which there are also disagreements) – the A. Rabīʿa (= A. ʿAzīz and Mʿāmar) and the A. Drīss (Ridwān and Sellāma).

The name Hamāma covered two series of what Gellner has termed "nested groups."[8] An individual designated as a Hamāmi would, by indicating another eponymous ancestor, immediately specify the subdivision to which he belongs, which in turn determines the closeness or distance of his relationship to other Hamāma. In other words, a tribe is not an aggregate of families. It consists rather of groups that are roughly equal – in size and in their position with respect to their ancestor – but separate. Separated both by a name that distinguishes them and by geographic distance, they are also separated in some cases by internecine quarrels, which the investigating officials termed *internal soffs*.

There were, in fact, rivalries that were known, assumed, and in some cases explained by their partisans. The Ridwān, for example, when speaking of themselves, related the quarrels that occurred within their own group: In 1796–7, the Awlād Masʿūd and the Horshān disputed the control of a water hole and settled their differences through armed combat. In 1817–18, it was the Awlād Mbārek who fought the Awlād Yūsif after a number of incidents of pillaging. And finally in 1864, the A. Masʿūd and the Horshān, who had been at each other's throats seventy years earlier, became allies against the Arua, whose camels they appropriated.

Whatever the origin of the quarrel, in every case it opposed not families or even less so, individuals, but placed one entire group in confrontation with another. These groups were equidistant from their ancestor: The first conflict opposed two segments situated at the third level of segmentation in relation to the Ridwān. The second conflict involved two segments, both closely related, situated at the fifth level. The situation was less clear in 1866: The opposing groups were not, according to this account, of the same genealogical rank. Other accounts, however, do place them on the same genealogical plane.

In any case, these episodes demonstrate that kinship does not preclude discord. Quite the contrary, one can readily say that it creates occasions for strife over water holes, grazing lands, and so on. They also show that violence is collective. The raids, like the retaliations, are group affairs.

The Ridwān tell us nothing more about their internal quarrels or about their relations with other branches of the Hamāma. However, accounts from other Hamāma groups reveal a series of conflicts. Some are of the same type as those exemplified by the Ridwān, opposing close offshoots of the same branch. Other oppositions belong to an entirely different category, in particular, the conflict that alienated the whole of the A. Rabīʿa from the whole of the A. Drīss. Here, according to the Mʿāmar, is the origin of "the enmity that has always separated the Ridwān from the A. Mʿāmar":

A descendant of Hamām, named Drīss, who was on his way to the holy cities with his ailing wife, was obliged to leave her with some members of the A. Rabīʿa – a Hamāmi who had also come from the Gharb (Faid banī Hamām) and had settled in the region now occupied by the A. Mʿāmar. While Drīss continued on his way to Mecca, his wife gave birth to a son, named Drīss, who was raised among the Rabīʿa, but who apparently did not receive the same care as the Awlād Rabīʿa.

On his return from his pilgrimage, Drīss found his son all grown and wanted to take him to Gharb al-Juālī (Morocco). Drīss ibn Drīss refused to leave his adoptive father.

"Stay then and populate this land. You will become the founder of a great family," were the prophetic words of the pilgrim. Rabiʿa (mistaken for a woman by Arabs who mispronounced his name) had two sons, ʿAzīz and Mʿāmar. Drīss had two sons, Ridwān and Sellāma. These four people gave their names to the four great tribes that today constitute the great family of Hamāma:

A. Rabīʿa — A. ʿAzīz / A. Mʿāmar

A. Drīss — A. Ridwān / A. Sellāma

> The difference in origin is largely responsible for the hostility that alienates the first two groups from the last two, and though they had on occasion been brought together by intermarriage, they have never had very friendly relations on a broad level.
>
> Even today, although the Mʿāmar and the Sellāma were for a time united under the same command, they are anything but friendly. This hostility was carried to such a point that when the A. Drīss were victims of a partial raid, the A. Rabīʿa often failed to come to their aid, and vice versa.[9]

Since the entire story is related by members of the A. Mʿāmar, this group comes off best, while the A. Drīss are virtual bastards. Filiation, if it is not matrilinear, is at least matrilocal, since Drīss, the legitimate father, returned to Morocco without his offspring. Compared to the A. Rabīʿa, they are in a subordinate position, since their settlement in the region was more recent than that of the A. Rabīʿa. And last, while they owe their life to the hospitality of the A. Rabīʿa, they are thankless wretches who show no gratitude whatever. As to the Mʿāmar, they claim patrilinear descent by pointing out the confusion over the sex of their Rabīʿa ancestor.

This story raises two points. The first is that the conflict revealed here is quite different from the ones seen earlier. Those were temporary, sporadic, variable, and took place in historic time, whereas this one refers to mythical time. It is therefore permanent, irreducible, and structural. Second, in the apparently symmetrical genealogical system, one sees that there is a latent, implied hierarchy. The Mʿāmar, authors of this account, consider themselves superior to the Ridwān.

We therefore see two types of oppositions: the first are occasional, in which alliances are made and broken without any duration; the others are structural, and existed between hereditary enemies. These latter oppositions can either remain on the symbolic level or, on a long-term basis, express themselves through the absence of relations – principally through the infrequency of intermarriage – or at their worst, explode in armed conflict.

If one were to diagram the filiation of the different segments according to the preceding account, one would arrive at Figure 2.3, Plan A. The explanation of the hostility between the two primary branches is completely different in another account, from which Plan B is drawn.

This is how that story of Plan B goes: "The Hamāma had a chief

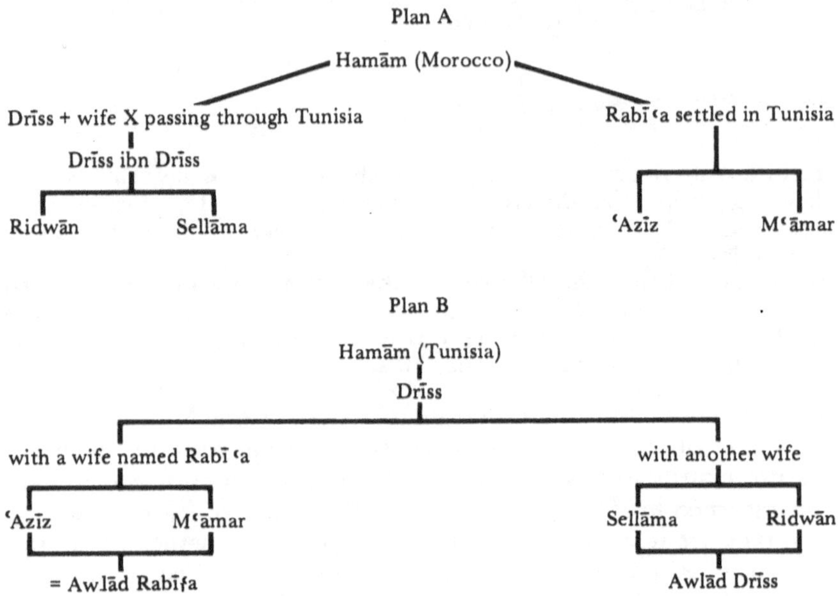

Fig. 2.3. Divergent accounts, opposing groups.

named Hamām, from whom they took the name Hamāma. This chief, on his arrival in the regency, had a son named Drīss, who himself had two sons, 'Azīz and M'āmar, from a previous wife, Rabī'a, followed by two more sons, Ridwān and Sellāma, from a second wife. These four are the heads of the four great tribes that today constitute the family of Hamāma. These two groups who decend from two different mothers, have always lived in great conflict."[10]

This new account presents none of the dissymmetries of the earlier one—no pseudobastard or patrilinear filiation raises one group above the other. All of the Hamāma, according to this version, descend from Drīss, the only son of Hamām: The symmetry between the two branches is perfect. It is Drīss's bigamy, and the resulting rivalry between the two wives, that accounts for the hostility between the two branches. The hierarchy implied by the first account is not entirely absent from this one, but it is turned around. Where the descendants of Drīss in the first account (Plan A) were the wards of Rabī'a, in the second version (Plan B) they descend directly from the founder, while the rival group takes the name of a wife. As a result, the superiority implied by the protagonists of the first account is questioned by the narrators of the second. What remains is the opposition between the two main branches. The explanation may vary, but the hostility endures and in both cases is openly acknowledged.

Other kinds of opposition are concealed: they are enacted without being formulated. In addition to the hostility that has appeared between the Awlād Rabīʿa and the A. Drīss, another set of antagonisms exists in the first group, disclosed by various remarks made by the A. Rabīʿa who, it will be remembered, are comprised of A. Mʿāmar and A. ʿAzīz.

"The Hamāma," relate the Mʿāmar, "came to the Faid banī Hamām in the Sāguiat al Hamra (southern Morocco). From the Faid banī Hamām into the territory of the regency came the Zawāra, the Awlād Slijān, Awlād ʿAkrīm, and Awlād Farhān. They all descended from Hamām, who gave his name to the family, and these are his only descendants."

The account goes on: "The Zawāra settled in the Sahara; it is they who provided the Hamāma with the first *qādis*. They have [a *zāwiya* a place of Moslem teaching; a mosque empowered to grant asylum] called Sidi Dahar on the border of the Frashīsh's territory. The Slijān fought alongside the Zawāra; they engendered the A. ʿMāmar. The A.ʿAkrīm and A. Farhān formed the A. Ridwān."[11]

This is a disturbing story, for it is completely irreconcilable with a subsequent passage from the same account that presents a genealogy quite different from the one forcefully put forth here – "and these are his only descendants" – to explain the hostility between the Drīss and the Rabīʿa. It is a questionable story, and for that reason a revealing one, since ʿAzīz is obliterated from this version. This omission tells us quite a lot about the relations between the ʿAzīz and the Mʿāmar. Appearing here as direct descendants of Hamām are groups that other accounts place in different positions: the Slijān, Zawāra, ʿAkrīm, and Farhān. Elsewhere they are listed as groups associated with the Hamāma but not descended from their founder, or else as full-blooded Hamāma but situated on the third or fourth rank in relation to their ancestor. And finally, this account confers authority on the Zawāra, from whom, to hear them tell it, the cadis of the tribe were always recruited.

And so, while the A. ʿAzīz are eliminated from Hamām's descendants, secondary groups are promoted to a rank all the way up to the founder of the tribe. This double manipulation of the genealogy is without a doubt an indication of the hostility between the two branches of the A. Rabīʿa, one which is not otherwise manifested.

When the A. ʿAzīz were questioned, the account changed again, but it nonetheless confirms the rivalry that had been disclosed. According to them, the Slijān, ʿAkarma, and Zawāra followed the Hamāma during their migrations. Presented in this way, they fall into a subordinate position, since the leadership of the migrations was always in the hands of the "authentic" Hamāma. They were therefore incapable of any independent political action. What is more, between Mʿāmar and ʿAzīz there is an evident inequality. The account reports that "ʿAzīz extended his authority over the Fitnāsah, Sobra, Zawāra, ʿĀkrama and Slijān." He thus inherited the power of his ancestor Hamām. ʿAzīz then led a new migration, bringing along additional secondary groups and affirming his authority through his victories over other tribes. The power finally passed over to his grandson, Belhādi, and subsequently to his descendants, the Awlād Belhādi, ʿAzīz's other offspring having been presented as inferior.

An undeniable arrogance emerges from all the sequences of the Awlād ʿAzīz account, further manifested by a strong tendency toward endogamy: "The A. ʿAzīz contract marriages between themselves without even going outside their individual fractions."

Thus the Awlād Mʿāmar and Awlād ʿAzīz present symmetrical and inverse images of themselves and of the secondary groups with whom they constitute the Awlād Rabīʿa. The balance of forces within the entire tribe is turned around depending on which of the accounts one accepts. According to one version, the A. Mʿāmar have the upper hand over the A. ʿAzīz; according to the other, the opposite is true. In this way, all the branches of a tribe, as traced by its members, would be articulated like a Calder mobile whose equilibrium requires an equal distribution of weight even though the individual parts are unequal, and the position of the parts changes constantly though the stress lines remain the same.

The tribe, a geometric entity of allegiances based on family relationships, is thus crisscrossed by conflicts. Some of them, of a circumstantial nature and without consequence, go back to historic time. The struggles that ensue correspond to explicit motives. Others, more lasting, go back to mythical times. Both types of conflict can give rise to the same forms of violence – in particular, the raid, a collective operation accompanied by looting. But the second type, even when not formally discernible, is structural; filiation is at the same time an affiliation. In other words, by definition, the members of a group stand united in their group's hostility to another group, and it matters little which chronicle records this. This permanent hostility, or feud, divides not only the major branches of a single tribe, but its respective subdivisions as well.

The tribe and others: the soffs. On occasion, rivals do join forces. It often happened, according to one account, that the A. Drīss were raided without receiving the support of the A. Rabīʿa, "but they were nevertheless allies when they were threatened by any serious invasion and when they participated in any major expedition." Just as within a tribe the offshoots of a branch are united in the event of conflict with an adversary branch, so the entire tribe stands together if a situation arises that opposes it to another tribe. In such a situation, the tribe is not isolated. It can count on the neutrality or support of other groups, as can its adversaries.

In studies on North Africa such alliances have become well known by the term *soff*.[12] The Hamāma, allies of the Jlāss and Naffāt, thus constitute the Husaynite soff. Their adversaries – the Banī Zīd, Frashīsh, and Mājer – are united in the Bashia soff. The names of these two leagues go back to the civil war of 1729–40, mentioned earlier, between the founder of the dynasty, Husayn, and his nephew, Ali Pāsha.

It is on this aspect of the relationship between tribes that one can suspect some bias on the part of the investigating officers. For their purpose in drawing up a memorandum on each group was to estimate the solidity of the French occupation of Tunisia and to calculate the likelihood of resistance, which is to say, the degree of solidarity among the tribes. Strategic concerns may have led the writers of these memoranda to overestimate the cohesion between those peoples and to perceive networks of alliance where there were merely occasional agreements. In fact, whereas the Hamāma openly distinguished between their allies and their enemies, some of the tribes interrogated evaded the question or declared that such alliances were no longer in effect or else that the old rivalries were now forgotten and unimportant.

With regard to the Hamāma, the alliances they recognized were expressed through economic cooperation and assistance in time of need. For example, the A. ʿAzīz stored their harvests with the sedentary peoples of Sened and Mech. In exchange, they protected them when rival tribes threatened them. For such tribes, hostility was manifested in the form of raids, whose result, if not purpose, was economic pillage and theft of herds.

Alliances and dissensions between different tribes seem barely distinguishable from what we have already seen within the Hamāma tribe. One would begin to doubt the veracity of the soffs if history did not come to the rescue of the tradition by revealing their dynamics and duration.

The first period of violent dissension occurred in 1729–40, during the quarrel between Husayn and Ali Pāsha. According to the historian Seghir ben Youssef,[13] who recounts these events in copious detail, the country was divided into two camps. On Husayn's side were the Awlād ʿŪn, the Jlāss, and the Hamāma, while Ali counted on the Methallith, the Awlād Saʿīd, the Sawāsi, and others. In fact, the two leagues rarely organized themselves into homogeneous armies led by the two adversaries. Generally, the adhesion of a tribe to either of the parties, or its alliance with other tribes, signified that it could raid an opposing tribe with the blessing of the pretender it supported. The Hanānsha and Awlād ʿAmār of the

Drīd, a chronicler relates, had joined with Ali Pāsha, "who authorized them to raid the Sharen and the Zawāra." Such brief engagements were also preferred to pitched battles. Furthermore, mobilization was brief, "each tribe leaving the field when it reached its own territory." Acknowledgment of a chief sanctioned rather than prohibited local strategy.

Twenty years later, Ali Pāsha's grandson rebelled against the descendants of Husayn. Among the rebel tribes were the Methallith, the Sawāsi, the A. Saʿīd, Frashīsh, Mājer, and Banī Zīd. On the loyalist side were the Hamāma, Awlād ʿŪn, Jlāss, and Naffāt.[14] Both sides remained faithful to their first allegiances.

For more than a century, the feuds seemed to subside. There is no trace of the rivalries between once-warring tribes until, suddenly, in 1864, a tremendous uprising ignited the country. After the first few months the insurgents broke ranks; some tribes went over to the bey to subjugate the others. On the bey's side, Husayn's descendant, the Awlād ʿŪn, Jlāss, and Hamāma suddenly reappeared. The insurgents again numbered among them the Methallith, A. Saʿīd, Sawāsi, and Banī Zīd.[15] After a century of virtual tranquility, the lines of fracture between the groups reappeared as in previous conflicts.

Even when the events that illustrate permanent hostility are forgotten or altered by time, the reality of the soffs is undeniable and their continuity remarkable. Opposition may be reactivated only sporadically, yet adherence to one league or another remains constant. "Anarchy," the perennial warfare between tribes or fragments of tribes, thus has its rules.

Apart from what they reveal about the relationships between tribes in times of war as in times of peace, these leagues also indicate the nature of relations maintained by the central power with the peoples of the hinterland. They are relations of alliance or hostility rather than of subjection. The loyalty of men of the tents is not based on their status as subjects, but on their voluntary accord with the dynasty. Unlike eighteenth-century Morocco, Tunisia did not have a dissident region that continuously challenged the central authority. All the tribes were subjects of the bey, and their obedience was expressed, first and foremost, as well as in other ways, by the payment of taxes. However, as seen by the tribes, their relationship with the central power was expressed in terms of accepted or rejected allegiance.

A structural space. If the history of the tribe has a beginning in time – the life of the founder – it also has a beginning in space. No matter which group was questioned, their account of tribal origins always spoke of an initial migration. For most of the Hamāma, that migration was a double one. During the first period, the tribe moved from east to west without stopping in Tunisia. During the second, they went from west to east within the regency. Though there is agreement about the general direction of the two migrations, the stopping places vary from one account to another. From the east, the starting place is given in some cases as Arabia, in others as Syria, and the place of arrival after the first migration is Algeria in some accounts, Morocco in others.

What does this migration mean? Once again, a "realistic" or historicist interpretation of the account is totally without interest. It is true that Tunisia received waves of migrants from the west, as from the east, but this is not the historic fact recorded by the myths of origin. Other tribes also begin their history with a major displacement. If these myths are to be trusted, Tunisia was once a magnificent plain, completely uninhabited, where all these groups – or rather the founders – converged simultaneously though not in concert.

Does this itinerary hold a religious significance? One would be tempted to think so. The Hejaz, birthplace of Islam, would also be the birthplace of the tribe. At the other extreme of the Moslem world, the famous Moroccan *sāguia*, holy place and western boundary of Islam, would be the starting point of the second migration. The two directions described in the account would thus indicate the limits of Moslem space, in which the Hamāma would situate themselves – which is what they did. However, this insertion within Islamic geography is only natural, for no other space is conceivable, and consequently it does not endow the geographic origin with any quality of prestige or glory. If some say they came from Arabia or the celebrated *sāguia*, others claim to have come from Syria or southern Algeria, neither of which has religious connotation.

What is most important in the account is not the place of origin, since it varies, but the very fact that there was a migration. It is as if migration legitimates the possession of lands, as if the arrival and settlement as a group establishes the right to occupy a specific territory.[16] Furthermore, the undertaking is collective, even when the eponymous founder is the initiator, a fact that strengthens the solidarity within the lineage. And it is through their participation in the various movements of the tribe that outside groups gain acceptance within it. This shared experience lays the foundation for the unity of the tribe. Just as genealogy describes fission in time, so migration traces secession in space.

The arrival in Tunisia does not, however, imply any conquest or military victory. Except for the A. ʿAzīz, who at the time of a third migration acquired their territory at the price of a confrontation with the Mājer, other groups present their arrival as a peaceful movement of transhumance rather than as an unleashing of invaders.

We see here two kinds of space. The first, vast, with ill-defined boundaries, nonetheless lies within the framework of Islam: the east and west

<table>
<tr><th colspan="3">SPACE</th></tr>
<tr><td rowspan="2">TIME</td><td>Founders</td><td>East → First migration. Bypasses Tunisia → West
Settlement
Tunisia ← Second migration ← West
Settlement within present boundaries</td></tr>
<tr><td>Lineages</td><td>Present-day territory
Partitioned according to genealogical divisions</td></tr>
</table>

Fig. 2.4. Space and genealogy.

from whence the ancestors of the tribe originated. The second, very precise, is the territory occupied by the tribe on its arrival. Its dimensions are not measured, either in days or in any other way. Topography – a stream, a mountain – provides no more than landmarks. The boundaries, like those of time, are social. The territory of the tribe ends where that of another tribe begins.

The tribe's territory was divided within perimeters established by time. Its various sections corresponded to the social structure. There were as many geographic units as there were social units. The distribution of the groups over the land reproduced the genealogical divisions already indicated. Two subdivisions of a lineage could not jointly inhabit the same territory. Genealogy is therefore a conceptualization of the arrangement of territorial segments (Fig. 2.4).

This space, although adequate for the social structure, was not closed off, however. Economic activities, and religious or political affinities, created bridges between tribal lands and neighboring regions. To start with the religious aspect, the Hamāma's territory held the tombs of saints, which were holy places of pilgrimage. Some, revered only by the Hamāma, were objects of a purely local cult. Others received the visits of neighboring tribes, even enemy tribes. So that, for example, on the lands of the Awlād Arua, the tomb of a holy man reputed to belong to the Mājer tribe drew believers from his own tribe as well as from the Jlāss. As for the Hamāma, they frequented holy places located on the neighboring territories of the Jlāss, their allies in the north, and particularly in the towns of Gafsa and El Ksar in the south. In this, religious activity was inseparable from commerce. Saints were visited when there was merchandise to exchange. That was when the Hamāma sold their wool. They entrusted their silos to the sedentary people of the region, while at the same time assuring them of protection.

The Hamāma maintained only limited commercial dealings with the cities of Sfax in the east and Kairouan in the north. Having no markets in their own territory, the Hamāma received neither migrants nor produce from other regions. They seem to have had no relations whatever with the Ifriqīya, in particular. Their entire existence was thus contained within the space belonging to the tribe, in coordination, however, with the villagers who bordered on their territory to the south.

From the particular to the general

Structural time, structural space, the pattern of relationships between the tribe and its neighbors, and within the tribe itself – these are the themes of the chronicle of the Hamāma. To determine in what way this tribe was typical, it is necessary to compare it with other tribes, not by retracing the same route for each of them, but simply by checking the recurring and variable features revealed in the totality of the collected oral traditions against those found in the history of the Hamāma.

The past as metaphor of the present

What becomes immediately obvious is that the morphology of the histories is always the same and in almost every case is genealogical. The chronicles of the Jlāss, the Naffāt, and others begin with a founder and then follow the same set of sequences as those recounted by the Hamāma: a time of ancestors and migration, a time of descendants, a chronological time containing a sequence of actual events. The trait common to all the tribes is the minimal variation in the span of mythical time, a period that for all the groups is quite brief. Among the Jlāss, for example, only five generations separate the living members from their ancestors. In measured time, the different histories cover one and a half to two centuries. Tunisia, uninhabited before the fifteenth century, would have first been populated, according to the chronicles, by the generation of founders. This is absurd, but it confirms that the past is a metaphor of the present, and a formalization of the social organization. The "passage" of time is an illusion.

Following mythical time, itself divided into one or two sequences depending on the tribe, is historic time, marked by a series of important events. The latter differs from the first in that it contains snatches of reality – civil wars, feuds between tribes, the famine and epidemic of 1867 – even when the facts were altered. Its duration, therefore, varies only slightly from one group to another, not exceeding 150 or 200 years. Beyond that limit, collective memory does not preserve or transmit dated facts. This "historic" sequence is not included in the genealogical one, but connects with it in an order of succession. The time of *n* generations separating the founder from his living descendants should also encompass recent chronology. It should therefore be possible to assign a given dated incident to the lifetime of an ancestor or to a particular generation.

But this is not the case. The genealogical series and the series of events follow one after the other. And yet the latter is also part of mythical time: The quarrels it relates prolong it and illustrate it. As in the case of legendary time, the function or result of the chronological sequence is to clarify the tribe's relations with other tribes and their respective subdivisions. Time is therefore not a continuum but a structural relationship between the first and the last terms of a line of filiation.[17]

An initial migration also appears in all the accounts and fulfills the same function: that of legitimizing the occupation of the land. Some tribes, however, such as the Drīd or the Riyāh who settled in the north, are not the owners of the land they farm. In order to explain their tenant status, the account of their migration is consequently modified as follows: The Riyāh relate that they originated in Arabia and came into the regency at the request of the pasha, whom they had helped. They remained allied with the bey, to whom they furnished troops on a regular basis. As compensation for their services, he is said to have ceded to them the lands they inhabit, in return for payment of a rental fee. The indignity of their position as tenant farmers is thus compensated for by the glory of having saved the monarch. A pathetic and meager compensation, when one recalls that the Riyāh were the most powerful tribe among the Hillalian invaders of the eleventh century; that they imposed an alliance on the last Zirid sovereign, took three of his daughters as wives, and conquered the greater part of his realm. Of this brilliant epic, no trace is to be found in the unpretentious nineteenth-century chronicle of the Riyāh.[18] Once again, the external origin of the group is a structural rather than an actual fact of history.

The Riyāh's amnesia regarding their own past glory is worth noting for it invalidates the hypothesis frequently offered to explain the agglutinative force of certain tribes, their power of attraction for others, and the resulting amplitude of the genealogical phenomenon. "We are in a land (in this case Algeria) where certain names are epic poems," wrote P. Bourdieu, who also reminds us that the poorest shepherd can boast of Hillalian ancestry. In Tunisia, not only has the epic been forgotten, but even groups like the Riyāh, who are entitled to it as a source of strength and pride, have lost all memory of it and have succumbed to fragmentation.

An order based on symmetrical and contradictory elements

With or without a founding ancestor, all the tribes manifest the same kind of organization based on symmetrical lineages reproduced by repeated fission. The symmetry and equality between groups of the same genealogical rank are mirrored by the same equality among subsequent ranks. Among the Jlāss, for example, there is no distinction between the

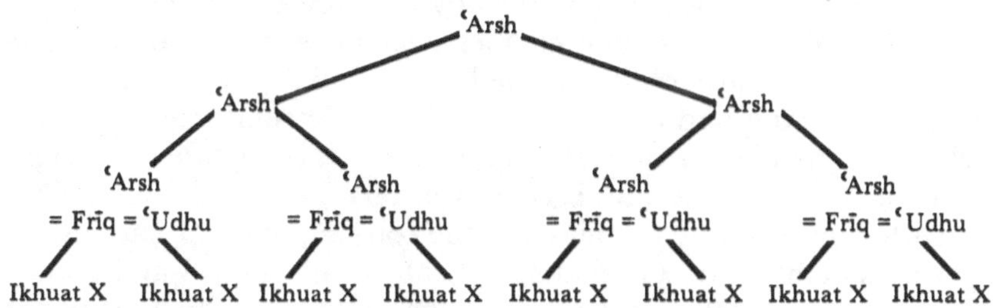

Fig. 2.5. Organigram of a tribe.

Awlād Shabīb and the Awlād Hillāl even though the latter are a subdivision of the former. This equivalence is further confirmed by the lexicography of these tribes. The same word, *'arsh*, designates groups of unequal dimensions and different positions within the genealogy. In an eighteenth-century document, the Jlāss are designated as a tribe, *'arsh*; the three branches that compose it – the Sindāssin, Awlād Idīr and Awlād Khalīfa – are also called *'arsh*. The later offshoots are *'arsh* as well. Beginning with the third rank, two words are used that are never applied to the first rank: *frīq* or *farqa*, subdivision, and *'udhu*, branch (Figure 2.5). From one text to another, however, these terms are occasionally replaced by the word *'arsh*, even to designate a smaller offshoot of the tribe. In short, these groups have no apparent autonomy; individuals are lost in the collective whole. If, in the case of the smallest unit, an individual does emerge, he is placed in a fraternal rather than a dominant relationship to the rest of his group. The enlarged family is referred to as "the brothers [*ikhuāt*] of so-and-so," or "sons [*awlād*] of so-and-so."

Sons or brothers, the members of a tribe are always represented as equals – equals, but opponents, as among the Hamāma. The chronicle of the Shāren is quite explicit on this point: "Twins were born," it relates, "joined by the thumb. An operation separated them, but the midwife predicted that divisiveness would arise between their descendants. The Shāren descend from one of the twins, the Wārgha from the other."[19]

What better illustration of the well-known Arab proverb: "I against my brother; my brother and I against my cousin; my cousin, my brother, and I against the world"?

The tribes of Tunisia consequently constitute a segmentary type of society in which politics, history, and economics are expressed in terms of genealogy, and political relationships are a function of genealogical distance. It is segmentary also because of its simultaneous dynamics of fusion and fission. A balance of forces is achieved through internal tension, and the group is both defined and preserved through its hostility to homologous groups.

This structure was already described by Peyssonnel in the eighteenth century with the acuteness that characterizes his entire account. "The bedouin Arabs of Barbary are divided into a number of nations, and these nations correspond to as many families as descend from the same branch. These families form small villages called *dawār*, made up of eight or ten tents, more or less, and each tent in turn holds a single family." So much for interlocking families and the consanguinity of nations. As for permanent hostility, or feuding, "Arabs often wage war between nations and reciprocally steal each other's animals... Their wars are rarely brutal; their only aim is loot and they rarely kill one another. They always respect the women, who are never mistreated."[20]

Variation of the model: the maraboutic lines

Maraboutic lines are a particular variant of the overall pattern traced for the tribes as a whole, not because of the sequences of their chronicles, but because of the functions of the individuals concerned. In the case of lay tribes, the functions of the ancestor or of his first descendants were simple and constantly repeated: (1) They gave the tribe its name; (2) they procreated; and (3) they led the migration and eventual settlement on their territory. These same three functions are also fulfilled by the founders of maraboutic lines. But in order for a tribe to have maraboutic status, it must also have a number of other attributes. For example, the history of the Mahādhba[21] begins, as does the Hamāma's, with an east–west migration all the way to Morocco, followed by a new trek toward the east. In this case, and in contrast to the Hamāma, space has a religious significance. The starting place was the holy city of Mecca, and the center of the second dispersion is Morocco, presented as a vast *zāwiya* whose chief is the sultan. The founder's journey to Tunisia also has religious overtones. Its purpose was to propagate the faith by two means: first by procreation, which engendered new tribes, and then by the conversion of adherents through missionary work. Proselytism was thus one of the functions of the founder.

"Having reached the place where the kubba of Sidi Mahadhab now stands, the holy dervish stopped. Water was abundant, pastureland close by, and in addition, the Methallith, who held the region, were eager to assure themselves of divine protection through the presence of the venerated marabout."

Another specific trait of maraboutic lines is the manner of settlement. Land is acquired not by merely occupying an uninhabited region, as in the case of lay tribes, but by donation. This comes from the piety of the tribe already settled there, but it also indicates a kind of reciprocity. In exchange for the land, the presence of the marabout guarantees divine protection for the donor.

The descendants of the family founded by Sidi Mahadhab claimed the genealogy traced in Figure 2.6. It reveals a new trait, particular to a maraboutic tribe: the prophetic origin of the ancestor. This filiation should confer a much more ancient past on the tribe than can be claimed by lay tribes, but in fact, from the daughter of the Prophet to Sidi Mahadhab, all they count is forty generations without going into detail. Descent from the Prophet is therefore a thinly camouflaged fiction.

The epic of the founder recapitulates all the major features of all the founding ancestors of tribes. But his origin, behavior, and actions add a religious coefficient to the corresponding attributes of lay founders.

The second sequence of the history is in turn richer than that of lay tribes. In order for a tribe to maintain its maraboutic status, the descendants of the marabout must also evidence holy characteristics. Along with their greater piety and wisdom, they also possess magical powers. For example, En-Nuwīqes, "the incomplete one," a descendant of Si Mahadhab, is said to have accomplished a miracle. After a long period of sterility, his wife gave birth to a child every seven months – a proof of God's recompense for the saint's piety, since saintliness implies wealth and fertility.

Several qualities distinguished the status of the tribe as a whole. First among them were the dispersion and the extent of spiritual influence. Maraboutic tribes had relatives and therefore allies throughout the country, from north to south. They also exercised a spiritual influence over those tribes who flocked to the marabout in pilgrimage. Another quality was their wealth, which was the result of the generous offerings of pilgrims and devotees generated by the marabout's prestige. Its extensive influence and wealth were in turn proofs that the tribe continued to enjoy divine blessings. And finally, pacifism was a maraboutic virtue. Men of piety were not men of war. This, however, did not protect them from attack. But being nonviolent, they responded to aggression with prayer. When they were raided by the Hamāma, their story goes, "the Mahādhba immediately took their prayer beads and went on a new kind of pilgrimage in search of their stolen camels. The miracle, it would seem, did take place, and the Hamāma, deeply moved, ended up by returning all or much of the loot."

Different traits thus distinguish this group as a maraboutic tribe. The Mahādhba do not, however, incorporate all the attributes of holy men. Other saintly lines, in their past as well as in the present functions, have specific characteristics of their status which the Mahādhba do not share. Many founders had miraculous powers. The founder of the tribe of Awlād Abū Ghānim[22] had the same past as Si Mahadhab (sharifian origin,

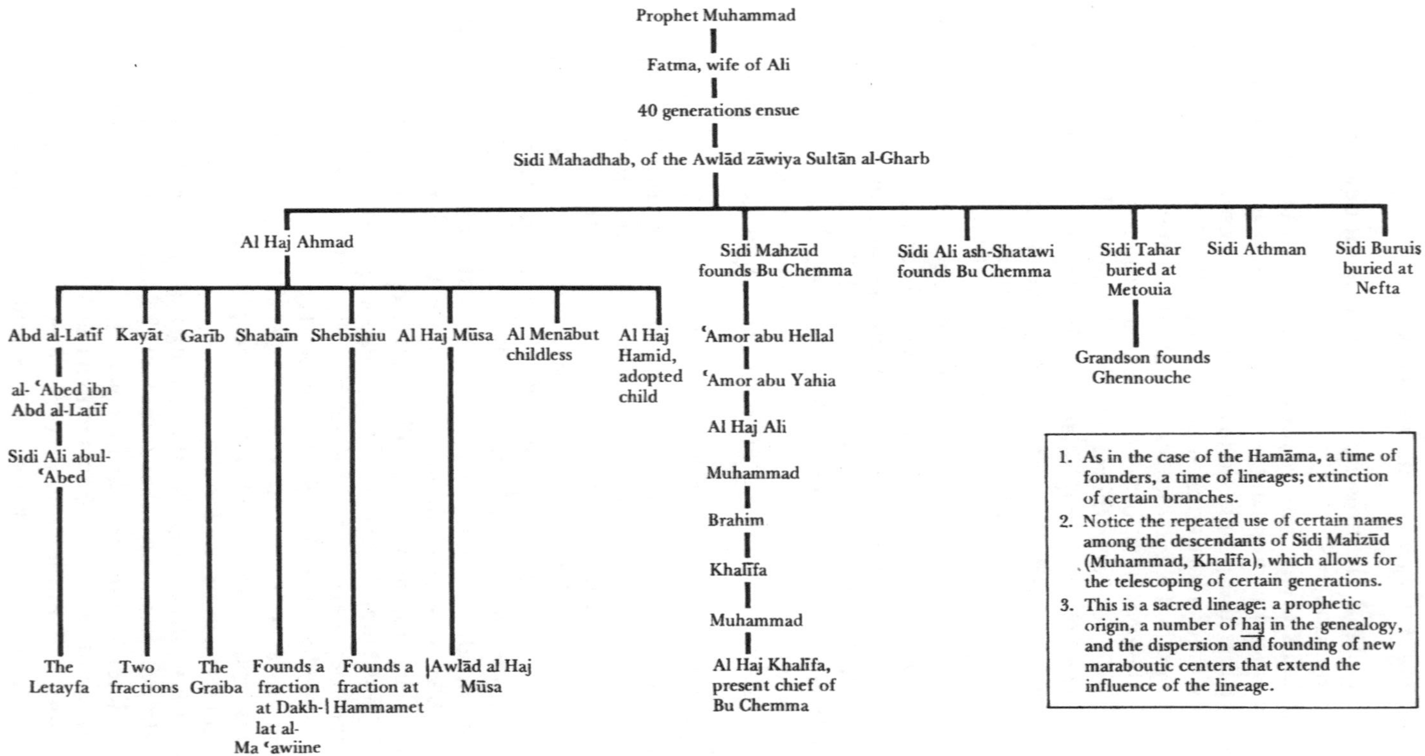

1. As in the case of the Hamāma, a time of founders, a time of lineages; extinction of certain branches.
2. Notice the repeated use of certain names among the descendants of Sidi Mahzūd (Muhammad, Khalīfa), which allows for the telescoping of certain generations.
3. This is a sacred lineage: a prophetic origin, a number of haj in the genealogy, and the dispersion and founding of new maraboutic centers that extend the influence of the lineage.

Fig. 2.6. Genealogy of a maraboutic group: the Mahādhba.

early settlement in Morocco before coming to Tunisia), but on his arrival in the regency, he accomplished many miracles. He was nourished by a camel who came every day to offer him her milk; he emerged uninjured from flames, changed into a crow, and saved the son of a prince from burning. The rest of his life story is comparable to that of Si Mahadhab, and he too received land on which to settle.

Other maraboutic lines, while not claiming descent from the Prophet, are entitled to the status of marabout because of the conduct of their ancestor. In short, the functions of these maraboutic tribes fall into three categories. They are, of course, religious. The tomb of the saint is a place of common worship and usually a place of learning. They are also political. The tomb can, on occasion, provide asylum; that is, it can protect the life of anyone who seeks refuge there. Generally speaking, maraboutic tribes do not get involved in tribal quarrels and can therefore serve as arbitrators. Furthermore, the annual pilgrimage hosted by these tribes provides an occasion to confirm and consolidate ties between allies. Finally, these holy men play a role in the protection and reproduction of wealth, either by safeguarding the grain left with them by neighboring tribes, or by enlisting divine favor on behalf of those who make offerings. However, as has already been noted, no single maraboutic tribe combines all of these functions.

Even though they span a much longer period and have a much richer content – including tales of wonders and miracles – the histories of maraboutic lineages belong to the same genre as those of lay tribes, and they reflect the same type of social organization. To assert this similarity already implies a considerable degree of generalization for eighteenth- and nineteenth-century Tunisia, since nomads were far more numerous than sedentary people and covered a greater geographic area. But does the same pattern fit settled groups? Or does the segmentary system no longer apply to them?

Another variant: the case of villagers

An answer to these questions can, in part, be found by examining the nineteenth-century local traditions of Gafsa and its surrounding region.[23]

"Five subdivisions live in this city whose names are Al Baldiya, Jbargu, Al Mnariyīn, Al Knānsa, and Al Jariyīn." This sentence reflects the same scheme we observed among the tent dwellers. The various quarters of Gafsa bear the name of the lineage groups that occupy them. The population did not identify itself in terms of social stratification or topographic distribution, but by a commonly recognized origin. The Baldiya, who occupied the northeast sector of the city, were the oldest unit and the most populous group. Living in the center, the Mnariyīn descended from four individuals who came from northern Tunisia and settled in Gafsa because they were well received by the earlier inhabitants. The third group had an ancestor, Ali Knawa, who left a *zāwiya* in Morocco, came to Tunisia, married a young woman from a maraboutic family, and thus founded the subdivision of the Knānsa who settled in southwest Gafsa and provided the city with its men of learning. The second and third subgroups were thus the result of the migration of an ancestor and the proliferation of his descendants, a familiar story of origin and scarcely different from that of tribal groups.

As for the Jariyīn, their ancestors were two men who left their native land to come to Gafsa where "they married two Mnariyīn girls and each had many offspring. One of their descendants, Abdallah Abu Bakr, achieved great prominence in the city because of his intelligence, learning, and wealth. He is said to have had four children. Still today, almost all the judicial positions are by members of that fraction." The elements of migration and proliferation in this account are quite standard. But its history also emphasizes the power of this group: many progeny, wisdom, and intermarriage with the Mnariyīn. Marked by misfortune, the background of the Jbargu is completely different. Their settlement was the result of a punishment – political, according to some, divine according to others. The chronicle relates that "this fraction was made up of people who were brigands and were obliged to live in the city of Gafsa by the sultan of Tunis, who had received complaints about the misdeeds of the Jbargu." In another account, "the inhabitants of Gafsa, and particularly the Jbargu, were decimated by cholera one year. The Jbargu, believing that the plague had hit them especially hard merely because they were living on the Jabal Mida, hastened to leave it and settled in the city proper."

To these five groups we must add the Turks, the families of nomadic tribes, the Jews who occupy a quarter on the eastern side of the city, and finally, the population of the suburb of Sidi Mansūr, 1.5 kilometers from Gafsa. "Sidi Mansūr traveled around the country some three centuries ago to spread the Moslem faith among the inhabitants. During one of his travels, he died at Tamaghza where he was buried. His children, not wishing to live far from their father's tomb, later carried the ashes of the marabout to Gafsa and buried them where the kubba of Sidi Mansūr stands today... They have always lived harmoniously with the people of Gafsa; every time that the Gafsans quarreled with their neighbors, the dwellers of Sidi Mansūr intervened and sought to reconcile the two sides." A void was thus filled: The five subdivisions had educated men among them, but no marabout. With Sidi Mansūr, propagator of the faith, and his descendants, arbitrators of conflicts, the picture is complete.

What is still missing is the nature of the relationships connecting the different groups that made up the population of Gafsa. We can only guess at what these relations were like inside the city. An alliance between the Jariyīn and the Mnariyīn is suggested by the marriage between the ancestor of the latter and the daughter of the former. One can also guess at the rejection of the Jbargu, ill-loved by the prince or by God, and at the power of the Baldiya, more ancient and more numerous. A whole interplay of relations is implied here but the details elude us. The picture is much clearer with regard to the relations between Gafsa and the surrounding villages and tribes, as for example its dealings with El Ksar, a nearby oasis.

El Ksar has seven subdivisions whose history follows the well-known pattern. One learns first that the inhabitants of the two places do business with each other but stay separate, "not mixing." This interaction is explained in the following way:

> Three centuries ago, all these subdivisions lived in Gafsa forming a single group because each of them felt too isolated in the city. The reason for their departure was that a son of the *qādi* of the city became the lover of a young girl belonging to this group. As a result, he was killed by members of her clan. After the murder, the inhabitants of Gafsa began persecuting the seven clans who, in search of peace, left Gafsa and settled outside the city near the Jabal Mida.
>
> Some time later, these people wished to put an end to the hostility between the Gafsans and themselves (they had even been prohibited from entering the mosques of the city), sent forty elders from the group to the *qādi* to pay a price for his son's blood. The *qādi* received them graciously, even inviting them to dinner, but he had poison put into everything they were served. The forty old men died within the same day. Their corpses were placed on mules and carried outside the city where they were dumped.
>
> The seven clans, seeing they could not be reconciled with Gafsa, wanted to settle even farther away from the city. And so, in agreement with the townspeople, they decided to roll a heavy stone for a full day. Wherever it stopped was where they would settle. When night fell, they stopped rolling the stone and built the village of El Ksar on the spot where they had stopped. For a long time, the Gafsans called them El Menzil (the transported ones).
>
> Two years later, to avenge the murder that had been perpetrated on forty of their own, the inhabitants of El Ksar attacked a large number of Gafsans who had assembled in one of the gardens of the oasis for a wedding, and killed almost every one of them. This garden, located on the road to Tozeur, still carries the name of Jnan al Moqtal (garden of the murder).

Though the past and the space that separates them are saturated with blood, the inhabitants of both places had been reconciled and were living in harmony when their history was compiled. As a matter of fact, these homicidal conflicts did not prevent the two towns from joining the same soff, having the same allies, and even the same enemies (specifically the Hamāma).

Gafsa has been deliberately selected. On an ancient site, whose history is far richer than its inhabitants relate, Gafsa is more than a village. With its garrison, its large and ethnically varied population, its numerous merchants and artisans, Gafsa can be considered a city. There are other possibilities of societal organization than those we have seen among the tribes. In this case, the translation of the societal structure into space, or the transposition of the social location into myth, is even clearer, if that is possible, than in the vast tribal territories.

Are we still too close to the desert? Villagers living near the capital see themselves no differently from the inhabitants of Gafsa and its surroundings. Must one stop at the edge of towns? That is not certain. As to structural time, we see indications of it even among the most literate. The historian Ibn Abi Dhiaf was of old Tunisian stock, we are told by Ahmed Abdesselem.[24] "His *nisba*, al-ʿŪni, relates him to the tribe of Awlād ʿŪn, who were settled in the region of Siliana, east of Le Kef. The Awlād ʿŪn were part of the tribal group of *husayniyya*, which means that they took sides with the founder of the Husaynite dynasty, Husayn Ibn Ali and his sons, in their struggle with their nephew and cousin, Ali Pāsha and his descendants... Among the Awlād ʿŪn, the family of Abi-d-Dhiaf seems to have been highly prestigious. It stemmed from a minor saint whose renown was not wide but was sufficient to prove that his descendants were not among the late-comers to the tribe." This *nisba*, the indication of ancestry in each individual's name, also assigns him his place in a network of family relationships and alliances. In all Arab societies, the name of the individual, whether town dweller or peasant, indicates paternity or filiation (abū or ibn). As Jean Cuisenier and André Miquel pointed out in a study on Arabic terminology of kinship, "Specification does not arise on the level of a single word, but on the level of an entire assemblage of words according to the nature of their concatenation; it points to the whole chain, not to the individual links."[25]

Structural space has been repeatedly observed, if not in Tunis, then at least in other Muslim cities. The absence of economic segregation in urban quarters, their organization on a family basis, their function (the quarter, an ethnic unity of residence and kinship is the basic unit of the city), their morphology, replication of the family module, and finally, the cleavages that reproduce and extend the cleavages of Bedouin society – all this recapitulates the social architecture observed in the hinterland. Cities, above all, large cities, are doubtless locales of social mobility, differences of fortune and education, various trades, in which other means of classification surely interfere with the horizontal representation provided by country people. If the city is in no way reducible to the model of the village or the tribe, the model nonetheless has undeniable extensions in the city.[26]

The dynamics of the system

Theoretically, the spread of the genealogical tree, beginning with a single root, should continue infinitely. The population has only to multiply and the tree becomes denser and denser. On looking more closely at the genealogy of the Hamāma, we observe two processes that limit the multiplication of the segments. First, at certain points along the ramification of the lineage, a mutation occurred that interrupted the development of the tree. A collective name replaced individual eponyms and was transmitted from generation to generation without producing new branches. Second, lacking descendants, certain families died out.

Anthropologists in the field have been able to observe the dynamics of the segmentary system. The fusion of two branches under a single name, the use of a limited stock of first names, repeated on many levels of the genealogy, thereby "telescoping" a number of generations – these are among the processes through which the tribe's cellular tissue is modified without assuming outsized proportions that would disrupt the functioning of a tribe as a cohesive unit. The ultimate process is the creation of a new tribe by secession. Studying the Bedouins of Cyrenaica, Peters uses the expression "area of ambiguity" for that part of a genealogy in which these manipulations occur. After the first five levels, which remain stable, the zone of turbulence and alteration begins.[27]

How does this apply to Tunisian tribes? How do they change in time while remaining intact? Is it possible to find over an extended period what the ethnologist observes in the field?

The Jlāss, who were first surveyed in 1724,[28] and again in 1860, and who were finally described in 1884–5, provide some basis for answering these questions since the arrangement of the tribal subgroups can be reconstructed for each of these dates. A comparison of these three documents reveals that between 1724 and 1860, and from 1860 to 1884–5, the key elements of their organization were stable (Tables 2.1–3). The Jlāss (level I) remained divided into three parts: the Awlād Idīr, Khalīfa, and Sindāssin (level II). Changes appear one rank below. Among the A. Idīr, four of the subdivisions on level III in 1724 are in the same position around 1860: the Nhār, Ziādna, ʿAdādja, and Mathanīn. One group, the Awlād Saʿīd, has disappeared. But five of the groups federated under the A. Saʿīd – which were therefore on the level IV – moved up to level III. As a result, the number of branches on level III more than doubled. Farther down, various possibilities appear on level IV: a few groups, less numerous, kept their position, such as the Awlād Hāj, Awlād Nsīr, and Mbārek of the Mathanīn. We have already seen a number of segments

Table 2.1. *Segments of the Jlāss tribe in 1724: the Awlād Idīr*

Level 1	Level II	Level III	Level IV	Level V
Jlāss	Idīr	ʿAdādja	ʿAthāmna	Individuals
			Ez-Zkhāna	
			Juāber	
		Mathanīn	Mhārza	
			A. Haj	
			A. Mbārek	
			A. Mqadīl	
			A. Nsīr	
			Srāhta	
		Nhār	ʿAlālqa	
			Shuāmākh	
			Dhifallah	
			A. ʿAshūr	
			Sahlāt	
			Tratīt	
		A. Saʿīd	ʿAtallah	
			A. ʿAlauna	
			A. Khshīn	
			A. Khalfallah	
			A. Kleib	
			Ruājah	
		Ziādna	Farjallah	
			Kshāna (?)	
			Shraitia	

Note: The major segments are arranged alphabetically to facilitate comparison.

elevated to level III; others disappeared while new families moved into level IV.

The disappearance of the Awlād Saʿīd and the elevation of its constituent groups recurred in 1884 with the Ziādna. They no longer appear in the genealogy but the segments they comprised, the Sellāhua and Kutra, rose from level IV to level III. Farther down, the Jwāwda left the Kutra to occupy a place beside them on the same level. The Nhār dropped down a rank, and the Awlād ʿAshūr and the Ruājah shifted to other segments.

Among the Sindāssin, seven segments of level III kept their place from 1724 to 1860, three disappeared, a similar number dropped to lower ranks, and two coalesced into a new clan. As in the case of the Awlād Idīr, there are many more modifications on the fourth level with the severance of some branches and the appearance of new ones. In 1885, although no notable change occurred, the Fdhūl, who had dropped from third to fourth rank between 1724 and 1860, regained their original position (Tables 2.4–6). The following interesting commentary illumi-

Table 2.2. *Segments of the Jlāss tribe in 1860: the Awlād Idīr*

Level I	Level II	Level III	Level IV	Level V
Jlāss	Idīr	ʿAdādja		
		Mathanīn	Uhibāt	
			A. Haj	
			A. Mbārek	
			A. Nsīr	
		Mqadīl		
		Nhār		
		Shuāmākh		
		A. ʿAshūr		
		Ṣahlāt		
		ʿAlāuna		
		A. Khshīn		
		A. Khalfallah		
		A. Kleib		
		Ruājah		
		Ziādna	Kutrā	Dhibāt
				Muisāt
				Jhināt
				Jwāuda
			Sellāhua	Farjallah
				Shraitīa

nates this shift: "The last subdivision, the Fdhūl, has long been associated with the Sindāssin. But even today they are considered outsiders by the Awlād Sindāssin who offer two different versions of their origin." According to one, they came from the Sahel two centuries ago and were attached by the beys to the administrative district of the Sindāssin. In a second version, a Sindāssin of the Awlād Shehīb was a shepherd for an outsider named Fadhil whose daughter he married, thus giving rise to the Fdhūl.

These stories represent the Fdhūl as outsiders and latecomers, whereas our documents attest to their cohabitation with other Jlāss segments for more than a century and a half. Their expulsion from the kinship group should be seen as a sign of some tension or conflict within the tribe.

Last, the Awlād Khalīfa shows the greatest stability. There were only minor changes in level III: Two families joined the groups listed in the 1724 census, all of whom were also present in 1860 and 1885. On the next level the changes were of the same order as in the other two lineages of the Jlāss (Tables 2.7–9).

Whether the appearance of new families compensated for the extinction of others is impossible to determine. What is clear is that the proliferation to which the system lends itself can be held in check by different means. In addition, although lateral or vertical shifts in the genealogical

Table 2.3. *Genealogy of the Jlāss tribe in 1884: the Awlād Idīr*

Level I	Level II	Level III	Level IV	Level V
Jlāss	Idīr	ʿAdādji	ʿAthmān	
			Zerāna	
		Bu Methnāna	Uhibāt	
			A. Haj	
			A. Mbārek	
			A. Mqadīl	
			A. Nsīr	
			A. ʿAshūr	
		Shāmkhi	Nhār	
			Sahlāt	
			Dhāhar	
			ʿAttaya	
		Al Khshīn	Rajāh	
			Bū Ghāba	
			Ruājah	
		Khalfallah		
		Kleib		
		Kutra	Duīb	4 groups
			Muisāt	3 groups
			Jhināt	3 groups
		Sellāhua	Farjallah	3 groups
			Sherārat	2 groups
			Shraitīa	6 groups
			Romdhān	3 groups
		Jwāwud		

scheme affected many segments, these groups nevertheless remained within the genealogy. Diachronic observation thus substantiates current ethnology. The "area of ambiguity" can be noted on the third level and increases as it descends through lower ones. The supporting beams of the structure, however, are never replaced. Furthermore, the unequal development of the segments – in volume, wealth, and prestige – led to the alterations of the genealogy over a period of time by means of restriction or absorption of the weaker segments.

Political institutions

"This nation is completely subjected to the bey of Tunis but governs itself," wrote a French observer at the end of the eighteenth century who lived near the Nafzah tribe.[29] This observation is echoed by a remark made by the bey who, on learning in the 1850s of the homicidal quarrels between two southern tribes (the Banī Zīd and the Hamāma), said, "*Beīn-athoum*, let them work it out among themselves."[30] It is indeed true that

Table 2.4. *Segments of the Jlāss tribe in 1724: the Awlād Sindāssin*

Level I	Level II	Level III	Level IV	Level V
Jlāss	Sindāssin	Awlād ʿĀmer		
		Fdhūl		
		Friwāt		
		Hadāia		
		Awlād Hāmed	Al Blāghsha	
			Awlād Bū ʿAbīd	
			Ikhuāt Tāleb Sālem	
		Hmāmda		
		Jrirāt	2 groups	
		Awlād Kʿūd		
		Mhafīdh		
		Msāʿīd	Ikhuāt al-Bakkūsh	
		Nqāqza		
		Nqāqta	Ikhuāt Belgacem Ahmad	
		Awlād Shehīb	ʿAbd es-Smīʿ	
			Awlād Ali Nsīr	
			ʿAtiya	
			Awlād Hellāl	
			Ikhuāt Sheikh al-Fāni	
			Fraiāt	
			Awlād Nāsr ibn Khīl	
			Rzāmta	
			Awlād Thābet	
			Zhirāt	
		Awlād Ūm Krīm		
		Awlād Zāid		

a centralized political authority, which functioned with undeniable regularity and efficiency, especially in fiscal matters, coexisted with an equally undeniable tribal autonomy. The decision-making centers were not to be found in the Bardo, the seat of the sovereign, or with the caid, the bey's delegate, who generally lived within his own district, but rather in the tribe and its segments.

Within the tribe there were two inherent oppositions: one, between men and women, the latter being totally excluded from power; and the other, between young men and their elders. This opposition becomes apparent from time to time during uprisings. Seghir ben Youssef, discussing Ali Pāsha's rebellion against his uncle, relates that the population of Jabal Waslāt was split. The older men were against the uprising, and the young were in favor of it. Reporting on a different revolt, another author, Hammūda Ibn ʿAbdalaziz, who knew neither Seghir ben Youssef nor his works, places the young men (*shabāb*), adolescents (*ahdāth*), and vagabonds (*sufahā*) on the side of the rebels. Those who held power

Table 2.5. *Segments of the Jlāss tribe in 1860: the Awlād Sindāssin*

Level I	Level II	Level III	Level IV	Level V
Jlāss	Sindāssin	A. ʿĀmer		
		Hadāia	Fuansīa	
			Huatfīa	
			Shmamqīa	
		A. Khīr	Jrirāt	
			Nqāqza	
			Tuāl	
		Mhafīdh	A. Sidi Ali ibn Sālem	
			A. Baniu	
			A. Draʿ	
			A. Dhifallah	
			A. Gharsallah	
			A. ʿIssāwi	
			A. Mahfūdh	
			A. Sʿūd	
		Msāʿīd	A. ʿAnāne	
			Aʿualīa	
			A. al-Bakkūsh	
			Bsilāt	
			Adh-Dhīb	
			Jlālba	
			Juamʿīa	
			Māiz	
			Mkhalfīa	
			A. Yūsif	
		Nqāqta	Brahmīa	
			A. Haj	
			A. Mesʿūd	
			Mnāsa	
			A. Nāsr	
			Qrirāt, Shuaūta, Trīf	
			A. Sʿīd	
			Ruashīa	
			Shuarbīa	
		A. Shehīb	ʿAjilāt	
			A. Brahīm	
			Fdhūl	
			Fraiāt	
			Ghrāba	
			A. Hellāl	
			Mtirāt	
			Sbaiʿiya	
			A. Zāir	
			Zuatnīa	
			Zwawda	
		A. Zāid		

Table 2.6. *Genealogy of the Jlāss tribe in 1885: the Awlād Sindāssin*

Level I	Level II	Level III	Level IV	Level V
Jlāss	Sindāssin	ʿAmer		
		Fdhūl		
		Hedaid	Farsīa	
			Huatfīa	
			Shmameq	
		Kheir	A. Ali ibn Khalfallah	
			A. ʿĀmer	
			Jrirāt	
			Nqāqza	
			Tuāl	
		Mahfūdh	A. Ali ibn Sālem	
			A. Bayu	
			Drāʿ	
			A. Dhifallah	
			A. Gharsallah	
			A. ʿIssāwi	
			A. Mahfūdh	
			A. Saʿdallah	
		Masʿūd	A. ʿAnāne	
			Aʿualīa	
			A. Bakkūsh	
			A. Brahīm	
			Bsilāt	
			Jlālba	
			Juamʿīa	
			Al Māiz	
			Mkhalfīa	
		Neqqati	Gatʿa	
			Juidāt	
			A. Mnāser	
			Saʿīd	
			Shuarbīa	
		Shehīb	Fdhūl	
			Zuatnīa	
		Zāid	7 groups	

(*dhawi al-ahkām*), the notables (*aʿyān*), prominent citizens (*wujūh āhl al-jabal*), and sheikhs are placed on the side of order. In a subsequent account of these events by the historian Ibn Abi Dhiaf, the same split appears: the young (*sibyān*) and the vagabonds are opposed to the notables (*aʿyān*).[31]

To associate wisdom with age and experience, and daring and excess with youth, might appear as a commonplace. But the unanimity of writers who, under very different circumstances, referred to the same cleavage is surely not without meaning. This opposition finds further

Table 2.7. *Segments of the Jlāss tribe in 1724: the Awlād Khalīfa*

Level I	Level II	Level III	Level IV	Level V
Jlāss	Khalīfa	Al ʿAzāza		
		Blāghta		
		Brikāt	A. Zāid	
			Qāsʿa	
		Hāmed	Bdārna	
			Forjān	
			Germāsa	
			Hmāmda	
		Muaghīr	Ikhuāt ʿAbbās	
			Ikhuāt Bū Ghāba	
			Ikhuāt Sheikh Mtāir	
		Mjābra		
		Mkhalīf		

confirmation in the linguistic sphere with the ambiguity of key terms such as *kabīr* and *sheikh.* The word *kabīr*, meaning both big and aged, designates the important members of a group. So, for example, Hammūda ibn ʿAbdalaziz speaks of *baʿdh akbār al-jabal*, a few elders from the mountains. Similarly, for a census or tax levy to be valid, the presence of elders is required and specified.[32] Or again, a solemn gathering of the Hamāma brings together their sheikhs and their *rjāl kbār*. The ambiguity of the word is most evident in this last example.[33] For if what determines the importance of the individuals designated as *kbār* is not apparent elsewhere, the syntagma *rājl kabīr*, in the dialect of Tunisia, indicates a man of years. Prestige is therefore associated with age.

This is even more obvious in the word *sheikh*. Once again, Peyssonnel understood it thoroughly in the eighteenth century, when he defined sheikh as "old, an old man, prince, scholar, chief. One chooses as sheikh an old man, or the most important man of the tribe, or the oldest of the *dāwār*."[34] The word connotes both considerable age and authority. Venerability may indeed be the result of other factors, such as wealth or knowledge, but once again, it is in terms of genealogy that politics expresses itself: Authority resides in the patriarch.

Peyssonnel also wrote: "Each nation has a sheikh who commands it, and each *dawār* has a sheikh of its own who is inferior to the sheikh of the nation." In other words, the distribution of authority followed the social structure: Each point of segmentation in the lineage was also an instance of decision. The tent was governed by the head of the enlarged family, the *dawār* by a sheikh, and all the *dawār* of a tribe by yet another sheikh. In politics one finds this same parity between homologous and

Table 2.8. *Segments of the Jlāss tribe in 1860: the Awlād Khalīfa*

Level I	Level II	Level III	Level IV	Level V
Jlāss	Khalīfa	Al ʿAjābna		
		Al ʿAzāza	Al Faqqa Al Khbūz Al Khdaimīa A. Bū Hlos	
		Bdārna	ʿArfāt Duairīa Kuāta Kraimīa Slāta Sūfr	
		Blāghta	Dhibāt Juāber Shramtīa	
		Brikāt	Al Khraishāt A. Zāid	3 groups 4 groups
		Forjān		
		Fuāid		
		Mjābra	ʿAbābsa Hmidāt Jbilāt Al Jazīra Triwāt	
		Mkhalīf	Hadāda A. ʿĀmer A. Bū Dhrāʿ A. Meskīn Ruaūna	
		Muaghīr	A. Haj A. Jumlīa A. Taʿmallah	
		Shtābra	3 groups	
		Suālem		
		Themāma		

equivalent segments, and the repetition of similar forms from one level to another. But each level had its own sphere of competence. If domestic problems were settled on a lower level, economic or political decisions were made on higher levels.

In view of the way in which authority is acquired and exercised, this kind of political organization under sheikhs cannot be regarded as chieftaincies, which imply a high degree of concentration along with a certain continuity of power. On the one hand, the sheikh was elected by his constituency – a group of equals who granted him power for only so

Table 2.9. *Genealogy of the Jlāss tribe in 1884: the Awlād Khalīfa*

Level I	Level II	Level III	Level IV	Level V
Jlāss	Khalīfa	Al ʿAjābna		
		Al ʿAzāza	Krūbes	
			Mtaigīa	
		Al Hāmed	Bdārna	
			Forjān	
		Blāghta		
		Al Brikāt	Krishāt	
			A. Zāid	
			ʿAfallah	
		Mjābra	Hmidāt	
			Jbilāt	
			Friwāt	
			Wamrīa	
		Mkhalīf	Hadāda	
			A. ʿĀmer	
			Ruaūna	
			Suālem	
		Al Muaghīr	A. al Haj	
			A. al Mtīr	
			A. Suīsi	
			Gesʿa	
			Jumlīa	
			Al Ufaid	
		A. Jamlīa		
		Al Shtābra		
		Al Themāma		

long as he remained the interpreter of their views. "The headmen," wrote an observer who lived with the Nafzah, "are really no more than the first among equals: they have very little influence over deliberations and can take no initiative without the unanimous consent of the tribe. This is why their assemblies are so noisy!"[35] Let us add that once elected, the sheikhs had no material means of coercion.

On the other hand, if the sheikh held power only on the level of the collectivity that installed him, he exercised it collegially on the level above. Here again, vocabulary is instructive: the assembly of sheikhs is not designated by the plural *shiūkh*, but by the collective *mshāyakh*, which suggests a collegial organization.

Every decision was made by assemblies, whether the issue was to conclude an agreement for the distribution of loot after a raid, to set the date for the seasonal migration of southern nomads, to begin agricultural activities, or to conclude a treaty or a truce between warring tribes.[36]

These gatherings were designated by the term *miʿād* and were an institution common to all the tribes of Tunisia. Was this some form of democracy? It was rather rule by gerontocracy, which was the repository of the group's fundamental values and traditions. Under different names, the rest of the Maghreb, both Arab and Berber, was governed by the same principles.

Having begun with an ideological discourse – the chronicles of origin – we can now discern an outline of a social structure that can be found from one end of the Muslim Mediterranean to the other; from the Berbers studied by Montagne, Hart, and Gellner, to the eastern Bedouins studied by Murphy, Kasdan, or Chelhod. Patrilinear descent, cohesion through tension, equality of segments and instability of power, fission and fusion – these principles are ubiquitous, which does not preclude many variations in the corpus of customs, or in the relationship between familial or local units and central authorities.

Have we confused the practices of these people with their idiom? Have we been taken in by their discourse and the image it projects? In this context, praxis and ideology are indivisible. Genealogy, an ideological construct, reveals itself not as an account of the past, but as an allegory of the present, a translation of political, religious, and matrimonial practices. At the same time, this construct contributes to the preservation and reproduction of the economic order and social praxis. We have seen how latent tensions could materialize at a time of widespread conflict, how in the long run modifications of segments of tribes could become imprinted on the genealogical design. Whether pertaining to political, matrimonial, or economic affairs, the genealogical structure provides a matrix for the many possible practices. The conflicting representation of the tradition is both figure and action.

In the sphere of economics, we have mentioned only – and at that, very briefly – the relationships of solidarity and exchange, or the rivalries between nomadic and settled tribes. More important were the relationships of production. As will be seen in the next chapter, the forms of ownership of land and the agricultural means of production, as well as forms of exploitation, were inseparable from the genealogical relationships that served as their buttress.

Part II

The people and the land

3. Structures of property, land ownership, and land tenure

The right to the land

The question of who had rights to the land was obscured by endless discussions, essays, and theories that were current during the colonial period and whose ultimate goal was colonization. This was no academic debate. Those who took part in it were less concerned with clarifying a legal point or undertaking a sociological survey concerning the distribution of land than with rendering the land transferable and thus accessible to colonists. In other words, the purpose was to define the status of the land and if need be, to modify it to make possible the transfer of ownership. Some lawyers considered this process illegitimate, for it meant the spoilation of the native population. But they too had a political bias and it was in terms of their defense of the peasants that they interpreted the law. With regard to Tunisia, an additional source of misunderstanding was to emerge from a half century of legal experience in Algeria. The overriding tendency of the French was to bring with them all the practices accumulated in the neighboring territories, thereby overlooking what was particular to Tunisia.[1]

The various categories of Tunisian laws and their application are themselves hardly crystal clear. The coexistence of Hanafite and Malikite codes, either of which could be chosen by the bey's subjects, along with the triple canonical basis of the legal system – the Koran, the Sunna, and jurisprudence – considerably complicated the situation. Moreover, in Tunisia as elsewhere, any legal prescription could be overturned, here more than elsewhere, since religious law competed with custom. Among Berber-speaking people of Algeria or Morocco, who had their own *qanūn* (written customs), the contradictions between the two were recognized and codified. Unlike the Berbers, the Arabic-speaking people of Tunisia did not commit their customs to writing. Nevertheless, one should not assume that they observed the letter of the written religious law. In the end, customs and laws were both modified by time.

Is the state the primary owner of Tunisian land?

The problem of the system of land ownership is thus a thorny one. The question begins with the bey: What were his rights to Tunisian land? Or, put differently, was the territory of the regency *kharaj* land? If it was, its status was that of a conquered territory, subject to a special land tax, in contrast to other Muslim lands that were taxed only with a tithe on their harvest. In this case, the land was a kind of *waqf* or trust consisting of inalienable and nontransferable property for the use of the community of believers for whom the sovereign was representative and guardian. If the peasants of Tunisia were paying the tax applicable to conquered land, they had only the right to tenancy on the land and to its permanent usufruct. Tunisia would then belong to a type of society known as "Oriental," in which the state was not only – as in all cases – the agency that levied taxes, but one that also exercised direct control over the most basic means of production: the land.[2]

To this fundamental question, jurists of the colonial period generally replied in the affirmative. On what grounds did they do so? To begin with, they answered that the situations in Tunisia and Algeria were identical. It had never been demonstrated, however, that Algeria was *kharaj* land before 1830. Second, there were texts, specifically by Sidi Khalil, that spoke of certain territories in the Muslim empire as *waqf*, but these referred to Syria and Iraq and not to the Maghreb. Maghrebi authors such as Ibn Abi Dinar Al Qairawāni and Ibn Khaldūn state that the *kharaj* was imposed on Christian and non-Muslim Berbers of North Africa. But was this tax continued, even after their conversion, while everywhere else it fell into disuse?

All things considered, there is nothing conclusive about this argument. Had they been more familiar with the practices of the Tunisian government, or with French texts of the eighteenth century, the defenders of the state's primary right to the land would have consolidated their position. In the French texts they would have found allusions to the *kharaj*. The beys, according to Saint Gervais, went out twice a year "to collect the *carache*." What European writers of the eighteenth century meant by this term was in fact a head tax. In the words of one writer, the bey is "like a tax collector, whose function is to exact the *caraj*, or tribute of the Moors, who are like peasants." This confirms another writer who speaks of the bey going "to collect the *carach* or head tax from the Moors of these lands."[3] There is consequently no doubt about the confusion here between a personal tax and a property tax.

In fiscal practice, however, an inequality between different categories of inhabitants already appears in our earliest evidence. In 1677–8, the tax on olive trees in the Sahel was less severe for Turks and some other categories of taxpayers than it was for *ra'iya*, the general mass of subjects who owned larger numbers of trees than the preceding categories, and were certainly more numerous. This differential is documented in a later ruling (1155 A.H or 1742) relating to the arable lands of the north. The rate of taxation on wheat or barley was lower if the taxpayer was a *mokhazni* or a *sherif*, and higher if he was a *ra'iya*. This ruling was unquestionably in effect and for a long period of time, since fiscal archives dating from the beginning of the nineteenth century still make the distinction between the two categories of taxpayers.[4]

On the other hand, the status of *kharaj* land was incompatible with the levying of a tithe, or *'ashr*. Land could not be subjected to the tax imposed on non-Muslims at the same time as its produce was subjected to the tax imposed on Muslims. In fact, an *'ashr* on barley, wheat, and other grains was levied regularly throughout the regency. And last, such a status would be contradictory to the existence of private property of the *mīlk* type, transferable to women as well as men. It was this latter category of land ownership that predominated in all regions inhabited by settled peoples.[5] Nomads would consequently be the only ones denied full ownership of the land on which they pitched their tents, and would only enjoy the right of unlimited occupation. But even among them, the inalienability of land was not constant, nor, as will be seen later, was the disinheritance of women.

Clearly, precolonial Tunisia cannot be considered *kharaj* land, nor the bey the primary owner of the land he governed. One may ask whether he was the owner of at least part of the land, in view of the dichotomy that prevailed – not in fiscal terms but in terms of the system of land holding – between two categories of land: "live" or cultivated lands, and "dead" or fallow lands that yield nothing to anyone. The former, with their trees, structures, and irrigation systems, bear the imprint of human labor. They are readily distinguishable by their orchards and gardens and fenced-in plots on the outskirts of villages and towns. As to the others, flocks may graze and water on them, but if they are not exploited on a regular basis, their ownership reverts to the state. But tilled lands, even if left fallow for a long period, and even if they were not enclosed by fences or terraces, for technical or sociological reasons, were not considered wastelands. A wheat field could be left unsown; that did not make it dead land. Land, inhabited for a long time even when not intensively cultivated, did not become vacant land.

Mīlk properties and 'arbi lands

Living land and dead land – of this antonymous pair, recognized by Islamic law, the second category further divides into *mīlk* lands and *habous* (or *waqf*) lands. Islamic law makes no other distinctions. In fact, fiscal archives, land deeds, and some surveys among the tribes brought to light another antonymous pair, one that opposed *mīlk* lands and a new category, that of *'arbi* – literally, Arab – lands[6] or to certain other lands, otherwise not qualified, said to belong to "the Awlād X," signifying that they belonged to a group and not to individuals. During the colonial period, such lands were designated as *collective*, which became the subject of contradictory legislation, recalling the more familiar notion of *'arsh* land, which originated in Algeria and was already questioned when Tunisia became a French protectorate.

What distinguished such lands from *mīlk* lands was the manner in which they were transmitted. Consanguinity established a right to the land. Each member of a tribe was automatically a co-owner of his lineage's territory. To put it more simply, the right to property was acquired through membership in a lineage. In this regard, the force of the agnatic principle applied equally to *mīlk* lands, whose laws of succession will be discussed later.

Another distinguishing factor was that proof and definition of a tribe's or subgroup's lands were based on common knowledge, on the consensus of neighbors who recognized their long-term occupation of the site. There was no need for any official deed. Ownership of *mīlk* land, on the other hand, could be attested to by a notarized deed, though this was not always necessary. A property could be wholly owned without any official document according to the same criteria as tribal property, namely, long-term occupation and common knowledge. What the deed provided was information regarding how the owner inherited the land, going back to the first owner of the property. This amounts to saying that the deed, by tracing the genealogy of the owner, merely proved, in writing, that a property had been held by a particular family, which, in the case of tribal lands, was accomplished through the oral tradition.[7] The deed, however, could also record an act of transfer or sale, whereas such transactions never established tribal property. In short, for tribal lands, an individual acquired the right to ownership by his membership in the group, and the group maintained that right by its long occupation of the land.

Although a segment or a tribe was not entitled to buy land collectively, they might however donate to a marabout, or even sell, a part of their land. The inalienability of landed property and the exclusion of women from the inheritance system – customary practices that led people to consider the status of the land as that of a *waqf* – had no strict legal basis. The case of lands situated in the territory of the Jundūbah illustrate this quite clearly. In 1780–7, thirteen proprietors belonging to the same subgroup of Awlād Abu Sālem sold a property of approximately eight "plows"* to a party outside the tribe. The thirteen sellers were recognized as owners by right of inheritance from their ancestors, according to Arab custom. What established ownership was thus the length of time a property had been occupied by the same lineage. And just as in the case of *mīlk* land, owners could transfer their property.

The reason for the sale was that the thirteen sellers had contracted a debt and given their land as collateral to their creditor. The purpose of the transaction was to repay part of this debt. However, the sale was contested by six members of the same tribe who claimed their share of the sale as joint owners through the same inheritance, and who made good their claim through the intermediary of a lawyer. Among them was a woman. The notarized document also provided for payments to other members of the subgroup, including several women. Here then we see the extent to which the land was considered indivisible among members of the same clan, a fact that prevented neither the mortgaging or sale of the land, nor the exclusion of women from rights to property. There is even a case on record of a woman who, in 1812–13, claimed her share of an inheritance, amounting to 1/588th of the land in question, and who obtained satisfaction with a compensation of fifteen piasters.[8]

This isolated example does not indicate how widespread such practices were, but it does bear witness to the fact that they existed.

On lands belonging to tribes or fractions of tribes, pastures were collective and the harvested fields left for general use.[9] Defending the common territory against trespassers was also a collective endeavor. As to the cultivation and care of trees, crops, and the use of water, customs varied according to natural conditions, and from one group to another. Among the Sindāssin of the Jlāss, for example, cultivated land was divided in a permanent and hereditary way for each family: The planting of trees and irrigation systems made these plots rigorously *mīlk* and their use was denied to other members of the tribe. Elsewhere, among the Frashīsh or Nafzāwah, a periodic apportionment was made by the *mi'ad* (tribal assembly) after the first rains. Shares were allocated to all males of fasting age, or to all males in general, or in proportion to the number of teams of oxen owned by an individual. The distribution in this case corresponded to units of production. Women, as nonproducers, were at a disadvantage, whereas male children, as eventual producers, were eligible for shares. In yet another group, the Sawāsi, a portion of its land consisted of permanent family farms. But the best plots, located in the lower valleys, were not allocated, "the group not wishing to leave to any one of its members any rights whatever to a particular lot." And finally,

*A measure based on the area that a plow could cover in one day. – Trans.

among other groups, particularly the Hamāma, agrarian "collectivism" was the rule at the level of the subgroup.

These forms of allocation and cultivation corresponded to ecological conditions and to a certain type of agrarian activity in which itinerant farming was made necessary by insufficient rainfall, and in which herding predominated over farming. As a consequence, collective rights held sway over the family unit, and it was difficult for strictly private property to gain a foothold. A scant population also served to keep these forms alive. Where people are few, the division of land is pointless. In densely settled regions, the relationship between collective rights and family-owned property was inverted: Collective lands were on the fringe of the gardens and served as pasture land or grain fields. Orchards, however, were *mīlk*.

The family principle nonetheless played a very important role here. The condition of joint ownership of these lands resided in the inextricable connections between numerous co-owners. In an eighteenth century inventory, one finds that a particular individual listed among his holdings "a quarter of joint property and a fifth of a quarter of half a jointly owned lot of virgin land with four olive trees" located near Tunis. In another case, the bey jointly owned thirty-seven gardens in the region of Bizerte with an equal number of co-owners.[10] Joint ownership could be dissolved by an act of division or by compensating the co-owners holding the smallest shares. This form of ownership was quite frequent and its significance in certain village lands will be discussed later.

The transfer of land and laws of inheritance

The priority of the group over the rights of the individual is equally operative in problems connected with the transfer of land. In the case of a land sale, for example, the transaction is licit but it could threaten the local community with disaggregation. This danger was forestalled by the right of preemption, or *shufʿa*, granted to the co-owners and heirs of the seller and, according to Hanafite law, to his neighbors as well as to the co-users of an easement.[11] Preemption was conferred on the condition that, within an agreed-upon period, the beneficiary of this right made known his intention to buy back the property and was able to pay the set price, and on the condition also that the seller had not instituted a procedure authorized by Hanafite law, namely, sale by *surra*. Such a sale occurred in 1790 when a buyer added to the sale price of a vegetable garden a handful of coins for distribution "to those who cannot easily be assembled,"[12] an act that deprived the beneficiary of the right of preemption from the possibility of offering the same price as the rival buyer.

In the case of inheritance, a few verses from the *Sura of Women* reveal the essential rulings regarding the transfer of property.[13]

To men, the share of what was left by parents and close relatives; and to women, a share of what was left by parents and close relatives, whether little or much: a specific share.

This is what God decrees that you do with regard to your children: to a son, a share equivalent to two daughters. If there are only daughters, even more than two, then to them two-thirds of the estate of the deceased, and if there is only one, then half to her. As to the mother and father of the deceased, to each one-fifth of the deceased's estate if he has a child; if he is childless and his parents inherit from him, then to his mother one-third, but if he has brothers, then his mother receives one-sixth, after the execution of the will he would have drawn up and the payment of debts. You do not know who among your offspring or forebears is more likely to be helpful to you. Consider this a decree from God. God remains all-knowing and wise, verily.

And to you, half of what your wives leave if they have no children. If they have a child, then one-quarter to you of their holdings, after execution of the will they drew up or payment of debts.

And to them, a quarter of what you leave if you have no children, but if you have a child, than an eighth to them of what you leave, after execution of your will and payment of debts.

And if a man has no heirs, offspring or forebears, or even a wife, but does have a brother or a sister, then to each of them a sixth, and if there are more than two, all will share in a third, after execution of the will and payment of debts.

To these verses of the Koran, the Sunna and the *shari'a* added numerous elaborations, including stipulations regarding the rights of other relatives. But the essentials are already there, establishing the rights of forebears and offspring. One can again see in these rules the congruence between land law and family structures. The preponderant rights of males in inheritance laws correspond to the patrilinear organization of the society, and the sharing of legacies by offspring and lateral relations to the agnatic order.

Added to this is the notion of *'asib*. Alongside heirs whose share is set by the Koran, certain rights are granted to an *'asib*, a relative whose relationship with the deceased has no intervening female generation. While a relative of a female line does not inherit, an *'asib* receives what remains of the estate after it has been distributed among the direct heirs. Here again we observe the strength of the family principle and of patrilinear kinship.

The strict application of these rules – even setting aside the hypothesis of a proliferation of males across the generations – would inevitably lead to the fragmentation and dispersion of estates. The laws do not limit the number of heirs, nor do they indicate at what degree of kinship the rights of inheritance cease. However, rules of exclusion do operate, thereby reducing the danger of splintering the land, and are summed up by this formula: "The nearest *ʿasib* excludes the furthest removed." Thus, the father excludes the grandfather, the brother excludes the sons of the brother, and so on. That still leaves a very large number of claimants for each legacy, requiring enormously ingenious calculations in each case. It is for this reason that a tradition of the Prophet claims that understanding the inheritance laws counts for half of all knowledge.

Let us take the theoretical case of an individual who dies leaving as heirs his mother, two widows, three daughters, and four brothers and one sister of the same parents. For the first three groups, the Koran prescribes a fixed share of the inheritance, which in this case will not thereby deplete the estate. The remainder goes to the fourth group, the *ʿasib*. The mother therefore receives one-sixth of the estate; the two wives, one-eighth, which they must share; the three daughters, two-thirds, which they too must divide.

What remains is one-twenty-fourth of the estate to be distributed among the five *ʿasib*, the male share being double that of the female share. The common denominator for all these fractions is 432, so that:

1. the mother receives 72/432 of the estate;
2. each widow, 27/432;
3. each daughter, 96/432;
4. each brother, 4/432; and
5. the sister, 2/432.

It is abundantly clear that a division of this kind would result in the total fragmentation of any estate.[14]

This example, based on the normative literature, can now be compared with the actual destiny of one or two estates. In 1764 a freed slave of Levantine origin, Mustafa ben Abderrahman al Hanafi el ʿOlj bought a certain property. As his name indicates, he followed the Hanafite rite, and his wealth would thus have been transmitted accordingly.[15] The property he acquired consisted of two pieces of land, each of which was "a jointly owned eighth of the jointly owned half" of two pieces of land. Consequently, at the time of acquisition, the heritage was already fairly complicated, since the new owner had become associated through joint ownership with other owners whose number and status remain unknown.

On his death, Mustafa ben Abderrahman left three heirs: his three children from the same wife, a son and two daughters. One of his daughters later died leaving as her heirs her brother and sister on the one side, and her husband on the other. Here began the dismemberment of the inheritance, for her husband remarried. He even had two wives, and the share of the estate that he received from his first wife was passed on to his descendants (eight grandchildren in 1850) who had no blood relationship whatever with the founder, Mustafa ben Abderrahman.

The founder's son left four children, each from a different woman, and a wife named Fafa. This resulted in a new fragmentation of the heritage when a part of Fafa's share passed, on her death, to her mother and brother, neither of whom had any kinship with the original owner. Let us skip the other episodes of transfer and division of the estate and arrive at 1850. There were eighteen heirs at that time, only five of whom were direct descendants of Mustafa ben Abderrahman al Hanafi. The property, however, was still jointly owned.

The transfer to lineages other than that of the original owner led to the dismembering of the estate. The natural epilogue of this story was the sale of bits and pieces, scattered among far too many co-owners, to a new buyer who reconstituted the property.

This example is an extreme case. For the fragmentation of property could be limited either by natural elimination, which gathered into the hands of a few heirs the shares of those who died without issue, or by financial elimination – buying out holders of infinitesimal shares – or by simply circumventing the laws of inheritance. Among the properties whose distribution we shall examine later, the weak position held by female proprietors indicates clearly enough that the letter of Koranic law was not rigorously observed. In these same areas, however, the proliferation of small plots and the number of joint owners confirm the tendency toward the fragmentation of patrimonies.

To this danger, the Kabyles* reacted with an explicit rejection of Koranic laws. "Inheritances are not to be divided according to Muslim law: we follow the wishes of the deceased," preemptorily declares the *qanūn* of Yakouren.[16] The "wishes of the deceased" can be seen in the customs that the *qanūn* set down and that excludes women from inheritance. Some of the customary codes even impose a financial penalty on anyone proposing to leave a share of his estate to a woman. This was a collective and codified response by a society to the contradictory implications of Koranic law, which although affirming the rights of kin, could lead to the opposite results. Endogamy was still another response to this threat.

Tunisians, whatever their rite, accepted Muslim law. But, like the Kabyles, they rejected the squandering of legacies, and so resorted to a means of individual defense: the establishment of a *habous*. The long history of a peasant family from the north is an excellent illustration of this strategy. Toward the end of the seventeenth, or beginning of the eighteenth century, a peasant died leaving a legacy of five properties west of Tunis on the road to Wadi Milian. Twice married, he had four

*Berbers of the coastal regions of Algeria. – Trans.

heirs: his two wives, a son, Kassem, and a daughter. On the death of his second wife, her estate was to be divided among her own daughter and two nephews. Kassem immediately forestalled the disintegration that threatened his father's legacy. As the direct heir of his father and his mother (since deceased), he bought the shares of the second wife's heirs. In 1723 the estate was thereby reconstituted.

This was when Kassem decided to set up a *habous* for all his properties. The *habous* is a type of religious trust through which this wealthy farmer "rendered forever nontransferable" all of his property for the benefit of his wife, his eight children named in the notarized document, and the children who may be born subsequently, "a boy being entitled to as much as two girls." The first protective clause stipulated that his wife could exercise her rights only so long as she remained his widow. In the event of remarriage, she would relinquish her share to her six grandchildren. The second stipulation: Whereas the male heirs had unqualified rights to their inheritance, the girls had rights to it while they remained unmarried. Although they lost their rights upon marrying, they could regain them if the marriage was broken.

The text further states that this gift was made for the benefit of "the children of his children ... their offspring, and the offspring of the offspring, as long as they multiply and their branches extend within Islam ... On the death of any beneficiary without issue, his share will go to the cobeneficiary of the same rank of kinship, or else to the nearest cobeneficiary."

One may legitimately wonder about the religious dimension of this trust. It is to be found in the following: In the event of the definitive extinction of all posterity, the lands would go to the *zāwiya* of Kassem's father, the revenues of which would be used to maintain the buildings or feed the guests of the oratory, with the understanding that the lands could never be sold or given away "until God inherits the earth and its fruits; for He is the best of heirs."

The evident intention of the testator was to preserve his estate for his descendants, to eliminate from the succession the husbands and children of his female offspring for the benefit of his descendants through the male line, and to prevent the sale, division or cession that could fragment the property.

This arrangement was entirely successful. In 1723 Kassem listed nine living heirs. During the eighteenth and nineteenth centuries, according to various extant documents, the property remained in the same family. Finally, in 1906 eight of Kassem's descendants were still owners and cultivators of this estate – more than 12,000 hectares of arable and hilly land, a fine patrimony that was kept admirably intact among the same number of beneficiaries as when their ancestor was alive.[17]

Aiming at the same goal, Tunisians and Kabyles adopted alternative strategies to perpetuate a man's patrimony within the same lineage. From a juridical standpoint, the classification of land takes the form of successive dichotomies: *kharaj* lands/*ʿashr* lands; dead lands/cultivated lands; *habous* lands/*mīlk* lands. According to the letter of the law, there are no further subcategories. But in practice, the *mīlk* system functions only in regions occupied by settled peoples where joint ownership remains within the framework of the extended family – the basic unit of production and consumption. In this framework the application of Koranic and post-Koranic law was possible, individual rights were identifiable, and land was transferable property. In tribal territories,[18] the difference of scale, co-ownership within the framework of the clan, made the processes envisioned by the law inapplicable and preserved the nontransferability and joint ownership of the land. Though these two systems differed, they were, as we have seen, not contradictory. But *ʿarbi* lands were, to borrow Marxist categories, based on "an archaic form of land ownership" more rigid and more resistant to change than family property of the *mīlk* type.[19]

Tribal lands in Tunisia at the beginning of this century covered six million hectares, or nearly half the surface of the country. But only two million, or one-fifth the national total, were arable. In the tribal sector social inequities based on the distribution of land were minimal. What, on the other hand, was the situation in settled regions, where the transferability of land could undermine equality of access to the land? Land ownership was not in itself a sufficient criterion to define social stratification. Other elements of differentiation, material or symbolic, must be taken into account. Information concerning these is, unfortunately, not available to us, whereas quantitative data on the division of land among the villagers can be found in abundance.

El Alia, Gabès, Msaken: typology of villages in the nineteenth century

The case of El Alia, an Andalusian village

Let us look at El Alia, situated between Bizerte and Porto Farina in a fertile region of cheerful villages surrounded by well-tended gardens, luxuriant orchards, and cultivated fields. The buildings and the size of these villages gave them the appearance of small towns. Some of the villages, such as Aousdja, El Alia, and Ras el Jebel, were the sites of weekly markets; the Friday market of Ras el Jebel drew a particularly large crowd.

Within these densely settled areas, each village specialized in a particular crop, without, however, giving up diversified farming. Raf Raf was known for the quality of its grapes and fruits, Ras el Jebel for its apricots, and El Alia for its olive trees.

This region, like most of the coastel Tell, is favored by low-lying hills whose slopes offer the best land for fruit trees and vineyards, by abundant rainfall with a total annual accumulation of 500 – 600 millimeters, and by the proximity of cities such as Bizerte and Tunis, which provided natural markets for the produce of this active district.[20] Its population was nurtured by the immigration of Moors, driven from Spain in the fourteenth century and especially in the early years of the seventeenth. Well into the nineteenth century, El Alia and neighboring villages were still considered Andalusian.

A population known as Andalusian. In this group of villages, El Alia was an agglomeration of more than 1,000 inhabitants during the nineteenth century, almost as populous as Porto Farina or Metlin, but less important than Raf Raf, Ras El Jebel, or Menzel Jemil.

Only 6.5 percent of the assessed landowners were in fact of Iberian origin.[21] El Alia had also absorbed immigrants from the west, villagers from central or southern regions, and even tribal people from the Hamāma, Mājer, and others, whom one would have thought unalterably devoted to their mobility yet who became settled fruit growers there. The population had thus grown out of various sources. In this, El Alia was not different from other so-called Andalusian villages, or from the rest of the northern part of the country, a zone that had received peasants from all over. The example of El Alia also confirms the pattern of the heterogeneity of rural communities in North Africa, even when a common ethnic or geographic origin was claimed.

Property census of 1844. In 1844, for purely fiscal reasons, two surveys of the property held by this relatively small though highly mixed population were conducted. The first listed the grapevines, the second the olive groves and irrigated lands. The third circle of village lands – that of plowlands – was not surveyed, but thanks to the tax records of the tithe imposed on cereal crops, we have some data almost contemporaneous with the surveys of 1844.[22]

They were taken with great accuracy. One ledger lists the irrigated plots owned by each proprietor, giving the precise location of each one in the area surrounding the village, its size, and the number of olive trees on it. The unit of length used to measure the irrigated lands was the "cord" of Tunis, which is about 25 meters long; the corresponding unit for surface measurement was the *merja*ʿ, about 625 square meters, or a sixth of a hectare. It was on the total number of *merja*ʿ*s* that each owner was taxed, at the rate of eight *nāsris* per year per *merja*ʿ.[23]

For the vineyards, which were listed in a second ledger, the survey followed the same pattern: A count was made of the number of rootstocks of each owner, and their location noted. There was no indication of the space occupied by the vineyards. But after consulting with thirty villagers – notaries, the Koranic schoolmaster, vineyard owners – the census takers determined that one *merja*ʿ of vines in El Alia averaged about 160 rootstocks.

It is possible on the basis of these two inventories to diagram the land holdings in El Alia by classifying the various owners according to the size and nature of their property. This task, however, is complicated by the existence of two particular categories of ownership. One is partnerships, which means that the name of the same person appears in different sections of the survey. For the purpose of calculation, it was therefore necessary to separate the partnerships and arbitrarily assign an equal share to each co-owner of the joint property.[24] The other problem, still harder to resolve, was that of inheritances, since the names of heirs were not listed. Some of them might already have appeared in the list of individual owners. Unlike the partnerships, which could be artificially dissolved, it was impossible to distinguish coheirs or to separate co-ownerships. Along with the single landowners, men or women, it was thus necessary to preserve this category in our tables.

Description of landholdings in El Alia. Once this preliminary arrangement of data is made, we can easily distinguish between rich and poor landowners, and identify those whose holdings were so large as to rank them far above the majority of villagers.

Of the 561 owners listed, one group clearly did not farm its own land. This included mosques, *zāwiya*, and the holy cities of Mecca and Medina, which received lands in donation. In El Alia, twenty-five of these religious foundations owned 9 percent of the olive trees and 7 percent of the irrigated land. The main mosque of the village had the largest share with 2.6 percent of the olive trees and 3.7 percent of the irrigated land. None of these foundations, however, had any vines; apparently the Koran's prohibition of wine extended to grapes as well.

In addition to these religious landholdings, which were not directly exploited by their owners, there were those belonging to urban landowners and dignitaries. They numbered no more than a dozen and accounted for 12.24 percent of the olive trees and 6.3 percent of the irrigated lands. Absentee landowners and religious foundations owned 21.31 percent of the olive trees and 13.34 percent of the irrigated lands.

Subtracted from the total of directly farmed properties, this represents a sizable portion of village lands.

These holdings, however, did not constitute latifundia, but had the same characteristics as the properties of the average villager in that they too consisted of scattered and multiple plots. One would search in vain for a domain all of a piece, for which tenants without permanent rights would pay rent to a landlord. This form of exploitation was to be found outside El Alia. A geographic study of the neighboring village of Galaat el Andleuss in the nineteenth century has shown that wheat fields belonging to the bey and his entourage were held and cultivated by landless peasants, leading its author to conclude that this was exploitation of the seignorial type.[25] Nothing of the kind existed in El Alia, an area of fragmented landholdings devoted to the intensive cultivation of olive and fruit trees. In addition, villagers were not required to offer services either in kind, in work, or in cash to any of the big landowners. There were no feudal preserves and no feudal rights. Evident inequalities nonetheless separated the members of village society. The average holding came to 52.7 *merja'‘s* per owner for irrigated land, 628 vinestocks, and 225 olive trees. A number of villagers went well beyond these figures in all three categories of property surveyed here, but they represented no more than 5.34 percent of all the landowners. Conversely, 45.81 percent did not reach the average in any of these categories. Nearly half the owners, 48.84 percent (Table 3.1), fell between the two groups.

The first inequality was magnified by a second disparity relating to the different types of holdings. Nearly half the landowners, 48.48 percent, had no vines, and nearly as many were without olive trees. Irrigated land seems to have been more evenly distributed since only 11.76 percent of the landowners did not possess any. Small landowners were well endowed in this regard since they comprised 45.65 percent of the owners of irrigated land. But they figure less prominently as owners of olive groves, among whom they appear as no more than 37.32 percent, and among vineyard owners, only 28.02 percent. If one measures the quantity of land or the trees they owned, their position drops even lower. Small landowners possessed only 7.76 percent of the vines, 6.05 percent of the olive trees, and 9.2 percent of the irrigated land. For them, the average size of a piece of property was about 10.5 *merja‘s* – slightly more than half a hectare – three dozen olive trees for those who had any, and 172 vinestocks. Nearly half the villagers, therefore, had meager holdings.

The second group, that of the middle rank, showed a better apportionment: 48.28 percent were owners of irrigated land, 58.68 percent owned olive groves, and 62 percent had vineyards. Their advantage over the small landowners is confirmed when one compares their share in the various categories of wealth (Table 3.1).

Table 3.1. *El Alia: distribution of property according to land wealth in 1840*

Types of landowners	Small	Middle-sized	Large	Total
Number	257	274	30	561
%	45.8	48.9	5.3	
Vineyards				
Landowners				
Number	81	179	29	289
%	28	62	10	
Root stocks				
Number	14,092	136,173	31,482	181,747
%	7.8	74.9	17.3	
Olive trees				
Landowners				
Number	111	157	30	298
%	37.2	58.7	10.1	
Trees				
Number	4,080	44,798	18,449	67,327
%	6.0	66.6	27.4	
Irrigated lands				
Landowners				
Number	226	239	30	495
%	45.7	48.3	6	
Fields				
Number of *merja*ʿ	2,379	15,503	8,117	26,000
%	9.2	59.6	31.2	

As for the big landowners, they numbered only thirty. One-third of all the irrigated lands, more than a quarter of the olive trees, and 17.3 percent of the vines belong to them.[26] Five of the seven notaries in the village were from this group.

The distribution of land and trees in El Alia therefore gives the impression of very marked social differences between a mass of scantily provisioned peasants and a minority of great landowners.

A peasantry of small plots. This picture should, however, be qualified and its apparent contrasts moderated. In the first place, of the landowners listed on the tax rolls, eighty were women. Of these, fifty-nine were classed as small landowners, constituting nearly a quarter of this category (22.95 percent). Needless to say, these women did not cultivate their own land. These plots were adjuncts to their fathers' holdings before their marriage and were added to their husbands' holdings after their marriage. The size of the group of small landowners must therefore be slightly reduced.

At the other extreme, the large landowners possessed an average of

211 *merja*ʿ of irrigated land, or a little more than 13 hectares. If one adds to that a few hectares of vineyard, the average area of their property rose to 14 hectares. These were not enormous estates. Of course, they comprised irrigated fields, from which the relentless efforts of the peasant extracted a much higher yield than from wheat fields. Also, the size of these holdings was undeniably larger than that of neighboring small farms. Nonetheless, an area of 14 hectares is still quite modest.

The mediocrity of farming techniques only added to the mediocre size of these properties, which were subdivided to the extreme. For the entire irrigated area, I counted 2,900 plots, each averaging just over one half of an hectare. Thus, the very notion of a large property is deceptive. For even the largest was broken up into scattered plots of curious shapes, no different from the adjacent gardens.

Did this village harbor landless peasants who do not appear in the assessment, but who must nevertheless be accounted for to determine levels of wealth? One need only remember the number of adults counted in El Alia: 253 men. In the inventory of property, we found 308 male owners, from which the number of those living outside the village must be subtracted. The number of owners is thus greater than the number of inhabitants. There is no margin here for the possibility of landless peasants.

Two studies of a more recent period of Tunisian history provide further evidence to corroborate this conclusion. The first, completed in 1954, centers on Aousdja, a village near El Alia. Forty-five percent of the land was then owned by absentee landlords or religious foundations. Nonetheless, write the authors, it is possible to "qualify the region of El Aousdja as one of owner exploitation, characterized by the total absence of tenant farming and the infrequency of agricultural associations."[27] Of course, proprietors who did not cultivate their lands themselves employed hired help. But the farm hands themselves were often small landowners. There is no doubt that in El Alia, a century ago, small landowners must have augmented their income in the same way by hiring themselves out to the large landowners.

In Galaat el Andleuss, the subject of the second study, property became extremely concentrated after the establishment of the protectorate. However, the practice of owner operation remained the general rule and gave way to leasing or sharecropping arrangements only in the case of properties larger than 100 hectares. In Galaat in 1965, there were many peasants without land, 300 as compared to 465 owners. However, since the end of the nineteenth century, the population of the village has more than quadrupled, and it is this demographic explosion that accounts for so large a group of peasants bereft of means of production. Toward the middle of the nineteenth century, the farmers of El Alia were a small-holding peasantry and minimally equipped, but they were not dispossessed of land.

The ownership of wheat land, whose distribution may well reveal the existence of a latifundian property not apparent until now, might serve as another basis of inequality. On the subject of plowland, available documentation, although precise, does not always agree with the data analyzed earlier. Tax registers indicate the amounts of wheat, barley, fava beans, and chaff that each proprietor had to pay after the harvests of 1846–59. Now, a compilation of landowners on these lists yielded 121 known from previous surveys, and a hundred or so do not correspond to the vineyard owners and fruit growers enumerated in these tax rolls. The explanation of this discrepancy is to be found in the caprices of Tunisian names. The first registers were drawn up to last, to serve from year to year, which explains the ample detail of the inventories: geographic origin, filiation, nickname – all were noted. For the tithe, on the other hand, register was intended to serve for no more than a single harvest. It was enough, therefore, to list just the name of the taxpayer.

However cursory these lists, they shed light on several points. To begin with, one notes the total absence of noncultivating proprietors among the grain producers: women, *habous*, townspeople, and heirs do not pay the tithe. This is a clear sign that wheat and pulse were cultivated for family consumption. Confirmation of this hypothesis can be found in the fact that the area sown was always small, in any case smaller than a *māshia* (± 10 hectares), the normal unit of tilled land. Although cereal crops did not occupy vast fields around El Alia, almost every man in the category of large landowner produced some, whereas five out of six small landowners did not. This new inequality does not alter our conclusion that the rural society of El Alia was a democracy of landowners who cultivated their own land. Although for many the land was meagerly distributed, it was distributed among all the inhabitants of the village. Of course, small producers also had to work on plots that did not belong to them, and differences of wealth distinguished rich and poor. But both possessed their means of production, that is, land and equipment, no matter how rudimentary.

Meager lands and primitive techniques imply direct cultivation and household farming, rendering the development of any agrarian capitalism impossible. Today, two kinds of large farms exist in the region. In the first, the traditional method of cultivation has been preserved. The lands are parceled out in microscopic plots. Techniques remain backward; the owners let out their lands to tenant farmers in return for a fixed rent. But nothing, not crops, methods, or yields, has changed when compared with the nineteenth century. In the second kind, in contrast, capitalist development has appeared: Irrigation is motorized, production is totally oriented toward the market; the lands have been reaggregated; the tenant has been replaced by the agricultural worker. In this new type, farming methods, crops, and social relations correspond to a capitalist structure that was unknown in the nineteenth century. Two hurdles have been surmounted: one, technical – low productivity resulting from the simple equipment used and the small dimensions of the farms; the other, demographic – the sparse population.

Are these conclusions applicable to other villages in the north? Is the distribution of wealth in El Alia typical? Other investigations undertaken in Cape Bon[28] lead us to reply in the affirmative. In Hammamet, where only the olive trees were assessed, one finds the same patterns of ownership and cultivation. Land was broken up into a profusion of lilliputian groves (almost 40 percent of the properties had fewer than twenty olive trees), and middle-sized properties were fairly numerous. The local mosque, as in El Alia, was the primary beneficiary of the inhabitants' piety, and all together the religious institutions owned nearly 10 percent of the trees. Here, however, large landowners were more numerous. If one subtracts women and *habous* properties from the figures, then men owning groves of more than 100 olive trees represent only 20 percent of the owners, but they control 69 percent of the trees.

The example of Hammamet also indicates the relative stability of these patterns. Around 1860 a new survey of olive groves was made. Innumerable details of sales, transfers of property, deaths of proprietors, and dispersal of their estates were recorded. Few properties still had the same dimensions. But the general outlines of the whole picture had not changed. The variations that had occurred, whether an increase or a decrease, resulted from biological rather than economic events. Death divides what life assembles. A certain Ali al-Ka'bi owned more than 1,500 olive trees in 1847. After his death and the division of his estate among all the eligible heirs, his undivided heritage comprised only 130 trees. Another individual declared 810 trees at the time of the first census. His heirs received only half that number in 1860. Conversely, fortunes were amassed in a few years.

Similarly, on investigating the most prosperous families, one sees that some consolidated their fortunes while the wealth of others crumbled. The Bu 'Askar had nineteen properties in 1847 divided into seventy-five parcels on which 1,600 olive trees were planted. In 1860 they had twice that number of parcels and more than 2,300 trees. The properties of the Khzīra increased from 1,300 to more than 2,000 olive trees. On the other hand, the Munq'i and the Na'na experienced a decline between the two surveys.

The interval of thirteen years between the two surveys is probably too short to disclose the meaning of a possible evolution. But from this example of Cape Bon we can at least assert the existence of a similarity between the structures observed in the villages of northern Tunisia.

The oasis of Gabès

In the south, Gabès, the ancient Tacape, although a single oasis located in a single wadi, consisted of three villages, Chenini, Jara, and Menzel, which shared and disputed its abundant water supply. Three communities lived in the same space, with nomads close by and ever present in the oasis, where they had plantations. This cohabitation wove a complex set of relationships that warrants the focus of our attention on Gabès. Whereas all the local produce was surveyed in El Alia, in Gabès only date trees were counted. It was indeed quite a significant oasis, numbering close to 200,000 trees in all its villages, and over 80,000 for Jara, Menzel, and Chenini alone.[29] But the oasis contained many other resources as well: fruit trees, vegetables, and tinctorial plants.[30] Furthermore, the dates were not of the same quality as those of the Jarīd and were not an item of interregional trade. The ownership of date palms is thus only a partial index of the wealth of Gabèsians, but it will have to suffice.

Different types of ownership. Nothing was more varied than the system of ownership in this oasis. The simplest form was that of private individual property. Although common in the oasis, it nonetheless coexisted with other types. The first was property shared among a number of individuals whose identity is revealed in the surveys, which makes calculation easy since one can extrapolate the dimensions of the property belonging to each of them by assuming that co-owners had equal shares. A variant of this type, but one that makes calculation more difficult, was the one in which property was shared among a number of individuals having equal rights, only one of whom was mentioned: "so-and-so and his brothers," or "so-and-so and those who accompany him." This held true for 11.4 percent of the proprietors in Jara,[31] 9.2 percent in Menzel, and 28.9 percent in Chenini. Our calculations necessarily leave out anonymous owners, but their existence should not be overlooked since it lowers the actual potential of each surveyed proprietor. The fourth type was property jointly held by members of the same family. This may apply to the children of a given proprietor or to the estate, with no way of knowing whether the name following the mention of "estate" refers to the heirs or to the deceased owner. It is not impossible that owners in this category also belong to the first category of individual landowners, which would make them appear twice in our calculations. Yet another

Table 3.2. *Oasis of Gabès: distribution of date trees according to types of property in 1840*

	Jara		Menzel		Chenini	
	Properties	Trees	Properties	Trees	Properties	Trees
Men	728	30,066	539	18,328.5	522	15,785
Women	38	898.5	46	627	37	512
Joint	176	9,146	128	3,787.5	104	3,063
Collective	27	1,550.5	22	998	13	881.5
Habous	27	2,679	20	1,849	16	779.5
Total	996	44,340	755	25,590	692	21,621

case is that of collective properties involving an entire group. Most often these owners, nomad or settled, are from outside the three villages under examination, but they can also be inhabitants. And finally, the last category included the mosques, *zāwiya*, and schools that were beneficiaries of donations – *waqf*.[32] This fact not only confuses our calculations but indicates above all that within the villages themselves, property alone – for we have not yet examined the different types of cultivation possible – created an intertwined network of relationships among the inhabitants. For each grove or garden there was often more than one claimant. In Chenini, where the phenomenon was most common, nearly half the gardens belonged to a number of owners whose levels of wealth were often markedly different.

Distribution of property. Certain properties consisted of many hundreds of date palms, whereas others amounted to no more than 10. In the village of Jara, where 996 properties were surveyed, the average was 44.5 date palms per property; in Menzel, with 755 properties, the average was 33.8; and in Chenini, it fell to 30.3 palms per property (see Table 3.2).

If, on the basis of these average figures, the properties are classified according to size, then five categories appear (Table 3.3). The smallest properties contained 10 date palms or less. Nearly a third of the properties in Menzel, more than a fourth in Chenini, and 17.46 percent in Jara, fell into this group. This was followed by properties consisting of 11–20 trees, still a low figure, but one that represented a quarter to a third of the properties in the three villages. The middle category covers properties with 21–50 trees. In Jara, a good third fell into this category, as did a large proportion of the properties in Chenini and Menzel. Properties with 51–100 trees constitute the fourth category and account for only 16.36 percent of the properties in Jara, 12.05 percent in Menzel,

Table 3.3. *Oasis of Gabès: size of properties in 1840*

	Jara		Menzel		Chenini	
Date trees	Number	%	Number	%	Number	%
10 Date trees	174	17.46	234	30.99	180	26.01
11–20 Date trees	231	23.19	199	26.35	211	30.49
21–50 Date trees	337	33.83	179	23.70	194	28.03
51–100 Date trees	163	16.36	91	12.05	74	10.69
+ 100	92	9.23	52	6.88	33	4.76
Total number of properties	997		755		692	

Note: Figures indicate the number of properties and the percentage of the total number of properties.

and 10.69 percent in Chenini. Finally, properties of larger dimensions form a fifth category, uncommon in all three villages, particularly in Chenini.

But such as they are, these figures do not account for the diversity of conditions among the various owners. A small property can have a different significance depending on whether it is owned by an oasis dweller or a nomad outside the village, by a woman, or by a religious institution. In the first case, the property was a primary means of livelihood; for the nomad it could be no more than an additional source of income. As for the mosque, though its holdings may be small in a given region, it could be the recipient of larger donations elsewhere.

Precise differences in wealth can therefore be determined only by an analysis of each type of property. We can begin with the men who made up the majority of owners, a large number of whom worked in the oasis. How was property distributed among these villagers?

In Jara, 127 men, or 17.44 percent, owned no more than 10 date palms (Tables 3.4–6); 23.62 percent owned between 10 and 20. Thus more than 40 percent of the male proprietors had scant holdings, and their property was considerably smaller than the general average for the oasis. In Menzel, small holdings were even more prevalent with 30.42 percent of the men in the first category and 25.97 percent in the second. More than half of all the men (56.21 percent) were thus in the category of small owners. The same proportions held for Chenini, where 56.7 percent of the men fell into the first two categories: 25.28 percent in

Table 3.4. *Oasis of Gabès (village of Jara): distribution of property in 1840*

	0–10 trees		11–20 trees		21–50 trees		51–100 trees		+ 100 trees	
	Properties	Trees	Properties	Trees	Properties	Trees	Properties	Trees	Properties	Trees
Men	127	865.5	172	2,638	255	8,386	116	8,290	58	9,886.5
Women	16	105.5	8	123	9	274	4	280	1	116
Joint	24	150.5	41	640	59	1,962.5	31	2,157	22	4,236
Collective	3	22	3	37	9	317	8	558	4	616.5
Habous	4	22	7	106.5	5	155.5	4	282	7	2,113
Total	174		231		337		163		92	

Table 3.5. *Oasis of Gabès (village of Menzel): distribution of property in 1840*

	0–10 trees		11–20 trees		21–50 trees		51–100 trees		+ 100 trees	
	Properties	Trees	Properties	Trees	Properties	Trees	Properties	Trees	Properties	Trees
Men	163	981	140	2,160	131	4,195.5	68	4,579	37	6,422
Women	27	116	13	195	4	102	1	63	1	151
Joint	35	232	36	535	33	298	18	1,201.5	6	826
Collective	2	11	6	89.5	7	208.5	4	248	3	441
Habous	7	41.5	4	59	4	129	0		5	1,623
Total	234		199		179		91		52	

Table 3.6. *Oasis of Gabès (village of Chenini): distribution of property in 1840*

	0–10 trees		11–20 trees		21–50 trees		51–100 trees		+ 100 trees	
	Properties	Trees	Properties	Trees	Properties	Trees	Properties	Trees	Properties	Trees
Men	132	798	164	2,457.5	139	4,307.5	63	4,329	24	3,893
Women	17	106	12	176	8	230	0		0	
Joint	25	147	32	516.5	36	1,170.5	7	552	4	677
Collective	2	12.5	2	27	5	165.5	2	195	2	481.5
Habous	4	17	1	19	6	160	2	132	3	451.5
Total	180		211		194		74		33	

the first and 31.41 percent in the second. The small owners held only 7.8 percent of the total number of date palms in Jara (where 11.6 percent of the trees belonged to men); in Menzel they controlled 12.2 percent of the trees in the oasis (17.1 percent belonged to men); and finally in Chenini, where the distribution was more equitable, they owned one-fifth of the date palms (20.61 percent belonging to men, or 15.4 percent of all the trees in the oasis).

Middle-sized proprietors were more numerous in Jara than in the other two villages: 35 percent of the men and 27.89 percent of the trees fell into the intermediate category of 21–50 trees. In Menzel and Chenini, a fourth of the owners were in this rank and held 22.88 percent of the trees in Menzel and 27.35 percent in Chenini.

In the higher categories, the number of proprietors fell sharply. There were nevertheless 117 men in Jara who owned 51–100 date trees and represented 16 percent of all the proprietors. In Menzel, they were no more than 12.61 percent and in Chenini, 12.05 percent. These well-to-do proprietors owned 27.07 percent of the trees in Jara, 24.92 percent in Menzel, and 27.36 percent in Chenini, respectively. Of the men of Jara, 7.97 percent belonged to this last category of owners of more than 100 date palms, and they controlled nearly a third of the oasis. In the neighboring villages there was an even heavier concentration of property: 6.86 percent of the men of Menzel owned 35 percent of the trees, and in Chenini 4.59 percent owned 24.66 percent.

To sum up, the distribution of ownership among male proprietors reveals a solid kernel of intermediate proprietors, a large number owning few trees, and at the opposite end of the scale, a minority that held a quarter to a third of all the trees.

Properties belonging to women do not reveal the same contrasts. They were few and of generally small proportions. Of the total number of properties enumerated in Jara, only 3.81 percent belonged to women, 6 percent in Menzel, and 5.3 percent in Chenini. Most of the properties owned by women consisted of less than 20 trees. Of the 121 female owners in the three villages combined, only 2 had more than 100 trees. In Chenini, not one owned more than 50. As in the case of El Alia, one can say that taken separately, these properties were inconsequential. They were valuable only insofar as they added to the household patrimony.

Jointly held property, fairly common in the three villages, represented 17.6 percent of all the property in Jara, 16.9 percent in Menzel, and 15 percent in Chenini. In Jara, the average of 52 trees per property was greater than for individually owned properties. This was not the case in Menzel or Chenini, where they numbered on average 29.5 and 29.4

trees, respectively. This was not very much if these properties were supposed to support a number of individuals, or even a number of families. For that matter, even in Jara, where these joint properties were larger than those of the other two villages, 37 percent fell into the category of small proprietors; in Menzel and Chenini more than half had fewer than 20 trees. Jointly owned properties were therefore no different than individually owned properties, either in their average size or in their distribution among the different categories of properties. Joint ownership did not, apparently, result in the consolidation of estates. It was in no way conducive to a regrouping of land nor did it prevent the dismemberment of patrimonies.

Collective property is an additional and new category. Here is where the nomads come in. They have long been held to have been the "lords" among oasis people and to have kept the poor settled peoples in thrall.[33] In fact, collective property was of comparatively little consequence in the oasis. In Jara, 3.4 percent of the date palms belonged to this category, 3.8 percent in Menzel, and 4.1 percent in Chenini. Of these, only a part belonged to the nomadic tribes of ʿAqarība, Mahādhba, or Hazem. The others were the property of settled peoples living outside the three villages. The average size of these properties – 57.4, 45.3, and 67.8 trees for each of the villages – although greater than those of the oasis dwellers, was still not particularly large. If the nomads had any hold over the oasis people, it was not economic in nature.

Religious property was the last type. In Jara, the largest single proprietor was the mosque of Sidi Driss, with 737 date palms, which exceeded by far the most prosperous single grove owned by Haj Mohammed Ibn Rehuma, who possessed 533 trees. Another major religious owner was the *madrasa* (religious college) of Gabès, which owned 450 date palms. Other mosques and oratories were less well endowed, some having only 5 or 6 trees. Generally speaking, the villagers of Jara relinquished their property for the benefit of local institutions – mosques and marabouts of the same oasis, readers of the Koran attached to those places of worship – whereas the religious metropolises in the regency (Tunis and Kairouan) received no donations whatever. Mecca and Medina were given a mere 124 date palms.

The situation was similar in Menzel. The great mosque alone had 536 trees, and the *madrasa*, which served Jara as well, had 446. In Chenini, the *madrasa* Lablabia was in possession of 68 date palms. Despite the generosity of oasis dwellers and the considerable proportions of certain religious properties, *waqf* properties all told did not comprise even 10 percent of the trees in the three villages. These holdings, however, were not directly exploited but constituted a first group of lands requiring the service of tenant farmers. They were not the only ones.

Nonexploiting proprietors, outsiders, and notables. Like religious institutions, groups from outside the oasis owned no more than a small portion of the trees. But members of these groups held, in addition, privately owned property within the oasis. The Naffāt, nomads whose territory lay south of Sfax, collectively owned 241 date palms in Chenini and 63 in Menzel (on the other hand, they owned nothing in Jara, where other groups from the Sfax region were landowners).[34] Added to this collective presence were some hundred members of the Naffāt tribe who owned 2,438 date palms in Chenini, while twelve other Naffāti owned 176 trees in Menzel. Similarly, the Hazem jointly owned trees in Jara and Chenini, but none in Menzel. Furthermore, twenty-two Hazami were proprietors in Jara, and twenty-six owned property in Chenini. Some, but not all, of the owners originating from nomadic tribes were probably settled in the oasis.

The population of the oasis included other outsiders as well. Just as in the Sahel, many exchanges occurred between the villages of the region. Inhabitants of Methouia, Ghennouche, and Mareth owned land and probably resided in Gabès; Jerbans were numerous in Menzel (fourteen individual properties belonged to them) and even more so in Jara (fifty-nine properties). On a broader scale, there were proprietors from Sfax and its surroundings, from Algeria, and even from Morocco. But there were none from northern Tunisia or from the Sahel.

It is in Chenini that the number of "foreign" owners (settled in the village or not) was the greatest: 176, whose holdings amounted to 4,590 date trees. The average size of their property (26 date palms) did not place these outsiders above the villagers. The same is true for Jara, where the number of outside-owned properties remained high (144, comprising 5,229 trees). With an average of 36.3 trees per owner, these "foreigners" were no richer in trees than the native inhabitants, or those reputed to be natives. The situation remained the same in Menzel, where two-thirds of the properties belonging to outsiders fell into the lower categories. If one Nefāsi had more than 500 trees, the others were distributed among the various categories according to the same proportions as the long-time residents of the oasis.

There was consequently no direct relationship between wealth and length of residence. Nothing distinguished the latecomers from those most solidly rooted. This fact is further confirmed among the inhabitants reputed to be pure Gabèsians, such as the Shemama in Menzel who, despite their age-old presence in the oasis, had only mediocre holdings.

Maraboutic descent offered no greater assurance of wealth. In Jara, where twenty-one *mrabet* (marabouts) were assessed, nine were in the category of middle-sized proprietors and the others were equally divided between large and small. The average size of their property – 40 date palms – was no different from that of "lay" owners. In Menzel only nine owners were marabouts. Their properties came to an average of 46 trees, or slightly more than that of other owners. But there as elsewhere, one does not find a concentration of property. The thirty-three marabouts of Chenini were more liberally endowed. With an average of more than 62 trees, they seemed prosperous; one of them had more than 600 date palms. But even in Chenini, fourteen *mrabet* had fewer than 20 trees.

It would seem, however, that knowledge and wealth went hand in hand. In Jara, ten *fqih* (learned men) were assessed of whom only one was a small owner. All the others fell into middle or upper brackets. The same was true for Chenini, where of twenty scholars, only four were in the lower categories. In Menzel, their holdings were more modest; none had more than a hundred date palms. With an average of thirty trees per capita, the learned men of Menzel were no better off then their neighbors.

Civil or judicial functions also granted certain rights to landed wealth. Not one of the fifteen sheikhs in Chenini was among the small proprietors of that village. This was equally true for the seven notaries. In Jara, there was only one notary and he figured among the intermediate owners. But the fifteen sheikhs were in the middle and upper categories and their average holdings exceeded 90 date trees. One of them, who served as a judge, had 470 trees. The sheikhs and notaries of Menzel were less wealthy. One of the two notaries and three of the six sheikhs had fewer than 20 trees.

Thus, without monopolizing knowledge or power, the largest proprietors nonetheless amassed both along with their landed wealth. In addition, they were in a better position than the other villagers to acquit themselves of their religious duties, particularly the pilgrimage to the holy cities. All of the Gabèsians were pious, as witnessed by the amount of land offered to the mosque and the school, and also as attested to by the practice of pilgrimages, even by small owners who were discouraged neither by the cost nor by the risks of the trip. Fifty-three owners from Jara went to Mecca, among whom twenty belonged to the lower ranks of proprietors. For the five levels of wealth that we have established, there was one *haj* for every sixteen or seventeen proprietors in the first four ranks. Among the rich, one large landowner in six accomplished the pilgrimage. Piety was even more fervent in Menzel, eighty-eight of whose inhabitants had earned the title of *haj*. One proprietor in nine of the lower categories had been to the holy places; one middle-rank proprietor in six; one in five among the fourth group; and among the rich, one out of two. And finally, in Chenini, the proportions are less surprising but still very high: forty-six villagers had made the pilgrimage among the rich, or one in four.

To complete this portrait of notables and affluent people, let us point out one last characteristic: the ubiquity of some proprietors who owned trees in two and even all three of the villages of the oasis. Half of them already had a solid fortune in one of the villages where they appeared on the census. On the basis of their plots in only one village, some might have passed for poor peasants, but once their various properties were added together, they turned out to be rather well off. They were, however, few in number, close to sixty in all, only four of whom held land in all three villages. The majority of the villagers clearly did not go beyond the limits of their village.

The disinherited. At the other extreme, who were the disinherited? A first, rough estimate of the relationship between the number of villagers and the number of proprietors is already indicative. In 1844, 1,732 male proprietors were enumerated, not counting those who appeared two or three times in the survey. Men from other places should be subtracted from this figure, but those who owned property jointly must be added to it. Let us suppose, for the convenience of calculation, that these two figures cancel each other out. There would therefore be about 1,700 landowners. In 1857, according to records for the poll tax,[35] there were 1,659 men in the three villages. Leaving aside the Jews and soldiers (*zawawa* and *sīpahi*) who were not peasants, we are left with 1,486 men. But we must allow for exemptions and frauds. If we add the 200 or 250 men who would make up the difference between the two figures, the coefficient of fraud and exemption is on the order of 14 – 15 percent. This is not excessive, since between the first and the second censuses there was a difference of 438 men, either because of fraud or negligence. If we accept this rough estimate, we can propose the following hypothesis: All inhabitants whose income did not derive from the army (*sipahi* and *zawawa*), from shopkeeping and craftsmanship (Jews and a few professional weavers and shoemakers), or from domestic service (slaves and their descendants) were landowners in the oasis.

Slaves were indeed very poorly off. Of the three villages, only six possessed any land. All fell into the lower categories, as did the Jews, who had no right at all to own land, although two of them in Jara did own six trees, and four others were left in charge of a few plots belonging to a Muslim. Jews and slaves, as one would suspect, could not live directly from the produce of the land.

As to the others, if they all owned land, they were separated by obvious differences that can be roughly estimated as follows: In the second half of the nineteenth century in Menzel and Chenini (the average was lower in Jara), the yield of each date tree was 7–8 *waiba* (280–300 liters) in good years, 3–4 *waiba* (120–160 liters) in bad years. Since good and bad years do not coincide for all the trees, let us postulate an average annual production of 2 hectoliters per tree.[36] The owner of more than 100 trees would thus harvest more than 200 hectoliters a year. Deducting the share of the *khammās* (a sharecropper who, etymologically, received one-fifth of the yield), that still left the owner about 17,000 liters of dates, or more than 45 liters a day – an abundant amount by any standards. At the same time, the proprietor of 10 date palms would have harvested 2,000 liters of dates. If he had not been employed as a *khammās* and had no irrigated crops, he had at his disposal 5 liters of dates per day, which meant he had nothing to sell and ate badly. A *khammās* was generally assigned about 100 trees, from which, in practice, he retained only one-seventh of the harvest as a wage, or approximately 3,000 liters of dates. This is vastly superior to the produce of the pitifully small plots of small landowners.

These inequalities were perhaps not noticed by the parties involved as clearly as they would have been if they had had our calculations and tables before their eyes, since there were no large holdings owned by a single person, and since large properties were broken up into the same tiny parcels as those owned by small landowners. It is also possible that horticulture, the primary activity of the oasis of Gabès, provided the small landowner with enough for his needs because it did not require extensive space. There is thus a certain unity in the social status for most of the inhabitants, but a disparity in resources and wealth. The society of the oasis thus reflects the same picture as that of the settled peoples of the north. But what about the Sahel?

Msaken, a large community in the Sahel

The final case to be examined is that of Msaken, a large community in the Sahel. Here the landscape was very different. Contrasted with the diversity of produce in El Alia or Gabès, the olive tree reigned here in monotonous supremacy. In every way – the specialization of agriculture, the antiquity, significance, and density of its settled population, and the intensity of exchange between the countryside and the urban markets that absorbed the oil, exporting most of it to Europe but retaining some of it for the local soap industry – the Sahel projected the image of a center of an advanced economy when compared to other regions of the country.

The Sahel is the long littoral eastern fringe of Tunisia between Djeradou and Ksour Essaf. Since antiquity, the economy has been based on the cultivation of olives. This tree finds in the Sahel the landscape, soil, and climate best suited to it – soft hills and rolling plains, a generally sandy soil (in Msaken, however, it is heavier, clayey), a gentle coastal climate, and enough rainfall (everywhere more than 300 millimeters per year) to compensate for the effects of the latitude. In addition to these naturally favorable conditions, the Sahelians were able to adopt the most suitable farming techniques – particularly water conservation, for springs are rare – through an ingenious system of collecting and storing rain water, thus creating an agrarian landscape entirely by hand.

In this region, even more than around Bizerte or Cape Bon, tent and village life was organized around a dense network of villages, hamlets, and towns. The two districts of Sousse and Monastir contained some fifty villages, most of which had a population in excess of 1,000 inhabitants. Around the middle of the nineteenth century, a number of these agglomerations assumed the proportions of towns. It should be added that agriculture was not the only occupation of the inhabitants. Skilled artisans, permanent or periodic markets, schools, and places of worship added vitality to these localities. The proportions of their mosques and the solidity of the buildings conferred an urban appearance on these villages. Culminating all this were the three ports of Sousse, Monastir, and Mahdia, squeezed inside their ramparts, but for the most part open to the sea and controlling the hinterland both administratively and economically. Sousse and Monastir were the seats of the caidate. This was where money and oil collected by revenue officials converged, where the oil market was organized, and where contacts between the rural society and the outside world were established.

From this region of the Sahel, Msaken has been selected as an exemplar for its immediate relationship with Sousse, only 12 kilometers away, where the effects on the local economy of the olive oil trade, and its integration in an "international market," can be directly observed. At the same time, the many opportunities for investment that might be found on the coast – shipping, trade, craftsmanship – were absent here. The olive trees remained the principal resource. A survey of the groves should therefore capture a faithful image of Msaken's wealth.

A curious community, Msaken – a secret town about which nothing was known before the seventeenth century, but which then was already the center of one of the largest olive groves in the Sahel.[37] European travelers knew nothing about it because entrance was forbidden to Christians and Jews alike. Even the French officers of native affairs, to whom we owe so much data, failed to describe it. Only Pellissier was familiar with it, and in the middle of the nineteenth century he estimated its population at 10,000.[38] He was not exaggerating the figure, for the census taken in the 1860s indicates a population of about 9,000.[39] Msaken was perhaps more populous than Sousse, the capital of the region. Divided into five quarters called *qsār* – which suggests a previous fortress-town – of considerable importance, the town covered a large area. Even recently, Msaken was found to be the second most spread-out city in the entire country after Tunis.[40] It nevertheless retained its rustic appearance. Already continental, it was poorly linked with other places in the Sahel. Situated in a region totally lacking in stone, the entire town was built of ocher-colored clay. Its huge houses, whose rooms were arranged around a large courtyard, revealed no more than tall blank walls to a stranger's glance.

Profile of Msaken's society. Msaken contained 2,436 properties amounting to 236,000 olive trees.[41] As was the case for the villages discussed earlier, these raw figures are misleading and require some adjustment. To begin with, because of the complexities of inheritance, some of the proprietors were probably counted twice, whereas joint ownerships allowed a few to slip by unnoticed. Let us once more assume that one compensated for the other. Another reason to distrust these figures is that in Msaken, as in the other villages, properties were rarely in the form of a single plot, and holdings were regularly dispersed and fragmented. Nevertheless, even at this first level of examination, the morphology of the region looks different from that of the other villages. Here it was not unusual to find large groves of 100–200 trees and even more. Similarly, disparities were more apparent than elsewhere. Individual plots and scanty properties lay side by side with extensive domains.

The first peculiarity of the area went along with the extreme specialization of the agriculture, the olive tree being the dominant product, whereas in Hammamet or El Alia it was part of a diversified agriculture in which fruit, grapevines, and vegetables also had a place. Concomitantly, average dimensions of the farms were completely different; they were distinctly larger than in the villages of the north. Here, the average size of the properties – summarily obtained by dividing the number of trees by the number of properties – came to 97 trees. Thus a peasant who in El Alia or Hammamet would have been a large landholder was in Msaken a member of the intermediate category of landowners.

The morphological differences between the parcels of land in the three villages, and the scale of dimensions of the properties, did not reflect merely a technical difference between kinds of production, but rather a social difference. For wealth in Msaken was distributed in quite another way than in the regions discussed earlier (see Fig. 3.1). With the average property containing 97 trees, the category of those people owning properties of approximately this size, 81–120 trees, was the smallest of the entire population: only 256. The bulk of Msaken's inhabitants was divided into two extremes. The first, and numerically greatest, consisted of small owners – less than 40 olive trees – who represented 40 percent of the total population. The second group, numerically more important but even more important economically, had large properties; at 513, or

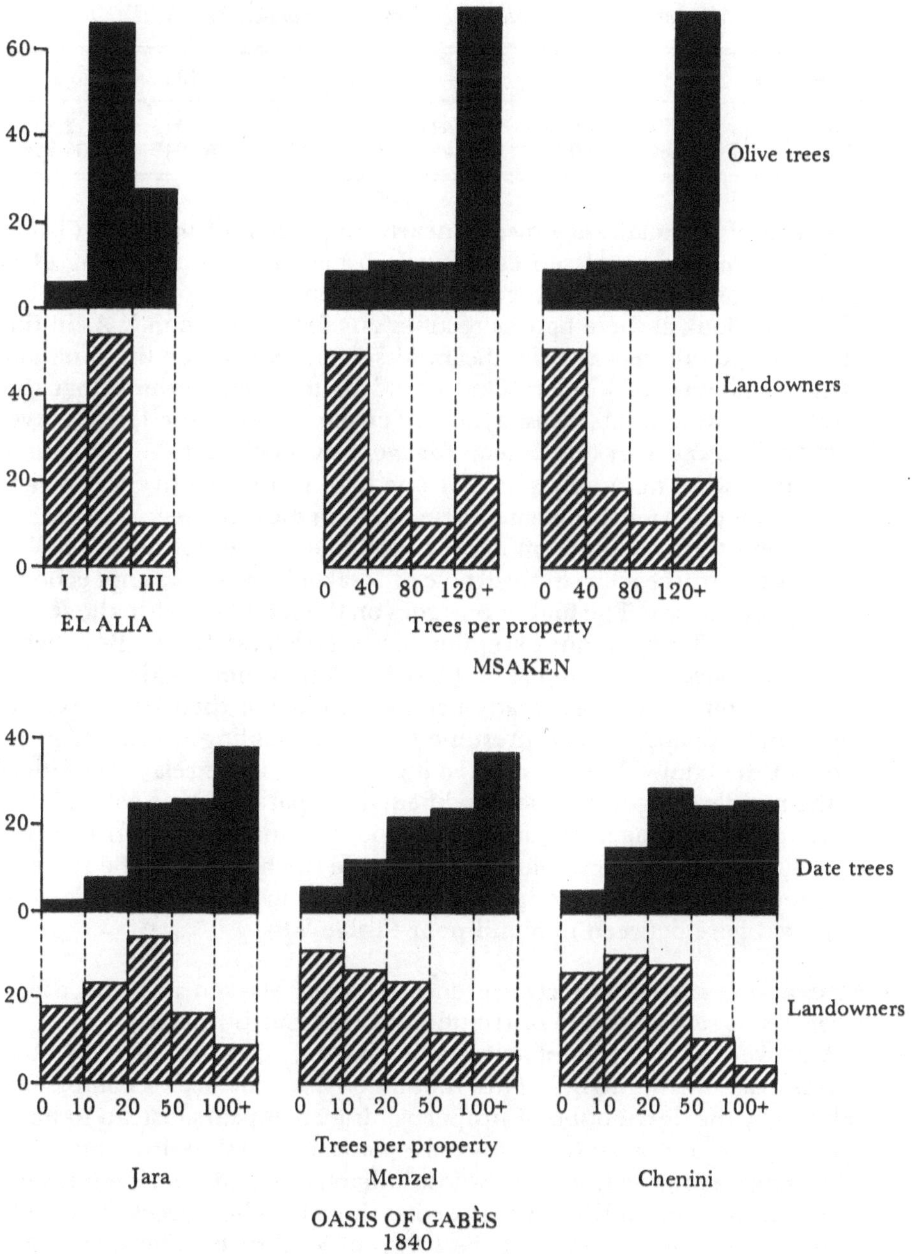

Fig. 3.1. Distribution of olive and date trees per property. (El Alia: I, small landowners; II, middle-sized landowners; III, large landowners.)

Table 3.7. *Msaken: number and dimensions of properties in 1840*

Dimensions	– 40	41–80	81–120	+ 120	Total
Number of properties	1,210	447	256	513	2,426
Number of olive trees	20,000	26,298	25,007	164,949	236,254

one-fifth of the total, they owned nearly 70 percent of the trees (Table 3.7). The middle rank, representing 10.5 percent and possessing 10.6 percent, was squeezed between the two extremes.

A closer look at these figures rectifies our first impression.[42] As in the other villages, there was a significant dissymmetry between the situation of men and that of women. One would be tempted to think that the Msakenites were doubly misogynous. Female owners were few (326 vs. 1,999 male owners, or one woman for every six men), and above all, their properties were miserably small. If one man in four or five was a rich landowner, only one woman in nineteen was in the top category, whereas 75 percent were counted among the very smallest landowners. The bipolarity of fortunes seen in the whole of Msaken's society was not echoed among the fair sex. The higher one goes on the scale of wealth, the fewer the women. There was one exception: a royal princess, ʿAicha Beya, who with 2,650 olive trees, was one of the richest landowners in Msaken.

These women, as has already been said, did not themselves exploit their land. Again, one can presume that their holdings were added to those of the family. With that taken into account, if the relative position of the middle categories is not modified, the separation between the two extremes is no longer as great. The poorest landowners represented only 40 percent of the whole and were twice the number of the richest. The remaining middle group, well represented in Gabès or El Alia, was squeezed here between rich and poor (Table 3.8).

Msaken, holy city. Another difference between Msaken and the other villages was related to the distribution of religious properties.

A proverb says of the inhabitants of Msaken, "Poor [*masākīn*] by day, knives [*sakākīn*] by night." This reputation for violence is completely refuted by the distribution of property. Msaken appears instead to have been a pious and austere town where places of worship, learning, and pilgrimage abounded, a town whose inhabitants generously endowed their own religious institutions as well as those of other places. Through such legacies one can guess at the forms of local piety. There was first of all the importance given to the cult of marabouts, some of whom had been as generously endowed as the largest mosques. Second, the cult was organized around family units: mosques and *zāwiyas* bore the names

Table 3.8. *Msaken: types of properties in 1840*

Dimensions	– 40	41–80	81–120	+ 120	Total
a. Number of properties					
Men, joint	925	385	226	463	1,999
Women	238	49	22	17	326
Waqf	47	13	8	33	101
b. Numbers of olive trees					
Men, joint	16,042	22,697	22,127	134,577	195,443
Women	3,558	2,886	2,121	5,783	14,348
Waqf	400	715	759	24,589	26,463

of the great families of Msaken, such as Rūīs, Chati, Qmādi. All told, there were 101 recipients of donations. Some of them were fragmented to the point of absurdity, for examples, one tree to Sidi al Hāni, one to the great mosque of Kerkenna. Three centers benefited particularly from the generosity of the faithful: the religious institutions of Sousse, with 2,000 trees; those of Kairouan; and the fifty-seven institutions of Msaken.

In Msaken, twenty of these foundations belonged to the upper rank of owners. Strangely enough, the great mosque, with its 550 olive trees, was not the richest landholder of the town. Nor was the great *zāwiya* of Sheikh Ali Ibn Khalifa, about which Pellissier wrote that it was famous throughout the land and made "of this rich and populous town the Benares of the south in the regency of Tunis."[43] The most enormous property belonged to the mosque of Sidi Sahib in Kairouan, which was endowed with a total of 13,000 trees.

Religious foundations accounted for 11.2 percent of the olive trees in the region, a proportion not much higher than that of other regions. But elsewhere, the produce of those donated lands in some way returned to the community. For the lands provided a means of sustaining the celebrants of the cults, the readers of the Koran, teachers of all grades, and so on. The situation was quite different in Msaken, where an institution totally outside the town benefited from the generosity of the town's believers. This fact, already replete with implications, is not unique. We shall come to the question of Kairouan later.

Powerful families and great fortunes. When examining the census, one is struck by the numerical importance of certain lineages in Msaken. The same names reappeared in every part of the Msaken forest: 120 properties belonged to the Mahjub family, 59 to the Qmādi, 55 to the Chati, 54 to the Rūīs, 55 to the Hmīla, 47 to the Abu Qdīda, 46 to the ʿAdhari,

43 to the Abu Hillāl. The names ʿAttīa, Trād, Karmūs, and still others were equally widespread throughout the region. Many of these families also had their own mosque, and in some cases a marabout as well among their kin.

The frequency of these names suggests sizable fortunes and the overall prosperity of the descendants of these lineages. Curiously, numerical size was not related to material wealth (see Fig. 3.2). Generally, the members of great families were distributed throughout the ranks of the scale of wealth with no break in continuity. Though some individuals might distinguish themselves from the group by owning 1,000 or more trees, most were at the base of the pyramid. Only the Qmādi had a large proportion of rich people in their family ranks. Ten of them had more than 200 trees. Two inheritances in the family consisted of single undivided groves, each containing 1,000 olive trees. Even the women were relatively better off than in most other families. They also had their own chapel, their own Koran readers, and other *habous* foundations. One can imagine the social importance of this group. The Qmādi combined numerical strength with material wealth.

This family was an exception. Other families – such as the Maqrūn, one of whose members was a leader in the revolution of 1864 – though smaller in size, could be very well off. Only four properties were listed in their name, but three of them contained more than 500 olive trees.

Along with these families, designated as native to Msaken, was a large number of proprietors whose origins were elsewhere but who nonetheless resided in Msaken. There were few nomads among them; only a few from the neighboring tribe of Jlāss had settled there. However, some twenty landowners came from other parts of the Sahel. Msaken also absorbed about ten Andalusians (this fact is noteworthy since the Iberian presence was rare in the Sahel), and the inhabitants of Jabal Waslāt (who owned seventy-three properties). Finally, and predominantly, natives of Kairouan – 128 men and 7 women – lived in Msaken and owned land there. They were wealthier than the natives. Their average property consisted of 118 trees, or quite a bit more than the average for natives of Msaken. Although 32 percent were in the small-owner category, 26.7 percent were among the richest. What is more, among the landowners in Msaken who lived outside the town, twenty-five were inhabitants of Kairouan, two lived in Sousse, and less than twenty in Tunis. It has already been mentioned that a large portion of the *habous* properties belonged to Kairouan institutions. All of these factors indicate the strong tie that bound these two cities. What does this signify? It highlights the fact that Kairouan, surrounded by a barren steppe, could generate only small revenues from its own hinterland, and that its crafts had greatly declined since this holy city ceased being the capital. Its inhabitants

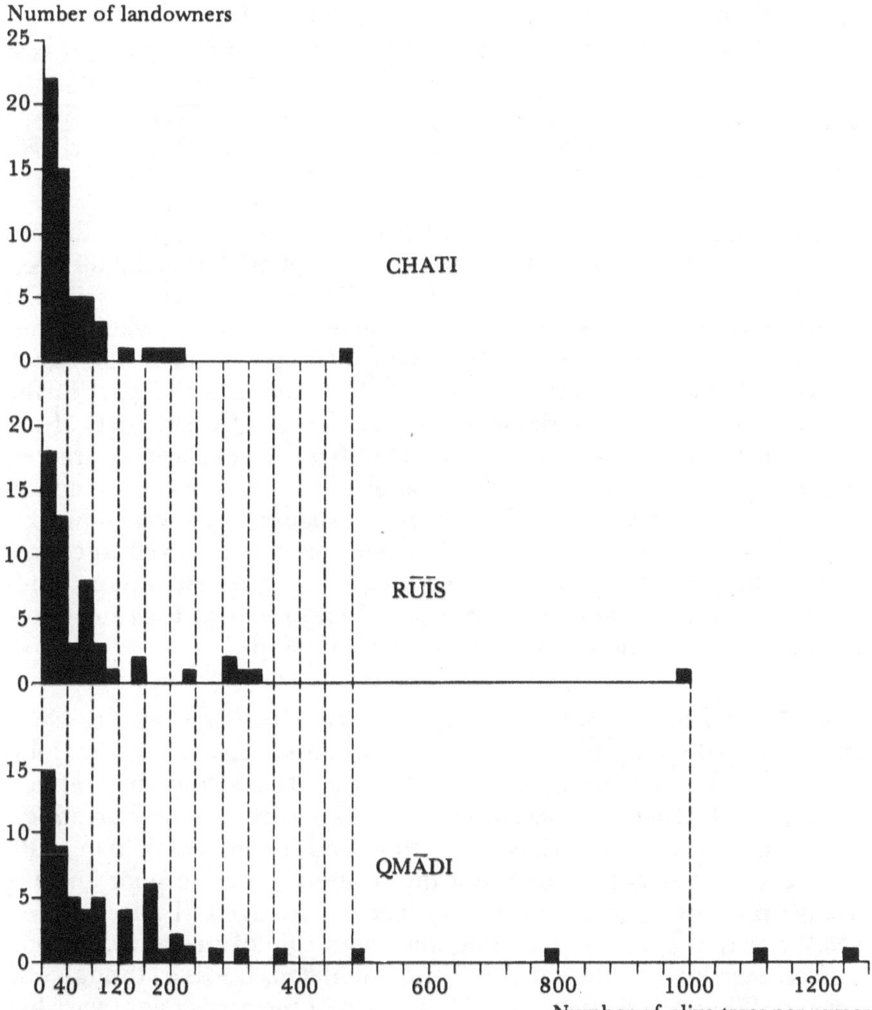

Fig. 3.2. Powerful families of Msaken.

therefore derived part of their income from their contacts with other centers of production, in this case, Msaken. What had occurred was a transfer of people to this large agglomeration in the Sahel, a shift of capital and investments to its olive groves, but also a transfer of profits from the lands of Msaken to the mosques and homes of Kairouan.

The inhabitants of Tunis also benefited from the prosperity of the Sahel and the activity of its inhabitants. Seventeen Msaken landowners lived in the capital, among them members of the bey's entourage. The

Table 3.9. *Number and dimensions of properties in 1859*

Dimensions	−40	48–80	81–120	+120	Total
No. of properties	1,206	434	253	481	2,374
No. of olive trees	20,236	25,405	25,171	158,796	229,608

caid, Muhammad ibn ʿAyād, owned 1,500 olive trees; the former Keeper of the Seal, Shākir Sāhib at-Tābiʿ, left an estate of more than 2,000 trees. Another concession to a prince had a similar number. Two sheikhs, a notary, and a *kātib* (scribe) were also among the owners in Msaken. Thus, notables from the capital extended their influence as far as the Sahel. Some of them, particularly caid ibn ʿAyād, took an active part in the olive oil business. A proprietor of olive groves in different parts of the Sahel, a tax collector, benefiting in addition from export licenses granted by the bey, ibn ʿAyād had at his disposal numerous ways of cornering the surplus agricultural production of the region. This was, however, an unusual case. In 1844 none of Msaken's proprietors lived in coastal towns. The inhabitants of Sousse were consistently absent among landholders in Msaken. The trade in olive oil had not – at least not yet – altered the distribution of wealth in the hinterland.

1840–59: structural stability. Twenty years after the first census, which was carefully kept up to date, a new one was undertaken.[44] As in Hammamet, there were innumerable changes in details, but their effects canceled each other out. Declaring more dead trees than new plantings, Msaken owners claimed to have a few thousand fewer trees than in 1840; a few dozen owners had died. But the relation of rich to poor and the relative proportion in each category had not changed (Tables 3.7 and 3.9).We may perhaps be touching here on a rule of preindustrial economics: Stability was the sum of changes in detail. It was as though one were shuffling a deck of cards: The position of the cards might vary but the deck remains intact. In the case of the land, the new shuffle resulted in a fragmentation of property, a tangle of farming units, and a distribution of plots complicated by the intricacies of inheritance.

A society more differentiated than elsewhere. Once again, let us ask the question, Were there landless peasants and pure rentiers? Hired hands and absentee landowners?

Rentier landlords there surely were, and first among them were the outsiders who did not reside in Msaken. There were many and they were rich. There were the mosques as well, particularly the one in Kairouan. Together they owned 40,000 trees at the time of the first census, or one-sixth of the olive groves in Msaken. That was a considerable part of the entire area. As for the very large landowners on the spot, household cultivation became impossible when properties assumed gigantic dimensions. Many – but how many? – had to entrust their trees to less prosperous peasants.

At the other end of the scale, the proliferation of miserable little plots with only a few trees clearly indicates that many peasants did not have the productive means necessary for their subsistence. A large number evidently had to hire themselves out to the major olive growers.

Elsewhere, in all the villages analyzed, the number of adult males and of landowners was more or less equal. Here, a significant disparity appeared. Excluding jointly owned properties, 1,570 male proprietors were counted. According to the censuses, there were more than 2,000 adult males in Msaken, and this figure does not take into account fraud and legal exemptions. The discrepancy is too great to be the result of chance alone or the carelessness of the scribes. Where other villages showed a common pattern, Msaken stood apart. Here, approximately 500 men, or one-fourth of the surveyed population, were landless. This was more or less the same as the number of large landowners. Did Msaken's religious and intellectual activities, its commerce and crafts employ that many workers? It is not impossible. In 1836–7, there were 227 weaving shops and 56 oil presses in the community.[45]

In other villages it was possible to conclude that the society, without being undifferentiated or homogeneous, showed no clear stratification. The differences in wealth did not alter the relationships of production. The contrasts were much greater in Msaken. The middle rank was compressed between the two outer groups – a host of peasants whose minuscule properties were incapable of feeding a family was bound to be dependent. At the other extreme was a dominant group, numerically larger, holding patrimonies far greater than in other regions. Here, the small independent producer did not comprise the majority.[46]

Whether this stratification was peculiar to the Sahel or to large communities is hard to say. We have tried in the course of our study to explain this type of structure. It may be that it existed elsewhere. In the absence of further investigation let us postulate that in the middle of the nineteenth century, the dominant type – that of independent, family-operated cultivation – did not exclude more differentiated structures.

Landlords and landless

In the north as in the south, and in the Sahel, the existence of rentier landlords is not in question. Religious organizations, urban notables, agents of the bey, and great families residing in the countryside owned a significant share of village lands. From another vantage point and with another lens, so to speak, we would like to take in the whole panorama of territory controlled by the great landowners and determine their extent. Can this be done? In the documentation currently available, only two families disclosed their properties: the bey's family and that of the Jallūli.[47]

Of the latter's activities and importance I have already written elsewhere.[48] The members of this family succeeded one another to the caidate of Sfax, and extended their power as far as the ʿAqarība tribe and the Sahel. Merchants trading with Malta and the Levant, shipbuilders participating in corsair expeditions against Christians, major agents of the bey capable of lending him money on occasion or offering him a slave from the Orient, the Jallūli also had a well established fortune in real estate. Between 1793–4 and 1843, Muhammad Jallūli owned a number of houses, apartments, shops, cafés, ovens, and a mill in Sfax, the family seat. He had houses and shops in Sousse and Ksour Essaf, oil presses all over the Sahel, and above all, a vast number of olive groves. The dimensions of the Jallūli family's groves were rarely known, and their revenues not at all.[49] But the geographic distribution of their lands speaks for itself: they were scattered throughout the whole of the Sahel as well as in the region of Sfax (Map 3.1). However small the income from any one of these groves, the sum total of income in money and produce that flowed into Sfax was surely enormous.

Far more eloquent than any inventory minutely compiled by an accountant, one anecdote bespeaks the affluence of these mighty caids. One day Jallūli was berated by the bey, Hammūda Pāsha, for not having invited him to his table. Jallūli at once replied that he would be delighted to welcome the bey at his Manouba country house. On the appointed day, the bey arrived to find that the meal had already been served and consisted of only one dish. When the lid was raised, the serving dish was found to be piled high with *mahbūb* (gold coins) in which a diamond nestled. The gift was worth 500,000 piasters. Satisfied, the bey returned to his own palace for lunch.[50]

This story is said to be authentic. As far as their fortune was concerned, the bey's family had no reason to be envious of the Jallūli. During the first half of the eighteenth century, Bey Husayn owned hundreds of properties in the region of Tunis, nearly as many near Bizerte, and about the same number near Béja (Maps 3.2, 3.3). His holdings extended as far as Sfax and Kairouan, where he had some forty properties. In contrast to the Jallūli, solidly entrenched in the Sahel, the bey of that time had no lands in that part of the country. Is it that we are lacking documentation? Administrative accounts of the period confirm the in-

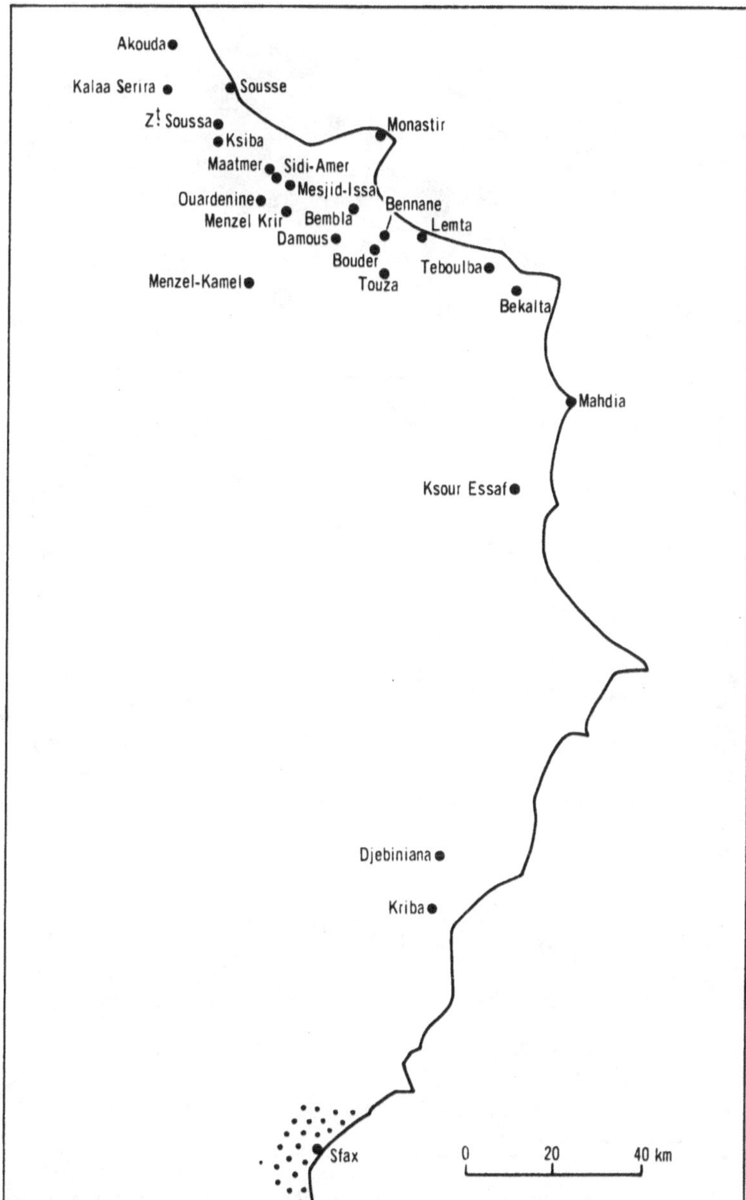

Map 3.1. Properties belonging to the Jallūli family at the beginning of the nineteenth century. (Z' signifies Zaouiet.)

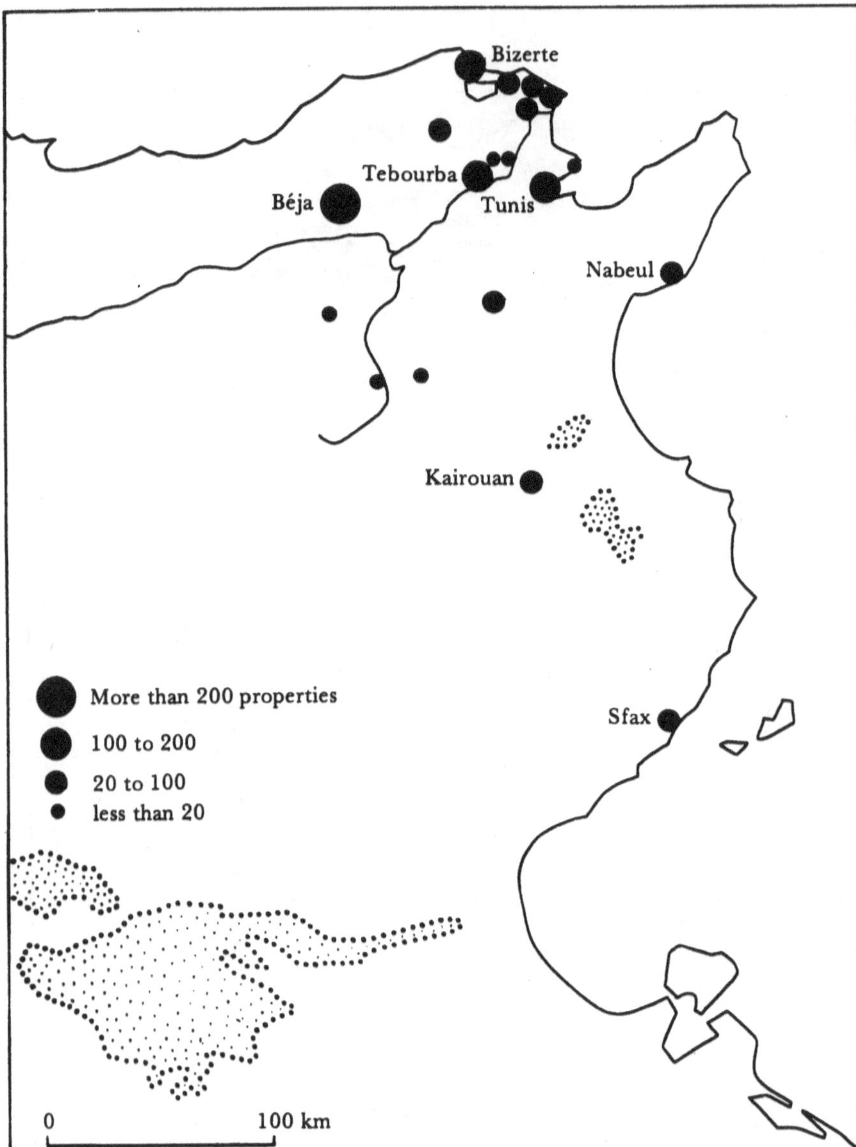

Map 3.2. Properties belonging to the bey at the beginning of the eighteenth century.

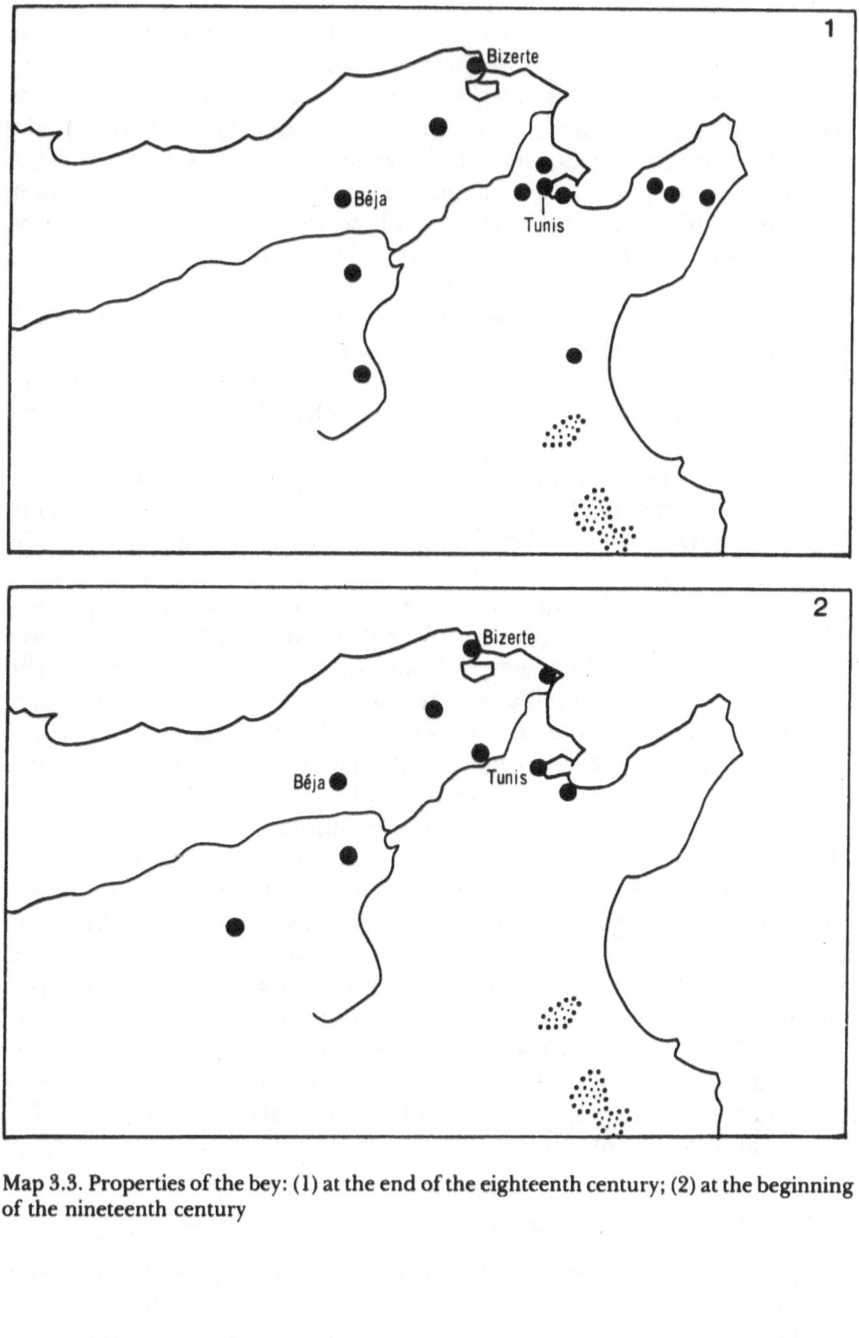

Map 3.3. Properties of the bey: (1) at the end of the eighteenth century; (2) at the beginning of the nineteenth century

ventories of holdings: It was primarily in Ifriqīya that the bey was a landowner, around towns and villages, and among tent dwellers. A generation later, in 1758–9, the properties belonging to Bey Husayn's four daughters still stretched across the same regions: the outskirts of Bizerte and Tunis, Cape Bon and, to the west, the territory of the Awlād Abu Salem. There was no extension at that time toward the steppes. A fresh inventory of properties "placed under the bey's supervision" between 1786 and 1795 shows that certain lands were transferred or disposed of, and others acquired, because of the absence of heirs, among them *habous* lands, since all the descendants of the marabout had died. The geographic distribution of these properties had not changed. It was only between 1838 and 1845, because oil sold to European merchants had become Tunisia's principal export, that the real estate of the ruling family extended into the Sahel where the bey bought a large number of olive groves.[51]

In truth, the bey did not wait until then to gain control of all kinds of lands. Whereas the Jallūli placed all their eggs in one basket, so to speak – in olive trees – the bey's holdings were far more diversified. His arable lands covered thousands of hectares; his olive groves came to thousands of trees; he owned orchards and vineyards. At Cape Bon alone, by the end of the eighteenth century, he had thirty-eight olive groves containing 24,000 trees. All told, his orchards amounted to the territory of a number of villages put together. Moreover, those writers who tried to evaluate the revenues of the regency placed the income from the bey's properties as one of the major sources of his treasury, followed only by the revenues generated from tithes and "caideries."[52]

With the beys and the Jallūli we are at the summit of the social pyramid. Their wealth attained extraordinary proportions. But these were not exceptional cases. Every rich city dweller described by travelers or chroniclers had some property in the country: A learned man, a reader of the Koran in the mosque of as-Zaytuna, had olive trees in Cape Bon; a perfume merchant in the bazaar of Tunis owned arable lands outside the capital, an area dotted with opulent country houses belonging to the city's leading citizens.[53] In Tunisia, as in other preindustrial societies, agricultural rents provided supplementary incomes for the urban well-to-do. Land was the ideal investment for officials of the regency, for artisans and merchants, and for learned men.

Methods of allocation and cultivation

In the villages whose nonexploiting proprietors could be estimated, about 10 percent of the lands were associated with religious institutions; a more variable and unverifiable percentage belonged to absentee landlords or to estates too extensive for direct cultivation. On these lands, there were three possible types of allocation. The most favorable arrangement for the landless or meagerly endowed peasant was to cultivate *habous* lands when they were not farmed by the maraboutic family itself. An *enzel* contract granted the tenant perpetual rights that could be passed on to heirs, transferred, or even sold, thereby assuring the tenant prolonged use of the land. He, in turn, had to pay an annual rent, in some cases in kind, in others in cash, the amount being usually small and, in any case, fixed once and for all. It was on this basis, for example, that a large part of the olive trees belonging to the great mosque of Hammamet was tended by the inhabitants of the town. *Enzel* provided the means for modifying the principle of nontransferability of *habous* lands and also, through the perpetuity of the lease and the fixed rental fee, prevented the aleatory gains that Islam prohibits.

Two kinds of contracts applied to groves and orchards: *musaqa*, under which the lessee contracted to irrigate a strip of land whose yield he would share with the owner; and *mugharsa*, under which the lessee contracted to plant trees. So long as they did not bear fruit, the *mugharsi* was entitled to the entire produce of the land around the fledgling tree and to the natural pastures the land provided. But when the trees began to produce fruit, the land was then shared between the initial owner and the lessee, who then became full owner of half the land he had fructified. Their association was terminated. This contract provided the means of acceding to property and corresponds to the canonic principle according to which the fructification of land establishes the right to ownership. Innumerable olive trees belonging to the bey were planted under such conditions.

On the plowlands, the mode of allocation was that of leaseholds. Leases were generally drawn up for one growing season (based on the Julian calendar, called *ʿajmi*) and went into effect in October. The validity of the contract could also extend for two or more years. If the rent was payable in cash, the owner had only to hand over the land and receive his rent either upon concluding the contract or in a number of payments.[54]

Since all these agreements were generally oral, it is very rare to find any record of them. There is, however, the case of a *māshia* of land, rented in 1799, for an unspecified period, by Ali ben-Saʿad al-Jandubi to Mohammad ibn Hsin al-Busalmi. The tenant, on concluding the contract before witnesses, paid 10 piasters (in the currency of the period). The same proprietor leased half a *māshia* for 3 piasters to someone who contracted to grow wheat and barley. Let us say that for one *māshia* of 10 hectares, the yield in cereals – half wheat, half barley – was about 1 *qafīz* (approximately 5 hectoliters). The first tenant harvested 10 *qafīz*, the second, half that amount. The price of a *qafīz* of barley at the time was about 20 piasters, and that of wheat between 22 and 49 piasters. The value of the total harvest came to about 300 piasters. For the first farmer, the rent was therefore 3 percent, for the second, 2 percent.

By the same calculations, in 1835–6 a rent of 15 piasters for a *māshia* came to 3 percent. This was the lowest rate. For other farms, the rent was 20 piasters per *māshia* in 1822–3, 45 piasters in 1836–7, which corresponded to a rate of 10 percent. These are individual cases that do not allow for general conclusions. They merely point to the diversity of tenure arrangements and indicate the order of magnitude of rental fees.

When the rent was to be paid in kind, the terms of the contract were completely different. In that case, the owner gave the tenant an advance and shared the costs of cultivation. He provided the seed and draft animals, the plows and yokes, in short, the basic input for the enterprise.[55] Under these conditions, the output was fairly considerable in proportion to the capital invested. On the lands of the bey, a tenant in the regions of Mateur and Bizerte owed 8 *qafīz* of wheat and 4 of barley per work unit; in Tunis and Cape Bon, 5 *qafīz* of wheat and 10 of barley; in Béja and Téboursouk, 8 of wheat and 25 of barley, or depending on the region, from 5.5 to 8 hectoliters of grain per hectare. These are Draconian conditions. Given the probable yields, this did not leave much for a tenant farmer. The proprietor probably took care of the wages of *khammās* and other workers involved in cultivation. One may presume that the tenant farmed more lands than he rented, for in fact, the total surface of the properties was one thing, the part actually leased – very much smaller – was another. Perhaps the tenant farmer was thus able to farm land that lay officially outside the lease.

These properties, like those whose rent was paid in cash, were up for auction every year. According to Ibn Abi Dhiaf, until 1759, a farmer was obliged to prolong his lease for several years if the bey did not find a higher-paying tenant at the time of its expiration. After that date, probably because of the relatively favorable demographic conditions of the regency during the second half of the eighteenth century, new tenants were readily available. The bey then freed the tenants from their obligation.

The actual period of occupation was, in fact, variable. Although certain properties changed hands very often, many tenants remained on the same land for a long time. A group of Libyans remained on the same estate in Cape Bon for seventy years. The bey's secretary, Sheikh Muhammad Lasram, and his family held the rights to one of the properties in the region of Mateur for sixty-four years. The descendant of a slave, Marzūq al Usīf, kept a farm of about 70 hectares for nineteen years.

Who were these tenants? In the region of Mateur, the bey owned fifty-one estates whose tenancy can be followed for nearly a century, between

1750 and 1830. The names of the tenants are recorded, but in 72 percent of the cases there is no other information about them. Among others, there were members of local tribes, specifically the Bjāwa, and immigrants from distant regions such as Libyans and Waslatiya. The other 28 percent consisted of members of the army and the civil service, a mixed group, some of whom were obscure guards, *sipahis*, or *khojas*. Others, on the contrary, were of the highest standing – the Keeper of the Seal, the bey's secretary, the *khasnadar* (finance minister). In Béja, the bey had forty properties whose tenants are recorded: 57 percent belonged to local tribes, 43 percent came from the administration and the army, among them the caid and the *kahia* of Béja, the Keeper of the Seal, and so on. The same holds true for the regions of Tunis, Bizerte, and Téboursouk, where the bey had other estates. For the tenants of the first group (peasants from the region, immigrants from other provinces), and for the poorer ones of the second, to rent a piece of land was a way of getting settled, of assuring themselves of a living by having access to land. For the others, the leasing of land, we can assume, was an investment. The actual cultivation was accomplished by others, and the lessee shared with the owner the rent obtained from the peasants who tilled the land. A white slave by the name of Sliman al Mamlūk, who became *khasnadar* and then a commander in the bey's army, leased the *henshīr* (estate) of Batan si Nasr, which varied between 25 and 40 hectares, for thirty-five years, and for four years the *henshīr* Shabra, which varied in extent from 45 to 60 hectares depending on the year. At the same time, he rented additional *henshīrs*: Mekkada (15–40 hectares), ʿAin el Baidha (15–20 hectares), and still others. Similarly, Lasram, the bey's *kātib*, leased a number of farms and for long periods. Both of these men, and many others – such as the Keepers of the Seal Youssef Khodja and Shākir – were among the highest officials of the regency and were important enough in the history of the country to have their biographies recorded by Ibn Abi Dhiaf. There is no doubt that for these "tenants," leasing lands from the bey was a way of increasing their already sizable income.

The khammās

Once land was leased, who was responsible for the harvest? To reply to this question let us turn to the decree of 1874 on agriculture, which established the rights and obligations of peasants involved in the cultivation of a plot of land, and particularly those of *khammās*. This worker was defined as "an associate having the right to one-fifth as compensation for his work."[56] A *khammās* was the one who provided the labor, and the owner, or the *fellah* who hired him, provided the other four elements necessary for farming: land, draft animals, plows and other implements, and seed. The *khammās* thus constituted one-fifth of the investment and his compensation amounted, theoretically, to one-fifth of the harvest.

The services that he owed were participation in plowing, planting, irrigation, weeding, protection of crops against birds, spring sowing, care and feeding of draft animals, rope making, participation in harvesting, threshing, basket making, the building of haystacks, which were protected with a coat of damp earth. This latter operation marked the completion of a season's work. The *khammās* was not required to participate in the construction of permanent structures (houses, fences, storehouses, silos, etc.), and if he did, he was entitled to additional remuneration. It was the master's duty to provide all the means of production.

The employer's obligations to the *khammās* were, first, to pay him an advance in cash; second, to provide beasts of burden to help transport his personal belongings to his new dwelling; and finally, to give him his share after the harvest. It was also proper for the landowner to pay his *khammās* in advance if he was not able to provide his own clothing.

The hiring of guardians and day laborers during periods of heavy work was also the responsibility of the employer, as was the payment of the scribe's fee for the contract outlining the *khammās*'s debt and the one assuring the *khammās* his share in the harvest.

The *khammās*, however, even when he had fulfilled all his duties, was still not free of his obligations. Before the end of the season, he had also to inform the farmer of his intention to leave, and above all, to reimburse the funds advanced to him. The keystone of this partnership was precisely the advance made to the *khammās*. Without an advance, there could be no contract. It was not the plot of land but the debt contracted before the work began that bound the *khammās* to the peasant who hired him. The law of 1874 made two important changes in the contractual arrangements. The first referred to the date inaugurating the growing season, which was moved back from October to September 1 – a seemingly insignificant measure but one that reduced the *khammās*'s freedom. Article 27 stipulated that the association could not be terminated during the month of September if the harvest had not been entirely garnered, and it could happen that the threshing was not completed by this date.

The second modification concerned the duration of the obligation, modifying a tradition of many centuries and a practice recognized throughout the Maghreb. According to Article 32, "The *khammās* can change his status only by becoming a farmer himself, and if this is not possible for him and he leaves his work to take another, or simply to be lazy, the caid will require him to renew his contract with the farmer for whom he worked, or to find the same employment with someone else." Prisoner of the advances he must reimburse before he may leave his creditor, the *khammās* became even more oppressed by these two rulings. Without anticipating an analysis of the changed circumstances that these measures reveal – changes that will be discussed later – it is nonetheless apparent that a contrast existed between the rulings of 1759, which eased the farmer's burden and probably corresponded to favorable agricultural conditions as well as greater density of lands, and those of the end of the nineteenth century, which indicate an attempt to bind the worker to the land in a situation in which a reduced labor force coincided with a contraction of plowlands.

The *khammās*, while defined as an "associate," was in fact a hireling paid in kind from the produce of his harvest. He did receive a fifth of the harvest, but only after the tithe and fodder for the animals needed for work during the summer had been deducted. In other words, once he was paid, the *khammās* would be hard put, especially in years of meager harvests, to repay his advance. In practice, however, the *khammās*'s share was not necessarily limited to a fifth; it could reach a quarter, or even a third of the harvest.[57] A similar arrangement also existed in the oasis where the *khammās* or *sherik* had to take care of the irrigation system and tend the date palms, fruit trees, and vegetables. His share was then rarely a fifth and varied according to the crop: for example, a quarter for fruits, a seventh for dates, and a third for grains and vegetables. Or else he might keep half of the vegetables, a fifth of the dates (plus the total harvest of a single tree), and a fourth of the corn. Local practices – the simple law of supply and demand – thus affected the specific conditions of the *khammās*.

Was the *khammās* a widespread phenomenon in the regency of Tunis? In the light of available information, it is impossible to provide a quantitative reply. Geographically, we know only that the *khammās* was rare or not present at all in many parts of the country, particularly in the Sahel and the steppes, where direct exploitation was the rule. Other types of contracts were more prevalent, such as the sharecropping association between one peasant who provided the land and half the seed, and another who provided draft animals and the labor of his own back. The *khammās*, on the other hand, was a central figure in the oases of the south. On the wheat fields of the north, landowners, among them the bey, also made much use of his services. All in all, the conditions pertaining to the country's sparse population, access to land ownership, and the abundance of land lead us to presume that the use of the *khammās* was quite limited before the advent of colonization.

4. ❧ Crops and techniques

The principal crops of the old regency were grain cereals. Although rainfall was uneven and land irregularly fertile throughout the country, all peasants nonetheless tried to raise wheat and barley. After the first rains, nomad and settled people alike took up their plows, tilled the soil, and sowed seed. Second in importance was the olive tree. Too numerous to count in the regions of Sousse, Monastir, or Mahdia, where there were immense forests of olive trees, they could as readily be found in the villages of the north as at the edge of the desert: in Jabal Matmata, the olive tree provided the major source of income. In this latitude, however, man's greatest achievement was the cultivation of the date palm, whose fruit was transported throughout the regency and to ports around the Mediterranean as well.

Grain, olives, and dates comprised the triad of Tunisia's basic crops, though not its total agriculture. There were also many other plants that required little space and grew virtually concealed among the other crops. Though inconspicuous, these plants were nonetheless important to the economy of the regions that produced them and to the peasants who cultivated them. We shall begin our inventory of the species grown in Tunisia with them.

Bountiful gardens: useful and edible plants

An inquiry into those gardens may be an excellent idea, but how is one to determine the thousand and one varieties of plants grown during the eighteenth century, and how, amid all that luxuriance, is one to distinguish between what was planted merely for the pleasure of sight and smell, and what had an alimentary, medicinal, or magical purpose? The most reliable source of information is Desfontaines,[1] a botanist and conscientious researcher, professor at the Museum of Paris, whose three copious volumes catalogue, describe, and depict the entire repertory of Algerian and Tunisian flora in the eighteenth century.

Cash crops

The first plants described by Desfontaines are two kinds of jasmine, whose flowers give off a sweet fragrance: *Mongorium sambac* and *Jasminum grandiflorum*. Of all the jasmines, these two are the loveliest.[2] Why, the reader will ask, mention plants that were clearly grown for pleasure? The reason is that these two jasmines were also the most useful, since an essence was extracted from them. Also cultivated in Tunisia were two kinds of roses, whose petals yielded a precious attar: the ordinary red rose and the white *nesri*, more costly and rarer, which "the wealthiest and most sensuous Moors" distilled at home for their personal use. And last, the orange blossom, which provided the fragrant orange-flower water.[3]

These products were used in baking and perfume, cooking, and toiletries.[4] They were precious commodities indeed, appearing among the gifts sent by the bey to the court of France. In 1729 Youssef Khodja presented twenty bottles of orange-flower water to the comte de Maurepas, and in 1776 the bey sent, among other local products, two cases of orange-flower water and a case of rose water.[5]

These were items of great luxury. Between 1748 and 1762 a *qintār* of 100 pounds of roses cost 18 to 25 piasters, or almost the price of a *qafīz* (over 500 liters) of wheat. From 1751 to 1762 orange blossoms cost approximately 5 piasters per 100 pounds. The ratio remained the same twenty years later.[6] As for the extracted essences, their price in the eighteenth century is not known, but some indication is provided by market prices in Tunis on April 16, 1850. A pound of rose water was then worth 3.5 piasters, the equivalent of 17.5 liters of wheat or couscous, or 32 liters of fava beans. On the very same date one could have bought a sheep for less than the price of 2 pounds of rose water.[7] These essences, moreover, were exported, albeit in small quantities. As of the eighteenth century, Leghorn, Genoa, and Marseille began receiving some flasks of orange-flower water. Leghorn continued to import this product until the middle of the nineteenth century, if not later.[8] The Levant, while producing some itself, also imported essences from Tunis because of their superior quality.

Roses, jasmine, and orange blossoms were therefore industrial plants, and all three were cultivated in the north, which is to say in the immediate environs of Tunis, or in the region of Cape Bon, where orange trees grew in profusion. Tinctorial plants such as indigo, madder, and henna were other industrial crops. The first was harvested in the region of Mahdia.[9] It was sown in May in irrigated fields. When the plant matured, it was pulled up, dried, and burned. Its ashes were collected in jars and water was added. This mixture was then boiled down to make a paste, which was then shaped into small tapered molds a few centimeters long. In this form indigo was brought to market. Though of mediocre quality, it was enough during the eighteenth and nineteenth centuries for the needs of the country. No indigo was imported from Europe; in fact, Tunisia exported some. At the beginning of the eighteeenth century, this product became a regular item of trade with Malta, which imported a few hundred molds of indigo every year. After 1725, for reasons unknown, shipments ceased, but in 1755 were resumed in small quantities and irregularly. Leghorn and other Italian cities also bought Tunisian indigo.

Henna is a plant of the oasis – *Lawsonia inermis*, the *cyprus* of the ancients – whose uses are innumerable. Women, wrote Desfontaines, tint the tips of their fingers and toes with it, stopping the practice only "if they have lost their husbands or parents." The hair of children up to the age of nine or ten was dyed with it. The backs, manes, and legs of horses were rubbed with henna.[10] It was believed by eighteenth- and nineteenth-century travelers that this was done for aesthetic reasons. But henna was used from one end of North Africa to the other, under the same circumstances, and for the same purposes. It was presumed to conciliate beneficent forces and repel evil ones. Its fumes were used to summon a loved one, or to expel evil spirits from a house about to be occupied. Everywhere henna was applied to the hands and feet of girls immediately following their engagement and on the eve of their wedding. A groom endowed with supernatural strength but threatened by evil influences was protected by having henna rubbed on three fingers of his right hand. Scattered on the steps of a traveler as he was leaving home, henna leaves warded off evil spirits.[11] *Al-henna min urāq al-jenna*, says an Arab proverb: Henna is among the herbs of paradise.

Henna was also used for therapeutic purposes. In the eighteenth century, its leaves were applied to fresh wounds to promote healing, and to tumors to shrink them.[12] In addition, henna was used to dye cloth.

Last among the dyes, madder was produced in the region of Gabès, specifically in the village of Methouia. From Tunis, in small quantities, it was exported to Leghorn and Marseille. Around 1880, 100 square meters of good soil could produce 60 kilograms of roots a year; poorer soil, 20.[13]

These three dye-producing plants – henna, indigo, and madder – needing little space, could provide the peasants who grew them with a product of great value, easily sold in urban markets, and were thus an assured means (before the appearance of synthetic dyes at the end of the nineteenth century) of obtaining the cash needed to pay taxes and buy consumer goods. Although these crops required great care and good soil, there was no need for equipment other than hands to seed, gather, grind, or crush; a simple implement to hoe the earth; baskets to gather henna leaves; and containers to collect the indigo ashes.

These were "cash crops" in that they were grown for the market. Their production was sufficient for the internal consumption of the country. This was not the case for textile plants, which Tunisia produced in quantities too small for an industry that was itself modest. The mulberry, for example, was grown in the region of Le Kef and in the countryside of Testour in order to raise silkworms. But Tunisia bought from the Levant the raw silk needed by the weavers of Tunis or Jerba. Cotton was also cultivated. Desfontaines saw beautiful cotton plantations near Bizerte, and others could be found in the Sahel as well, between Sousse and Mahdia. Production apparently exceeded domestic needs since Leghorn imported bales of cotton from Tunis during the eighteenth century. Tunis nonetheless imported some from Egypt. In addition, the regency produced small amounts of flax in Cape Bon (in the village of Beni Khiar), in the region of Mahdia, and in Ghennouche, in the Gabès oasis.

Around 1880, this crop covered only two hectares in the oasis and produced about 6,000 kilograms of fiber, or about 4,000 kilograms of yarn per year,[14] which is not very much. Although this cannot be verified, the peasants who grew it claimed that in earlier periods, flax was more plentiful. There was never enough to keep the looms of Sousse and Sfax busy. It was Alexandria that supplied the regency with flax throughout the eighteenth century.

Yet another industrial crop was tobacco, two varieties of which were grown in Tunisia on the humid and fertile soil of the northwest coast.[15] In the eighteenth century, Tunisia exported tobacco to Genoa, Leghorn, and Malta. Even sugar cane was grown. This plant, which in the climate of Tunisia was at the outer limits of its natural environment, did indeed flourish in the eighteenth and nineteenth centuries, in the country gardens of Tunis and Cape Bon.[16]

It should be pointed out that all these specialized crops, however useful, were not of major importance in the economy of the country as a whole, or even in the villages themselves – only a few villages cultivated them – since cash crops never gave rise to a single-crop agriculture.

Vegetable crops

In Tunisia, as in other parts of the Mediterranean basin, vegetables were the most widely cultivated crops. Virtually every village was replete with gardens producing all the common Mediterranean vegetables, from carrots and turnips to cabbages and leeks. Tunisia, however, grew some varieties of vegetables and condiments that were not found on the western shores of the Mediterranean. Peppers, for example, were grown in most vegetable gardens, but more abundantly on the oasis of Gabès, and particularly in the village of Oudref, where they were raised with care for export to the rest of the regency. Okra, *Hibiscus esculentus*, used in stews, was another, and *mulukhiya* (mallow), whose dried and pulverized leaves were reserved for certain festive meals.

There were also many herbs: tarragon and sage, grown near Gafsa; saffron produced near Le Kef and Testour; fennel and coriander from the region of Mahdia. Fennel, an ingredient used in baking and cooking, was also used to flavor a liquor distilled from figs or dates. Coriander, both the plant and the seed, commonly known as a spice, was supposed to relieve stomach upsets and purify the blood. Its uses ranged from healing sick animals to fattening girls of marriageable age. Fenugreek was another highly prized plant. It was eaten raw as a vegetable; dried, pulverized, and mixed with water and sugar, it became a sweet, though somewhat bitter, pastry. The seed was also used to freshen the mouth and enrich animal feed. The value of these plants was not merely nutritional. Their symbolic qualities were appreciated as much as their flavor.

Fruit trees

Tunisian orchards were comparable to those of Mediterranean Europe. All kinds of fruit trees flourished in Tunisia and many of them were grown in multiple varieties: four kinds of plums, four kinds of apples, two kinds of apricots and pears, and so on. Grapes, which became so important in the colonial economy, were already widely grown in the eighteenth century. Near the capital, trellised vines produced fine grapes, some of which were harvested for drying as raisins. Vineyards were also abundant around Bizerte and in Cape Bon. The islands of Kerkenna and Jerba produced grapes as well, particularly Jerba, whose raisins, *zebīb*, were sold to distant buyers. In the oases, vines were grown around the trunks of palm trees, or strung on wires between the trees.

All these varieties grew alongside fruits from warmer climates and from the steppe. Limes and lemons, citron, and oranges flourished primarily in the north (the regions of Tunis, Bizerte, and Cape Bon), forming a magnificent forest around the village of Menzel bou Zelfa. Orange and lemon trees could also be found in the Sahel of Sousse and Monastir, and even in the shade of the palm trees of Jarīd and Gabès.

Pomegranate trees, grown in various places in the regency, covered vast surfaces near the capital, especially at La Marsa, where they stood aligned by the thousands, providing fruit and a rind that served as a dye for wool and basketry. The almond tree was more at home in the latitude of Mahdia and Sfax, as was the pistachio, which grew only in the region of Sfax. Another fruit tree that grew in irrigated regions as commonly in the dryer steppes was the carob, which could reach 8–10 meters in height. It provided a refreshing drink and fruit for people and shade and valuable forage for animals.

From north to south there was no orchard without fig trees. In Tozeur half a dozen varieties were cultivated and since each variety ripened at a different time, figs were available from May to the end of summer. Among the ʿAkkārah of the Zarzis Peninsula, 10,000 fig trees were counted around 1880. In villages in the deep south – those of the Jabal Matmata – fig trees were a major resource. "This mountainside abounds in olives and figs," an anonymous writer observed in 1715.[17] At least five varieties were grown, and the harvest was carefully preserved or taken to urban markets, where it was bartered for barley, wheat, and dates.

The simultaneous presence – from the gardens of the north and the Sahel to the oases of the south – of so many different fruits gave European travelers an impression of delightful profusion. "Their gardens are merely enclosures with trees planted irregularly, lacking paths or separations," wrote a French traveler, who added, "one nonetheless notices a certain splendor in this superabundance and natural disorder."[18] It was, in fact, unusual for any one crop to predominate or to cover an extensive uninterrupted area.

All kinds of fruit trees coexisted and, beneath them, all kinds of vegetables. Thus the oasis dwellers of Tozeur had their date palms growing together with olive trees, grapevines, all the plants of a vegetable garden, and all the fruit trees of temperate climates, and even the banana tree, "the pharaoh's palm,"[19] which was well adapted and produced excellent fruit.

The prickly pear cactus, which encircles trees and vegetables, served as an impenetrable barrier around gardens and orchards. Prevalent throughout the country, cactus plantings were even made by nomads on their pasture lands. For them, these nutritive fruits were essential during the summer. The dethorned leaves were used as forage. Among settled groups, the prickly pear served the same purpose, primarily to keep animals away from the trees and vegetable patches.

Needless to say, the most important purpose of fruits and vegetables was to provide variety in the diet. They also compensated for deficiencies of basic foodstuffs and provided food during periods of want. Along with oil, olives, and grains – the staples of every household – figs, tomatoes, peppers, okra, and mallow were stored, thus assuring subsistence even in regions least suited to agriculture. Like those basic commodities of oil, grains, dates, wool, and products of animal husbandry, some of these products, because they were specialized, provided a means of exchange for the peasants who offered them for sale. Just as floral essences and industrial plants gave rise to interregional and even international trade, so did the specialized products of a particular region – grapes from one locale, pomegranates or figs from another, melons and watermelons from a third. The quality and quantity of these foodstuffs made possible the exchange that was necessary for the equilibrium of peasant life.

In this way, the economy of sedentary groups, far from being autarchic, always had an outlet, either to other local economies, which provided supplementary products, or to the town, which provided money, luxury items, and manufactured goods. Any village always had something to sell to its nomadic neighbors, or to the nearest town. None of these specialized crops mattered in terms of the general macroeconomy of the country. Had there been a shortage of figs from the Jabal Matmata, or melons from Sfax, the country would have remained unaffected. On the local level, however, that of a microeconomy, such products were the safeguards without which people at the mercy of a capricious climate and poor equipment would have been unable to secure their subsistence.

The olive tree

Widely cultivated, the olive tree was probably the earliest tree to be domesticated and surely the most useful. It provided wood for fuel, olives for food, and oil for cooking and illumination. The by-products from pressed olives fed humans and animals. Oil, one of the principal resources of Tunisia, was its primary export in the nineteenth century. Olive growing was anything but monotonous, however. Varieties of olives and techniques of cultivation and extraction varied from one grove to another.

The olive tree was densely planted in three major areas. The first, in the north, extended from Bizerte to Cape Bon. Large groves of tens of thousands of trees surrounded the villages near Bizerte, Tebourba, Tunis, and Zaghouan in 1840. Luxuriant plantings covered the countryside near the towns located at the base of Cape Bon and along its eastern shore. "Beautiful olive groves," wrote Peyssonnel, "stretch from one sea to another, carefully aligned and well pruned."[20] The prosperity of this northern sector owed much to the Moors who had fled Spain, recolonized the villages of the north, and improved both horticulture and arboriculture. The presence of smaller groves in certain areas of the Medjerdah Valley can also be explained by the settlement of Andalusians in the villages of Téboursouk, Testour, Slouguia, and others.

This region received enough regular rainfall so that olive trees did well without irrigation. The trees were planted more closely there than elsewhere, and peasants could intersperse grain crops.

From the time of Bey Husayn, the plantings in the north were subject to a particular form of administrative control. Cultivation was regulated. Skilled workers were responsible for maintaining the groves – two tillings a year and pruning – and guards policed them. A director was given judicial powers to punish trespassers. In 1870 a new decree was passed aimed at improving olive production: Pruning methods were improved, beating the trees was prohibited, intercrop plantings were reduced, and grazing was not permitted until the harvest was completed.

However well groomed the groves of the north, they could not match those of the Sahel, the ideal region for the cultivation of the olive tree. This second belt stretched from Kalaa Kebira to Ksour Essaf, extending in width as much as 15–20 kilometers. The entire littoral was covered with an unbroken forest of olive trees. Olive growing dominated every other activity there. The prosperity of the region antedated the arrival of the Andalusians and may have begun at the time of Roman colonization. Without going back that far, one fact is certain: The geography of olive production had not changed since the end of the seventeenth century.[21] A document of 1678, based on an earlier survey of olive trees made under Othman Dey, listed twenty-six producing localities in the canton of Sousse, and twenty-nine in the canton of Monastir (see Map 4.1). These were virtually the same villages and towns that were subjected to a new tax on olive trees in 1841. There were some changes in the relative importance of the villages, but the major centers of production remained the same, including Sousse and Monastir, of course, as well as Msaken, Moknine, Djemmal, the two Kalaas, and Akouda. However, during the 150 years that separated the two surveys, the number of olive trees had considerably increased. Whereas the two cantons put together had fewer than 300,000 trees in 1678, there were three million in 1840. It was precisely this prodigious expansion of olive growing in the Sahel that led to an updating of tax records and to the creation of a new *qanūn* for olive trees.[22]

The Sahel, the olive-growing region par excellence, extended to the north through the small groves of Hergla, Takrouna, and Djeradou, and to the south, through large plantations near Sfax. Around 1840, long before the intensive twentieth-century colonization of the region, those groves already contained hundreds of thousands of trees.

At this latitude, despite coastal humidity, irrigation was necessary. At the base of each tree, peasants dug a small trench to hold water. On nearby slopes, they contained the runoff by digging diagonal trenches and sent water to the trees in channels that were scoured out at the end of each summer. Here the *shamlāli* variety, famous for its superior oil,

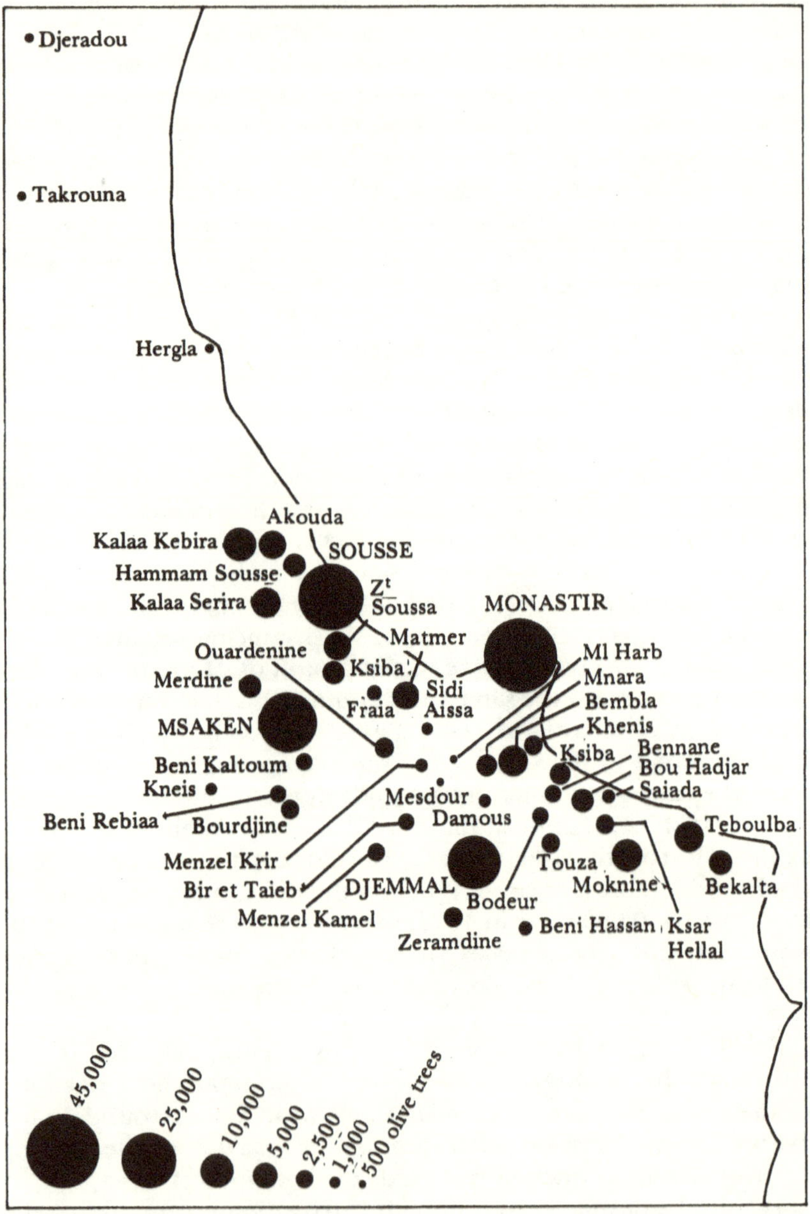

Map 4.1. Continuity of settled life in the Sahel: villages and olive groves at the end of the seventeenth century.

was preferred to all others. The trees were spaced, and intercrops were reduced, but crops that required irrigation benefited the tree and increased the yield. The soil was burned and plowed twice a year, even three times in the region of Sfax, and the trees were pruned annually.

In the long chain of oases in the south, olive growing was also important and in some places – Oudiane, near Tozeur, Zarzis, and Jerba – was the principal activity. Farther south, in the Jabal Matmata, the economy of the settled population depended on olive growing. Whereas in the oases the trees enjoyed continuous irrigation, in the Jabal, painstaking work was required to store water. The peasants dammed up the ravines with stone barriers to collect streams and the silt they carried. It was in those ravines, behind the terraces, that the trees were planted. There were even some olive trees in central Tunisia.

The harvest extended over a period of months and generated great activity in the groves. Nomads came to participate in the work; business agents, notaries, and landowners rushed to collect reimbursement of advances or rents from tenants and to make sure that contracts with peasants were observed. Both men and women took part in the harvest, the men beating the trees while the women swept the felled olives onto mats and sifted them to remove the dust. They were then carried on mule- or camelback to the presses. There, depending on the locality, the olives underwent extraction by various techniques, not all of them equally efficient. In one of the villages near Bizerte, Galaat el Andleuss, the olives were piled into a basin hewn in the rock, where they were crushed with a large stone. The basin was then filled with water so that the oil floating on top would run off into a lower basin for collection. Nomads of the Jlāss tribe used this same method.

Another technique, particularly common in the Jarīd, was to grind the olives under a stone cylinder, a *qarqība*, which the women rolled over a stone slab. The oil expressed was blotted with a tampon of wool, which was squeezed into an urn. The first pressing produced the best and most fragrant oil. The residue from the first pressing was then taken to the river, washed, and pressed again. The oil that floated to the top was skimmed with a ladle, but in this rudimentary procedure most of the oil was lost in the water.

A method of extraction used throughout the regency was the animal-drawn press. It consisted of a circular, concave slab with an upright pole in the center that was secured to a wall. A horizontal axle, attached to the pole, passed through the conical grindstone, which rolled over the slab, pulled by a camel. After the first and most delicate oil was extracted, the residue was pressed in vats, which produced common-grade oil. A third pressing yielded a low-grade oil, which in the Sahel was mixed with barley flour to make bread.

These archaic techniques led Desfontaines to write at the end of the eighteenth century, "This shows, it may be said in passing, how backward these people are, even in the arts of basic needs."[23] As a matter of fact, this kind of press, which produces the highest yield, was an exact replica of the kind used in Roman Africa, and despite its antiquity it was nevertheless the most sophisticated as well as the most profitable for its owner. Providing service for peasants without presses of their own, owners of such presses furnished the animals and maintenance necessary for operation in exchange for which they took a share of the oil and its by-products. In spite of their meager production, these presses also supported the export trade.

The date palm

If one can speak of perfection in the realm of agriculture, it is the date palm of the Jarīd that achieves it. All travelers, European or other, attested to this and recalled with amazement the variety of its fruits, the many uses of its by-products, and the excellent techniques for its irrigation, fertilization, and reproduction. Let us turn once again to Desfontaines, who concludes his *Flora atlantica* with an entry filled with admiration for the date palm, *Phoenix dactylifera*, in a beautiful piece of writing in which his habitual concern for detail does not mar the powerful impression made on him by the oasis.[24]

> Date palms grow all throughout the Barbary Coast, but it is only at the fringe of the desert that they are cultivated with the greatest care and most assiduous activity. There, under a blazing sun, they produce healthy, succulent fruits, whereas in the north, so much more temperate and more generously endowed with the bounties of the earth, their fruits are always unripe, shriveled, and of poor quality, making the date palm an ornament for the home or garden rather than a resource for public or private use.
>
> This strip bordering on the great desert and Atlas Mountains, virtually the only inhabited area in the region, is very poor in the fruits of Ceres. Sandy soil, dried and almost destroyed by the heat of the fiery sun, too infrequently watered and cooled by beneficial showers, yields with great labor a mediocre harvest of maize, barley, or sorghum. The palm tree, all by itself, abundantly, and as it were, openheartedly, replaces them and provides the basic foodstuffs as well as other commodities necessary for life...
>
> I have seen the most beautiful palms in the region known as *Blet el Gerid*, and especially around Elhammah, Tozzer, Loudian, Nefta, Nefsa, etc., where there are ample springs of brackish water and streams. It is not unusual for the circumference of a palm grove to measure a myriameter [10,000 meters]. The villages nearby are heavily populated and the inhabitants are healthy and vigorous.
>
> Inaccessible to the rays of the sun, the palm groves in this torrid region offer inhabitants, travelers, and animals welcome shade. Under their dense cover, orange, lemon, pomegranate, olive, and almond trees grow helter skelter along with grape vines that wind their way up the trunks of the palm trees. All these

trees, protected by shade, can produce the sweetest fruits. An amazing variety of fruits and flowers gladdens the eye, while the happy chirping of birds, attracted by the shade, water, and food, delights the ear.

This generous tree yields first of all its fruit: "Fifteen to twenty varieties differentiated by their size, their color, their flavor, etc., and designated by specific names." An Italian traveler of the seventeenth century counted even more varieties – no less than thirty-nine – all of which he described.[25]

The date palm provided in addition a great number of other products and by-products, which Desfontaines discusses.

Dates are dried naturally: They are exposed to the burning sun for a few days until they are completely dry and are then crushed into flour. Thus prepared, they can be kept without spoiling and are very useful to travelers who undertake long journeys across the vast expanse of the desert. This flour is eaten diluted with a bit of water. This simple food can nourish one for months and admirably maintain the strength of a traveler.

The softer varieties of dates are piled into earthenware jars, which are perforated at the bottom, in which they are compressed under a weight. The liquid pulp, separated from the skin, fibers, and pit, passes through the openings and is collected below. This substance, known as date honey, has a pleasing taste.

Also from dates, a liquor is extracted that is not at all unpleasant. Astringent and soothing, dates have a medicinal use: they relieve colic, soothe intestinal pain, and are also used with great success as salves that heal wounds and ulcers.

Not even the pits go to waste. Crushed or softened in water over a number of days, they provide a nutritious and not unsavory food for sheep and camels.

The flowers, enveloped in their sheath, are also edible and are very tender when young; they are said to have aphrodisiac properties. The sheaths of females are also edible and tasty...

The ribs of the fronds, softened in water and ground in a mortar, are reduced to a fiber from which rope and shoes are made.

The young fronds, as yet undeveloped and thus very tender, are delicious with salt, vinegar, and oil. The heart, or inner substance, of young palms is also edible and quite tasty.

The tendrils that emerge from the base of the petioles on each side are good for rope. The twigs of the petioles are used for fencing around houses and gardens. From leaves softened in water, baskets and all kinds of woven items are made that are very common throughout the Barbary Coast and are very useful.

The wood of old palm trees, very solid and hard, is used to build houses and is reputed to last forever. It burns slowly without a flame, but its embers are very hot.

There is more still: A liquid, called palm milk, is tapped from the trunk. All the branches are cut; a circular trench is dug out with a knife, just beneath the top of the tree; a bucket attached to a cord is placed in the opening; a number of incisions are made on the denuded head of the trunk, which is then covered with fronds so that it does not dry out in the heat of the sun. A syrup drips from the incisions in the hole and from the hole into the bucket. It is sweet, rather pleasant, and milky. It is given to sick people, but must be drunk within twenty-four hours, for it sours quickly, especially in warm weather. Male palms and sterile old females are selected for this purpose, for the tree dies quickly, or lasts only a few years. . . .

There is no tree in so extreme a climate whose benefits are as vast and whose uses as precious to man as the date palm.

In regions where the date palm did not flourish as in the Jarīd, and where dates were neither comparable in quality nor even edible, it was grown nonetheless for all the products it provided for human beings, beasts, and artisanry. Those benefits, particularly in the oases, were achieved at the price of very hard work and constant care. In the spring, and above all in the summer, the trees had to be watered regularly, as did the crops beneath them. The peasants therefore had to look after the irrigation canals, dikes, and levees that surrounded the base of the trunks. With spring came the period of reproduction and pollination. Reproduction was accomplished by means of seeds or cuttings. Pollination, which took place after flowering, was accomplished by removing the male flowers and successively fertilizing each female cluster with their pollen. In the fall, the dates were harvested – a new labor and a dangerous one for the pickers who had to climb each tree a number of times in order to gather the fruits.

The palm workers climb the trees by holding on with their hands and feet to the nodes which circle the trunk in gradations, or by means of a rope, both ends securely tied, which goes around the man's chest and the trunk of the tree. Then, his feet against the trunk, the rope between his hands, he repeatedly flings it toward the upper part of the tree, and with astonishing agility, reaches the top. The trees are climbed a number of times as the fruits ripen. Often, the date pickers are seriously wounded by the very hard spines that grow on either side of the lower stem of the frond. The dates dry in the sun for a few days and are then placed in baskets made of palm fronds, or in sheepskins that give an unpleasant smell and taste, which can be nauseating.

At the same time, the oasis dwellers did not neglect the other trees, which also required pruning and watering, and whose fruit also had to be picked and stored; nor could they overlook the other vegetable crops, or the barley and alfalfa grown for fodder.

In the mid-nineteenth century, there were over a million date palms in all of the oases, distributed as follows:[26]

Tozeur and environs	770,000
Gabès and environs	190,000
Nafzāwah	140,000
Gafsa and environs	30,000

The Jarīd, which owes its very name to the palm tree, was the principal producing region, and Tozeur was the largest date market at harvest time. Many merchants came there to take the dates to cities and ports. Nomads arrived to offer their produce or their services. The Khamāmsa and Dufān, tribes from the Sers plain in the north, brought their surplus grain to the Jarīd in exchange for dates, part of which they used, the rest sold in the markets of the Medjerdah Valley. The Awlād Sidi ʿAbīd, nomadic camel breeders whose only resource was their herds, served as intermediaries between north and south. They brought dates to the north and grain to the Jarīdians, whose markets they regularly patronized. The Naffāt came to barter their animals for dates. As for the Mʿāmar and Sellama of the Hamāma tribe, they took part in the harvesting and were paid in dates.

This was also the time for the bey's annual expedition to collect taxes in the southern part of the regency, a portion of which was received in dates and went largely to pay the tribal cavalry that accompanied the bey's army. Dates were thus redistributed throughout the country. From Tunis and Sfax they were exported to Malta, Italy, and France, and not only the *degla*, still found in French markets, but also the *horra* and, in Malta, the less expensive pressed dates. This was a modest but a steady commerce. Under the French flag alone, an average of 200–300 metric quintals of dates was exported yearly.

The search for water

The profusion of plants, flowers, and trees contrasted sharply with the poverty of equipment used in tending them. An inventory of these tools shows them to be very rudimentary: baskets and earthenware containers for harvesting the produce; long poles for beating the olives, or if the tree was treated more gently, rams' horns that were slipped on like gloves, allowing for less brutal picking; implements with metal blades for hoeing, weeding, and trimming branches. Prickly pears bristling with thorns "were gathered with a pole split into three or four tines, the separations held open by a piece of wood or a stone forced into the middle."[27] Such equipment did little to increase the farmer's productivity. Gardening, in the strictest sense, was manual labor.

The farmer's ingenuity manifested itself in the realm of small-scale waterworks. Added to the various techniques for collecting and storing water, mentioned earlier in connection with olive and date growing, were those for drawing water. In the north, mules or camels turned the water wheels. Elsewhere, scaffolding was built over wells, with a transverse rod to which a rope was attached. The hanging water skins dipped and poured alternately by means of an animal pulling at the rope while continuously climbing and descending a slope constructed below the well. A man led the animal, accompanying it in the tedious work each time it climbed up and down.

In subdesert zones, *foggara* (underground conduits), which were inspected through vertical peepholes, carried water from the foothills to the irrigable land. There, as in other oases, it was less a question of digging for water than of assuring its equitable and regular distribution during periods of scarcity.[28] In Gabès, for example, the wadi was divided into two branches, each part of the oasis receiving water from the main branch for a certain number of days, after which the water was directed elsewhere for a given period. The main branch ended in a kind of crow's foot from which a number of irrigation ditches radiated, watering altogether about thirty gardens. When they were saturated, the water was rechanneled into the main branch and directed toward another crow's foot from which it radiated anew. If the lower gardens had not received enough water, they had a priority when their turn came around the next time. In Tozeur, the wadi was divided into canals, each one of them divided into ditches, which were dammed up with notched palm trunks. The quantity of water distributed was calculated in units of time. For the duration of one week, the gardens were watered alternately by day or by night to compensate for the unevenness of the days and nights. Lesser subdivisions were provided by the five daily prayers and by the phases of the rising sun and the shadow it cast.

The notches in the palm dams could be opened or closed, like sluices. They brought water to the canals, or *sāguias*, which carried it to the gardens. Each farmer had a right to a fixed share of water. In this region, water was private property to which one obtained a title in due and proper form, just as for a *mīlk* property. The allotment required very careful control. It was overseen by a council selected among the farmers – owners or one-fifth tenant farmers – assisted by "elders," the *kbār*, who watched over the farm hands, had them scour the ditches and drainage conduits, convoked them for maintenance work in the oasis, and punished their misdemeanors. Still others were entrusted with surveillance of the water, day and night, and the footbridges that spanned the canals. All of these people were remunerated in kind at the time of the harvest.

What is noteworthy about this is not the refinement of techniques but the importance of the social element in the operation of this agriculture. In El Hamma near Gabès, control of the water, defined to the last detail, was rigorously observed without recourse to any magistrate. The inhabitants maintained the irrigation system and controlled the distribution of water. These "hydraulic societies" functioned without the state. The power of the system did not reside in any governmental machinery, or in any machinery at all, but rather in the human collectivity that formulated its rules and applied itself to carrying them out. In the absence of a strong political power or a powerful administration, the organization of a system of irrigation required a high degree of social cohesion. A geographer once quipped that ground water in the oasis was not a natural phenomenon but a social factor. Indeed, when social control becomes inoperative and looks to other objectives – maximum profit in minimum time – the water table changes and with it the soil and the trees. This, in short, is the history of the Jarīd over the last decades.

The major crops: wheat and barley

Among the grains, barley, not wheat, was the most important. Both were sown in the fall whereas the others – maize, sorghum, and millet – were planted in April. Other grains or legumes were also grown: Italian millet (*Panicum italicum*), beans, peas, lentils, pearl millet (*Pennisettum*) – a profusion of species, and for each one, innumerable varieties. Does this indicate abundance, or rather the absence of any selection?

In fact, both in agricultural activity as well as in rural space, barley and wheat took pride of place. The barley grown was *Hordeum hexasticum*, which thrives in areas with light rainfall. As for wheat, it was always durum wheat (*Triticum durum*), of which there were many varieties. Even though there was no selection of variety, not all cereals could grow equally well in all soils; cultivation depended on a certain number of rules. The first was that all peasants produced some, however small the quantity. Among all the villages and tribes registered under the regency, only the Awlād Sidi ʿAbīd refrained almost completely from growing cereal crops. A tribe of herders with maraboutic status, which allowed them to have peaceful relations with other villagers or pastoralists, they specialized in trade between north and south, preferring to obtain their grain through trade rather than cultivate it themselves. Apart from this exception, there were no peasants who did not raise grain. Conversely, there were no peasants who devoted all their land and labor to it.

Grain farming was always associated with animal husbandry and complementary crops. Grain was first and foremost a subsistence crop. The overriding concern of the peasants was to provide for their own alimentary needs, however intense the pressure from urban centers or urban landowners, and however favorable the natural conditions for other cash crops.

Everywhere, the rule was that wheat was always grown with barley but never took precedence over it, even in the best of soils. In northern and central regions, villagers and tent dwellers planted both in equal quantities. This held as true for the fertile valley of the Medjerdah as for the plains inhabited by the Awlād Abū Ghānim, the Awlād ʿAyār, the Jlāss, and so on. In the south, in the region of Mahdia and the low plains of the Sawāsi or the Methallith, or in the high plains of the Hamāma, barley won out over wheat (see Map 4.2).

Barley was indeed the ideal crop for desert fringes. It required less

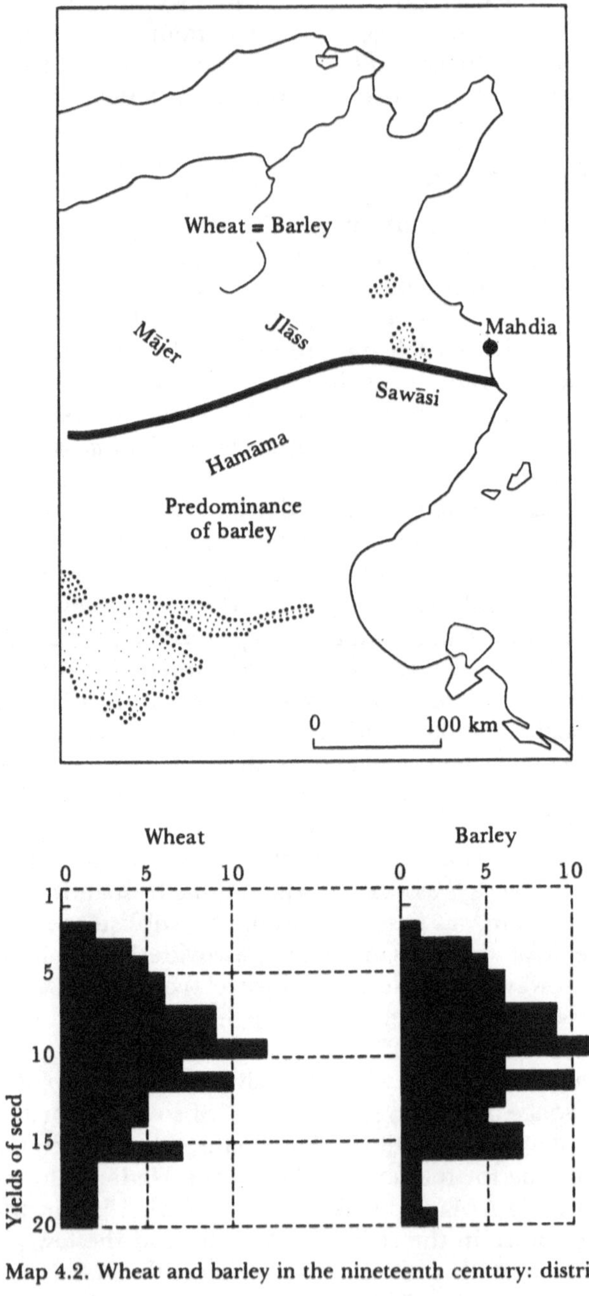

Map 4.2. Wheat and barley in the nineteenth century: distribution and yields.

Table 4.1. *Agrarian lexicon: terms for the land*

	Differentiated	
Undifferentiated	Wheat land	Irrigated land
ʿArd, land	Land suitable for plowing	Planted land
Treīfa, plot		*Gharsa*, planting
Qatʿa, plot	*Henshīr, Shāʿba*	*Jnīna*, garden
Juz'a, piece of land	Parcel	*Sānia*, garden
Barnūssa, triangular piece	*Feddan*, field	*Hūsh*, enclosure
ʿUlīja, land in the bend of river		
Mūdhāʿ, *buqʿa*, place		
Technique	Yoked animals	Hoe
Agrarian measure	*Māshia*	*Merjaʿ*
Morphology	Open field	Enclosure

water than other cereals, and its early ripening partially protected it from the dry season.[29] Tolerant of saline soils, it could adapt to poor soils whose salts rose through evaporation. These observations, only recently brought to light by botanists, must have been recognized empirically by Tunisian peasants since some groups completely abandoned the production of wheat, such as the inhabitants of the Kerkenna Islands, and in the south, the oases of El Hamma near Gabès.

Another rule was that almost every orchard owner grew some irrigated maize, sorghum, and millet. These spring crops required water and the preparation of plots surrounded by earthen levees, the proximity of wells or wadis, and the maintenance of ditches to carry water to the fields. But these spring cereals had the advantage of making up for the losses that a dry autumn or winter could have caused.

A final general rule concerned the great variation in wheat crops from year to year, which depended on the previous year's reserves and above all on the first rains. On farms given over entirely to cereal crops the lack of rainfall or its late arrival resulted in a reduction of the planting area. Among garden farmers, for whom wheat production was secondary, inadequate autumn rain led them to abandon plowing altogether. Conversely, when there was early and ample rainfall, all types of farmers planted cereal crops.

Definition of a field: the agrarian lexicon

The cultivation of wheat began with marking out a field and plowing a furrow that delimited the area to be sown. This surface was known by a number of names (see Table 4.1). As elsewhere, the rural vocabulary was rich in terms that designate a piece of land.[30] Whether notaries or scribes drafted the lease, inventory of holdings, or title of ownership to define the land in question, they all drew from a wealth of terms designating a field. Let us see how this lexicon was organized and according to which principles.

To begin with, there were general terms for any piece of land, such as *feddan*, a field, which in Tunisia did not denote, as in Egypt or Libya, a unit of cultivation; a piece of land, *qatʿa*; a plot of land, *treīfa*; a place, *buqʿa, mūdhāʿ*; a parcel, *juz'a*, which I found used only in the region of Kairouan. Some of these terms were also found by Jacques Berque in the Moroccan Gharb in the twentieth century where a plot was called *bqāʿa* or *qtāʿa*. But in Morocco, the two words indicated ownership; they designated the master's field rather than the simple sectioning of the landscape.[31] Not so in Tunisia.

A more descriptive vocabulary than the preceding was also in use. A triangular plot, analogous to a *bournous*, was called *barnūssa*; a long plot was a *shrāk*; *ʿulīja* suggested a piece of land within the bend of a wadi.

All these terms were scarcely differentiated and were used indiscriminately for wheat fields, orchards, vegetable gardens, and even fallow land. The term *henshīr*, on the other hand, was in a category by itself. It never designated a single continuous plantation, but could comprise within its boundaries fields, plots, or pieces of land; in other words, unlike the other units, it could be subdivided. The *henshīr* thus traces a wide-meshed pattern on the landscape, whereas the other divisions sketch a more tightly knitted design. The vocabulary already offers the first hints of a hierarchy.

There were also antonymic expressions that contrasted the different kinds of land according to their use. "A piece of land suitable for sowing and plowing" was by definition not irrigated, as opposed to the *sānia* (or its diminutive *suīnia*), or *jnān* (*jnīna*), even when the latter did not have a single tree. What distinguished irrigable land from plowland was not the presence or absence of a well. Whereas gardens and orchards were always enclosed spaces, a field might be marked by boundary stones but was rarely surrounded by a hedge.[32] Also enclosed was the *hūsh*, an area planted with olive trees and grapevines, which might be found in the midst of open, unfenced fields.

The vocabulary never indicated, as in ancien régime France or neighboring Italy, a relationship of man with land or the type of land tenure. There was no equivalent for "manse," *mezzadria*, and so forth, to suggest the status of the occupant. A single term indicated the nature of ownership: *henshīr*. Peyssonnel had already observed this during his trip between Le Kef and Tunis: "Henser, which signifies a field to which is added the name of the owner, as in *enseir sidy Mamout*, the field of sidy Mahmout, or the name of some marabout who may be buried there."[33]

A single word referred to the action of man on nature; *gharsa*, a planted area. The term *shrāk* suggested a partnership, the root *sharaka* meaning "to associate." But as a general rule, the numerous words for field did not denote any social unit.

Nor was there any precise designation for the juridical status of the land, except for the notion of *anqādh*. *Anqādh*, corresponding roughly to the idea of usufruct, referred to trees, buildings, or wells that belonged to a private party who enjoyed their use, though they were situated on land owned by a religious institution. For example, among the lands possessed by the bey in the region of Tebourba, one finds a reference to "the usufruct [*anqādh*] of an area planted with 106 olive trees in exchange for the annual payment of one piaster to the great mosque of Tebourba."

In short, the vocabulary was largely undifferentiated. At most, it was specified by some indication of form or quality. Social connotations were rare. Yet the list of words for a field, though long, is insufficient for it is taken out of the context in which these words were used. The word for field never stood alone. It was always accompanied or followed by a phrase that qualified and explained it. The verbal network around it must therefore be reconstructed.

In order of frequency, when a property was mentioned, it was first named and located. For example, in 1726–7, among the properties belonging to the bey there was "an estate of bare land suitable for a plowing west of Tunis, called *Tbūltush*"; or, "a white (empty) field called *al-Ubha*, in the *Aqrās* bordering on the Medjerdah"; or else, "a bare garden where there is a well, west of *blād maīna*, called *sāniat as-sarha*."[34] These topographic and toponymic indications always concluded with the enumeration of properties bordering on the cardinal points. It was the neighboring lands rather than physical landmarks – road, road marker, or tree – that delimited a property. At the other end of the Maghreb, Jacques Berque observed a similar phenomenon among the Berbers of the High Atlas. Their plots, he wrote, "are not determined by a particular spatial framework so much as by the way one plot right holder's fits in with other right holder's."[35] In this way, social references were joined with physical ones.

Other factors, not always mentioned, concerned the content of the land (e.g., bare, planted, fallow, etc.). But even when all of these qualifications were provided – location, form contours, content – none of them indicated the measure of the land. Nonetheless, technical criteria or more abstract procedures were not unknown.

There were several types of technical criteria. The dimensions of a piece of land could be expressed in terms of the quantity of seed it could take. For example, "this parcel of bare land, suitable for farming," and delimited by its boundaries with neighboring properties, was termed "capable of taking two *qafīz* of barley seed."[36] Another example speaks of a piece of land belonging in 1758–9 to Jalīla Khdūja, daughter, of Bey Husayn, that "contained eight measures of wheat." This method of measurement was rarely used. Instead, the usual unit of measurement was the yoked pair, *māshia*, which designates both the yoked animals and the surface they could plow in a season. The corresponding surface varied from region to region: 8 hectares in one place, 12 or more in another. Some properties were measured in *māshia*. The bey owned twenty-one properties in the territory of the Awlād Abu Sālem, which in 1773–4 covered an area of 246 *māshia* or more than 2,500 hectares. During the same period, in the canton of Krib, he owned thirty-one plowlands covering a total surface of 608 *māshia*, or more than 6,000 hectares. These figures were in no way systematic, however, and within the total inventory of the bey's holdings were even exceptional.

In any case, a *māshia* did not designate a field, but rather the plowed surface within the field. It was used to refer to a work unit in tenant-farming contracts. When a farmer leased a property, he contracted to plow not the total area of the land, but a certain number of *māshia*. In contracts for lands belonging to the bey, the size of the surface leased and the corresponding rent were always mentioned. However, this was not always the rule for other landowners. A lease did not necessarily include a reference to the number of yokes used. In twenty-six leases for wheat land drawn up during the first half of the nineteenth century, only ten specified the surface rented. The others merely stipulated the amount of the rent.

The *māshia* was also a fiscal unit. It was on the number of *māshia* sown, not on the size of the property, that the tax on the harvest was calculated.

As a technical unit, the *māshia* could only be used for arable lands – to measure a *henshīr* and its subdivisions, for instance – but was not applicable to orchards, in which case the number of trees provided their dimensions. In Tebourba, El Qantra, and Djedeida, in 1726–7 the bey owned nearly 200 farms containing more than 14,000 olive trees. In this case the assessment was precise, but once again the quantification was unusual. In the environs of Tunis, where the bey's holdings were also inventoried, of the seventy-three properties listed, the number of olive trees was counted on only seven of them. In Rades, where eighty-eight properties were assessed, the plantings were never counted, though most contained orchards.

And finally, when abstract criteria were adopted, the dimensions of the land were measured and the surface calculated. In such a case the unit was the *merja'*,[37] which, according to a definition found in a legal document, was calculated "on the basis of a rope known as the rope of

Table 4.2. *Properties of the bey: modes of measurement*

Date	1726–7	Undetermined	1776–7	Total
Number of properties				
Inventoried	846	65	576	1,487
Measured	267	0	226	493
Dimensions expressed in:				
Seed capacity	0	0	0	0
Māshia	0	0	97	97
*Merja*ʿ	56	5	30	91
Rope	2	0	0	2
Number of trees	209	0	99	308

the diwan, used for agricultural measurement, 50 cubits long, taking as the unit of measurement the Arabic cubit used in trade."[38] Translated into the metric system, a rope of 50 cubits is about 25 meters long. A *merja*ʿ is therefore 625 square meters and it takes sixteen to make a hectare, which is one-tenth the size of a *māshia*, or plowing unit. These two units corresponded, in fact, to two different systems. The *merja*ʿ was used for enclosed surfaces associated, in every case in which I have ever seen it used, with land given over to vegetable gardens and orchards, all carefully divided. A *māshia*, in contrast, referred to open spaces that could be plowed.

Neither of these measurements was used to identify a piece of land. The shift in meaning that takes place in the case of the French *arpent* (about an acre) or *journal* (the size of a field a man can plow in a day) is inoperative here. A Tunisian peasant would never call himself the owner of a given number of *māshia* or *merja*ʿ.

The frequency of using various procedures can be assessed on the basis of a homogeneous sample: the inventory of properties belonging to the bey in the eighteenth century. Table 4.2 calls for a number of observations. To begin with, of all the properties, only one-third were measured. At the time of the survey, the olive trees on the property in Tebourba were counted, but there were no such data for other olive-growing regions (Bizerte, Tunis, Cape Bon). A more rigorous, detailed account was made in 1776–7. As for arable lands, they were *never* measured in 1726–7. In the second survey, the number of *māshia* of good wheat fields located in the territory of the Awlād Abu Salem was systematically counted, but of 219 fields near Béja, only 36 were measured. Thus, during the eighteenth century, there was no movement from descriptive to quantitative definitions. Subsequent surveys, and later archives, show no change in this respect during the nineteenth century.

To conclude this inventory of terms and modes of designating a field, one can state that they constituted a heterogeneous lexical ensemble.

Nonetheless, a polar division does emerge between the dry wheat fields and the irrigated lands. There is a difference of scale. The former were loosely laid out, whereas the latter were divided into small, tight plots. This also corresponds to a difference in technique. The first was cultivated by draft animals, the second by the manual labor of peasants. There is, in addition, a contrast in landscape. The first was an open field; the second was closed and compartmentalized.

The fact that land was rarely measured not only indicates that eighteenth- and even nineteenth-century Tunisia was in a prestatistical era, but also reveals that, from a legal standpoint, even when a written document was available the oral record took precedence. Since deeds provided no more than a description of the land without any graphic representation, the consensus of neighbors was required to establish the boundaries of a property, especially in the case of wheat fields where no enclosure delimited the plot.

From a sociological standpoint as well, property rights ended where a neighbor's began. Such properties were in turn determined by their position between other properties. Parcels of land were defined by their neighbors more than by the extent of their surface. Cultivated lands were thus the juxtaposition in space of similar units, which corresponded to the image society had of itself. It also suggests comparisons with tribal lands: Between plots of cultivated land and tribal land there was a difference of scale rather than nature. Tribal lands were also defined by those of neighboring tribes. In this system, one missing factor is revealing: There was nothing to indicate the status of the cultivator, whether tenant, owner, or sharecropper. If semantics translates the social condition, and if language reveals a society's system of collective representation, then we may conclude that in their relationship to each other and to the land Tunisians of the eighteenth and nineteenth centuries were theoretically equal.

Cycle of labor: agricultural methods

There is yet another notion missing in the agrarian vocabulary, that of the *mtīra*, the plot marked off by the farmer before plowing the first furrow. Jacques Berque found both the word and the practice in the Moroccan Gharb. In Tunisia, William Marçais also observed it in the countryside of Takrouna, where it corresponded to a plot four to five paces by twenty to thirty paces, as did Pierre Bardin in the high plains of the Medjerdah.[39] The word *mtīra* indicates a relationship of work between the farmer and the land, but the root also brings to mind the word for rain, *matar*. The boundaries of the plot are in fact more determined by rainfall than by any right of property or occupation.

The word *mtīra* may have been lacking in the vocabulary of the eighteenth and nineteenth centuries (possibly because of the kind of archives we found), but the practice itself had not changed. The peasants waited for the first rain to water the soil before marking out the fields to be plowed. In the climate of Tunisia, this meant September to October, although rains could be delayed until December or January. Any later and plowing was given up.

Techniques and rituals intermingled then, and for the protagonists they contributed in equal measure to the success of the harvest. Before plowing could begin, male relatives had to assemble. The farmer shared food with them on the field, which also received a portion of wheat gruel, or a few pomegranates whose abundant seeds assured a prolific harvest. The father anointed the animals' yoke with the gruel and crushed a pomegranate on the handle of the plow. Animals, implements, earth, and men were thus associated in the enterprise of reproducing nature's bounty.

Two weeks after the first plowing, the wheat was sown and covered over by a second plowing perpendicular to the first. Two or three weeks later, it was time for barley as well as lentils and chickpeas. In the intervening period, fava beans were planted. They required only a single plowing. If the rains came early, these tasks were completed by mid-November.[40] As for seeds, the peasants were satisfied with any healthy seed from the last or next-to-last harvest, no matter what the variety. Once the planting was done, the farmer let nature take its course. He weeded, chased off sparrows, turned over the soil in the bean field, and above all waited for rain. In some regions, however, the farmers compensated for the meagerness of rain with irrigation systems. The fields were then marked out into squares, surrounded by gullies to carry water from the wadis or wells, and inundated five or six times from the moment the wheat began to sprout until the spike was formed. Spring planting also required repeated watering between seeding and maturation.

Barley, the last to be planted, was the first grain to be harvested – as of March in the south and by the end of April or early May in areas of greater rainfall. The wheat harvest followed a month later. The upper third of the stalks was cut, tied, and carried to the *mandra*, a threshing floor smeared with cow dung, where the grain was beaten. Oxen pulled a *jarrūsha*, a sled fitted with blades and sharp stones that crushed the chaff and released the grains. Once that was done, the wheat was fanned by being tossed with rakes against the wind. The kernels fell free of the chaff and dust and were then ready to be stored or milled. Spring wheat was harvested in August.

After the harvest, the peasant's concern was to feed and replenish the earth. Two kinds of fertilizers were used. The first was ashes from burned thatch and brush. This practice was recalled by an agent from the Compagnie d'Afrique who complained of the intense heat caused by the fires the peasants lit: "This prodigious elevation of temperature was caused by fires from the mountains, fanned by wind off the land, which the Moors light every year at this time to avoid the nuisance of scything the straw left from the wheat which they cut below the spike; to open up paths in order to see through the brush that covers their valleys, their mountains, and their plains; and to keep away from their homes the wild beasts that occasionally cause damage."[41] In one fell swoop, the ground was cleared and enriched with potassium. Another fertilizing technique, much more widespread, was the use of manure. Either the farm animals were left on the harvested fields, or a reciprocal exchange took place between nomads and settled peoples. Nomads came during the period of harvesting to take part in the work. To the settled farmers, they brought their labor and the manure of their animals. In exchange their animals were allowed to graze, and once the work was finished the nomads took with them provisions of grain. This kind of barter was not accidental. The nomad did not offer his services only when drought drove him from the steppe, or when the promise of a good harvest in the north summoned farmhands from other regions. In the eighteenth and nineteenth centuries, such migrations were organized and collective.

The land was left fallow after harvesting. Was the rotation biennial or triennial? There was no regular rotation, but rather a kind of shifting cultivation that varied according to the amount of the first rainfall and that, given the abundance of land, did not exhaust the soil. In the event of ample rainfall the same plot could be planted two years in succession. But the general rule was one of rotation with no regular periodicity.

Cycle of labor: farm implements

The harvest was brought in with sickles, a small implement with an angled blade. The threshing was accomplished either by the treading of animals led around the floor or by the use of the *jarrūsha*. In short, the equipment of the field worker was as rudimentary as that of the fruit and vegetable grower. Of all the means of production, the most sophisticated was the plow, an implement Tunisia shared with other Mediterranean countries and that is still in use today. At plowing time – despite the competition of the so-called vineyard plow made entirely of metal and gaining in use – one can still see peasants breaking the soil with wooden plows of traditional types. These peasants allow us "to read history backward," and to interrogate the present in order to discover the past.[42]

These traditional plows varied from region to region. In the northwest and in a part of the eastern Sahel, the tooth plow was used. Its handle and beam fit separately on the frame or the tooth.[43] This model in turn

Table 4.3. *Size of the tooth plow, regional differences*

	Length of parts		
Villages	Pole and beam	Frame and share	Handle
North			
Fernana	250 cm	100 cm	70 cm
Aīn Draham	250 cm	100 cm	80 cm
South			
Sfax	81 cm	54 cm	76 cm
Jerba	80 cm (approx.)		
Oudref	80 cm (approx.)		

had other variations. It was larger in the north than elsewhere and there were differences in details of the parts and their assembly (Table 4.3). In all samples from the eastern region, from Nabeul to Jerba and Oudref, the pole is not fastened to the frame by an assembly bolt. From Nabeul to Jerba the beam and pole are furthermore separate parts, and the frame has two wooden flaps that serve as the moldboard. In Aīn Draham, as in Fernana, in contrast, a single piece of wood is hewn to constitute both the pole and the beam; it fits into the frame and is held by a wooden bolt. This model has no moldboard. These variations are the result of differences in soil conditions and draft animals. A pair of camels or oxen is needed in the north, whereas a lighter yoke is sufficient for the looser soils of the east.

The differences are greater between models of the second type, the swing plow. This is used in the Andalusian villages of the north, in Cape Bon, the Sahel and the center, the steppes, and all the way to the *qsūr* of the deep south (Map 4.3). The general structure of this plow is the same as the other (see Figs. 4.1, 4.2): a curved beam, the end of which fits into the handle and is attached to the frame; a metal bolt between the beam and the frame; a ring, also metal, at the base of the beam. The swing plow of the *qsūr* looks like a toy compared to the one from the north. All the parts are shorter than the other model, with the exception of the handle, whose length is invariable and corresponds to the position of the body and the hand of the field worker (Table 4.4).

This increase in the size of the various parts corresponds to an increase in the weight of the implement: It is very light in the south, 6–8 kilograms in the center of the country, and heavier in the north. The frame of the southern plow is a solid block, roughly triangular, and cut at a right angle in the upper part. It is attached to the lower part of the beam without fitting into it. In the north, the frame is a long piece of wood that fits into the beam and is fastened to the handle by a wooden bolt.

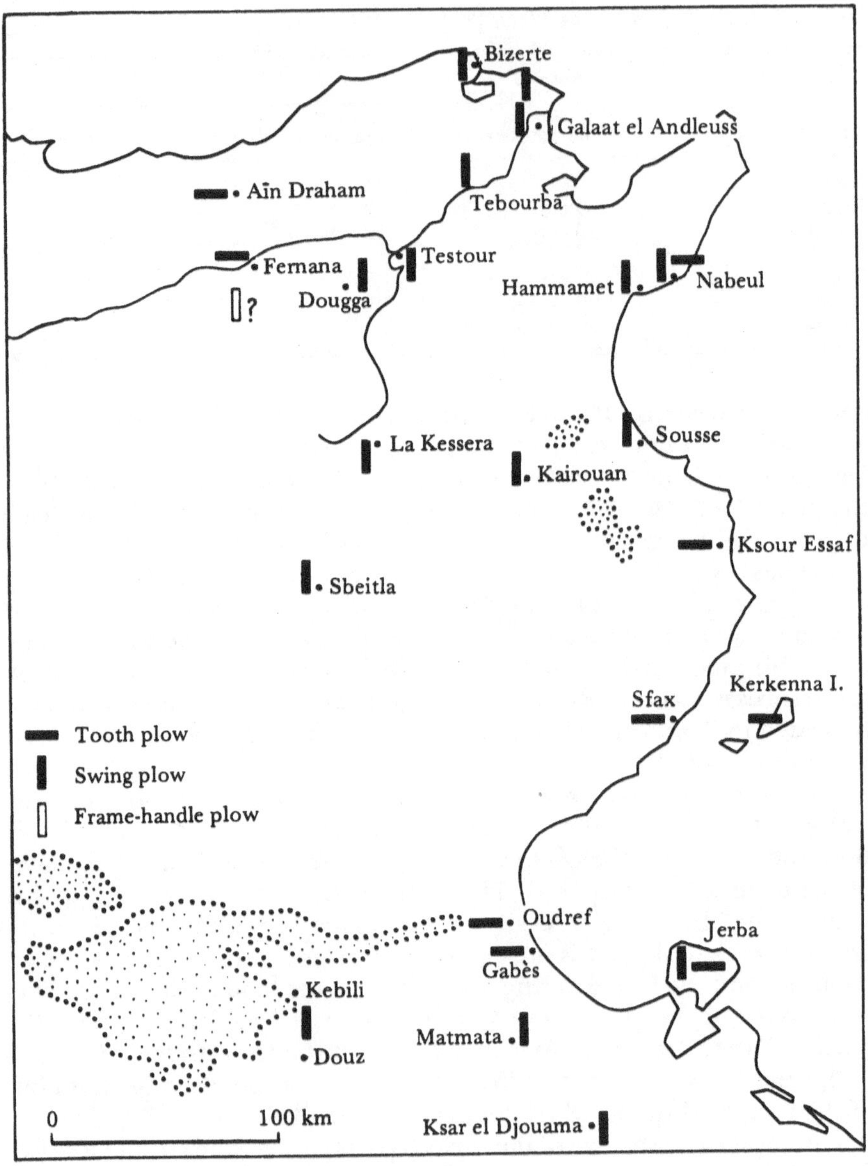

Map 4.3. Typology of plows, twentieth century.

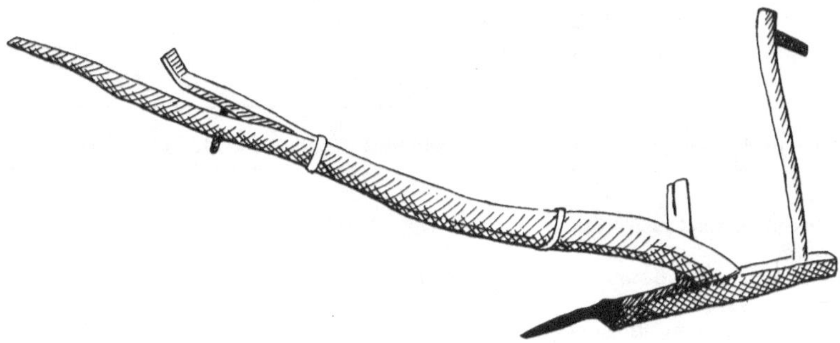

Fig. 4.1. Tooth plow.

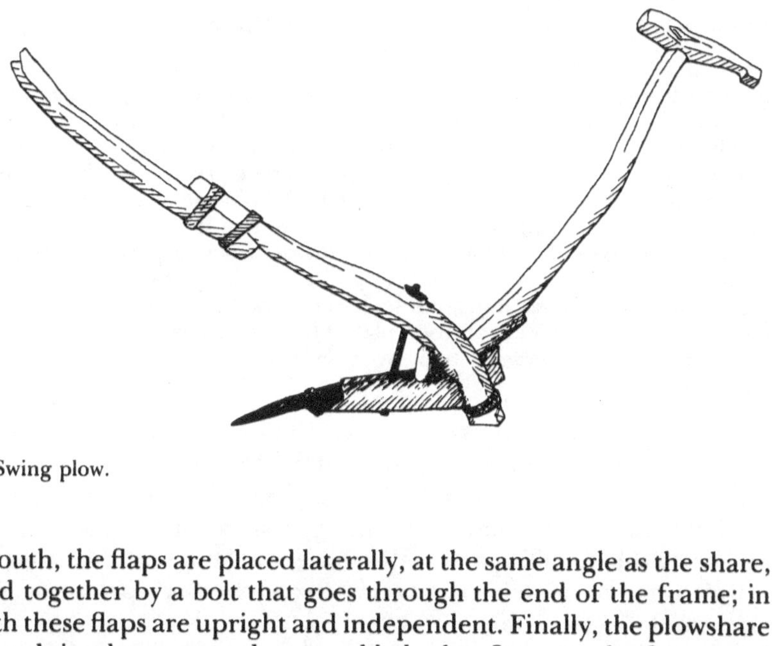

Fig. 4.2. Swing plow.

In the south, the flaps are placed laterally, at the same angle as the share, and held together by a bolt that goes through the end of the frame; in the north these flaps are upright and independent. Finally, the plowshare in the south is a large curved convex blade that fits onto the frame and part of the handle. In the north, it is a flat blade at the end of a long stem placed in a ridge hollowed into the upper surface of the frame, which fits onto the handle. In short, it is a crude implement made to scrape the hard dry soil of southern regions. It is more flexible in the north. In both types of plows described, the power diminishes as one descends into less fertile regions. Both adapt to the more fragile soil that is less suited for plowing, as they do to the constraints of a climate that prohibits large-scale farming and requires constant movement to fields watered by rainfall.

Table 4.4. *Size of the swing plow, regional differences*

	Length of parts		
Villages	Pole and beam	Frame and share	Handle
North			
Testour, Galaat el Andleuss	Nearly 300 cm	60 cm	80 cm
Center			
La Kessera, Kairouan	Approx. 150 cm		80 cm
South			
Kasr el Djouama, Matmata	70 cm	40 cm	80 cm

The Tunisian peasant used a third kind of plow, the frame-handle plow, accurately described by an eighteenth-century French author:

Their draft animal is the camel. The plow used is very different from ours; it has no wheels, and consists of only five principal parts. A single piece bent almost at a right angle constitutes the body. There is one pole at the rear that serves as a handle. The lower part is designed to hold a plowshare. The pole is slightly curved, split at the end, and fits into the angle of the plow where it is held by a large wooden wedge. Four holes at the back hold the bolt, which takes the pull of the oxen; the depth of the blade is determined by how far forward or back the bolt is placed. The plowshare, the third principal part, is obtuse, convex, smaller than the one on our plows, and has the shape of a large trowel. I have seen some in certain cantons that look like wedges. Finally, the fourth and fifth parts consist of two pieces of wood placed below at sharp angles to the underside of the plow; these serve to turn over on either side the earth broken by the plowshare."[44]

This is a valuable and accurate description. However, it describes an implement that, although widely used in Morocco and Algeria, is hardly known in present-day Tunisia.[45] In any case, the different components of these implements have not changed since the eighteenth century, especially the metallic parts – the share, the bolt, and the assembly ring – which had to be delivered every year to the bey's palace by Tunisian blacksmiths[46] (see Table 4.5).

Identical types of plows were known in North Africa from the time of Rome and Carthage, and for millennia Tunisian peasants remained faithful to these devices. Many accusations have been brought against this primitive, lightweight swing plow that only scratches the surface of the soil and yields small harvests. Ever since the eighteenth century, European observers have considered it inferior to the heavier implement used in northern Europe that could plow more deeply. Now that natural conservation is as much a concern as increased production, there is no question that the swing plow was less harmful to the soil, that it slowed erosion, and prevented a too rapid evaporation of soil moisture. Re-

Table 4.5. *Terms designating the different parts of the plow*[47]

	Eighteenth century	Twentieth century	Locality
Plow	*mhrāth*	*mhrāth*	Everywhere
		shāʿba	Sfax
Handle	*qerrās*	*guerrēs*	Testour, Kairouan, Biskra, Touggourt
		dhrā	Galaat el Andleuss, Mecheria; in Biskra, the term means "beam"
		muzeraq	Sbeītla
		mozrag	Nafzāwah
Handlebar		*shāshiya*	Testour, Sfax
Beam	*rkba*	*rekba*	Kairouan, Kasr el Djouama, Fezzan
Pole		*ngūd*	Testour
		magwad	Nafzāwah
		timūn	Galaat el Andleuss, Infi, Tindouf, Chaouīa
Frame		*gāʿda*	Testour, Sfax, Kairouan, Kasr el Djouama
Share	*sekka*	*sekka*	Everywhere
Moldboard		*ūdhneīn*	Testour, Galaat el Andleuss, Algeria
Bolt	*mejmaʿ*	*mejmaʿ*	Testour, Kairouan
		beskūl	Testour
		beshkūr	Kairouan
Assembly ring	*hilq*	*hilg*	Testour; in Nafzāwah it designates the bolt
		shrīku	Galaat el Andleuss

quiring only light draft animals, easy to construct, and inexpensive to replace, it was clearly the implement best suited to the household economy of precolonial Tunisia.

Food storage

Techniques for storing grain were similarly millennial. The most characteristic in North Africa, particularly in subdesert regions, were fortified granaries, citadel-silos, which were at the same time collective storehouses, the sites of markets and meetings, as well as symbols of "the independence and economic prosperity of the community."[48] In Tunisia, on ʿAkkārah tribal lands, Zarzis was a collection of hamlets (gāsr Awlād abu Ali, gāsr Muansa, gāsr Awlād Saʿīd, etc.) that served as storehouses rather than as dwellings. These granaries were made up of small stone structures, attached to each other, that held the reserves of the different clans. In Medenine and Metameur, these hive-shaped granaries were stacked on several levels. Other *qsūr* in the Aʿrādh were perched on heights, such as in Djouama and Zemmour. Jean Despois, who is responsible for the most detailed descriptions of these granaries, stresses that they were fortified, indicated by the term *qāsr* (pronounced *gāsr* here) and the structure.[49] During more bellicose and distant periods, these constructions doubtless served as fortresses. In the nineteenth century, their use as collective granaries was predominant. Indeed, an entire subgroup, even a whole tribe, could place its total stock under communal guard. This did not hinder the storage of family reserves for immediate use, which, in the case of nomads, were packed in sacks and earthenware jars, or in the case of sedentary people, stored in urns of considerable size, often 2 meters high or more. Among nomads, the bulk of their reserves was placed in these granaries to avoid carrying loads of grain and oil from camp to camp. Surveillance was entrusted, in Medenine, to groups of marabouts who camped nearby. Elsewhere, this was accomplished by a small number of guards, clearly indicating that the primary purpose was to stockpile produce in one place rather than to assure its vigorous defense. There were other means for storing grain, more widespread than these fortified granaries, called *matmūra*, which were also grouped together but were not fortified. They were roofed pits dug into the earth. The walls were lined with a coating that protected the grain from rodents and humidity. These pits generally held a *qafīz* of barley or wheat and were usually placed close to one another. Desfontaines saw as many as three hundred in one spot.[50] This was an efficient method, for if the upper layer fermented and became a crust, it protected the remainder of the grain, which could usually keep without spoiling for a number of years, provided care had been taken to store it when it was completely dry.

The Wārgha or Awlād Yaqūb in the north, like the Frashīsh and the Jlāss in the center, or the Sawāsi in the east, had their silos grouped together in a small number of known locations on their territories. In some cases, as among the ʿAqarība, the tomb of the eponymous saint protected the wheat, barley, and straw stored in these silos when the tribe moved to another camp. In others, the grain was left unguarded. This is borne out by the experience of Ismāʿil Ibn Yūnis, the grandson of Bey Ali Pāsha, who crossed the border between the regencies of Tripoli and Tunis in 1759 in an attempt to seize power. Exhausted after crossing the desert for many days, he accidentally came upon the silos of a border tribe. His horse's hoof struck the stone that closed one of the subterranean silos, revealing vast supplies of barley that restored both men and beasts.[51]

The Awlād Saʿīd, tent dwellers in the Sahel, stored their provisions in the villages of Kalaa Kebira, Kalaa Serira, and Akouda. We have already mentioned that the Hamāma entrusted their provisions to the safekeeping of villagers in the region of Gafsa. The use of collective granaries was thus another aspect of the close relations between nomads and settled peoples.

These pits, like the threshing device used to separate the wheat or the plow or the oil press previously discussed, had been known since antiquity, and Pliny, among others, furnished a description of them. "Opulence in the garden, traditionalism in the field," writes André Miquel to characterize agriculture in Islamic lands.[52] Indeed, the profusion of varieties goes hand in hand with a remarkable inertia with regard to means of production and farming methods.

Production and yield

All through the cycle of farming, from the first plowing to the grinding of grain, the land remained vulnerable to any number of natural and other dangers. The principal enemy, evidently, was drought. If the autumn was too dry, the earth was parched and the plowing had to be delayed or given up completely. Even after sowing, the clouds were anxiously watched, and until harvest time, peasants continued to cast worried glances at the sky. If the rains were heavy in winter, a good harvest could be expected. If, on the other hand, after a rainy autumn, there was little rain between February and April, the wheat dried on the stalk and the harvest was lost. This is how barley and fava beans were scorched before the spring of 1811, and in 1829, the grain sown in the autumn was destroyed by drought during the following winter and spring.

When fair, dry weather persisted, prayer ceased being an individual activity. People would then assemble to implore God together, or seek the intercession of marabouts, offering in sacrifice an animal whose meat was shared. Each community practiced these propitiatory rites. On occasion, they became affairs of state. In the autumn of 1716, for example, rain was sorely needed. In December, the bey went to the tomb of a saint at the head of a great procession – 6,000, wrote one eyewitness – to ask for rain. The sky remained unheeding. Five months later, "the barley has dried on the stalk and the wheat will be lost if we are without rain for another week. No one has ever seen winds so hot at this season. These same winds from the south have completely scorched the entire grain harvest around Tripoli."[53] Alarmed, the bey asked the French consul to have prayers said in the French chapel to implore God's help. The Jews, for their part, fasted for three days and held a procession around their cemeteries in the hope of obtaining rain. Vain hope. The drought lasted into summer and the harvest was lost.

There are proverbs that express this expectation of beneficial rains during the ripening period: "March rain, pure gold" – *mtar mārs, dheb khalas*; "April showers make the stem rise from the bottom of the well" – *mtar abrīl, tallaʿ sbūla min qaʿ al-bīr.* Already in the sixteenth century, Leo Africanus remarked that "if the season is not wet between the 25th of April and the 5th of May, the harvest will be small and the rain that falls during that season is called *naisan* by the inhabitants of that region, rain which they consider blessed by God." A proverb still current today echoes that notion: "The rain of *nisān* fills glasses" – *matrat nisān, timla l-kisān.*[54]

A dry season could have lasting effects, for crop failure meant no seed for the following year. After the meager harvest of the summer of 1779, plowing was reduced for lack of seed. The same thing happened in 1821, when the harvest was good but not ample because there had not been enough seed to sow. And in 1839, it happened again after two years of shortage.

Although a lack of rainfall was the greatest threat to crops, an excess of water was equally feared. The year 1761–2 was a year of rot. Rain fell almost continuously from August to May. Grain was spoiled, and peasants in the north were unable to pay their taxes.[55] More often, early spring storms accompanied by hail destroyed the harvest or made the grain unsuitable for storage. In 1714 torrential rains fell; the wheat survived but the barley was damaged. Similarly, in 1783 hail pummeled the gathered sheaves and the uncut wheat. These disasters occurred endlessly. In 1844 a writer from Tunis relates that once again "the hopes raised by the favorable appearance of last spring's harvest have, alas, not materialized. Violent rainstorms that fell during the month of May have caused the barley, already cut, to rot, and have severely damaged the wheat, still standing and almost ripe. This misfortune will result in a cereal crop insufficient to feed the population."[56]

A hot sun after a shower, or the sirocco, which shrivels wheat, represented further natural threats, along with locusts, frequent in the seventeenth, but less common in the eighteenth, century. In 1700 they invaded the central part of the country and the Sahel, where crops were already suffering from lack of rain. For a long while locusts were totally absent. Then in 1764, after six months of intense drought – it was as hot in February as it usually was in June – they appeared as far north as Tunis. "On the 24th [February] at ten in the morning," a witness related, "the sky was darkened by a cloud of locusts which obscured the horizon; in the two and a half hours that the passage of these insects lasted, the sun was not visible for even a moment. It was fortunate that not too many fell in the countryside and that people hastened to catch them, far less to prevent the harm they would have done than to live on them for a few days."[57]

The plague was apparently spectacular but the damage was insignificant. Once again locusts spared Tunisia for many years. Not until 1845 were they seen again, when enormous hordes descended on the region of Gafsa. March 3–5 they attacked the Sahel of Sousse. Their flight covered an area 4 leagues long by 300 meters wide. On April 19 they were in Tunis, where they remained for six hours. After destroying farms near the capital they headed west, but at the end of the following month, they reappeared over Tunis, darkening the sky from ten in the morning until four in the afternoon. They came again in April and May of 1849 in the north. Soldiers tried to push them into ditches and crush them, but to no avail. It was necessary to wait for heavy rains before the insects could be carried off by the streams.[58]

Locusts, whose appearance coincided with periods of drought that made them come north from the Sahara, thus exacerbated the effects of inadequate rainfall. When they struck, farm animals were deprived of forage, people of crops, and both of water, for the locusts contaminated wells and wadis.

Added to these various plagues that beset humans, animals, and crops were such social evils as wars with neighbors, internal struggles, and the like. If the Algerian army threatened to invade Tunisia, as happened in 1701, no crops were sown in the north, or else the wheat, unharvested for lack of time, was burned. During the civil war in particular, first in 1729 and 1730, then in 1736–8, peasants gave up sowing crops in the east and in the south, and the fertile regions of Béja remained partially uncultivated. Generalized sowing was not resumed until the autumn of 1740 when domestic peace was restored. Then a bountiful harvest made it possible to forget the privations that had been endured.[59]

Did the sum of all these calamities prevent Tunisia from feeding its people? The countryside of Europe under the ancien régime also suffered various disasters – poorly distributed rainfall, excessive cold and periods of excessive drought, the passage of armies, and excessive taxation. Was Tunisia more seriously affected? In other words, was average agricultural production sufficient for the needs of the country?

This fundamental question cannot be answered conclusively. The volume of production is not known. The few estimated figures provided by contemporary observers are not very illuminating; they were purely speculative calculations made by men who knew only the northern part of the country, who were unaware of how much the bey and his agents collected under the cover of the tithe, and who continued to repeat the same figures from year to year.[60]

In the absence of a direct route to forming an opinion, we shall have to make a few detours, take note of what contemporaries said about crop yields, and observe in the reality of today such facts as will allow us to interpret the reality of yesterday.

With respect to yields, contemporaries made their calculations on the basis of the volume of seed sown, not on the surface plowed, and they were justified in so doing, for as we have seen, the unit of plowing varied according to the space involved. Nor was this the only variable. Units of measure were unequal. The volume of grain was expressed in *qafīz*, which contains sixteen *waiba*, each of which consists of twelve *saʿa*. In Tunis, the *qafīz* referred to in the sale of grain ran between 5.6 hectoliters and 5.2 hectoliters. In fact, there was no instrument of measure that corresponded to a *qafīz*. A *waiba*, in the form of a truncated cone, was used and held 32–33 liters of grain, roughly 25–27 kilograms of wheat, and 20–22 kilograms of barley. But these figures applied to the standard of Tunis, the *qafīz tūnsi*. The *qafīz bāji* – of Béja – was twice as large. Either measure could be used, depending on the region. In the Sahel of Monastir, at the end of the nineteenth century, a *waiba* of wheat weighed 30 kilograms, a *waiba* of barley, 22.5. It was therefore the *qafīz tūnsi* that served as the unit of measure. Among the Awlād Sindāssin, near Kairouan, the *qafīz bāji* was used instead. In Gafsa and Le Kef, yet another *qafīz* was used, roughly three times greater than the one used in Tunis. Thus, the same terms cover a number of very different realities. As a general rule, the measure became greater the farther one went from the capital.

Another variable was the density of sowing. In the region of Béja, or among the Awlād ʿŪn and the Awlād ʿAyār, twelve *waiba* of each grain were sown, amounting to 600 kilograms of wheat and 480 of barley, for each *māshia* of 12 hectares. In Monastir, the *māshia* was sown with 120 kilograms of wheat and 90 of barley. Near Sfax, the same amount of barley was sown as in Monastir, but twice as much wheat. Closely sown in the northern parts of the regency, crops grew more spaced as the land grew increasingly arid. There is nothing unusual about this practice since wheat and barley, through their ability to send off many shoots, adapt to the greater or lesser degree of rainfall. When the soil gets enough water, each seed can produce a number of stalks and as many spikes. In a bad year, a seed will produce a single stalk or none at all. Widely spaced sowing in regions of inadequate or irregular rainfall thus allows the grain to sucker in proportion to the amount of water received.

For each seed sown, according to Shaw in 1743, 8–12 stalks were harvested; 20–39, Poiron stated in the middle of the eighteenth century; 20, 30, and up to 60, said de Saizieu, the French consul in 1776; and Desfontaines, who was not given to hyperbole (and who worked from actual experiments measuring the yield in semolina and flour from harvested grain), claimed "from 12–20 for one seed in good soil." He added, however: "I have been assured that in a few cantons, the soil can yield up to 50 and more," and in the region of Tunis, in a good year, he said there could be 80 and 100 times the quantity sown.

At the beginning of the nineteenth century, Frank provided figures of 8–12 stalks to 1 seed. The French consul in 1815, Devoize, spoke of yields of 20–60 to 1. A few years later, Ferrier, an Englishman, wrote that the yield in wheat, previously 30 to 1, had fallen to 10 or 15 to 1, but that it had remained two-thirds higher for barley. And finally, even Pellissier, who generally presented a rather somber picture of the regency in the middle of the nineteenth century, indicated a yield of 16 to 1.[61]

These were impressive yields. Contemporaries attributed them to the natural fertility of the soil, "enriched by the nitrogen it contained," to the air also "impregnated with a significant amount of nitrogen," to the lightness of the soil making it easy to plow, to the mildness of the climate, which favored vegetation, to the practice of allowing the earth to lie fallow for a number of consecutive years in view of its abundance, and finally, to the quality of the grain itself since one seed could produce a large number of spikes.

How credible are these figures and the various proofs offered in their support? Today, many of the arguments of the eighteenth century are used, not to prove the fertility of the soil in North Africa, but the uncertainty of the yields. Where the mildness of the climate was praised, aridity is now blamed. Lightness of soil? This is now synonymous with fragility. Presence of salts? They sterilize the earth. What is certain is that soil erosion is a recent calamity, concurrent with heavier machinery and methods of cultivation that deplete the soil, with increased population, and the settlement of once nomadic shepherds.

It should also be added that travelers of the eighteenth and nineteenth centuries knew their classics too well, particularly Pliny and his *Natural History*. Desfontaines and Frank, extremely cautious when reporting the observations of their contemporaries, granted total credibility to Pliny's famous formulas, "Regio . . . fertilitatis eximiae, cum centesime fruge agricolis foenus reddente terra"; "contra in Byzacio Africae illum centena quinquagena fruge fertilem campum"; "sisit aptem solum quale in Byzacio Africae campo, centeni quinquaginta modii reddantur."[62]

What about the yields of the eighteenth and early nineteenth centuries? For comparison with more recent observations, let us first look at the most reliable figures, those provided by such trustworthy authors as Desfontaines, Frank, and Pellissier. Yields ran between 8 and 20 to 1.

The second series of figures comes from data collected by French officers between 1885 and 1887 for the entire country. In each of the areas where they conducted their surveys, they took care to note the maximum and minimum yields, distinguishing between barley and wheat. Leaving aside the excessive figures – 30 to 1 for wheat, more for barley – proposed for the lower plains of the Kairouan region, that still leaves the ranges of yields shown on the graph accompanying Map 4.2.

For wheat, three figures are more frequently cited than others: 10, 12, and 16, the officers leaning toward the first, the peasants toward the latter two because of the subdivision of the *qafīz*. These are questionable estimates, more revealing of the way the observers counted than of the actual yield. The French officers, familiar with the decimal system, tended to make their estimates in round numbers, whereas the peasants, accustomed to the subdivisions of the *qafīz* into quarters or sixteenths, inclined toward the figures of 12 and 16. However, 8–12 is the most common range – in 49 cases out of 101, or nearly half. For barley, the figures are somewhat higher: out of 98 harvests, 22 had yield-to-seed ratios of less than 8 to 1, 44 fell between 8 and 12, and 30 surpassed 12 to 1.

This second series of observations coincides with the first on one point, but not on others. As in the first series, yields of 8–20 comprise the largest number of cases cited. But within this very broad range 8–12 seems to be the more frequent. On the other hand, before 1850 there is no record of poor harvests, whereas after that date one-fifth of the figures listed fall below a ratio of 8 to 1. What the second scale reveals – and the first camouflages – is the vast discrepancy between yields, in other words, the irregularities of harvests. Seeds might produce 16, 18, or 20 to 1, but they could also fall to 3 or 4 to 1, and even to zero. In the second series of observations, the range of yields therefore broadened. Emphasis was placed on a level lower than the one indicated by the first observers. That level is nonetheless quite high, which raises a certain amount of doubt. Should we accept it as accurate? A new piece of evidence seems to confirm this. The payments required of farmers working on the bey's lands in the eighteenth and nineteenth centuries allow us to estimate the level of minimal yields. In the region of Tunis, the owner received 5 *qafīz* of wheat and 10 of barley per *māshia* – in other words, 20.5 quintals of wheat and 32.5 of barley for a surface of about 10 hectares.[63] This amounts, all in all, to more than 5 quintals of grain per hectare. Now, the farmer must have withheld his own share, the share of the *khammās* he employed, and the amount needed to pay the tithe on the harvest. In that case, the yield was surely greater than 5 quintals per hectare, or else the farmer would have been unable to feed his family or pay his debts. In other regions the farmer owed, and did indeed pay, 8 *qafīz* of wheat and 4 of barley per *māshia*, or approximately 30 quintals of grain for 10 hectares. Here too, the yield must necessarily have been greater than 4 quintals per hectare for the farmer to have covered his expenses.

Without being able to propose a definitive figure, it is nonetheless possible to state that the precolonial yield of grain was higher than 4 or 5 quintals per hectare, at least in the northern part of the country, which is where the estates whose accounts were preserved were located.

Let us compare those figures with current yields. In 1950–4, agriculture in the modern sector, which benefited from good soil and large machinery, obtained in the north yields of 6–12 quintals of barley. In the south, the average fell to 6 quintals per hectare for both wheat and barley.[64] The peasants of precolonial Tunisia could not have achieved such yields given the limitations of their technology. On the other hand, with the traditional methods of the mid-nineteenth century, the average yield of durum wheat was from 4.2–5.3 quintals per hectare, and 4.1–5.8 for barley. In the south, the yield was barely 1 quintal per hectare, if we are to believe the farmers of the region.[65]

These are surely very low yields. In 1950–4, cultivation had spread to lands unsuited to wheat where it was "almost absurd," wrote Jean Poncet. Even in the best of soils, rotation of crops and allowing fields to lie fallow were rarely practiced. The yields obtained by traditional agriculture in the middle of the twentieth century were therefore lower than those obtained with the same methods by peasants of the eighteenth and nineteenth centuries.

The difference is to be found elsewhere – in the method of calculating the yield, not in the reality of production. As a ratio of the surface cultivated, it was certainly a poor yield. But was this the case in relation to the volume of seed sown? Let us return to the figures cited earlier: 490 kilograms of seed per *māshia* in the region of Kairouan, or less than 50 kilograms per hectare. If the yield was from 10–12 to 1, it corresponded to little more than 5 or 6 quintals per hectare. A yield of 8 to 1 would mean only 3.2 quintals per hectare, a figure no one would question. There is consequently nothing contradictory in the surprisingly high estimates of the past and the pessimistic observations of the present. Let us go further: Since the grain was sparsely sown, cultivation was not as absurd as was claimed. In the event of a poor harvest, losses were small. In a wet year, vigorous suckering increased production.[66] There is no other way to explain why the Tunisian peasant persisted in growing a crop that was a continual failure.

As to the exceptional yields, they are plausible. Desfontaines was not inventing when he spoke of yields of one hundred times the seed, nor was Grenville Temple, who saw 97 shoots on a single stalk of barley in the lands of the Sawāsi. In 1912, northwest of Kairouan, a single grain of wheat, according to Jean Despois, produced 250 stalks with spikes, or 8,000 kernels. The same year, and in a nearby region, 120 spikes were obtained from one grain of barley, or 4,000 grains. These remarkable yields were obtained during exceptional years, on small surfaces, and in the steppe, where seed is widely scattered. However, "yields of 100 to 1, extraordinary as they may be, should not be considered abnormal."[67]

To sum up briefly, yesterday as today, yields are aleatory. They are low when measured in terms of the area planted, high in terms of the seed sown, but in good years and bad can adequately recompense the farmer for his labors.

Herding techniques

Most Tunisians lived in tents amid herds of animals. Since villagers also raised animals, livestock was doubtless an important resource under the old regency. It is, however, the least documented since the first census was taken after a series of disasters – the revolt of 1864 and its merciless repression, epidemics, animal diseases, and famine[68] – in short, at a time when little was left of Tunisian livestock. Fifteen years later, the French occupation caused a migration of people and animals toward Libya. When new counts were made,[69] the herds had barely been replenished. Their makeup and distribution were very likely changed by the intervening turmoil. Let us therefore regard the data provided by these estimations as indicating a range of magnitude rather than as a precise account.

In the country as a whole, there was no regional specialization. The same species were raised everywhere: sheep and goats, camels, horses, donkeys, mules, and cattle. The camel – the dromedary, to be precise – was everywhere. "It is the camel who carries grain and all produce from the countryside into all the villages, who is loaded with all the provisions for the camps, who brings in the taxes in kind, turns the mills of the town. In a country like this one where wagons are unknown, where dirt paths in winter are nothing but water and mud, these sure-footed animals are indispensable."[70] Nonetheless, from north to south, there was not a single camel-breeding tribe in the country, nor a single tribe that specialized in horse breeding. Tunisia was the kingdom of small livestock, and the nomad a pedestrian. During the 1880s, one group was relatively well supplied with mounts – the Awlād Sidi ʿAbīd. For the 2,700 individuals counted at that time, there were 2,070 camels, or three mounts for every four members of the tribe. This is a record number. The Awlād Sidi ʿAbīd happened to be specialized in transport, specifically between the Tell region and the oases. However, they owned more sheep than anything else – nearly 17,000, along with 4,500 goats, or eight head of small livestock per capita. Even among them, small livestock outnumbered camels. Another mounted tribe was the Drīd, auxiliaries of the bey. Around 1880 they had approximately 1,000 horses and 2,000 camels for a population of 10,000, and ten times as much small livestock. The Frashīsh, one rank below them, had one camel for every three members of the tribe, which clearly represents more than one for every adult male. Among the Mājer, their neighbors, there was one for every five, and among the Jlāss, their enemies, the same number, while the Hamāma, who were better supplied, had two for every five members. In all these tribes of the steppe, small livestock was much more numerous. There were more than 150,000 head among the Frashīsh, more than 100,000 among the Jlāss, and more than 50,000 among the Mājer.

Almost everywhere, sheep predominated over goats in ratios of 2 to 1 and 5 to 1. There were several varieties, distinguishable by the color of the coat and the quality of the wool. The fatty excrescence of the tail increased in quantity as one moved from north to south. North of a line stretching from Le Kef to Sousse, the animals were larger and stronger than in the south, their wool long, straight, and coarse. In the south, they were small, but their long tails provided a large amount of fat, which Bedouins found delectable. The sheep had a curly and extremely fine coat that was suited to the female weavers of the Jarīd and Jerba. Though these sheep were not castrated, they produced tastier meat than those of the north.[71]

When it came to climbing slopes and grazing on bushes and shrubs, the goat had it all over the sheep among the Mogod, near Le Kef and Zaghouan in Cape Bon. The inhabitants of the Jabal Waslāt must have been goatherds, since in their new settlements, after expulsion from their Jabal, the number of goats exceeded that of cattle. The little goat was still more prevalent in many villages of the deep south: the regions of Gabès, Gafsa, and the Jarīd. This animal, so bitterly accused of causing damage to trees, demonstrates a sobriety and a resistance to dryness that – all things being equal – are on a par with those of the camel.

Cattle fell far behind the other species. They held first place only in the plains of Mateur and were numerous around Bizerte. In the north, wherever goats reigned supreme, cattle could also be counted by the thousands.

The camel was useful for the long haul. Otherwise, from house to garden, from one plot to another, from the village to the souk, the donkey was the ideal vehicle, preferred to the horse or mule, which required more care. Roughly speaking, statistics for the end of the nineteenth century suggest one donkey per house or tent. This association of human beings and donkey in North Africa goes back to Neolithic times. Along with the donkey, the sheep has been domesticated since the beginnings of agriculture. Neither the horse nor the camel – both introduced in North Africa at a later date – has replaced them.

Techniques of animal husbandry were similarly ancient. There was no shelter for animals, with the exception of newborn lambs, which were taken into the dwelling. The others endured the cold out in the open, and in some years, in the north, succumbed to it as was the case in 1715, 1731, 1740, 1809, and 1841.[72] At most, a fence of thorns kept the animals from escaping. No forage was stored. The animals ate whatever they found in their wanderings. Every summer brought back thirst and hunger, and not until November or December was the herd restored to its full number. Nor was there any selection or control of breeding. A ram was let loose among thirty ewes and was replaced every five years. A few animal diseases could be treated: Mange, which destroys the sheep's coat, was cured by rubbing an infusion of tobacco leaves on the afflicted animal; and an animal suffering from plague could be saved if the symptomatic pustule was lanced in time. Applications of tar on the skin of dromedaries rid them of parasites.[73]

The same simplicity entered into the preparation of dairy products. It was the woman who milked the animals. To make butter, milk was enclosed in a goatskin that was suspended by its two ends and squeezed to extract the residual milk. *Smen* was obtained by bringing the butter to a boil and carefully pouring the liquid into jars after salt had been added. This salted butter, much appreciated in cooking, was brought to the markets of Mateur and Béja, sent as far as Malta and Leghorn, and regularly requisitioned, in the guise of taxes, by the bey's administration. As for cheese, herders used the flower of the wild artichoke to thicken milk and then poured the clotted milk into small baskets in which it drained.

However rudimentary these techniques, herding lent a rhythm to the lives of the pastoralists – their daily movements, their seasonal activities, and their dwellings. In their daily routine, the herds were taken out to graze after the sun had risen, when the dew had evaporated, for it was thought to be unhealthful for the animals. The herd was brought back at sunset and kept near the tents for the night. As for seasonal migrations, let us take the Awlād Mʿāmar and the Sellama, of the Hamāma tribe, as examples. In the autumn, the families came together for plowing and sowing. Winter was a time of dispersion. Some went to more distant pastures, others headed for the Jarīd where they brought in the date harvest and bartered produce. In the spring everyone returned to the fields for the harvest. The shearing took place in April and May, as it did for all the tribes. Everywhere this event was the occasion for great rejoicing. The day of the shearing was fixed by common accord for each sheep raiser. As in the case of plowing and harvesting, the same recip-

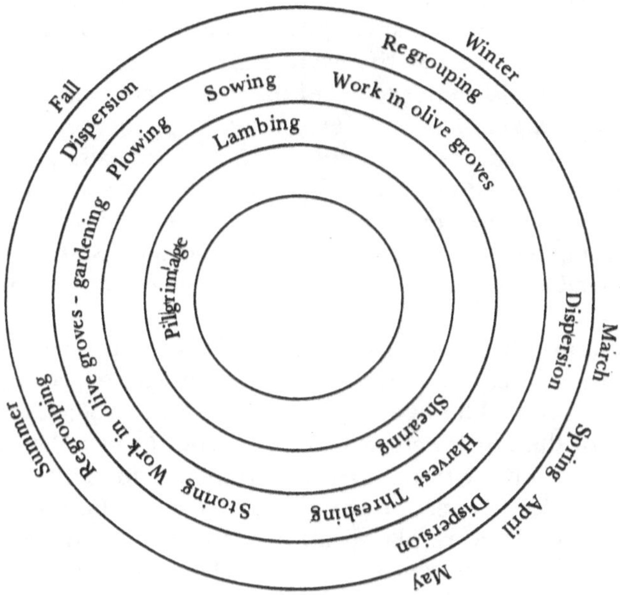

Fig. 4.3. The ʿAqarība tribe: cycle of displacements and labors.

rocal aid, *maʿūna*, was organized. The men sheared and sang, the women prepared the couscous while making the ululating sound of happy occasions.

In the same way the ʿAqarība, from around Sfax, alternately dispersed and reassembled, but for briefer periods. In October and November, they went off to plow and sow, each clan having its own terrain. In the winter there was a general reunion near the olive groves for the olive harvest. In March a new migration sent them off in various directions to pasture lands. As of April, the approach of the harvest sent them back into the fields. Since the threshing grounds and silos were scattered all over their territory, one part of the families remained to beat out the grain while the other brought in the harvest. And finally in summer the ʿAqarība returned to the shade of their olive trees and tended their gardens. It was a time of pilgrimage, feasts, and holidays (Fig. 4.3).

The needs of the livestock also determined agreements between nomadic tribes, shepherds, and peasants. The direction of collective migrations fell to the chief shepherd, called by his constituents *qaid al ʿazīb*. He supervised the order of transhumance, settled arguments, and saw to good relations with the inhabitants of the regions traversed. Although the tribes spent most of their time on their own territory, regular displacements, in accordance with specific agreements, were necessary for certain groups who lived under extremely severe conditions. The tribes of the Aʿrādh went up in the spring to the pastures around Sfax, the territory of the Methallīth and the Mahādhba. Conversely, the Wartan sent their herds south in winter to avoid the intense cold, and the Qoʿūb and Quazīn, on payment of a fee, offered their hospitality to neighboring tribes as summer approached. For their part, the villagers placed their herds in the care of herding groups who were compensated according to the growth of the herd, or of herders lent by the nomads in a kind of au pair arrangement in which they were fed and clothed by their hosts and received a certain percentage of the animals born during their contract.

Finally, pastoralists lived in tents, the "house of hair" carried by camels from one campsite to another. It was the women who sewed, repaired, and pitched the tents. The opening faced south as protection against the cool winds of the north and west, and in order to face the direction of prayer and the holy cities. Vertical curtains divided the tent into apartments – one, for women, on the east, the *sherqui*, and the other for men, the *gherbi*. Hooks were placed on the tent poles to hang utensils, weapons, and baskets. The tent was never isolated. It was the segment of a circle, the *dawār*, which brought together a number of families of the same subgroup. Peyssonnel saw the encampments of "a very numerous nation of Arabs," on the edge of the Silian wadi, in the plain of Sers: forty *dawār*, each consisting of thirty or forty tents. Later, Shaw saw migratory villages that had a few hundred tents.[74] In the winter, if the tribe had to spend a number of months in the same place, then sturdier dwellings were built, huts, made of dried earth mixed with straw. This was the *mashta*, the winter habitation, fragile and frequently rebuilt.

In all of this, was it the animals who moved man from place to place, or did man move as a way of adapting to harsh nature and making use of all available resources despite his fairly primitive techniques? For the nomads of subdesert fringes and high steppes, natural aridity was the real motive for their activities and mobility. This was less true of the north and the coastal regions where two types of economy coexisted side by side. One was the intensive agriculture of a population of gardeners wresting endless varieties of produce from tiny plots, and the other an extensive agriculture and herding of barely domesticated flocks on the part of vast groupings of nomads and seminomads. Were these two economies in competition? In fact, as we have already mentioned, political and economic arrangements existed between these two populations. Moreover, nomads could be farmers at certain times and pitch their tents near settled peoples in order to share their work and their produce. Above all, they participated in the same social organization and were steeped in the same culture.

Rural industry

In addition to seeing to all the farm work, Tunisian peasants also took an active part in industrial production. By virtue of the technical level it presupposes, and the relationship it implies between town and countryside, this fact is one of the major characteristics defining the dominant mode of production in precolonial Tunisia.

Textiles: a case in point

Fabric production was certainly the most important of Tunisian industries.[75] One might say that there is nothing very special about this, since in the economy of the ancien régime, whose structure was long since described by Ernest Labrousse, the industry that ranked above all others was indeed that of textiles. This was even more true in Tunisia, not only because of the number of workers it employed and its distribution throughout the country, but beyond that, because of the number of needs it fulfilled. To begin with, it provided nomads – the majority of the population – with their dwelling, the tent, an assemblage of *fleij*, long brown bands of woven goat and camel hair. Looms also produced the principal parts of its interior furnishings, such as the wool *ktīfa* that nomads spread out on the floor of their tent, the rugs of low pile or heavy yarn that were used by settled peoples as well and could take the place of a chair or a bed, and the blankets and hangings of various sizes and styles, some of pure wool, and others alternately banded in wool and silk. Objects for domestic use were in part a mixture of goat hair and wool: storage sacks, pack saddles, prayer rugs, and so on. Also woven, of course, was clothing. Often, it was no more than a large length of wool that was simply draped around the body such as *hawlis*, or black and white *wazras, haiks, sefsāris*, and the like. There was also the burnous, the essential item of masculine attire – a large cape of a single seamless piece of wool.

The textile industry was predominantly rural. Production was organized in three different forms. For the most part, fabrics were woven by nomads and villagers for their personal use. This activity was geographically dispersed since nearly all the pastoralists and many villagers participated in it (see Map 4.4a). It was also a household industry, in which the division of labor did not follow the lines of peasant versus artisan, but of man versus woman. Whereas men took care of farming and herding, women, in addition to their household tasks, spun the wool, dyed it, and wove it. In this sharing of chores, the life of the tent was divided into two spaces. The masculine side was devoted to hospitality and palaver, and the feminine side was taken up with cooking and weav-

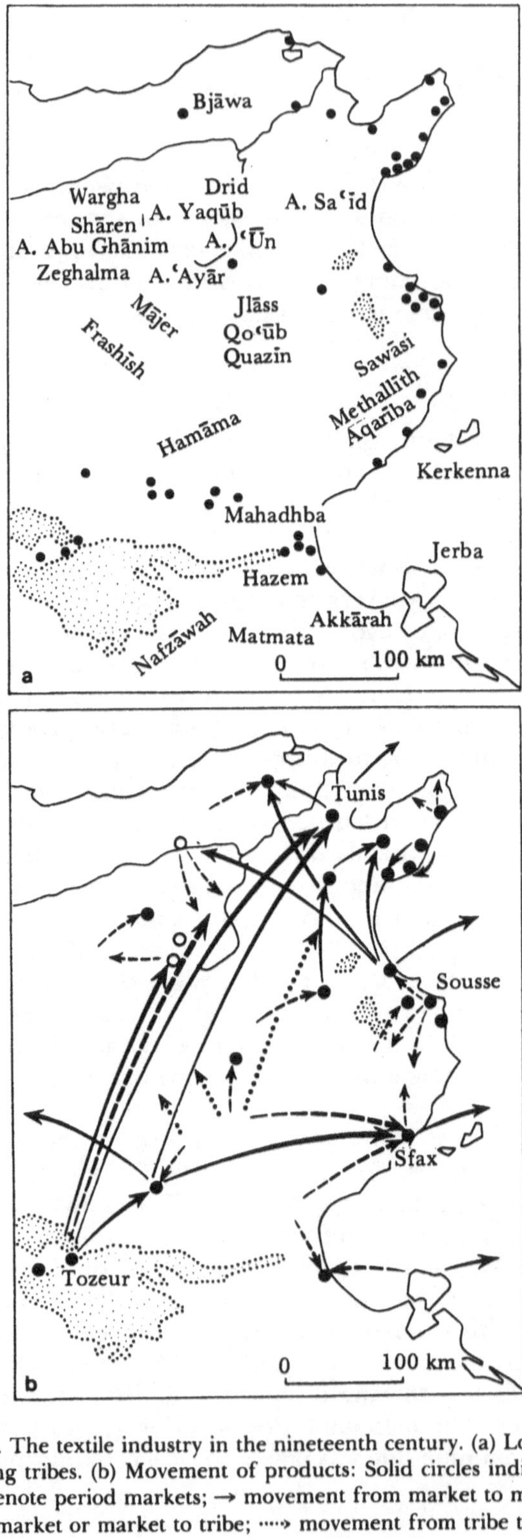

Map 4.4. The textile industry in the nineteenth century. (a) Localities of production and producing tribes. (b) Movement of products: Solid circles indicate urban markets; open circles denote period markets; → movement from market to market; --→ movement from tribe to market or market to tribe; ····→ movement from tribe to tribe

ing. Among settled peoples as well, it was in the women's quarters that the loom stood. There was little specialization among those female weavers. They engaged in every stage of clothmaking – spinning, dying, weaving – thereby providing all the clothing and furnishings for the tent and thus fulfilling virtually all the needs of their group. The loom itself seems to have been produced locally.

The Hamāma provide an interesting exception to this pattern. In some tribes, men were specialized in the making of *ktīfa* – the huge Bedouin rugs – and traveled from place to place, working on special order. They were the guests of their clients for the duration of their work, which was preceded and followed by a sacrifice.[76] Aside from this case, family activity aiming at self-sufficiency was almost universal in the Tunisian countryside. Except when poverty compelled some families to bring their products to market, or when the output exceeded the needs of the family, cloth was rarely put up for sale. This is how the Awlād Idīr of the Jlāss sold their surplus in Kairouan, or the Sawāsi went to Djemmal to sell a few *fleij* woven by the women of the tribe, along with food products. One has only to compare the areas of production with the distribution of the textile industry to see how unimportant these exchanges were.

Manufacturing in the southern oases fell into a second category. There, production was primarily intended for sale. But it remained a specialty of women and was thus spread out in family workshops.[77] Although this category was similar to the first, it was very different in purpose. Aimed at the market, production was more specialized. Gafsa was known for its *farashīya*, long coverings in bright colors; El Oudiane and Tozeur were reputed for the fine quality of their burnouses. Particularly esteemed among the goods coming from Nefta were fabrics of mixed wool and silk, especially *haiks* worn by women. Is it appropriate to designate this form of production as a rural industry? From a geographic standpoint, the answer is not certain. Although Tozeur, Nefta, and Gafsa were towns, they did not monopolize the entire production. The surrounding villages took an active part in the industry. From a sociological viewpoint, there can be little doubt that it was a rural activity, since the weavers were the wives, sisters, and mothers of peasants. This cottage industry was not the sole source of family income. As in the first type of textile production, the only division of labor was between the sexes.

Textile making had a long tradition in the south. Already in the sixteenth century, Leo Africanus spoke of the fabrics of Gafsa. Looms were already working as far back in the Husaynite period as one can go. The bey received burnouses and *wazra* from Tozeur, Nefta, and many villages of the Jarīd, *sefsāri* from the same places and from Gafsa, and still other burnouses from the Aʿrādh.[78] In addition to these purchases, the bey

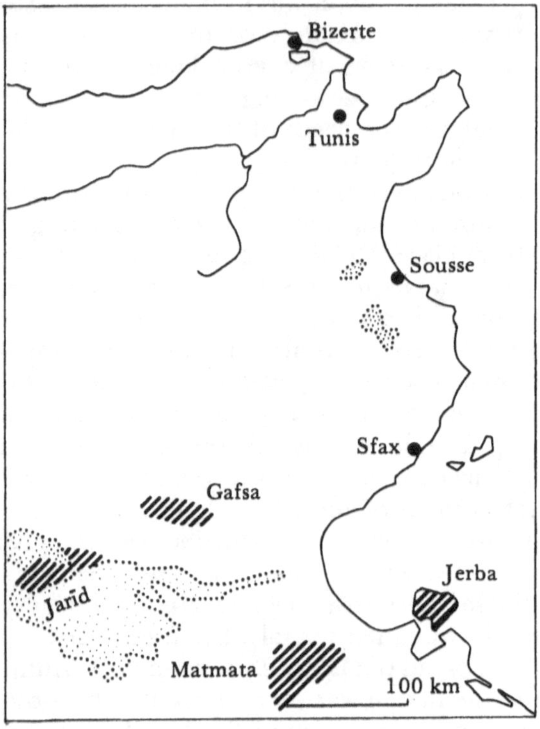

Map 4.5. The textile industry in the eighteenth century: localities producing fabrics for the bey.

each year levied – at a price that remained unchanged throughout the eighteenth century – hundreds of lengths of cloth produced in the villages and towns of the Jarīd. This was the only region of the country subjected to this form of tax paid in kind. It was evidently a manufacturing region that must have held first place in the wool market (Map 4.5). Production nonetheless continued to be organized within a domestic framework, the occupation of artisan never becoming separate from that of farmer.[79]

The third type of organization was found in the coastal regions: Jerba, the Sahel, and Cape Bon (Map 4.4a). There weaving was the occupation of permanent craftsmen who were weavers by profession and no longer worked in the fields. Women might spin the wool, but the weaving shops were outside the home and occupied a separate space. On Jerba, where a few hundred were counted in the census at the end of the nineteenth century, weavers were scattered all over the island. But elsewhere, a topographic clustering of crafts took place on a specific street or square. Thus Kourba, a small settlement on Cape Bon, had sixty weavers by the beginning of the protectorate, Kelibia more than forty, and Beni Khiar eighty. This was not yet the urban souk in which artisans of a single trade are under the control of a syndic. But it was not far removed from a typically urban form of production.

Towns such as Bizerte, Tunis, Nabeul, Sousse, Sfax, and Kairouan also produced cloth, but they were far from monopolizing the industry. One can be fairly certain that in precolonial Tunisia, a large part of the textile production was outside their control. There was no division of labor between town and country, which would have given the former a monopoly – or a simple primacy – over industrial production, placing the latter in a position of dependence. The countryside was not the third world of the town. Peasants no doubt provided raw materials to the towns and came away with certain finished products. To confine ourselves to the textile industry, Tunis, Sousse, Sfax, Kairouan, Gafsa, Tozeur, Moknine, and other settlements in the cantons of Monastir used wool brought by tribal herders into their workshops. Without the fleece brought by the shepherds, urban looms would have fallen idle. But the peasants managed to fulfill most of their needs without having recourse to the artisans in the towns, who predominated only in the production of certain types of cloth. Linen and cotton, in particular, were produced only in such urban centers as Bizerte, Nabeul, Sousse, and Sfax. Commercial ports, these last two received raw materials from the Levant and specialized in weaving.[80] But Jerba, which also imported silk, made a specialty of certain luxurious fabrics intended for export. Although its shawls of fine wool were worn by many persons of rank, even the bey, this Jerban production did not give rise to an urban concentration.[81]

Nor did the cities control the distribution of products. Since the household type of production was by far the most widespread, there was nothing that could be called a Tunisian "market" for the textile industry. In most cases, textiles were not really commodities since they did not go through commercial channels. Fabrics made to be sold took other routes that did not necessarily pass through towns. It is generally true that towns, inasmuch as they had permanent markets, were a secure outlet for the products of rural artisans. In the bazaars of Tunis, Sousse, and Sfax, one could readily find fabrics coming from producing regions as remote as the Jarīd or the Aʿrādh. Other, smaller centers siphoned off the products of their regions as in Nabeul, Tozeur, Gabès, and even Le Kef or Zaghouan, which had no textile artisanry of their own. On the other hand, the three large ports saw to the exportation of fabrics from the countryside and reshipped woolstuffs from Jerba and the Jarīd to Leghorn and the Levant. In 1864 it was estimated that Sfax had exported locally produced woolens valued at 270,000 francs, and fine woolens from the Jarīd worth 300,000 francs. Sfax, Sousse, and Tunis thus served as intermediaries for the industry of the hinterlands.[82] In such transactions one can easily imagine "the typical mechanisms of exploitation of the country by the city,"[83] for the isolated peasants had to rely on the better-organized townspeople.

Nevertheless, the distribution of textiles outside their places of production could also circumvent the towns, either because of the state's levies, or because the fabrics were brought to weekly rural markets by peddlers coming from producing regions. Or, trade could be even more direct. The seasonal displacements of nomads gave them the opportunity to buy fabrics, sell their own surplus, and exchange the wool from their herds. Their convergence in the south for the date harvest was at the same time a period of intense activity for the artisans of the Jarīd. Manufacturing followed the same rhythm as farming and herding.

Other industries

We have dwelt at length on the textile industry because it seemed exemplary. We can now list other branches of industry and describe them briefly. Two among them – basketweaving and pottery – offer analogies with textile production, and not only because of the place they held in the material life of the people. Nomadic or settled groups were often capable of producing themselves the objects for their basic needs. Cooking utensils, the brazier, the pots used for storing oil, grain, olives, and figs – all this paraphernalia was made of fired or dried clay. They were crude products that the women fashioned out of local materials. This domestic activity was less widespread than weaving and did not exclude production on a larger scale by professional potters. Some centers such as Tunis, Kairouan, Nefta, and El Oudiane catered only to their own region. Others sent their pots all over the regency. Zaghouan made ordinary unglazed dishes. Testour produced stew pots, vases, pans, and above all, the rounded tiles used by the inhabitants of Andalusian villages for roofing. Bizerte specialized in glazed pottery. In a country without coopers or glaziers, it was the potters of Jerba who made the amphorae, pitchers, and pots of all sizes in which liquids and solids were stored and transported. Their pots were carried into every part of the regency and even beyond, to Algeria and the Levant. Nabeul, characterized by Shaw when he visited there in 1727 as "a flourishing town because of its industrious inhabitants and long famous for its earthenware," was the great center of ceramics. Its construction materials, tiles, and earthenware or enameled dishes were sought after by all the regions of the country.[84]

All in all, the production of pottery was more concentrated geographically and more specialized technically than the textile industry.

Cordage and basketweaving did not suffer from a lack of raw materials. Artisans could use the esparto grass in the steppes, the leaves and fibers from palm trees and cactus plants, and reeds in zones of rainfall. The products of this craft were as numerous as their uses. Ropes served for hanging utensils, connecting implements, and fettering animals. Nomads kept their grain in huge baskets similar to amphorae. Saddle bags were used for carrying earth, manure, and other heavy items. There were also single and double hods, nets of esparto grass for binding straw, and so on. All kinds of bags made of braided esparto or palm were used to hold lightweight materials. Mats were required for the noblest of purposes – to cover the columns and floors of mosques – as well as for the humblest. They were placed on the benches of cafés, public baths, barbershops, and in the hallways of private houses. They served as beds; they were placed at the opening of bread ovens to lay down the hot loaves; on ships, wheat and barley were transported in them.

Since basketmaking was less widespread than clothweaving, production was much more commercialized. A few groups wove mats and bags only for their own use – the Mājer, Frashīsh, Wārgha, Shāren – whereas all the others sold a portion of their output. The mats of Djeradou, Takrouna, and Zriba reached a market as distant as Tunis, and those of the ʿAqarība and Mahādhba were sold in Sfax. The Awlād ʿAyār brought theirs to Ksour and Sousse. Unlike clothweaving, basketmaking was a masculine occupation. Filling leisure time in winter, it was not always separate from agriculture. But for certain items, it became an independent trade that employed a large number of hands for specialized production as in Soma (on Cape Bon) or near Gabès, in the towns of Ghennouche, with a specialty of esparto bags, and Methouia, which in 1880 had forty-odd looms and exported its mats to various urban centers. Basketmaking was the primary industry of Kerkenna, which supplemented the meager resources provided by agriculture by exporting its baskets. In Mahares, near Sfax, this was the major industry of the village where more than fifty basketmakers worked on the square or in the streets, making decorated reed mats that were then taken to Sfax and from there to the rest of the country.[85]

Basketry, unlike ceramics, was primarily a rural industry. Nabeul was the only important city in which the craft was widely practiced. Equally rural were other small crafts that provided supplementary income for impoverished families. After the growing season, poor peasants sold coal, tar, or plaster at urban markets. As for farm implements, they were rarely made by urban artisans. In centers such as Bizerte, Tunis, or Sfax, blacksmiths forged the metal parts of plows and yokes for their own regions, but for the rest – the body of the plow, pitchforks, spades, threshing boards – the material was so rudimentary that peasants themselves could tinker with them. Millstones, on the other hand, always came from the same region. The Hamāma and the village of El Guettar provided them for all the families of Tunisia.

In all this, it was the countryside that imposed its rhythm and its forms. To be more precise, it was the tribal group, or in the village, the family group, that was the fundamental unit of production, even in the case of manufactured objects. Rural or familial, these cottage industries generated neither industrial nor commercial capitalism, since the volume of commodities was small compared to the volume of goods intended for personal consumption. Nor did they create a contradiction between town and country. Certain industries were the absolute monopoly of towns – tanning and leather crafts, the manufacture of tarboosh, perfumes, copperware, weapons. Peasants, however, frequented urban markets primarily for nonessential items. If the harvest was poor, they did not go into town but postponed their purchases. Thus, the towns were somewhat hampered in their function of transforming raw materials into manufactured goods.

Villages and tribes were without blacksmiths, carpenters, masons, or roofers. The peasant was all of them combined. Horse-driven mills generally associated with bakeries; oil presses that exceeded the needs of their owners existed in all the urban centers and villages of any importance. In 1836–7, 567 oil presses were counted in the districts of Sousse and Monastir.[86] The bey owned some throughout the area of the Sahel and in a few villages of Cape Bon. This provided an additional source of income, but even more, it was a way of keeping track of the production of those who used them. However, no one was obliged to use them. The extraction of oil or the milling of grain could be done at home. One can understand the equilibrium resulting from this kind of social structure and its potential for reproduction, not only because the family group satisfied its own needs, but also because its specialty, however modest, created a currency for barter. This is reminiscent of neighboring Algeria, where the skilled Kabyle artisans, armorers, blacksmiths, and even minters produced for townspeople, and the craftsmen of the Beni Abbes made weapons, gunpowder, and burnouses, which were sold throughout the province of Contstantine.[87] There, as in Tunisia, the countryside provided objects for barter and supplied its own needs as well as those of the townspeople. There are doubtless other similarities in the rest of the Mediterranean basin, but none in the manorial economy of the feudal system such as described by W. Kula, or in Western Europe, even when it was still largely agrarian. For rural industry in Europe was separate from farm work, and certain of its branches fell under the control of capitalism.

5. The rhythms and networks of daily life

Eating habits and rituals

Products used

A glance at the local market. Considering the range of animal and vegetable products available in the country, the diet of Tunisians would not seem to have been severely lacking in anything. Carbohydrates? Barley and wheat were widely grown under the old regency and were supplemented here and there by maize, sorghum, and various legumes. Vitamins? They were provided by figs, dates, and the large variety of fruits already mentioned. Proteins? In a country where there were more nomadic herders than villagers there should have been no lack of meat. Salt? Along the east coast and near the oases, salt was extracted from *sebkhas*, either for use by the locals or as barter for wheat and barley.[1] The nutritional potential was therefore sufficiently varied, in theory at least, to satisfy today's standards. As to satisfying the needs of the people, that is less certain. For a people to be well fed, the volume of production has to be adequate and products must be available and distributed in such a way as to assure a certain measure of equality among consumers. Certain products, not native to the country, are presumed to have been unavailable at local markets: imported luxury products, now in daily use, such as tea, coffee, and sugar.

Imported products: luxury items. Regarding sugar, the energy food par excellence, Fernand Braudel, speaking of Europe, wrote that it was "a luxury before the 16th century."[2] In Tunisia, it was still a luxury three centuries later.

French merchant ships brought it to Tunisia from the colonies, thereby providing for the fortunate historian some documentation on imports.[3] During the first quarter of the eighteenth century, Tunisia imported, on the average, less than 100 quintals a year, Marseille weight. In 1720, a record year, the figures exceeded 230 Marseille quintals. Let us suppose that the population at the time was about one million inhabitants (a very low figure). Sugar consumption would thus be less than 5 grams per person per year, which amounts to saying that the Tunisians used none at all. In the second quarter of the eighteenth century, imports increased considerably: 844 quintals in 1736. From 1735 to 1739, however, the average annual consumption was 540 quintals, or 27 grams per person per year: still a ridiculously small amount.

The increase in consumption continued: 33,000 pounds of sugar were imported in 1784; 110,000 in 1785; 157,636 in 1786. The annual ration remained low: less than 80 grams per person.

Available documentation forces us to make another leap in time, bringing us to 1824. Tunisia imported 2,348 metric quintals of sugar that year, and 1,520 in 1826. Imports thus doubled or tripled during the years preceding the French Revolution. The average hypothetical ration went up to 200 grams per person per year.

In conclusion let us look at a piece of statistical documentation, "A General Survey of the Production and Consumption of Sugar during the Year 1846." The writer of the report, estimating too generously a population of two million inhabitants, says, "Consumers constitute approximately one-fifth of the population." The average individual consumption would therefore be 1,820 grams. If the olive harvest was good and business brisk, the consumption of sugar increased, if the price was right.

There was thus an undeniable increase in the consumption of sugar but not enough to consider sugar part of the habitual diet of the country as a whole. It was still a luxury item, the predilection of city dwellers, but unknown to peasants.

In the eighteenth century, sugar was still a royal treat. It appears among the gifts sent by the court of France to the court of the bey to conclude the peace treaty of 1741. Along with rare cloth and works of silver and gold, Ali Pāsha received thirty-six cases of fruit preserves and thirty loaves of sugar. On that occasion his elder son, the *khasnadar*, the *kahia*, the great scholars, and other ministers also received sugar, in smaller quantities however.[4] For the Ramadan of 1775, gifts from the French consul to the high officials of the regency consisted once again of sugar, syrup, jam, and coffee. A year later, the bey's son-in-law was offered a number of cases of jams, fruit in syrup, sugared almonds, prunes, and chocolate; powdered sugar and sugar in loaves; and coffee, etc. These delicacies did not rank in any way below the silverware, fine fabrics, and porcelain tableware offered to the bey.

Sugar was a precious commodity, a rare one until recent times. In mid-twentieth-century Morocco, as reported by Jouin, pious men preferred to drink coffee sweetened with honey or, lacking honey, sucked a date while sipping their coffee. Sugar was still suspected of being impure. Sharing this fear of uncleanliness, the Jews of Tunisia sweetened their coffee with dates rather than with sugar, especially at Passover.[5]

Let us leave aside for the moment dates, honey, raisins, and other sugar substitutes. Although North Africa contributed to the spread of sugar and even sugar cane, sugar came into use slowly and very late. What is most important is that following the great discoveries, Europe became the monopolistic supplier of sugar. From then on the consumer market was marginal and dependent.

Coffee had a similar fate. Whatever its date of appearance and place of birth, Arabia was the center of diffusion for coffee,[6] and it is from Arabic that it got its name. It was known in Cairo at the beginning of the sixteenth century and spread during that same time to Constantinople where coffee houses began to open. In the West, it appeared somewhat later. After a sumptuous repast that was offered to the Spaniard Adorno in Tunis at the end of the fifteenth century, poppy seeds were served to help him sleep; no stimulants, no coffee. And Adorno reports: "The Moors know no other drink but milk or water. The rich and the great sometimes drink a wine made of dried grapes. On occasion, they also drink sweetened water or syrup."[7] Later neither Leo the African nor Marmol, though keen observers of culinary customs and table manners, mentioned coffee. But it must have entered North Africa for, in the first half of the seventeenth century, it was a common beverage among townspeople, who also used tobacco. "Outside the shops," wrote Father Dan in 1637, "they chat and drink coffee [*cavé*] out of tiny porcelain cups, and an alcohol, which are served by a number of taverns. This *cavé* is a kind of drink, black as ink, which they consider very healthful and which quenches the thirst. They drink it in small sips and indulge in this charming occupation for two or three hours a day, the rest of which is spent taking tobacco in smoke."[8]

The Reverend Father Dan experienced the same surprise over these common customs of the inhabitants of Barbary as did Pietro della Valle, his contemporary, when he described a café in Constantinople. In France the first coffee peddlers appeared at the end of the seventeenth century, and the first shops around 1670. In North Africa the habit of taking coffee in public places was already developed in the first half of the century.[9] Also in the seventeenth century, any refreshment offered a visitor by the bey or other court personalities consisted first of all, and almost exclusively, of coffee. When a special envoy of the vizier of Candia was received by the bey in 1667, he was served a cup of coffee, followed by orange-flower water to perfume his hands and face, then a *sciarbet*, a lemon-flavored sherbet.[10] In 1724 the envoy of the French king, when received at the Bardo, was offered coffee. The ceremony would be endlessly repeated over the centuries. Offering coffee thus became a ritual of etiquette in Tunis. In addition to the capital, Soliman, Bizerte, Nabeul, Mahdia, Sousse, Monastir, and other cities had one or more cafés, places for socializing and relaxing.[11] Peyssonnel describes the café in Soliman in 1724: "That is where the Moors meet to chat, eat sweets made of honey and flour, smoke tobacco, drink coffee, and listen to the music of such instruments as guitars, oboes, and others, in the custom of the region."[12]

Did the custom of coffee houses cross the city line and extend into the countryside? It was only among townspeople that European travelers drank coffee. Elsewhere, pure water and soured milk were the only drinks served.

Importation figures measure the spread of coffee in rural regions. During the first quarter of the eighteenth century Tunisia received none from France. Perhaps coffee came directly from the Orient. Later, from Marseille, Genoa, and Leghorn, Tunisia received nearly 300 quintals of coffee a year between 1735 and 1739. Like the importation of sugar, that of coffee increased steadily. On the eve of the French Revolution, Tunisia was buying around 500 metric quintals of coffee per year, and twice as much in 1824–6. If only adults drank coffee, the hypothetical average would be comparable to that of sugar: low. Until well into the nineteenth century, coffee was assuredly not in daily use, nor even frequently used in the Tunisian countryside. The geographic diffusion of coffee was rapid though its social diffusion was delayed.

Tea, another stimulant, which replaced coffee as the national beverage, was unknown in the eighteenth century; its appearance is very recent. In 1761 it was still an object of curiosity. The chance occurrence of a shipwreck brought about its discovery. In the cargo of a ship that ran aground on the shores of the regency, according to the chronicler Seghir ben Youssef, "little tin boxes were found containing small round leaves, like the leaves of the caper bush; when they were brought to Béja, the tradesmen said it was tea and that infusions could be made of it and drunk like coffee."[13]

This discovery seems to have had no consequence. Tea is absent on bills of lading before 1739; later, a few dozen pounds were brought in. During the first half of the nineteenth century, it was still unknown to merchants. I found it listed among the products used in the palace of the bey, but in the pharmacy, not in the kitchen. Moreover, it appeared in a quantity comparable to that of the rarest spices – a few boxes. (In fact, it was no different in the French provinces, where tea was "still sold by apothecaries as a cure for indigestion"; Balzac's Madame de Bargeton was the innovator in Angoulême who offered "a reception with ices, cakes and tea.")[14] In 1850 in the markets of Kairouan and Sfax, a traveler who took note of the cost of foodstuffs found that coffee could be bought but not tea, whereas in Tunis two types of tea could be found.[15]

The success of tea in the regency of Tunis was thus late and sudden. In 1937 the country imported nearly 2,000 tons. One could do without food more readily than without tea. In order to purchase it, Jlāss shepherds sold off their butter at the market. Health services sent up a cry of alarm: Tea consumption had become a national epidemic. Family budgets were endangered by the intrusion of this new plant.[16]

It seems that this sudden passion was a direct effect of the colonial wars. In 1911, during the war between Italy and Turkey, Tunisia took in refugees from Libya who were fleeing the Italian army and who brought with them the custom of drinking green tea. Eastern Algeria was also belatedly conquered by tea.[17] In the west, however, it was already known to Moroccans by the beginning of the eighteenth century. Once again, the gifts offered the sovereign indicate the tastes of the ruling classes and date the spread of certain products: In 1719 the ambassador from England offered the king of Morocco various presents, among which were 20 pounds of tea and 200 pounds of sugar loaves; in the king's entourage tea was also offered as a gift. In 1777 the Swedish ambassador and later the Dutch commander brought the king of Morocco cases of rare tea and loaves of sugar.[18] In Tunisia coffee then held the primary position with one exception: In 1766 a new consul, fittingly English, offered among other gifts a case of tea and granulated sugar.[19] In the western Maghreb tea was widely drunk among the rich by the beginning of the eighteenth century. Before the end of the nineteenth century, it was drunk throughout the country and commonly used even by the people at the beginning of the twentieth century.[20]

Tea, coffee, sugar – three products whose conquest of the Maghreb was slow – remained, during the precolonial period, costly items. The Maghreb does not disprove the general rule that says that luxury items filter down from higher to lower ranks of society.[21] But it applied to the Maghreb long after it did to Europe, and then, under Europe's control. Tea plus sugar in the west, coffee plus sugar in the east – both required money, access to markets, European sea captains, and merchants who ruled over international trade. Even before the colonial conquest, the adoption of new foodstuffs already threatened the region with economic dependence and alienation, which Maghreb writers soon noticed and expressed in verse:[22]

> As for tea, you see,
> The Christian, who knows full well you are his enemy,
> Catches you with his cannon balls and his bales of tea,
> Lures you into ambushes on the platters of the scale.
> The enemy catches you in the belly. He knows that is where

> Death comes fast, in the belly, where the heart and liver are.
> The Christian strikes, he aims well. He brings sugar loaves.
> If your well-being were at stake, he would send nothing.

A poisoned gift, but with limited jeopardy, it may be said. For the Maghrebian lived primarily on his grain. In his daily diet, he did without those foreign delicacies and was satisfied with the produce of his labor.

Usual diet

Preparation: the kitchen, the women's domain. Daily food fell to women to prepare. In the country there was no baker, no miller. The man was the producer: He plowed, sowed, gathered, and harvested. If the fields needed water, it was the man who provided it. The woman, on the other hand, ground the grain, kneaded the dough, baked the bread, and cooked the food. She gathered the wood for the hearth. "And that is not all: for at the end of the day," like the women in Genesis, "they strap their nursing babies to their back and walk two or three miles from home in search of water."[23] The division of labor, as can be seen, was based not on differing strength (women also did heavy work), but rather on a division of space between the outside world, accessible to men, and the domestic world, from which women could escape for specific and limited purposes. The same division of labor, moreover, occurs all over the Muslim Mediterranean.

When a man moved from place to place he did no more cooking than at home. Dates, in pre-Islamic Arabia, constituted the classic provision for those who set off on a journey.[24] They still do in Tunisia, in subdesert regions. There was also something called *bsīssa*; a flour made of roasted barley, wheat, and anise seed. Mixed with water, it became a porridge to which olive oil, sugar, or honey could be added. Requiring no cooking, this was the food of nomads when they traveled. Another food that required no preparation was ground dried dates mixed with water.

In towns the situation was entirely different; there all the food-producing trades were always practiced by men. Bakers, butchers, grilled sausage or fritter merchants, water carriers, coffeeshop owners, sellers of roasted chickpeas – these shopkeepers and street merchants provided families with supplementary food and fed primarily the vagrant population of a city. The main function of food preparation, as in rural areas, remained the task of women.

Couscous, the national dish. For townspeople and country people, rich and poor, couscous provided the bulk of their nutrition. It required long preparation, which was never done alone. Had grain been set aside after the harvest? Then one called on relatives and neighbors who came to sort the grain, grind it, and sift it to obtain the size suitable for couscous, for *mhamos* (a coarser couscous), flours, and so on. If, however, the grain was ground just before the couscous was prepared, then this was done by the immediate family.

The hand mill known in antiquity was still in use. It consisted of two cylindrical grindstones, one of which held a vertical axle. To that axle was attached the moving grindstone, perforated in the center, with a wooden or metal handle at the end. To grind wheat, two women placed themselves on either side of the grindstone, poured grain into the center hole of the upper piece, and turned it vigorously. Custom dictated that this work began with a prayer, which the two women would intone during the entire operation.[25] It was therefore a religious task, accomplished according to a precise ritual. Other steps in the preparation of couscous were done the same way. After sifting the wheat, the women moistened it to roll it; if possible a few drops of rainwater, collected during the month of Nisan and kept in a flacon, were added, the water of the month of May being particularly beneficial. Once the semolina was rolled, it was placed in a couscousier, in which it was steamed over a broth containing vegetables and meat. It was wise not to mention anything sad, which could be a bad omen, but to speak of prosperity, abundance, and of pious and therefore benevolent people. Once served, the couscous was more than a simple means of surviving. Turned onto a large round platter, moistened with broth, garnished with vegetables and meat, it was eaten communally, each diner taking a bit of couscous with his right hand that he quickly rolled and swallowed. It was not polite to eat everything on the platter, since the leftovers are supposed to have some magical properties. After each diner had eaten, he or she thanked God with another prayer.[26]

Food eaten in common is quite clearly a symbol of communion, of kinship, not just familiarity and, even less, poverty. European travelers rarely perceived this since they felt a certain repulsion at the thought of eating from the same bowl, without a spoon or a napkin (although before and after the meal a pitcher was brought to the table so that everyone could rinse his hands). "Their uncleanliness made us somewhat sick to our stomachs," wrote a priest ransoming captives,[27] after seeing the Moors eat with their fingers from the same plate. And another was astonished by the table manners of the sovereign, which were hardly different from those of his humblest subjects.[28]

To close this digression on culinary customs and their significance, couscous, from its preparation to its consumption, was bathed in a religious aura. It was also known as *taʿām*, the perfect food, and associated with almost every collective holiday and ceremony: On the pilgrimages to local marabouts, the inauguration of a new house, Monday and Friday evenings, specially blessed by the *sunna* (and Friday evening, the eve of the Sabbath among Jews), couscous was preferred to other dishes.

It was not, however, the only common dish, or the only one with a symbolic value. Cereals also served as the basis for other dishes frequently prepared. In the form of noodles, porridge, bread, or couscous, they comprised the basic diet. In this Tunisian peasants shared the habits of all preindustrial populations. Generally, vegetable products held a greater place in the diet than meats, which were rarely eaten and were not equally desirable: Beef was disliked and calves were never slaughtered for meat. Mutton, on the other hand, was much appreciated, as were the meat and fat of camels. In desert regions, even dog flesh was eaten – an ancient habit that Muslim jurists tolerate with indulgence.[29] Finally, all sorts of fowl could be put in the stewpot. It was in the form of stews, slowly simmered and seasoned with various spices, that meat was served, whether fresh or preserved. Grilled sausages were an urban food. *Mechoui*, familiar to many foreigners, was an improvised dish of spit-roasted lamb offered to a stranger.

Other animal products were butter, churned by the women in an udder, and salted. It was eaten by nomadic shepherds, whereas olive oil was preferred by settled people. *Liya*, the fat of sheep tails, however, was universally enjoyed. It was stored when a sheep was slaughtered; salted meat was preserved in it; food was cooked in it. Its strong odor was infinitely preferred to that of other fats.[30]

An inventory of foods known to have been used in the eighteenth and nineteenth centuries covers a geographic area extending beyond the Maghreb, and a period of time that goes back much further, that cannot be detailed here and that, in any case, offers only a partial view of daily eating habits. What remains to be seen is when meals were eaten, what foods made up a meal, and what their variations were depending on social class, region, agricultural season, or religious calendar.

Variations in consumption. The first difference was that of sex. This factor did not affect the ordinary diet, but it appeared in situations when a woman required special treatment: before marriage, or after childbirth, for example. Certain foods, reputed to be good for fertility, were evidently reserved for women: plants believed to cure sterility, such as *Mercurialis annua*, or to enhance conception, or even encourage the conception of male children, such as the musk bugle, or *Centaurea suffriticora*. Plants reputed to be aphrodisiac, such as terfas, a mushroom that when cooked gives off an odor of sperm, and the flowers of the male palm tree, were reserved for men.[31] In addition, husbands "use a certain confection of herbs that delights the whole body and gives pleasure to women, so that having eaten no more than an ounce of it, one is cheerful the rest of the day."[32] The herb in question is hashish, which the Tunisians borrowed from the Turks. One can nevertheless assume that this pleasure was neither frequent nor common.

Otherwise, in terms of their basic diet, nothing distinguished the eating habits of women from those of men. Social differences, one might guess, were much more marked.

Peyssonnel, a physician, tried to classify the diets he had observed in Tunisia, from the wealthiest to the poorest, the most varied to the most limited.[33] Heading the list, as one would expect, was the table of the sovereign. The bey had either a pilaf of rice, or a couscous garnished with boiled meat, as well as other preparations of meat: roast chicken, skewered chunks of lamb, or grape leaves filled with chopped meat and cooked under embers. In addition, there were fruits, white bread, pastries, and as a beverage, pure water taken at the end of the meal. A second diet was that of the Moors, meaning townspeople. For them there was no rice, a costly item, but rather couscous with boiled meat, such as the bey ate, or *bazine*, with butter or honey, occasionally eggs or fish, and fruit. Like the bey, they usually drank water and sometimes soured milk. Country people had a more frugal diet: neither rice nor even couscous. *Bsīssa* with water or milk, or *aʿsīda* with oil, comprised their usual diet, occasionally supplemented with eggs and fruits. "One cannot lead a more miserable life than these Moorish Bedouins," Peyssonnel commented. The people of the Jarīd were even more deprived: They lived on dates and locusts. In the land of dates, there were still old people who had never seen bread.

Peyssonnel's typology is both sociological and geographic. One ate worse in the country than in town, in desert regions than in the rest of the country. But the general conclusion Peyssonnel reaches is that, on the whole, the range of possibilities was extremely narrow: Nutrition was mediocre everywhere and, despite a diet richer in meat and more varied, the sovereign was nevertheless poorly fed: "The bey fares no better than others."

What is the significance of this classification and this global judgment? Should we accept, correct, or reject Peyssonnel's eyewitness account? Let us take the case of desert people. Desfontaines, who was in the southern part of the regency in 1784 and seems on the whole to have been a keen observer, says, as did Peyssonnel, whom he had not read, that the inhabitants of the Jarīd live on barley, dates, and locusts, which they preserved in large quantities in salt. A century later, officials who lived in the country for longer periods and were able to make more careful surveys repeated that dates were just about the only mainstay of the inhabitants, even richer ones, who at least supplemented their diet with milk.

These observations are once again confirmed – this time supported by statistics – by more recent investigations. In 1955 a vast survey was undertaken covering the entire country, involving doctors, dietitians, and sociologists,[34] which resulted in the division of the country into four alimentary regions. One of them, combining oases and subdesert areas into one zone, was characterized by the primary position held by dates in the daily diet, which in the other regions was held by cereals; in second place were the important nutrients provided by locusts and prickly pears. In other words, today as yesterday the nutrition of predesert regions is poor in grains and even more so in meat; monotonous, despite the presence, in oases at least, of vegetables; and highly deficient.

Peyssonnel's observations regarding the Bedouins are perhaps less precise, or should at least be corrected, with the help of information he himself provided. The cooking implements of the Bedouins consisted chiefly of an earthenware pot and a sieve that fit into it, which clearly indicates that country people, like townspeople and the bey, also ate couscous.[35] The "average" family took two meals. The first, a cold meal eaten in the morning or at midday, consisted of bread and olives, or bread dipped in a mixture of butter and honey, and a bowl of yogurt. The second, eaten at sunset, was hot and more copious, consisting some days of couscous enriched with vegetables and spices, and others of *aʿsīda*, or other stews and porridges already mentioned. A variant among the rich was a midday meal consisting, like dinner, of couscous or some other gruel and meat. Among the poor, the variant was one meal instead of two. In that case the Bedouin went out to gather the supplementary foods that could allay his hunger: carob and prickly pear in summer; the sweet fruit of the *Ziziphus lotus* in winter; roots and leaves of the *Atractylis gummifera* – the "white chameleon" – which was made into a soup; during years of famine, the roots of *Arum alisarum*, after extracting its bitter purgative juice by drying it; cardoon, and so on.[36]

For the most part, the same diet was found among townspeople: meals reduced in number and content among the poor; three meals and more numerous dishes among the rich, among whom the presentation of food allowed a prescribed order. Here, for example, is the menu of a sheikh in Soliman in 1845: to begin with, a noodle soup, followed by a stew of meat and vegetables; next a couscous, heavily spiced. Pastries were served for dessert.[37] This "diachronic combination of dishes," according to Maxime Rodinson's formula, was traditional, particularly the couscous, which was always served before dessert.

As to the bey, it is true, as Peyssonnel remarked, that his diet differed little from that of his subjects. Not even holidays were occasions for lavish meals. If the month of Ramadan was outstandingly rich in pastries,[38] the daily menu was meager and the servants so few that the bey had to hire additional help just for the holidays. Hammūda Pāsha, for example, when his nephews were circumcised, had to hire – as would any middle-class inhabitant of Tunis – Jewish cooks as caterers.[39] There is a vast difference between this kind of culinary austerity and the ostentatious pomp of the last Hafsid rulers. Like their Eastern counterparts, they loved exotic dishes, rich and savory food, requiring a large and skilled staff. "To judge it," Montaigne wrote, having read Paolo Giovo's *Histories*, "I would like to have had a taste of the art of those cooks who know how to marry strange scents with the savor of meats, as was especially noted at the table of the King of Thunes who, in our time, landed in Naples to meet with Emperor Charles. His meats were stuffed with fragrant herbs and spices of such costliness that a peacock and two pheasants came to one hundred ducats for the preparation customary for these fowl, and when carved, filled not only the hall, but all the chambers of his palace, and even the houses nearby, with a fragrance that did not readily disappear."[40]

There was nothing like that in the eighteenth and nineteenth centuries. Frugality was not, however, a sign of stinginess in the beys of the Husaynite dynasty. Nor were menus any different in Algiers or Morocco. A contemporary of Hammūda Pāsha's, Sultan Moulay Slimane, was usually satisfied with a simple couscous. What caused this change of taste, or ethics? Culinary opulence is a spectacle, a symbol of power. Perhaps the circumscribed life of the Maghreb rulers did not require ostentation. One can imagine that if relations with the sultan of Constantinople had been closer, if contact with the courts of other Islamic and Christian lands had been more frequent, the taste for novelty, opulence, and rarity would not have been lost.

A portion of couscous with meat, vegetables, spices, and so forth amounts in today's terms to 1,500 calories, depending on the meat used. For proper nourishment, Tunisians would have had to eat a daily ration of couscous, and find an additional thousand calories in bread, milk, and the foods of their first meal. This figure does not seem to me to have been reached in precolonial Tunisia.

All things considered, Peyssonnel's diagnosis seems to hold: general frugality, malnutrition in certain regions, probable undernourishment during periods of want – before the date harvest in the south and in winter elsewhere – and famine. But the monotony and simplicity of daily food were in part compensated for by the abundance of holidays and the intensity of culinary exchanges to which family and religious ceremonies gave rise.

Religious holidays and agrarian holidays: the semiology of eating habits

On such occasions the symbolism of foods appeared most clearly, and a system of correspondence came into play, based on the analogy of colors, smells, and forms. Sweet, green, and multiple (fruits with seeds, grains, etc.) augured happiness and plenty; black and bitter, on the other hand, were unlucky and were reserved for times of mourning and penitence.

To begin with Islamic celebrations, on the last day of the Hegiran year it was customary to serve a couscous prepared with preserved meat that came from the sacrifice of *Aid el kebir*, which took place twenty days before. Then, on the morning of the new year, dates and honey were eaten for their sweetness, and milk was drunk as an omen of peace. At noon, the ritual meal was a stew of mallow, color symbolism endowing this green food with the promise of prosperity.[41] In the water used to cook this plant, eggs were boiled, intended to be eaten the next day as a symbol of wealth during the year to come. During the first days of the year couscous was avoided since this dish, although generally festive, must be cooked in a closed utensil, whereas it was desirable to begin the year under the sign of openness.

The *ʿashūra*, the tenth day of the year, was also a feast day. The day before, one ate chicken and a thick soup with noodles, to which country people added eggs. The day of the holiday one ate, and offered to friends, particularly to children, dried fruits, walnuts, almonds, raisins, and so on. In the country, masquerades took place on this day, and children received musical instruments and toys. The holiday doubtless harks back to a pre-Islamic ceremony that marked the death of the preceding year and the birth of the new. It also commemorates a tragic event, the death of Husayn, grandson of the Prophet, at the battle of Kerbala.

For the *Mawlad*, the holiday celebrating the birth of the Prophet, the meal consisted of *aʿsīda*, in Morocco as well as Tunisia. The month of fasting, the Ramadan, was simultaneously a month of culinary opulence. Even the poor had meat every evening. The fast was broken by a swallow of water and a few dates. After a pause, a meal was served that required no particular food or dish. However, during the evening, large quantities of sweets were served. The household ledgers of the bey give a good idea of the nature of this extravagance: one can see the amounts spent every year during Ramadan for *zlābia*, nougat, and other sweets. The month ended in the *Aid-es-seghir*. At that time the chief concern was to renew one's clothing rather than serve rich foods. Nonetheless, family visits provided the occasion for eating sweets.

On the most important of all holidays, the *Aid el kebir*, it was customary to commemorate the sacrifice of Abraham by slaughtering an animal whose meat was eaten by the family, a part distributed among the needy, and a part preserved for the last day of the year.

The Hegiran calendar, based on the lunar cycle, runs counter to the farmer's almanac as it does to the Julian year: the cycle of Islam coexists with the cycle of agriculture. It too was marked by culinary rituals. For example, on the first of May and the days immediately following, large quantities of sausages were eaten and houses were decorated with flowers and fruits.[42] This was a period of outdoor festivals, races, the distribution of dried fruits and marmalades: the typical country fair. Along with these regularly recurring holidays were ceremonies that accompany farm work: The *a'sīda* was shared by the peasants associated in field work and harvesting; an animal was sacrificed and the meat shared when rain was lacking and the intercession of a local marabout had been deemed necessary; another sacrifice was performed at the time of the annual pilgrimage to a favorite shrine. The form of this ritual, though not known by the same name, is reminiscent of the *tīmechret* of the Kabyles, who shared the meat with no distinction of rank or wealth among all the members of the community.[43]

There was also feasting at the time of family celebrations each time a member of the group had a change of status. Birth, circumcision, and marriage were the occasion of feasts marked by great prodigality, especially in sweets. Even death brought together the family of the deceased around repasts that were frugal to start with (bread and olives were passed around after the funeral), becoming ampler later on: Relatives brought food to the immediate family of the deceased, which was reciprocated at the end of the mourning period. Two or three months later the women immediately related to the deceased met at the cemetery for a funereal meal.[44]

The decision to start something, such as the departure for summer pastures or the weaving of a rug for the tent, was an event to celebrate. The arrival of an unexpected guest could also be cause to celebrate. All observers have remarked that the notion of hospitality was generally spread throughout the Maghreb, and beyond, in other lands of Islam, whether the guest was a Christian or a pauper. But most of those European travelers were mistaken about the nature of this welcome, seeing in it only a form of politeness, the application of a rule of good manners. The reception always followed the same order. Let us turn to the eighteenth-century English traveler, Dr. Shaw: "When we arrived at the tent the master brought us a pitcher of milk, a basket of figs, grapes, dates, and other dried fruits."[45] This first collation is the same one described earlier for the beginning of the year for the Tunisian Muslim; it is the food offering presented in Morocco to the traveler or pilgrim on his return home, to the newly betrothed, to the people who assist in piercing the ears of a young girl. The intention is always the same: Milk, sweet fruits, and foods with seeds symbolize the peace and prosperity that should accompany entrance or reentrance into the group or the departure from it. "He then went to select a lamb, a sheep or a goat from his herd," Shaw continues, "depending on the number of the company, and having killed it, gives it to his wife who immediately boils half of it, which she serves with the cuscasowe [*sic*] keeping the rest for a communal meal of kabab the day after, which was served for our lunch or dinner." The sacrifice of an animal and a meal taken together were more important as a ritual of communion than was the quality or quantity of the meal. Hospitality was therefore the restoration of order disturbed by the arrival of the stranger; the sealing of an alliance by the sharing of a meal; or the reduction of the mysterious, sacred mission carried by the stranger and his eruption into the family circle. The code of good manners was thus first of all a religious code.

Reciprocal exchanges, pilgrimages, and processions

The life of the Tunisian peasant unfolded in a religious climate. The day was measured by the five prayers; the Hegiran calendar announced the feast days, the month of fasting, the date of pilgrimage. First names given to children evoked the Prophet, his family, and his most prestigious namesakes. There is no clergy in Islam to assist the dying or officiate at weddings, but every act, public or private, every public address began or ended with a prayer to God. Education was based on holy writ: Law, ethics, and even aesthetics were for the most part commanded by the Koran. Within the living space of the peasant, each village had its mosque; each *dawār*, a tent that served in its place: It was a school and a place for meditation through which boys attained, and adults maintained, membership in the great community of believers. The world of rituals goes beyond the world of Islam. As with culinary customs, other practices were based on a dual system: Along with Islamic time was ecological time, solar time, which had its own rites and in which believers managed to insert a deviated Islam, interpreted according to their needs. Days and months were affected by a positive or negative sign that encouraged or inhibited all undertakings. Thursday and Sunday were preferred for the initiation of any action. The beginning of the Muslim year and the *mayou* of the solar calendar were unpropitious for beginnings.

Work and prayer, agricultural rituals and Muslim dogma are divisions well suited to analysis. In fact, all aspects of reality, all of life's moments, provide an even greater complexity of meanings. No social activity was without religious connotation, no gesture of piety was without a social context. Mention was made earlier of the alimentary obligation occasioned by certain holidays. They were not the only ones. Such obligations were part of an entire system of regulated exchanges that older documentation generally neglected but that recent ethnology has brought to light. Within the circle of family relations or the level of the village, cooperation was organized for both masculine and feminine labors. The men plowed, harvested, and threshed, gathered olives, sheared sheep, and constructed houses; the women prepared the reserves of food and set up the looms – all of which activities were publicly announced and collectively undertaken at the home of the man or woman who invited the relatives and neighbors. It was the obligation of the host family to feed the co-workers and to reciprocate the same service when the occasion arose.[46]

Joint aid, *maʿūna*, also occurs at the time of important events in the life of the family: birth, circumcision, marriage. Peyssonnel describes how on the day of a wedding, the guests come bearing gifts which a scribe lists "so that they can be reciprocated when the guests marry off their daughters."[47] Later observations confirm and amplify Peyssonnel's. At Zarzis, for example, at the beginning of the century, when a wedding day was set, the women got together to grind the wheat for the couscous that would be served at the wedding feast. Four days before the wedding, the nuptial tent was set up by the widows and divorcees, and the men brought the wood for the evening fire. When the parents of the bride and groom received their relatives and friends, they all came laden with food: meat, wheat, and so on. In Gafsa, when a marriage contract was concluded the presents were displayed with all the food and henna given by family and friends and were then carried to the house of the bride. During the feast that preceded the wedding, each guest gave the bride silver coins whose sum total was announced publicly. When the bride came into the nuptial chamber, "the women present her with butter that they rub on a piece of wood that is on the hearth, asking aloud that God fulfill their wishes for the newlyweds by blessing their marriage, and by increasing their herd so that the milk will rise all the way to the roof of their tent. After that, the bride is lowered from her horse and is given a wooden peg, which she herself places in the ground, intended to teach her that, just as the peg cannot come out of the ground unless pulled, so the woman may not leave her husband unless he sends her away."[48] It was the Reverend Father Dan who in 1637 described this rite and interpreted it. Three centuries later one finds the same story, word for word, in the Nafzāwah, with the slight difference that the phallic symbol is clearly recognizable: "I planted a stick and gave birth to a boy," says the bride. Earlier, she broke an egg, tinted with henna or saffron, against the lintel of the door or against a wall – a complementary symbol of her fecundity and, if the egg stuck to the wall, of the solidity of the marriage.[49]

These same events recurred, the same obligations were undertaken and discharged, over and over again, whether in conjunction with family celebrations or with activities that appeared to be strictly economic. This circulation of goods and services occurred between members of the same collectivity, familial or local. Relationships among kin, or more broadly, among neighbors, imposed these manifestations of solidarity. When, for example, construction of a house began, it was indeed a building enterprise and masons were needed for their technical ability. But their collaboration was gratuitous, and the direction and execution of the work fell to the head of the family, assisted by his family and friends. The construction of a house, which established a new family unit both in space and in matter, was therefore a social affair. The very word *tuīza* or *maʿūna* designates not only exchanges of productive work but exchanges at holidays as well.

This complex mutual assistance allows for a circulation of wealth, a redistribution of goods, and a regrouping of abilities and has, in a sense, an economic function. The creation of obligations among the members of a community strengthens relations and confirms the place of each individual within the society. Whoever exempts himself, or challenges the norm by not repaying what he received and beyond, undermines the entire social fabric, which demands repayment, or excludes himself. These practices therefore permit a social order to maintain itself while testing itself, and to perpetuate itself. In that transfer of goods and services there are, moreover, some participants who are not present, or at least are not visible. Occult forces, which can be malevolent, affect every moment of the life of the group and the individual. In these societies, strained by lines of fission and rupture, close relatives or neighbors can be bringers and accomplices of misfortune. To participate in the collective enterprise is therefore to collaborate in the preservation of harmony. To refuse to do so is to deliberately prevent things from developing according to the normal order; it is to instigate trouble and disoblige the collectivity. This explains the choice of gifts: grains, whose multiplicity augurs wealth; henna, whose prophylactic properties are well known; and silver coins.

To ward off hostile forces, envious people, or the "evil eye," there were gestures and behavior codified by the group: words – propitiatory formulas and exorcisms; and silences – words one would avoid pronouncing, subjects one would abstain from broaching. And finally there were signs all around: for example, the five fingers of the open hand, painted or molded on the front of the house. To protect themselves against spells Father Dan notes, "They always have a few hands represented on the walls of their houses, be they only of thatch, and for this very reason, they give silver or copper coins to small children who wear them on their bonnets."[50] Five is a lucky number; the five fingers were powerful enough to blind an evildoer. The dried tongue of a chameleon, worn around the neck, had the same effect; a passage from the Koran, slipped inside the skullcap or worn over the heart, prevented misfortune. Similar amulets were placed around the necks of horses and sheep.

The soil and all surrounding space were not merely physical phenomena. When a man opened a field with a first plowing, the help of his kin increased not only his physical strength but also his chances of a good harvest.[51] And the meal taken communally on the field was shared as much with the soil, to which the wife offered a portion of her *aʿsīda* by burying it at the end of a furrow, as with the workers.

Nature was the hiding place of *jnūn*, indefinite beings who can be good but when injured bring sickness, misery, or death. And since there was always the chance of crushing those tiny creatures, who sometimes took the shape of a toad, a worm, or an insect, their wrathful actions had either to be accomplished or dispelled by sacrifices and fumigations of incense and aromatic plants, or else one rid oneself of their spell by dancing.[52]

Space was inhabited by latent forces. Still visible today, mausoleums are perched on heights, erected in deserted places. Invariably, those familiar with the region will explain that they are shrines to a traveler, a pilgrim who died on that spot, offered by the inhabitants as a tomb. The propensity of those pilgrims to die all alone on elevations is most curious! A similar common practice regarding saints of the Maghreb was to situate their burial place wherever the animal carrying their remains stopped. On that spot, as for the pilgrims, the faithful constructed, not the modest tomb they erect for themselves, but a veritable dwelling, visible to all. There was a cult of the tombs of saints, but not of those of unknown travelers. The shrine erected in their honor was not without meaning, however. It protected the space around it and delivered the inhabitants of the region from the dangers that lurk everywhere.

Natural elements, people, and things were thus subject to evil, to ambiguous signs, which at the very least had to be neutralized, and at best, domesticated in the most concrete meaning of the word: One turned negative forces to profit, changed the direction of the vector, transformed a hostile space into a refuge, a stranger into someone familiar, a foreigner into an ally.

In the final analysis, these precautions, these provisions, which governed work, food preparations, and discourse, point to the constant anxiety of a vulnerable people, their uncertainty in the face of a material world that their technical means were inadequate to daunt. "Charming superstitions," Father Dan continually remarks; superstructures, our contemporaries would say, inseparable, in fact, from the precariousness of material life.

Exterior space was marked with these protective tombs (*kubbas*). But the poles to which the piety of believers gravitated were the *zāwiyas*, at the same time the tomb of a saint, the residence of his or her descendants, a shrine, and a hospice for pilgrims. The sainted men and women buried there were in many cases miracle workers and healers. A few have already been mentioned. There were others. For instance, Sidi Mansūr, in Gafsa, restored life to a traveler's camel; Sidi Khalifa, in the region of Sfax, increased the volume of grain for a taxpayer hard put to pay the tithe. Saida Um Yahia, in the same region, freed a fugitive prisoner pursued by the bey's guards. Even after death, the marabouts continued to exercise their power: Anyone taking a false oath on the tomb of Sidi Mansūr died before long. The same punishment awaited anyone stealing from silos near the tomb of Saida Um Yahia. The tomb of Sidi el Hani offered a cure to the sick and to sterile women. These tombs inspired such confidence that the peasants built their silos there and left them unguarded, under the watchful care of the saints, as in Mech, where the inhabitants were away for part of the year, or at Hazeg near Sfax.[53]

Although villagers generally found a local marabout to honor, some of these pious figures, more venerated than others and renowned for their ability to cure specific ills, occasioned the displacement of the villagers themselves. As for the nomads, they offered yearly homage to a marabout of their devotion. At fixed periods, they made a pilgrimage to the shrine, bearing food and animals to be sacrificed and shared with the progeny of the saint. The annual *ziāra* took place in May, before the harvest, to guarantee its success, or in the autumn, after plowing, to give thanks to the saint. The political and social function of these saints and saintly places has already been discussed; they were products of the Maghreb, completely alien to Muslim orthodoxy. They also ensured the continuity and abundance of resources and the health of the believers who enlist their intercession. Between them and the peasants a relationship was established on the model of the one between the peasants themselves: Along with presents, the latter offered a *maʿūna* in work, an obligation of gratuitous services on the lands of the *zāwiya*. The reciprocity in this case was of an entirely different nature, since the services rendered by the marabout were not the same as those offered by the peasants in exchange. The same vocabulary of reciprocity was used though a relationship of inequality entered into the practice.

In Morocco shrines fulfilled the same purpose and were often protectors of markets as well. Located on boundaries between warring groups, they assured peaceful transactions. This was not the case in Tunisia, where commercial exchanges – limited by the near self-sufficiency of the economy and the frugality of eating and dressing – could easily take place in villages, rural markets, or towns. The transfer of basic products did not have to occur in a souk or with money. When the Hamāma went to Gafsa and Tozeur, it was partly in the form of barter that the animals, wool, or grindstones were exchanged for dates. When some of the Hamāma went to bring in the harvest in the north, and other nomads harvested grain followed by olives in the Sahel, they were paid in kind for their work. As to the markets, they had more than an economic function. In the rural souks frequented by the members of different groups, meeting was an occasion to identify and differentiate themselves, by their products as much as by their clothes and their tattoos, which indicated the geographic origin of each.[54] In monoethnic markets, a fortiori, more news than products was exchanged. Among the Mogod, for example, at the Friday souk, the elders discussed the tribe's general concerns and fixed the price to be asked at the market of Mateur, where the Mogod used to trade. Among the Wārgha there were even two markets: one, where merchandise was brought, produce was bought, and implements forged in the twenty or so tents that served as shops; the other, where gossip was exchanged and quarrels settled. The market in this case functioned as a forum, a public square. It had its counterpart in the Moroccan Atlas, and in the Algerian Tell where a citizen was expected to attend the souk even if he had nothing to buy or sell.[55]

Just as the pilgrimage, a gesture of piety, had a social, political, and economic significance, so in many cases coming to the market had a political and social meaning.

Part III

A society in the process of underdevelopment

Up to this point, we have tried to reveal the structures of rural Tunisian society through a synchronic analysis. By structures, we mean that which lasts, in the sense understood by Fernand Braudel and historians: age-old techniques, direct relationships between people and land, and between the people themselves, which are not given to abrupt change; changes in detail that, all in all, modify neither social relations nor basic living conditions. We mean structures also in the sense understood by the other social sciences: the cohesive parts of a whole, the purpose of the analysis being not only to isolate the parts but, even more, to clarify their relationship to one another. In the case of Tunisia, the system of lineage, with its network of alliances and rivalries, underlay the appropriation of land and provided a framework within which production as well as the circulation of people and products could be organized. It also shaped the social praxis all the way to outbreaks of violence.

This society, whose description may suggest some kind of inert machine, nonetheless had its own dynamism and was also affected by the dynamism of other groups with which it had relations. It is therefore advisable to examine it in another setting, a vaster one, whose boundaries are marked by the cities – particularly the capital, and the reigning power – and by the Mediterranean ports; we must examine the society over time as well, each level of analysis having its own chronology, the different sequences fitting into an overall scheme.

We shall begin by evaluating the growth potential of the population across the ebb and flow of epidemics and then move to the rhythms of the agrarian economy, such as can be ascertained from changes in price, variations in areas cultivated, and revenues from taxes. A third factor is maritime trade, insofar as it affected rural life. And finally, we shall look at the changes that occurred in the relationship between the state and the population, particularly regarding the modification of fiscal policy.

6. Demographic calamities and economic conjuncture in the eighteenth and nineteenth centuries[1]

The recurrence of plague at the end of the eighteenth century

With regard to demography, contemporary observers of the eighteenth century stated that the population was growing, whereas all those of the nineteenth persisted in claiming that the population was declining. Epidemiologic history seems to prove each group right. After the dreadful plague of 1702–5 had devastated the country, as it had Libya and Egypt, Tunisia was spared until 1784. It enjoyed a long respite that allowed for an increase in the population. Toward the end of the eighteenth century, however, a severe famine in 1776–9 was followed by a new outbreak of plague in 1784–5, then again from 1794 to 1800, and once more in 1818–20. The plague abated, relayed as a recurring calamity by cholera, which first broke out in 1849–50.

It is not possible to measure the effects of these diseases, which were exacerbated by poor harvests. But what can be said, to begin with, is that Tunisia belongs in a category whose ancient demographic structure, marked by the periodic renewal of terrible crises, continued all through the nineteenth century. In Western Europe, the cholera outbreak of 1830 left a lasting memory because of its pandemic nature, and also because it was an outrage. Western Europe, free of the plague, no longer remembered the kind of widespread mortality that such a disease could cause. But in the Mediterranean? Let us look at the Mediterranean countries and at a calendar of epidemics (Maps 6.1–3). The eastern and southern parts of the basin had no respite. The presence of the disease was so constant that one cannot even speak of an alternating cycle of good years and tragic years. Those countries remained endemic breeding grounds. The population was constantly threatened. Whole generations were wiped out by the repeated passage of these diseases; they could be replaced only by a very high birth rate.

Is this continuity of demographic crises the cause or the symptom of the delayed economic and social development of these regions? It is too soon to tell. One can, in any case, accept that a demography of this kind[2]

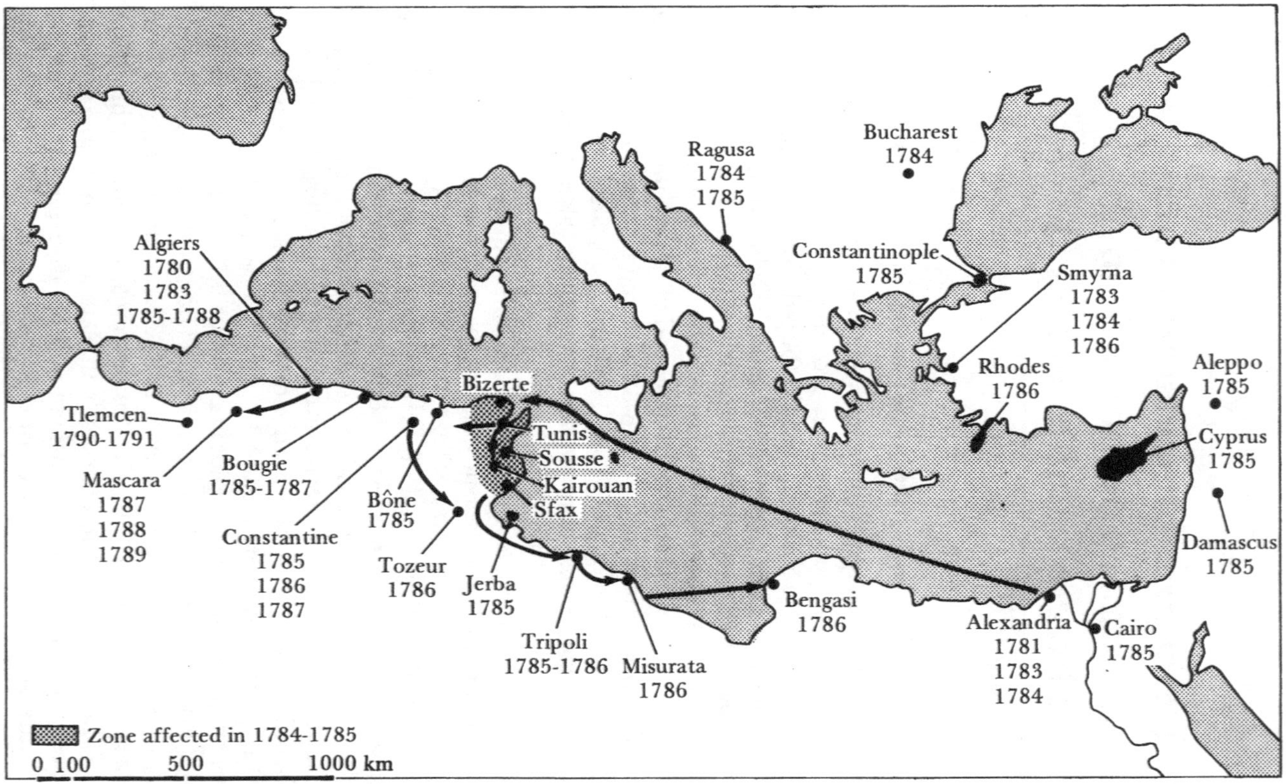

Map 6.1. Incidences of plague in the Mediterranean basin, 1780–9.

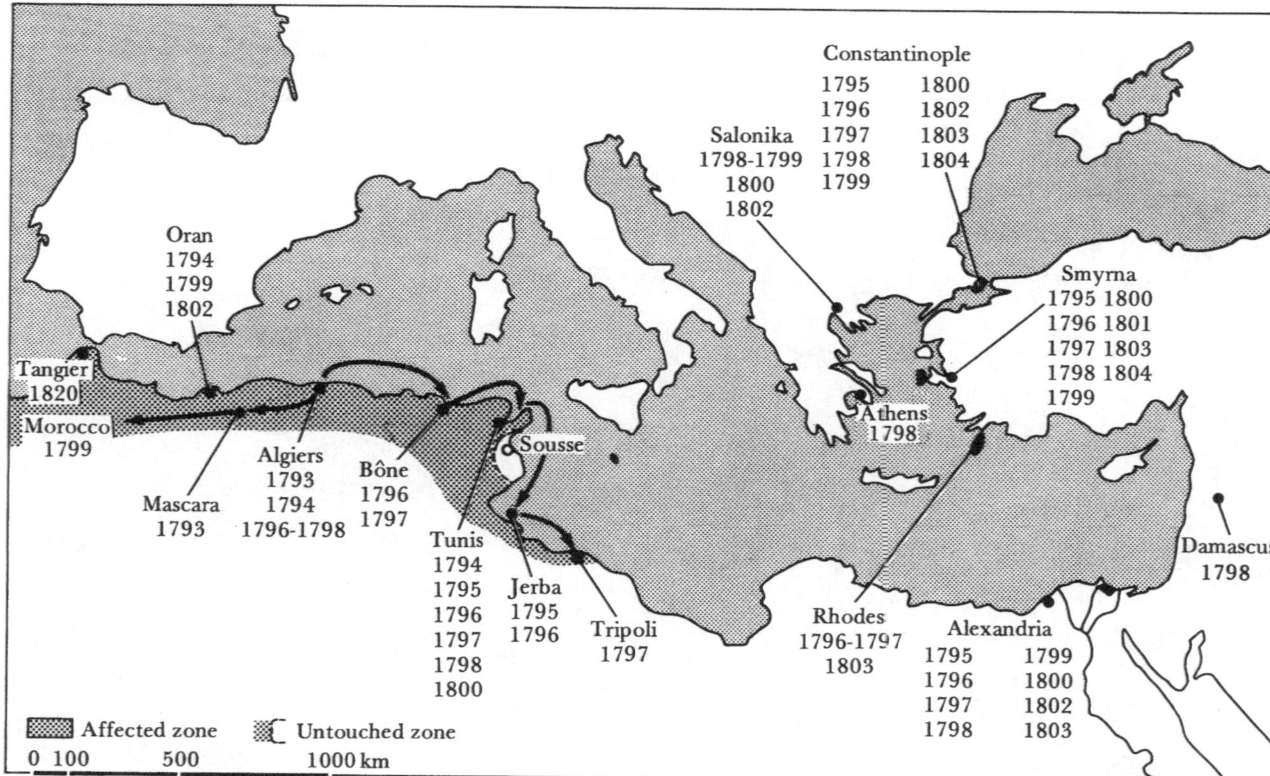

Map 6.2. Incidences of plague in the Mediterranean basin, 1793–1804.

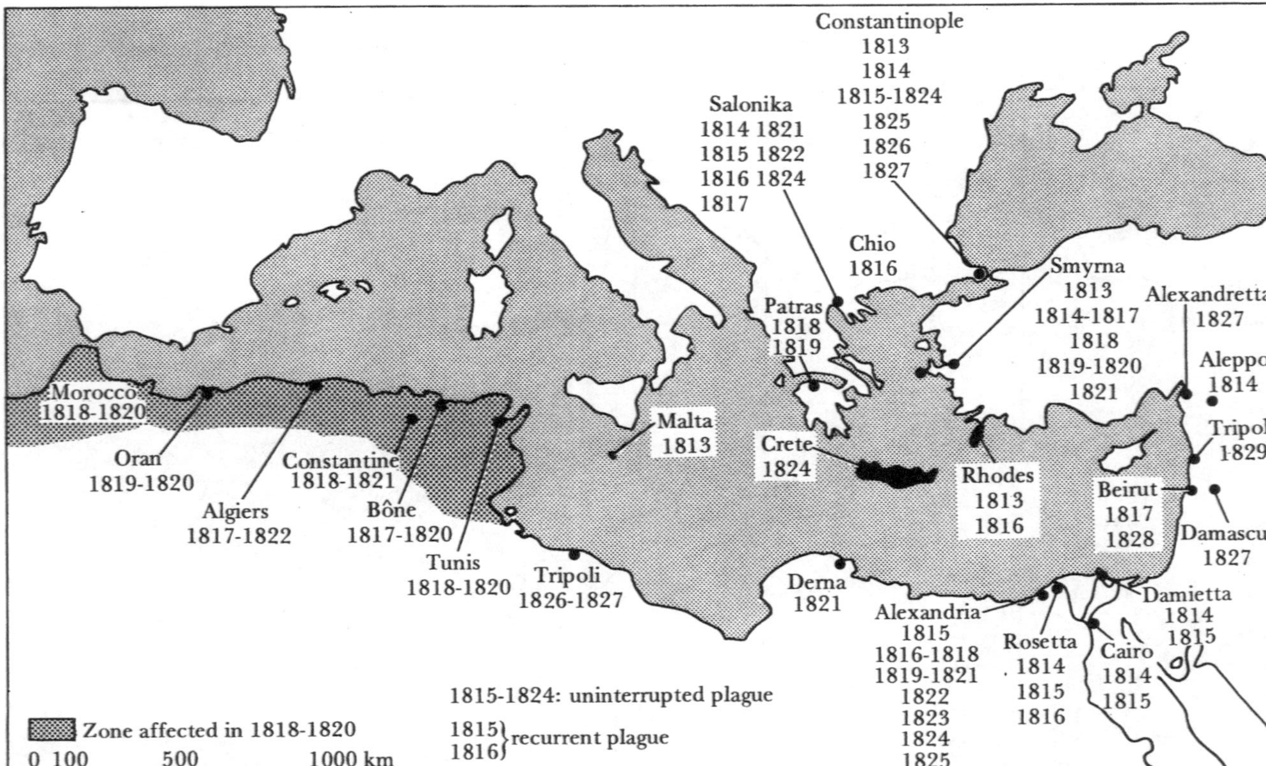

Map 6.3. Incidences of plague in the Mediterranean basin, 1813–30.

gives rise to a cumulative process. If the poverty of the people made them vulnerable to disease, the terrible tolls it took inhibited the activation of the social body. The distance that European progress created between developed and underdeveloped countries was thereby increased. Today one of the dominant characteristics of underdevelopment is the contradiction between an exploding population and the relative rigidity of its resources. It is perhaps not paradoxical to say that this underdevelopment grew out of an inverse conjuncture. In North Africa a "heavy" demography, that is, the number of people and their pressure, varied little from one generation to the next. In northwestern Europe, a progressive demography, the multiplication of people, encouraged economic growth and made it possible.

The age pyramid in 1862 and the problem of repopulation

The frequency of demographic disasters raises the question of the replacement of generations. After enduring such repeated attacks of epidemics and famines, is a population not worn out? Can it renew itself? The construction and analysis of an age pyramid for 1862 provide a unique and valuable method for arriving at an answer. It would indeed have been helpful to have a later census to compare with the one taken in 1862 and measure more carefully the actual possibilities for the replacement of the generations. Since this census is not available, we shall have to make do with the single census of 1862. Comparative data from three regional groups at least provide for greater substantiation in the discussion.

The first region, Cape Bon, is already familiar.[3] The second, five villages in the region of Porto Farina, was systematically surveyed for the ages of the male population at the same time as Cape Bon: In all, 2,000 individuals were accounted for. And finally, dispersed among twelve villages or hamlets, the Waslatiya constitute the third group investigated: 1,125 males.[4]

These surveys reveal a great many anomalies. Allowance must be made for fraud, willful or not, and for the army. Fraud can cause whole families to disappear. In Hammamet, for example, the number of adult males exceeded 600 in two censuses,[5] but in the one that interests us, there were barely 400. However, even though the heads of families and their children eluded the count, that should not modify the profile of the pyramid. A second source of error is that some children born during the year of the census do not appear in it. There will thus be figures in the category zero to one year old that are lower than they should be. In addition, a preference for round numbers, "the decimal appeal," is evident, particularly after the age of twenty. And finally, in view of the tax affecting men over the age of eighteen in Porto Farina, one can expect an inflation of figures in categories immediately preceding the taxable age. This reprieve secured by fraudulent reports does not appear in other surveys, however. On the contrary, since conscription takes young men, the pyramid is artificially indented, as in the case of the Waslatiya, 200 of whom were in the army, as well as Porto Farina and Galaat el Andleuss, with 143 conscripts. Since their age was not indicated, it is not possible to fill the gap on the pyramid left by their departure.

These irregularities do not prevent the observation of common factors in all three groups. The first, already stressed by Ganiage, is the wide spread at the base of the pyramid, indicating a high birth rate. The proportion of youths below the age of twenty is 62.8 percent, 50 percent, and 50.7 percent respectively, in the three groups under consideration. Since old men represent less than 10 percent of the population, this distribution, as Ganiage points out, relates the age pyramid with the "young" model of the demographers. That it is young is clear, but is it progressive? For one thing, a sudden and deep indentation appears in all three pyramids, pointing to a high incidence of mortality. For another, deep indentations appear in some other age groups indicating, despite the fraudulent reports already mentioned, the demographic catastrophes that followed one another during the preceding decades. Some were synchronous with the three pyramids, and others were staggered.

A calculation of the number of births during the twenty years preceding the census revealed unfavorable years in all three groups: the crisis of 1855–6 caused by cholera and felt everywhere; the epidemic of 1850, unequally reflected in the three groups; in 1848–9, smallpox caused an indentation in the curves; and in 1845–6, a childhood disease must have reduced the number of survivors of those years. Everywhere one can see the proximity and frequency of crises, the brevity of periods of respite, and the rapid reduction of population.

Comparison with the age pyramid for Tunisia a century later, although methodologically imprecise, is at least useful in revealing certain phenomena.[6] To begin with, the birth rate was and remained high. On the other hand, the more recent pyramid is much less concave than the earlier one; mortality decreased considerably over the century, and all the age categories benefited from this progress (Fig. 6.1). The drop in mortality would seem to be responsible for the sizable demographic growth during the century. Although the replacement of generations is now more than amply assured, the contrast between the two pyramids confirms our doubts about the dynamism of the Tunisian population around 1860. Whereas children under the age of ten represented 33–45 percent of the population in 1862 (31 percent in 1956), youths between fifteen and nineteen accounted for only 7–7.6 percent, as opposed

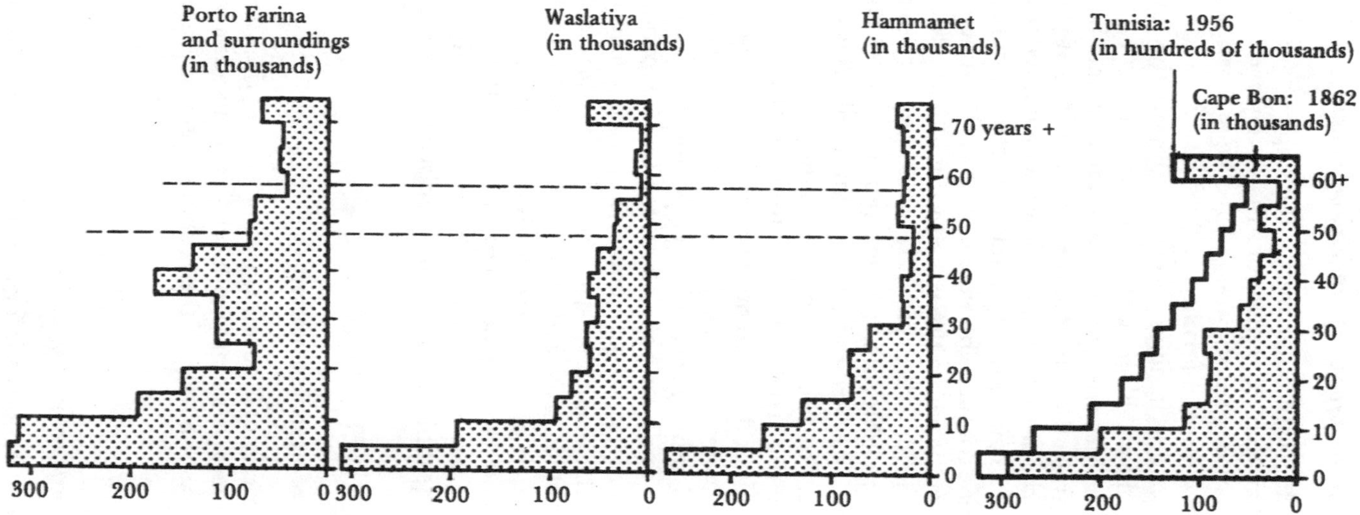

Fig. 6.1. Age pyramid for 1862 and 1956.

to 9.4 percent in 1956. In other words, the hope of survival was small, probably lower than that of populations that today are the most underdeveloped. Population growth would have been possible only under conditions of above-normal fertility.

The history of a few families serves to support this hypothesis. In notarized documents establishing the origin of properties, the history of these landholders is reconstructed down to the first one; in other words, these documents trace the entire succession and indicate who was married and who had children. One can follow over a number of generations whether each time a couple was formed, it succeeded in replacing itself. In the first case, nine couples who were married in the nineteenth century had fifteen children of whom three died without issue; twelve survived, but were less prolific than their parents. In another, eleven couples were formed between the eighteenth and nineteenth centuries, corresponding to five generations. They produced twenty-three children, of whom three died without issue. For twenty-two parents there were twenty children, the same rate as for the first example. On the basis of seven contemporary samples (eighteenth and nineteenth centuries) the replacement of generations was barely assured, despite simultaneous or successive polygamy.[7]

We would need other surveys to verify this one. It is nonetheless probable that the Tunisian population, far from expanding, was in a phase of regression. Is this an anomaly? Xavier Yacono was able to demonstrate that the demography of Algeria was regressive from 1830 to 1870.[8] The troubles provoked by French occupation were doubtless responsible for much of this decrease. But that is not the only cause, since epidemics and famines occurred at almost the same time as in Tunisia. It is therefore not unreasonable to propose the hypothesis of a negative demographic variation in Tunisia during the nineteenth century.

The two periods of agrarian activity

If the eighteenth century permits a somewhat optimistic view of the population of Tunisia, the nineteenth century demands a more cautious diagnosis. What was the state of the economy, and how are we to judge it?

First index of economic activity: prices[9]

The first instrument in determining the health of the economy is a history of prices. However, there is nothing in the archives that makes possible the reconstruction of a homogeneous, coherent, and trustworthy series.

Information is irregular and of varying quality, adequate merely to trace a few curves that can suggest general trends; to seek out the overall relationship between products and the changes in that relationship over a period of time; and finally, to find the major accidents, if the curves agree enough to make them emerge.

Let us take four basic products: wheat, barley, olive oil, and dried beans (Fig. 6.2).[10] The curves indicate, first of all, a general increase in base prices between the beginning of the eighteenth century and the nineteenth. Wheat falls into roughly three periods: the early eighteenth century, for which the few available figures are below ten riāls (or Tunisian piasters); from 1735 to the end of the century, with figures grouped between twenty and forty riāls; and the third period, the beginning of the nineteenth century, when a *qafīz* of wheat exceeded fifty riāls. Superimposed on the curve for wheat, the curve for barley tells the same story: prices quintupled in a century. Both grains show a more marked increase in 1739–42, 1776–9, and 1803–6. The curves drop between 1760 and 1762, and again in 1770–1. For dried beans, the curves cover a shorter period and confirm the increase observed in the first two commodities. The same holds true for oil: The price of a *mtār* more than doubled between the first and third quarters of the century. This was followed by a period of relative stability, and then, after 1805, prices started to climb again.

Let us now look at secondary products: honey, raisins, almonds, and dates. The figures are more accurate and the monthly entries more regular, making it possible to calculate average prices. On all these curves, the trend toward increased prices is confirmed, though to a lesser degree than for basic products. Rice, a supplementary food and a strategic one (it was the mainstay of seafaring pirates), increased as much as domestic products. Also in line with the price of basic products is wool.

These curves reveal three critical moments when prices increased dramatically. First, from 1739 to 1742, the price of wheat, followed by barley and rice, doubled suddenly. The three curves drop simultaneously from 1760 to 1762, and again in 1770–1, suggesting a period of abundance on the marketplace. A new crisis in subsistence began in 1776: four years of high prices for wheat and barley. In 1770–8, beans followed the trend, then rice in 1779, and dates and honey in 1779–80. In 1778, grain, beans, and honey all became costly when the crisis reached its peak. The third phase of troubles occurred between 1803 and 1806 with a rise in the prices of barley and wheat.

As proof of validity, do our curves concur with the accounts of contemporaries? They note first of all a crisis in subsistence foods at the beginning of the century that had not been apparent in the absence of quantitative data. All the disasters that befell the country occurred to-

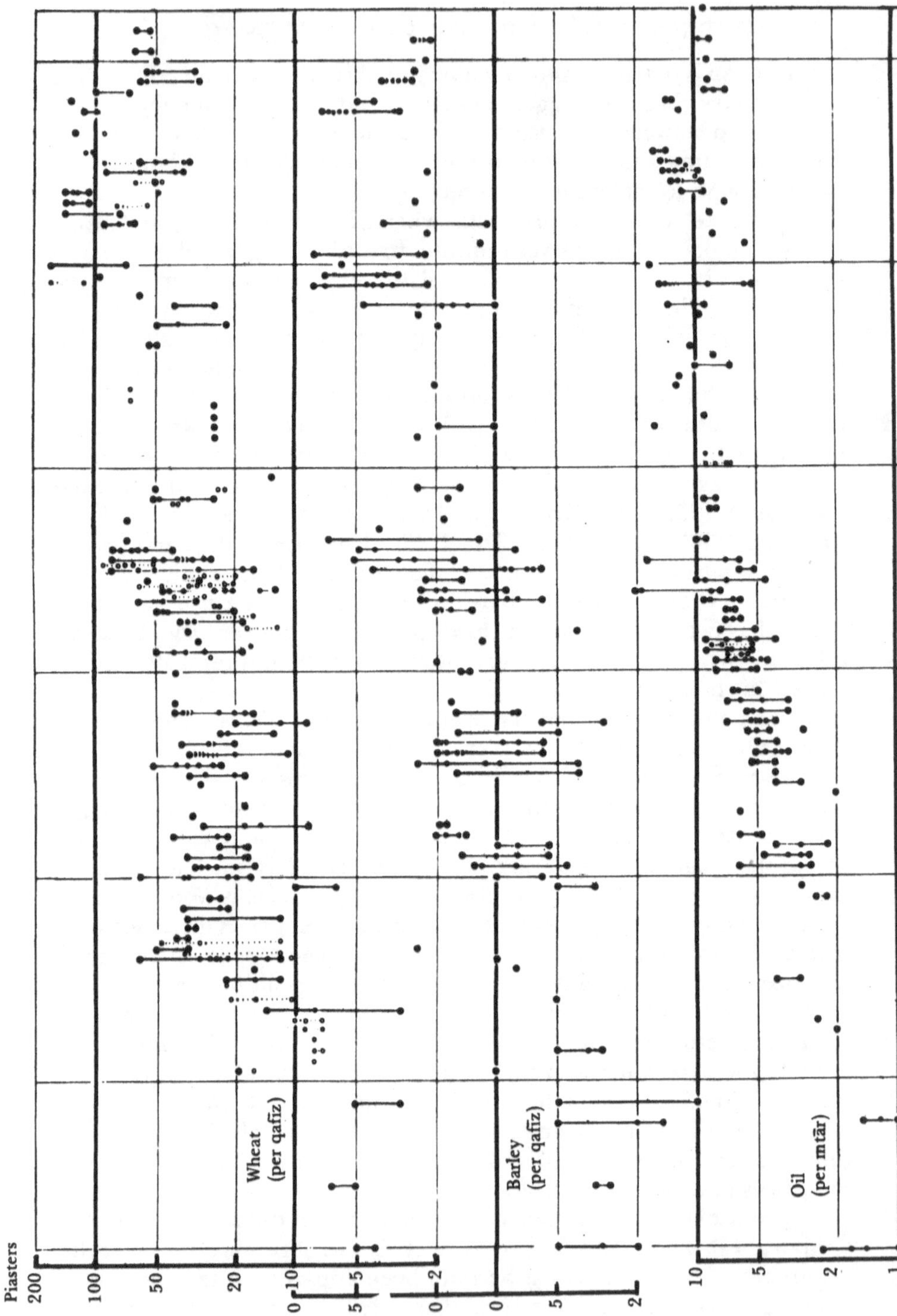
Piasters
Wheat (per qafīz)
Barley (per qafīz)
Oil (per mtār)
200
100
50
20
10
5
2
1

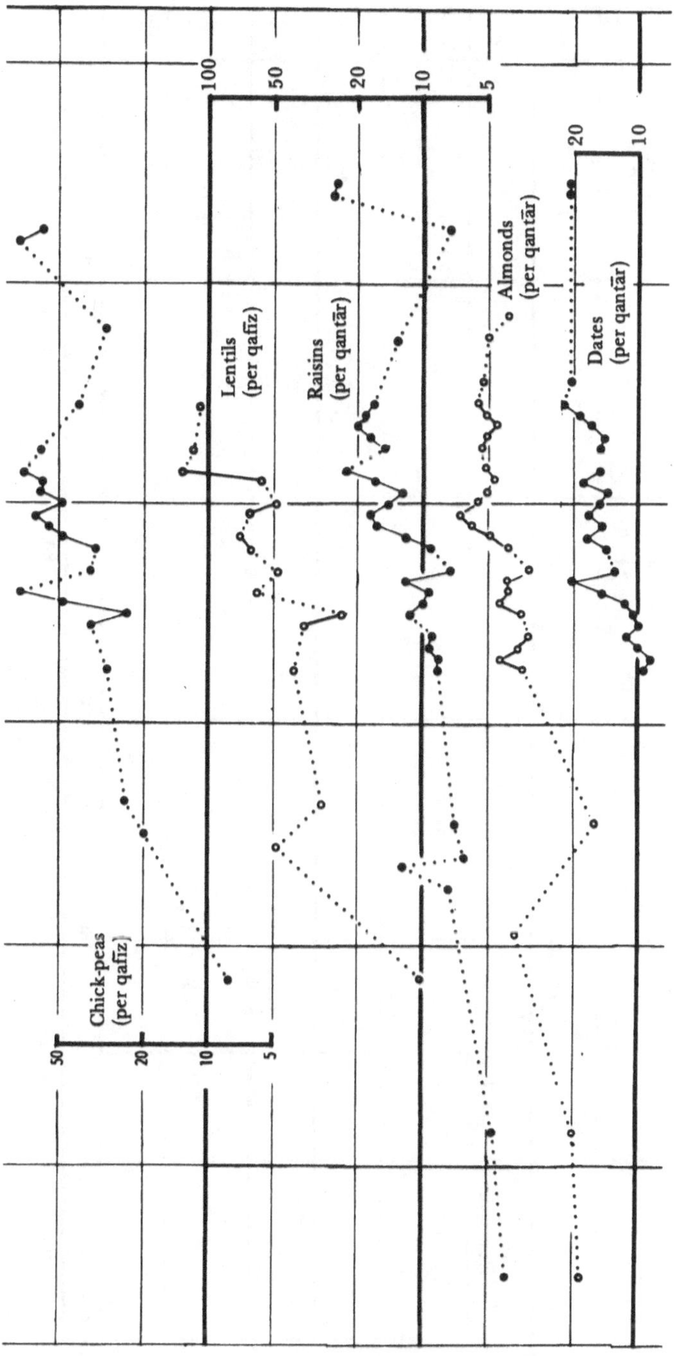

Fig. 6.2. Nominal prices (*continued on next page*).

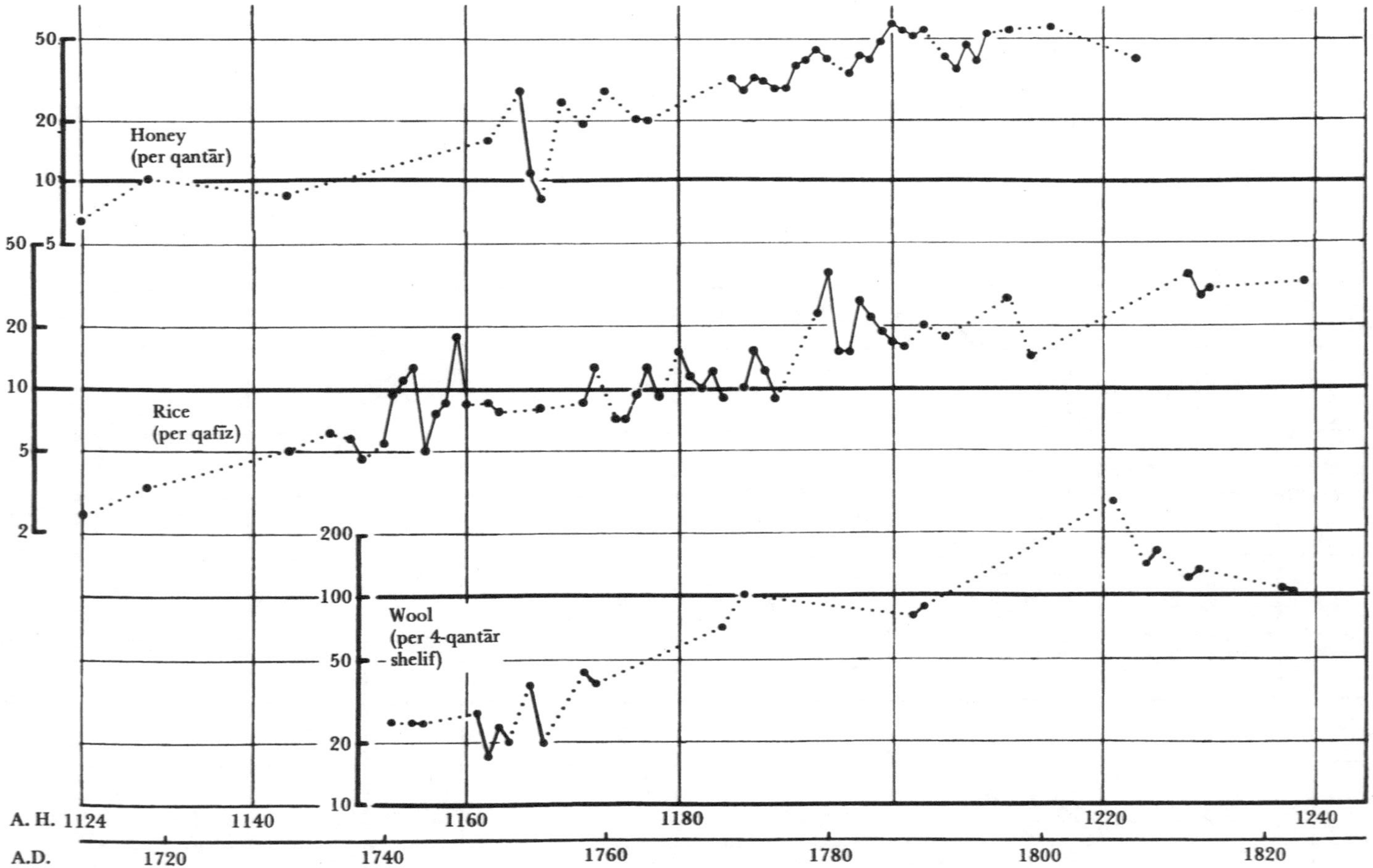

Fig. 6.2. Nominal prices.

gether. In 1701 the harvest was small. Little was sown because an invasion from Algeria was feared. In the autumn of 1701 the rains did not come until December, the threat of war still hung over the country, and planting was curtailed. In the spring locusts devastated the harvest, prices soared, and famine set in, which the bey tried to alleviate by requisitioning cargos of wheat from the Levant destined for Marseille. Tunis imported grain from Smyrna. In the summer of 1703 the harvest was poor. The country had emptied its reserves.[11]

In 1709 plenty reigned in the land. Genoa and France outdid each other in their purchase of grain. In December 1709 the Compagnie d'Afrique had no more room in its station at Cape Negre to store grain. "We send away Moors who bring more every day," while famine raged in France. In January, an urgent request was made for additional ships, since all the company's vessels were already overloaded. In 1719 another bumper harvest coincided with a famine in Provence. In the interim, we learn, crops failed in 1717 because of a severe drought.[12]

Contemporary accounts confirm the price curves: hardships in 1729–30, prosperity in the three following years. Then, a civil war and a new threat of invasion from Algiers caused a reduction in sowing and production. During the first quarter of 1737, Tunisia imported fava beans, barley, and wheat, indicating that reserves from the preceding summer had been depleted. On our curves, the prices of wheat and barley took a sharp rise. They did not reach those of the crisis years of 1739–41. As of the winter of 1740, contemporary witnesses speak of the depletion of reserves from the last harvest, a prolonged drought, and the absence of a new harvest. In fact, in February "people everywhere are dying of hunger." In Cape Negre, far from exporting grain, agents of the royal company were bringing it in from Marseille.[13]

As to falling curves of 1746 and the low point of 1747 contemporaries say nothing. They do confirm, however, the penury of the year 1758: Barley reached twenty-five riāls and wheat was twice as much. From 1766 to 1772 there is general optimism about the regularity of sowing, the extension of plowlands, and the volume of harvests. Prices went up, but not excessively.[14]

The terrible famine of 1776–9 caused a reversal of the conjuncture. The dryness of the winter of 1776 became alarming; by the summer it was evident that "the harvest this year will be half of last year's." The situation worsened the following year. In 1777 and 1778 contemporaries describe the grain shortage from Libya to Morocco, the poor quality of bread, pillaged caravans, seizures of hidden wheat, and popular uprisings. In Tunis, five hangings took place before order was restored. Exports, needless to say, were halted. Wheat even had to be imported from the Levant and from Europe.[15] On our curves, spiraling prices indicate the disappearance of basic foods.

A new crisis occurred in 1804–6: The harvest was no sooner brought in than grain disappeared from the markets. In August 1804, "it is only through brawls and riots that the Moors manage to grab a bit of wheat, far below their needs." The price of a *qafīz* of wheat, which had fallen below 50 riāls after the last famine, rose to 168 in 1804. Tunisia was not the only country to suffer from famine at the time. In 1805 people were dying of hunger in Constantine.[16]

Contemporaries thus confirm the oscillations in conjuncture that are traced by our curves. The increase in basic prices over the century was apparent to them as well. The chronicler Seghir ben Youssef cites figures and regrets the good old days of Bey Husayn (1705–35), a time of plenty and low prices. "Ever since 1726–7, when food prices had remained low and that year particularly so," he wrote in 1763–4, "prices have not stopped rising." His contemporary, the historian and minister, Hammūda lbn ʿAbdalaziz, did more than merely take note of the rise in prices; he interpreted it approvingly. According to him, price increases affected all products: cloth, mounts, implements, fruit, condiments, and above all, land. There was less of an increase in grain prices because of bumper crops. This overall increase, he argues, was beneficent; it encouraged economic activity, developed consumption, and promoted the exportation of grain and the importation of foreign goods. However, the discrepancy between the increased price of land, draft animals, and labor, on the one hand, and the price of wheat on the other, ultimately discouraged the farmer. After having benefited from an extension of cultivated land, the country suffered yet another reduction in sowing in 1776. This discussion of the symptoms and effects of economic growth has a modern ring, and the author provides the explanation: For several decades, there had been no war, no epidemic, no famine in the country.

Rising prices would thus be a symptom of economic growth. Before endorsing Ibn ʿAbdalaziz's analysis, let us amend nominal prices in terms of the real value of the Tunisian piaster (Fig. 6.3).

The curves tend to follow a horizontal line, illustrating an unusual case of a history of frozen prices. If honey, raisins, and dates confirm the increase at the end of the century, prices of other products undergo short-term oscillations that reflect the quality of the harvests but not at all the rising trend indicated by nominal prices. Contemporaries could indeed feel the effects of that increase, which expressed only the depreciation of Tunisian currency.[17] Although nominal prices may suggest growth, real prices reveal a fundamental immobility.

Second index: cultivated surfaces

Let us not lose sight of the fact that the economy of the regency was essentially a subsistence economy; services – herding, farm labor, and so on – were reciprocal or were repaid in kind; many exchanges took place in barter. In short, the circulation of money was limited to a very small segment of the population. Consequently, the price of food on the marketplace can provide only lateral information on the situation in the countryside.

If we wish to approach the reality of economic life more closely, we should, and can, follow other paths than the one laid out by a history of prices. A profile of agrarian activity can be traced from data provided by the bey's holdings. They were leased each year, the rent was in produce, and the rate did not vary. What did change, however, was the area cultivated. Variations in plowland can thus serve as an index of the economic conjuncture in the countryside.

Managerial accounts from a certain number of the bey's domains were kept more or less continuously from the middle of the eighteenth century to 1840.[18] These properties were all situated north of the ridge, in the most temperate part of the country, where the annual rainfall is 400–600 millimeters. They were all plowlands, or if there were other crops, they were not part of the tithe. The production was therefore homogeneous and consequently provides valid evidence of the prosperity or penury experienced in Ifriqīya during the eighteenth and nineteenth centuries.

Translated into curves, the changes in cultivated areas on these properties indicate first of all the wide range of variations. One enormous farm of more than 100 hectares was reduced drastically: Ras el ʿAin, in the region of Mateur, covering eleven plow units (or roughly 110 hectares) in 1774–81, shrank to three units seven years later; left fallow in 1826–7, the farm was expanded once again to 70 hectares in 1829. The *henshīr* Derqīsh, in the region of Tunis, went from the extremes of half a *māshia* in 1805 to 56 *māshia* in 1814. El Hauāria, in the canton of Béja, was less than 20 hectares in 1780–83; between 1786 and 1793, it tripled; it quadrupled two years later; and was seven times greater in 1800. These jumps are not exceptional. On the contrary, for most of the estates there were years of expansion and periods of contraction (Fig. 6.4).

In addition to the amplitude of these variations, the curves indicate two successive, contradictory trends: a marked increase in cultivated lands and their general reduction.

There are few continuous data for the first decades of the eighteenth century, but the results agree.[19] Seven properties in the region of Tunis

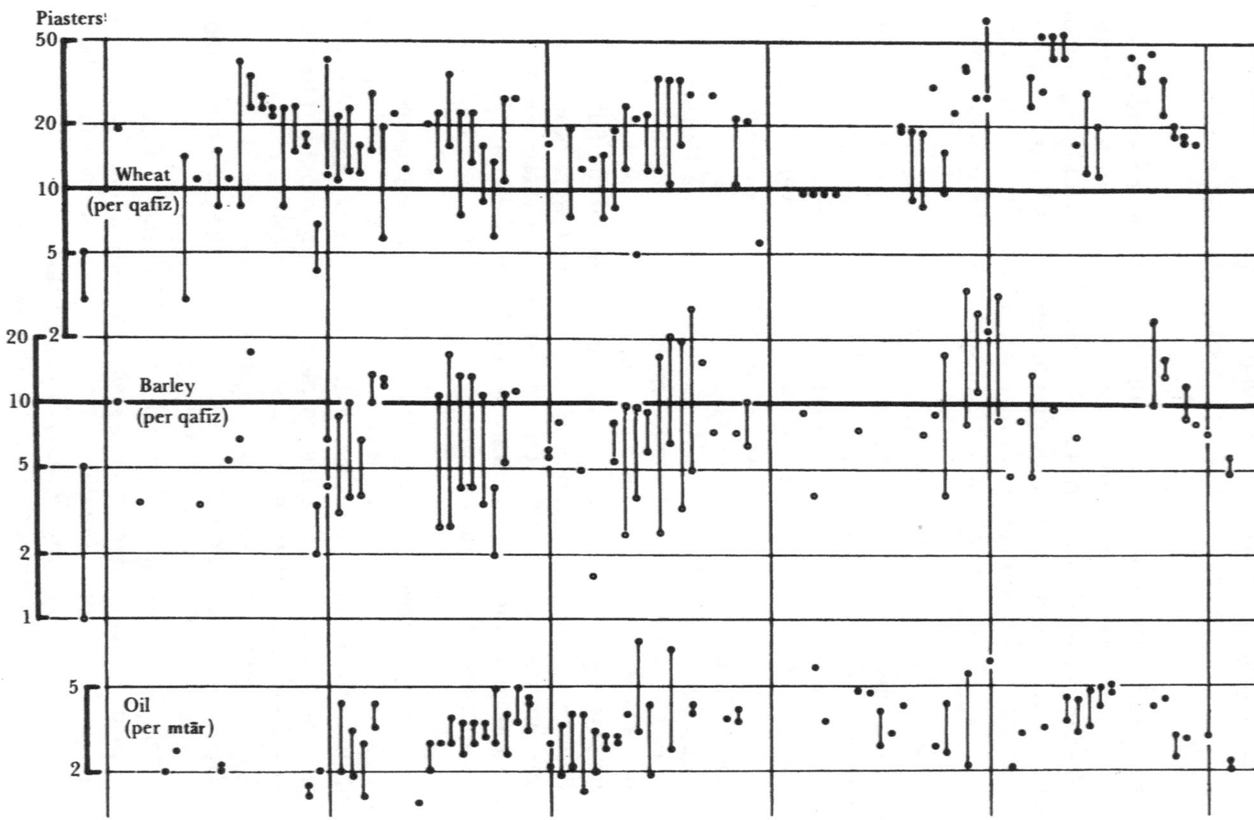
Piasters
50
20
10
5
2
Wheat
(per qafīz)
20
10
5
2
1
Barley
(per qafīz)
5
2
Oil
(per mtār)

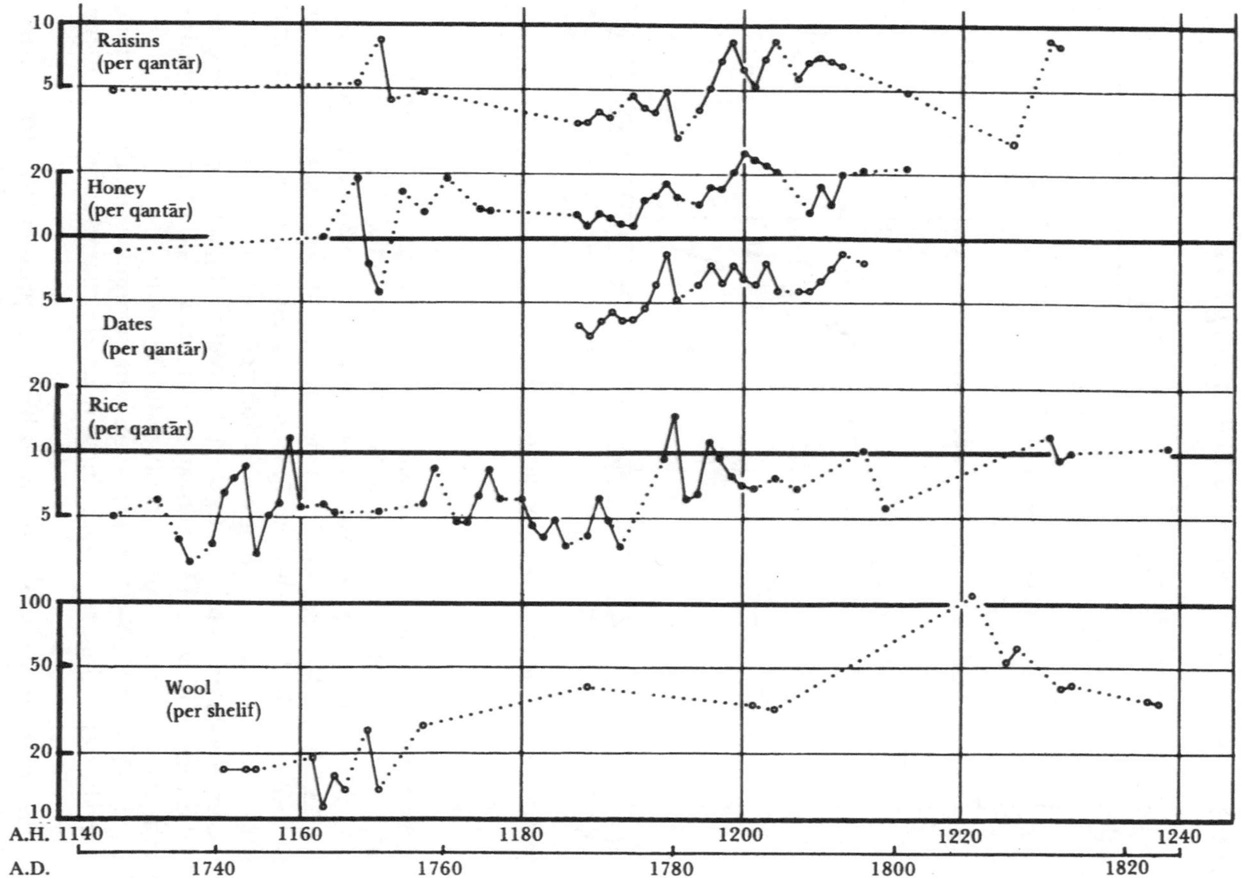

Fig. 6.3. Deflated prices.

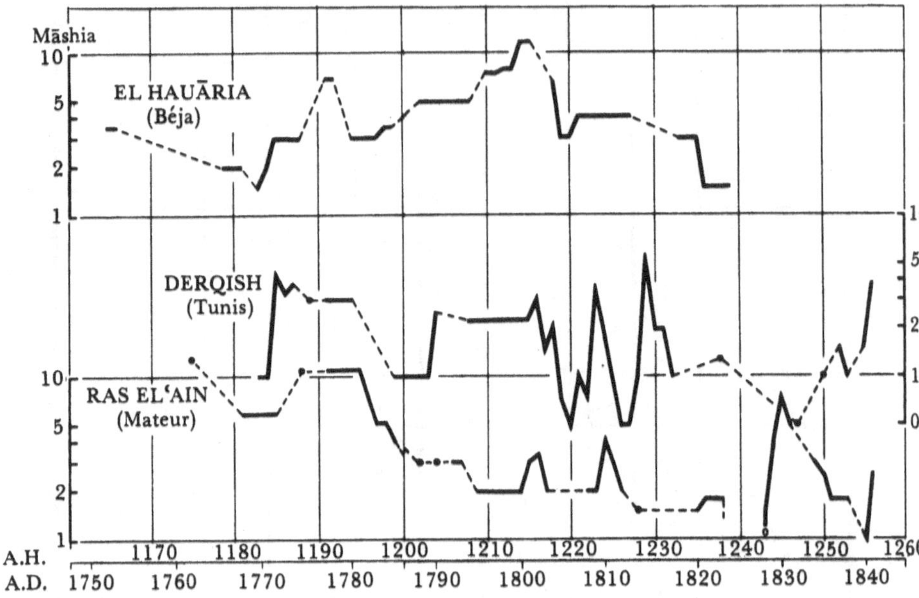

Fig. 6.4. Surfaces cultivated: extent of variations (I).

covered 35 *māshia* in 1717–18, and 41, twenty years later. Five, whose cultivated area reached 22 hectares in 1717, extended to 35.5 in 1761–3. In the region of Mateur, seven estates went from 31 *māshia* in 1725–6 to 53.5 in 1751–2. Six were recorded in 1737–8; their surface was then 49.5 *māshia*, which increased to 71 *māshia* fifteen years later. Eight farms, of 275 hectares in 1737–8, grew to 465 hectares in 1761. Even if these discontinuous reference points do not reveal changes in detail, the general direction is clear: The cultivation of land was increasingly intensive from the first decades of the century to the sixth.

For the years 1753–74, information is more regular and the variations both shorter and more visible: These years are characterized by stability (Fig. 6.5).

This tranquil phase was followed by a few prosperous years during which the size of farms grew considerably. Beginning in 1769, and above all between 1770 and 1774, most of the farms in the region of Mateur reached their maximum dimensions. A sampling of seven estates attests to an increase in surface greater than 30 percent. A similarly vigorous increase occurred in the region of Bizerte. Comparison with later years marks 1774 as the apogee in the expansion of cultivated lands around

Tunis. The estates in Béja, however, do not seem to have participated in this growth. Their dimensions did not change during those years.

Contemporaries had already observed that stability was followed by abundance. Four consecutive years had bountiful harvests: 1766, 1767, 1768, and 1769. In 1767 the French consul predicted that the country had reserves for ten years! If prosperity in 1773 and 1774 was less widespread, because of little rain in certain regions, 1775 was once again a year of bumper crops.

As a result, the ban on exporting grain was lifted. Except during winter months, when the bey waited for the forecast of the next harvest before allowing any grain to leave the country, the regency exported it every year. Tunisian grain went to Europe, which was always ready to buy, and to the Levant as well. Though itself normally an exporter of wheat, the Levant made massive purchases in 1769, and again from 1771 to 1773.[20] The enormous growth in commercial activity between 1771 and 1775 and the related increase in grain sales, which filled the holds of four out of five French ships, reflect the prodigality of farm production. What was true for the regency of Tunis was equally true for the rest of the Barbary Coast. Analyzing grain trade in Marseille, R. Romano noted that imports from North Africa, scattered from 1756 to 1768, became heavier and more continuous from 1768 to 1777. The agricultural and commercial prosperity of Tunisia was thus shared by the regency of Algiers at least in its eastern sector.

The authorization to export grain and the briskness of trade boosted the economy, encouraged farming, raised prices, and enriched the ruler – who sold export licenses – along with his subjects. Urban activities enjoyed a similar prosperity in 1769–74.[21] There was even an upheaval in the thinking of Tunisians, who gave in to the delusions of a consumer economy. The French consul, de Saizieu (in agreement, moreover, with Hammūda Ibn ʿAbdelaziz), was astonished by the sudden passion for European products.

> I can scarcely imagine the effect and suddenness of this revolution in the minds and opinions of the leaders as well as the people of Tunis, whom I knew as sober, peaceful, and miserable up until the time when produce from the regency attracted a host of ships and foreigners from all nations, providing it in less than four years with such a quantity of gold, silver, and precious goods that it has the highest standard of wealth and trade in the Levant. But this situation can only last so long as European consumption and the shortfall of its harvests require the purchase of foodstuffs produced by the Barbary Coast and from which the bey derives the chief principal profit through the prodigious royalties he gets from their exportation.[22]

In fact, without any change in European needs, as projected by the consul, a change in conjuncture occurred in Tunisia that shattered the

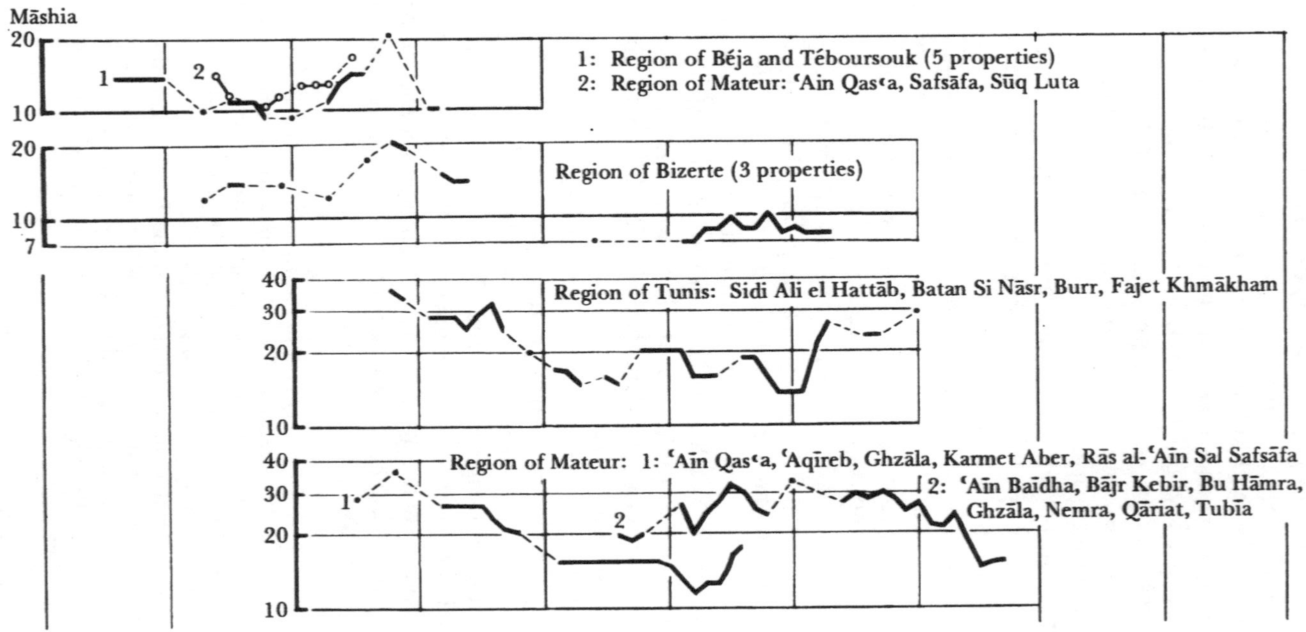

Māshia
20
10
1
2
1: Region of Béja and Téboursouk (5 properties)
2: Region of Mateur: ʿAin Qasʿa, Safsāfa, Sūq Luta
20
10
7
Region of Bizerte (3 properties)
40
30
20
10
Region of Tunis: Sidi Ali el Hattāb, Batan Si Nāsr, Burr, Fajet Khmākham
40
30
20
10
Region of Mateur: 1: ʿAīn Qasʿa, ʿAqīreb, Ghzāla, Karmet Aber, Rās al-ʿAīn Sal Safsāfa
2: ʿAīn Baīdha, Bājr Kebir, Bu Hāmra, Ghzāla, Nemra, Qāriat, Tubīa
1
2

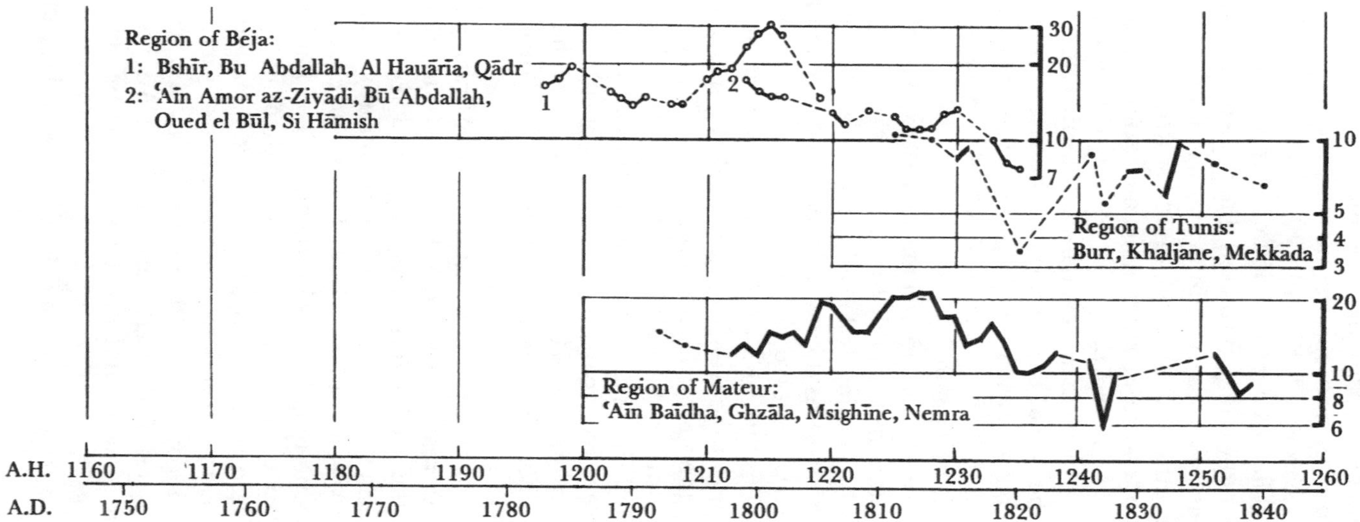

Fig. 6.5. Surfaces cultivated: extent of variations (II).

movement of economic expansion. A period of reduced farming set in. After 1775, and in all the cantons, the curves indicate first of all a trough whose bottom lies between 1785 and 1795. As an example, properties in Mateur can be followed over a period of twenty years. After the peak in 1774 (thirty-six plow units), farmland diminished radically by 25 percent in 1778 (twenty-six units), continuing at that level until 1781. Then there was a new contraction: In 1786, the cultivated area of all six properties amounted to less than sixteen units and remained that way for a number of years. The lowest point did not occur until 1797, when the six farms came to no more than eleven units. The first signs of an upturn first appeared at the end of the century. In the case of other properties, the upward trend began earlier – in 1796 – but was irregular. The years 1797–8, 1802–3, and 1806–8 were marked by new lows. The level of 1774 was never reached again.

In Bizerte, not even this improvement took place. Farms remained in the depressed conditions of 1788 for twenty years and more.[23] Near Tunis the decline in farming followed the same pattern as at Mateur. The decade of 1785–94 was the most dismal. The increase in cultivated land that had begun was interrupted in 1797–9 and particularly in 1804–6. The years 1800–1, 1808, and 1814 seem to have been more favorable. Between the bottom of the trend and the peak, figures doubled.

In Téboursouk the lowest figures date from 1783–4. The level remained very low during the following decade. The situation righted itself beginning in 1796 and continuing into 1805. Conversely, 1806, 1807, and 1808 were bad years. The same conjuncture can be seen in Béja: The curves drop in 1784 and 1785, poor conditions remaining stable until 1796. There the respite was short-lived. A steady decline can be seen after 1800.

Not all these trends have the same meaning. The first drops registered correspond to those years of crisis that befell the country from 1776 to 1778. The scarcity of seed determined the reduction in sowing and the consequent shrinkage of farmland. Harvests improved from 1779 to 1784 and rainfall was abundant. Nevertheless our curves continue to fall. This drop has nothing to do with drought. The harvests were said to be "promising, if there are hands to bring them in." For it was the plague that paralyzed rural activity and, even after abating, it continued to exercise prolonged effects on the cultivation of land. If the rural sector was slow to recover, it was doubtless due to new outcrops of the epidemic until the end of the eighteenth century. Another shortage in 1804 discouraged plowing and can be seen on our curves for Béja, Mateur, and Tunis.

To summarize, during the second half of the eighteenth century –

under the reign of Ali Bey – agricultural activity was helped by abundant rainfall and stimulated by grain trade. "Ever since the reign of Ali Bey, the father of Hamoudeh Pasha," wrote a French observer, "very considerable improvements have taken place in the kingdom. It is estimated that cultivated land increased more than a third, through the export of grain and oil that is allowed every year."[24] With the first famine of 1776–8, a succession of demographic and climactic disasters slowed activity.

As for the first half of the nineteenth century, from 1815 to 1840 there was no durable improvement of conditions. If we compare the levels for 1752–76 and 1805–29, the worst years of the first period equal the best of the second. *Henshīrs* in the regions of Tunis (Bechatr, Morra), Mateur (ʿUilīa, Sushāna, Ghzāla, Safsāfa, Tuīrq), and Bizerte (Ghirāṇ) admirably illustrate this fact. The total averages for all these properties is 43.2 *māshia* for the first period and 23.4 for the second. These figures, however modest, measure the reduction of plowlands.

As for 1858, we have only sketchy information but it is nonetheless eloquent. All the farms shrank to ridiculous dimensions. Ghirān, the most prosperous, was not even three units. By the middle of the nineteenth century, the trend to reduced farmland had not been reversed. Thirty years later, French officials in their investigations in the north of the regency still observed the great number of oversized farms, the limited cultivation, and the expanse of lands left fallow.[25]

Various factors were responsible for this collapse. Once again, we can point to consecutive years of lean cattle. After a mediocre harvest in 1815 the country experienced three years of famine in 1816, 1817, and 1818. In the year 1817, to relieve the famine, Bey Husayn sold wheat from his own lands below market prices. He chartered ships to bring in grain from Italy and Alexandria. There were additional imports in 1818.[26] The plague, it will be remembered, began its ravages at that time and lasted until 1820. Then, in 1820, drought destroyed the harvests and food had to be imported once again. It is not surprising to see farming reduced, particularly during the years 1819–21. In 1821 the harvest was good but not abundant. Fields had been left fallow for want of seed.

For the whole first third of the nineteenth century, only 1824 and 1826 produced good harvests, at which time Tunisia was once again in a position to export grain: nearly 100,000 hectoliters of wheat and barley in 1824, and 347,000 in 1826. These years were followed by a mediocre harvest in 1827, and none at all in 1828 and 1829. In 1830 drought burned and sterilized the fields. Is there any need to continue this chronology? Statements from contemporaries are so unanimous that one becomes distrustful, suspecting the repetition of a received idea among the European colony of Tunis. However, figures justify their pessimism. The historian Ibn Abi Dhiaf relates how, under the reign of Ahmad Bey, he was obliged to show the minister Kheireddin the farm ledgers: The *henshīrs* were "white," barren.[27] These are the ledgers we consulted. In the first part of the nineteenth century, Tunisia had little manpower, cultivated surfaces were reduced, and the country was no longer able to produce enough for its needs.

Between the middle of the eighteenth century and the middle of the nineteenth, the reigns of Muhammad and Ali corresponded to a period of prosperity. Hammūda Pāsha (1782–1814) began his in an unfavorable conjuncture. Then there were a few years of recuperation, during which the curves remained fluctuating, the situation uncertain. During subsequent reigns, that period would be remembered as one of plenty. In fact, after the death of Hammūda Pāsha the reduction of cultivated land attests to the grave economic recession that beset the regency of Tunis.

Final index: revenue from the tithe

While waiting for the disparate and discontinuous series of data on the tithe to be completed one day, let us use them in the meantime as signposts (Figs. 6.6, 6.7).[28] The first fact to emerge is, once again, the extreme irregularity of production. Barley harvests vary in ratios of 1 to 12 in Monastir, 1 to 25 in the north; wheat varies from 1 to 30 in the north, and even more in Sfax, where, in certain years, there was no harvest at all. Crops sown between 1780 and 1782 brought nothing into the treasury.

In the Sahel, during the second half of the eighteenth century, there were a few good years from 1751 to 1755, but 1750 was a disaster and three bad harvests followed one after the other between 1756 and 1758. In the north, the curve reached its highest peak around 1760. Bad harvests occurred in 1791 and 1808, years that other indexes have not revealed as particularly short. For 1816–19 the curves fall sharply, confirming the conjunction of a terrible drought with an epidemic of plague. In Testour, as the scribe clearly points out, many threshing floors were empty in 1819 and 1820; in Slouguia, all of them were. This village, which had 50–100 taxpayers, depending on the year, had *not one* in 1819 and 1820.

In Cape Bon, the treasury benefited from three good years: 1810, 1815, and 1844. In the intervening years the curves were concave. For the peasants, it was surely a period of recession and uncertainty. Oil had

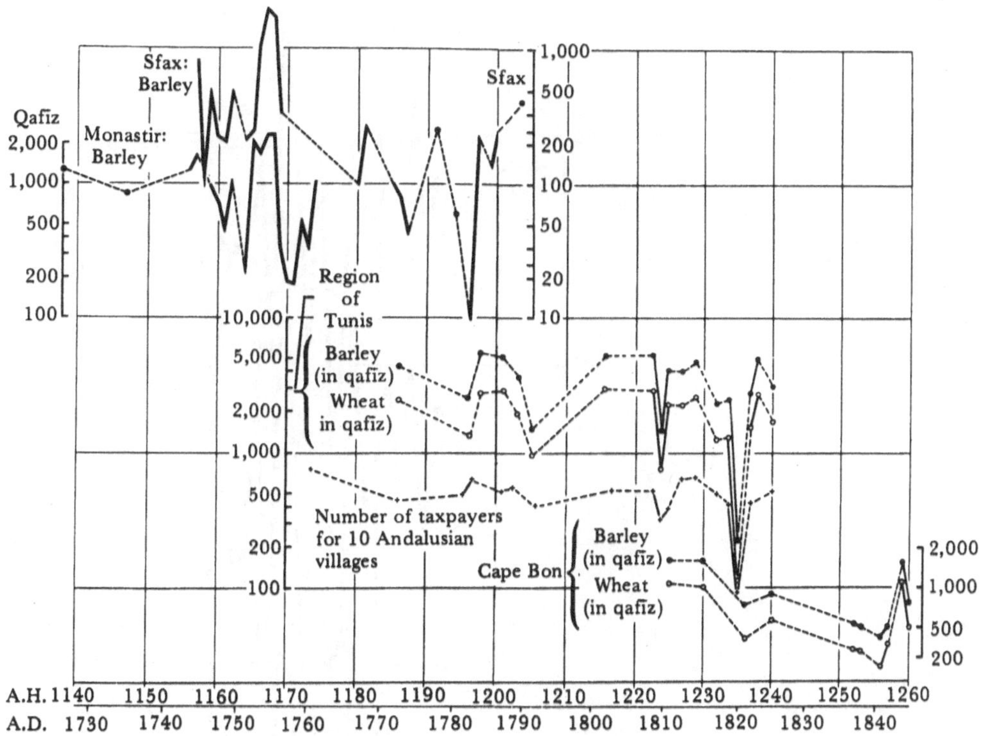

Fig. 6.6. The tithe on grains.

two good years in 1826 and 1832, each followed by poor olive harvests, whose consequences will be seen shortly.

Alimentary shortfalls and demographic crises therefore came together beginning in 1775. From a demographic viewpoint, peace had reigned over the land since the beginning of the century. As of 1784, catastrophes occurred at closer intervals, which drained the population and thus canceled the upward trend. From an economic point of view, the progress made in farming reached its peak around 1775. Then the whole mechanism halted and reversed direction. The misery that settled on the land during 1776–80 initiated a crisis, which was followed by a general reduction in planting, and consequently in production. Although never regular in the eighteenth century, when years of plenty alternated with years of penury, in the nineteenth century inadequate harvests had become chronic and abundance was exceptional. The multiplication and

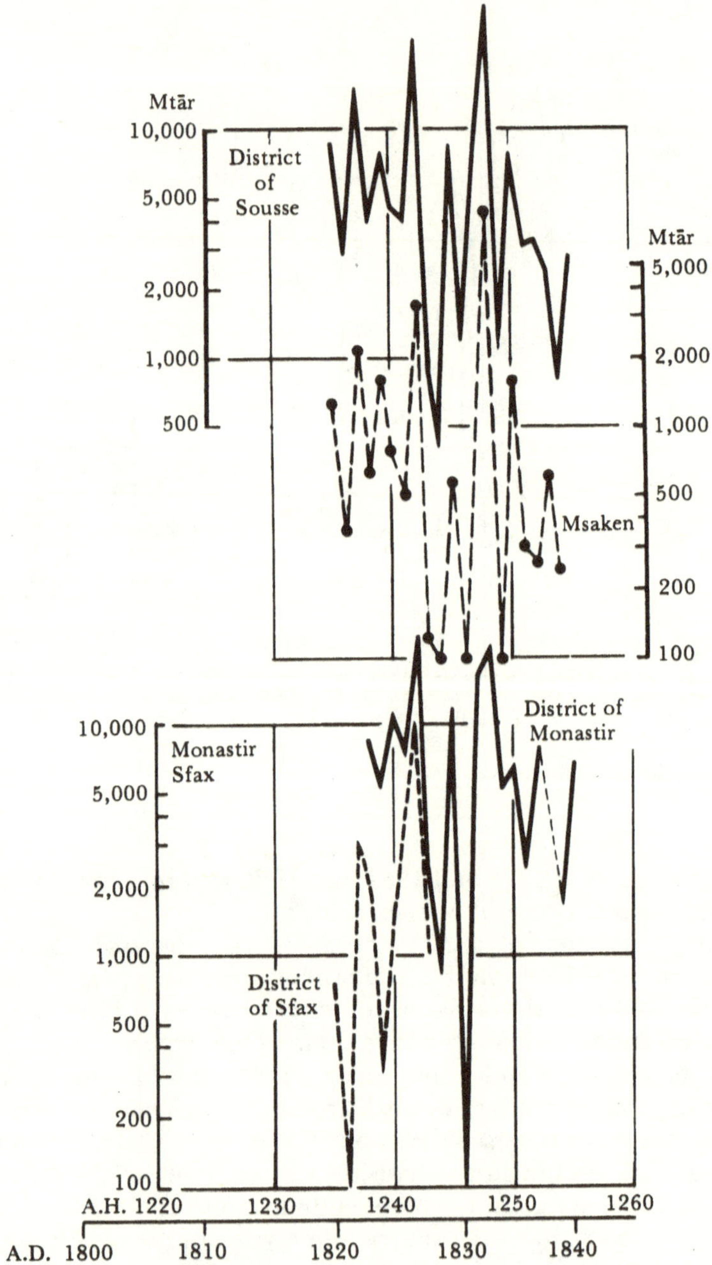

Fig. 6.7. The tithe on oil.

concentration of disastrous events mark the last decades of the eighteenth century and most of the nineteenth century.

Simultaneously, other factors aggravated the situation: modifications in trade between Tunisia and Europe and changes in fiscal practices.

7. ❧ The advent of a trade economy

To examine the economic exchanges between Tunisia and Europe is also to study how one economic system fits into other systems, in this case, how the Tunisian economy related to European capitalism that continued its irresistible expansion on the other side of the Mediterranean. By what means was commerce organized, what products were involved, and what effects did it have on the social fabric of Tunisia?

Leaving the lightly traced path of rural history, we now rejoin an itinerary marked out by the numerous works of economic historians, from Masson to Debbasch and other more recent writers. Having already presented the mechanisms of a trade economy in an earlier book, I shall try not to repeat the results of those analyses. Let us merely see what elements most directly affected the Tunisian peasants.

Instruments of payment and exchange

Currencies circulating in the eighteenth and nineteenth centuries

What currencies were used for payment, trade, and public accounts? As far back as I was able to go – the end of the seventeenth century – in examining fiscal practices under the regency,[1] I found mention of two currencies, the *riāl* and the *dinār*. The second was also known as *dahab*, gold. For example, the personal tax was five dahabs per "house," or "room," whereas the tax on olive trees was expressed in riāls, and its subdivision *nāsris*. These two monies can be found throughout the eighteenth century. Their rate of exchange never varied: 100 riāls equaled 162 dinārs, or 100 dinārs were worth 61.5 riāls.[2]

The silver riāl and gold dinār constituted the "national" currency. But this is not the only money mentioned in payments made to and by the bey. Around the mid-eighteenth century, the doubloon and half-doubloon, the *bunduqi* or Venetian sequin, the *sharifi*, i.e., the Ottoman gold coin, and the *sma'ili*, which is probably identical to a coin of Moroccan provenance, were also in use in the Bardo. Some years later, along with the Venetian and Turkish sequins, one also finds the *funduqli* sequin, another gold coin from Istanbul, the sharifi from Tripoli and Algiers, and later, the *qurūsh*, a silver coin worth forty *paras* minted in Istanbul, circulating in the palace. At the close of the century, the Venetian sequin was still in use, along with the *dūro*, or *riāl dūro*, the Sevillian piaster.

In the world of commerce, a large number of different currencies was known, negotiated, and shipped. The gold coin of the country was called *sultani*, or *sultanin*, or Barbary sequin, or else *zermabub* sequin, *mahbūb*, or "gold sequin stamped in Tunis." Silver money, the riāl, was known as the aspre piaster, since the piaster was divided into *aspres*, or nāsris. Among other coins either used or actually struck in the Mediterranean basin, the most frequently mentioned were the Venetian sequin and the "hard" piaster. The first was referred to all through the eighteenth century and well into the nineteenth – a valuable coin that survived the subjection of the Venetian republic, the disappearance of its flag, and the decline of its commerce. The most precious coin was the Sevillian or Mexican piaster, the "hard" piaster, or "real" piaster, when it was not clipped. It prevailed over all other currencies and Tunisians wanted to be paid in this coin, preferring it to the gold currencies that were offered to them. The choice is paradoxical since Tunisia had very few direct contacts with the Iberian peninsula, and Spain was the very symbol of the Christian enemy. At the beginning of the seventeenth century, mention of the Sevillian piaster was still accompanied by the formula: "Minted by the enemy of religion, the Christian, may God destroy him."[3] The primacy of Spanish coins in North Africa was not a new phenomenon, and the highly prized silver pieces were simply replacements for the Spanish gold coins that had invaded the North African market in the sixteenth century.[4]

The coexistence of all these coins caused no little confusion in the commercial world. Variations in exchange rates, the circulation of clipped coins, and the introduction of counterfeit coins added to the complication of monetary exchanges. In addition, Tunisian money was not always in the form of actual coins. Units of account were used to denominate certain transactions at the same time metallic money was circulating.

Tunisian coinage from the eighteenth to the middle of the nineteenth centuries[5]

At the beginning of the eighteenth century, although no coin called dinār was being struck, the gold sultani certainly existed. It was a round piece of approximately 3.5 grams with a gold content of 950. The bey also minted the half-sultani, a gold piece 29 millimeters in diameter, weighing 1.75 grams with the same gold content as the sultani. On the face of these coins, as on all the coins struck in Tunis, the legend gave the name of the reigning sultan. The coinage was therefore modified with each change of ruler in Istanbul, whereas the succession of beys was not reflected on Tunisian money. This fidelity to the "Sultan of the two continents and sovereign of the two seas" lasted until the second half of the nineteenth century. Not until Muhammad Bey (1855–9) was the name of the Tunisian sovereign stamped on the coins of the regency. However, the autonomy of the Tunisian money appeared on the obverse of the coins, where the formula "struck in Tunis" followed the date of the minting.

The silver piaster, in contrast to the gold sequin, was a fictitious coin. In reality, only its lower multiples – known as aspres by Europeans – small square pieces of silver, roughly cut, whose weight varied between 0.35 and 0.55 grams, were actually struck. Nāsris of the same type, square-cut,[6] had been struck in the seventeenth century, and even before, under the Hafsids.[7] These real monies were for common, everyday transactions. But what about large payments?

During the first years of the century, the "hard" Sevillian piaster was the common currency and had to be bought outside the country or obtained through trade. In 1714 the bey undertook to substitute a Tunisian currency for this foreign money as a means of payment. Ordering the withdrawal of "hard" piasters, he required all payments to be made in aspres. This operation had a number of advantages: For one, as soon as piasters were recalled, hoarded coins would pour back into the market; for another, the yearly outflow of piasters caused by the pilgrimage to Mecca would be avoided. Another advantage was recounted in a contemporary account: "By abolishing piasters, the bey restored the manufacture of caps to his country, in that *hajis* [pilgrims] and other people obliged to go to the Levant, presently take cases of caps instead of piasters."[8] Similarly, Christian sea captains who received payment in local currency for their freight charges had to use their aspres to buy local merchandise. Thanks to the abolition of Spanish money, commerce and artisanry received a boost. Indeed, aspres were struck in large numbers, since that was the only currency accepted in payment. But it is easy to see that these lightweight coins were not convenient for large-scale commerce. And more important, in the weeks following his decision, the bey was unable to inhibit the increase in silver prices and the disappearance of the white metal.

Finally, in 1725, the quarter-piaster was inaugurated, a coin 25 millimeters in diameter, weighing 5.55 grams, with a gold content of 650. As far as we know, it was struck again in 1727 and in 1728. The other actual currency in use consisted of small copper coins, called *bourbes* in

French documents. In 1703 they had been recalled and reminted and their weight standardized at 1.8 grams. They were worth a twelfth of an aspre.

Under the reign of Ali Pāsha, Tunisia's monetary system expanded, but its currency was depreciating. The bey struck half-sultanis of reduced weight, content, and size. They were only 15 millimeters in diameter, weighed 1.5 grams, and had a gold content of 935. In 1735 and in following years the bey also struck a silver quarter-piaster of the same size and weight as that of his predecessor's quarter-piaster, but of lower silver content (440, which amounts to billon). During the same reign there were a number of monetary innovations. The bey created coins worth an eighth of a piaster in 1738, the *qarūba*, worth one-sixteenth of a piaster in 1739, and the half-qarūba, a round coin of the same alloy as the first (440), in 1748. This small coin, 11 millimeters in diameter, was the smallest silver coin struck by Ali Pāsha. The square nāsri was no longer minted.

The nāsri was strange not only in shape. In a system of progression by multiples of two, the nāsri was worth one-fifteenth of a riāl. This anomaly stemmed from the fact that since the seventeenth century the metallic standard for currency had changed. Silver had replaced gold. At the beginning of the sixteenth century, Leo Africanus wrote, "The king of Thunes [Tunis] still mints another silver coin called *nāsri* . . . thirty or thirty-two of which make one of their ducats."[9] The nāsri was then a subdivision in silver of the gold coin, and since the ratio of the former to the latter was 32 to 1, this brings us back to the progression by multiples of two. Fixed since the sixteenth century, this ratio remained constant, but when the silver riāl overtook the dinār in a ratio that also remained stable, the nāsri became a fifty-second part of a riāl. One can understand, therefore, why Ali Pāsha, when completing and simplifying the monetary system, stopped minting the nāsri (see Table 7.1).

Under the reign of Ali Bey (1759–82), the Tunisian mint was kept very busy with the new emission of gold coins, the repeated minting of silver coins, and the creation of new coins. The half-sultani, which had not been struck for some time, reappeared in five successive mintings beginning in 1771. Its weight fell to 1.3 grams and its gold content to 895.[11] In 1767 gold sultanis of the same content as the half-sultani and twice as heavy were minted twice, and then again in 1183 A.H./1769–70 and 1186 A.H./1772–3. Silver coins were not subject to any change during the first years of the bey's reign. The qarūba, in particular, struck each year until 1764–5, was exactly the same as during the preceding reign. The great innovation was the creation in 1766 of a piaster that ceased being a money of account. Pieces of one piaster were created and were struck ten more times until 1780. Large pieces, 35 millimeters in

Table 7.1. *The Tunisian monetary system in the eighteenth century: silver money (number of pieces needed to make a riāl)*

	Riāl	Half-riāl	Quarter piaster	One-eighth piaster	Qarūba	Half-qarūba	Nāsri
Husayn (1705–35)	—	—	4	—	—	—	52
Ali Pāsha (1735–56)	—	—	4	8	16	32	—
Ali Bey (1759–82)	1	2	—	—	16	—	52[10]
Hammūda Pāsha (1782–1814)	1	2	4	—	—	—	—

diameter, they weighed more than 15 grams. But the metal content of silver coins decreased; it was now only 390.[12] The half-piaster, issued in 1773 and struck a number of times until 1780, was of the same billon and weighed 7.6 grams. Copper coins – *fals* and *qāfsi* – struck almost every year, did not change during that long reign so rich in monetary innovations.[13]

Under Hammūda Pāsha, although monetary activity remained very intense, manipulation of the coining also increased. Gold was no longer struck, but the silver piaster was produced many times. In the first issues of his reign, it increased in weight, reaching 16 grams with no diminution in silver content. Beginning with 1789, this coinage underwent steady alteration. The *bū shershūr* piaster kept its dimensions and its weight until 1813 and then fell in content. The half-piaster, on the other hand, after having increased in weight between 1782 and 1788, fell in content in 1791, 1792, and 1793, and then also in weight starting in 1795. Having the same silver content as the piaster (340), it weighed no more than 7.5 grams. And finally, the quarter-piaster struck in 1808 had the same silver content and weighed only 3.5 grams. In one century, this coin lost almost half its silver content and a third of its weight. Even copper money, the fals, dropped from 3.75 to 3 grams.

Tunisian money depreciated even further after the reign of Hammūda Pāsha. In 1815, the metal content fell to 300. During the reign of Husayn Bey (1824–35), the coins decreased in weight, size, and silver content, reaching a low of 286. The weight of piasters fell to 11.5 grams in 1825 and 11 in 1829. Demi-piasters dropped to 5.5 and 5 grams and the quarter-piasters to 2.7 and 1.3. The qarūba, which had kept its dimensions (14 millimeters), lost half its weight and, like the other coins, was of low-grade billon. In 1828 a measure to save the money was instituted but was not followed through. The bey created the double piaster of 38 millimeters, weighing 23 grams. His successors, Mustapha (1835–7) and Ahmad (1837–55), abandoned this heavy coin and returned to the piaster and its lower multiples.

The exchange rate

Plotting the decrease in the intrinsic value of these coins is enough to indicate the steady deterioration of Tunisian currency, slow at first, and then accelerating toward the end of Hammūda Pāsha's reign. In itself, that would not have been so catastrophic had the other currencies of the Mediterranean basin followed the same downward trend. It is in relation to the Turkish, Egyptian, and Venetian sequin or the Spanish piaster that the weakening of Tunisian money has to be evaluated. The remarkable stability of the Venetian sequin is well known. If we take the

Table 7.2. *Rates of depreciation of the Tunisian piaster*

A.H.	A.D.	Weight in grams	Content (%)	Index
1138	1725	22.2	650	1.0000
1148	1735	22.2	440	0.6769
1179	1766	15.2	390	0.4108
1196	1782	16.0	390	0.4324
1203	1789	16.0	340	0.3769
1228	1813	16.0	300	0.3326
1241	1825	11.5	286	0.2279
1244	1829	11.0	286	0.2180

value of the Tunisian piaster of 1725 as a basis for comparison (at the time, only the half-piaster was being minted), we see that it fell from 1 in 1725 to 0.38 in 1800 and continued its decline after this date (Table 7.2). In Cairo, the silver para went from 1 to 0.20 between the beginning of the eighteenth century and the French occupation in 1798.[14] In a chronology reminiscent of that of the Tunisian piaster – Cairo enjoyed a long period of monetary stability between 1756 and 1790, as did Tunis between 1766 and the end of the century – the Egyptian para fell even lower than the Tunisian riāl. In Istanbul, the Ottoman piaster collapsed during the last quarter of the eighteenth century. From a value of 1 in 1717, it fell to 0.39 in 1799. Following a different chronology from that of Tunisian currency, the decline was slower but similar in scope. Monies of the eastern Mediterranean basin thus followed a parallel destiny (see Fig. 7.1).

Intrinsic value is one thing, exchange rate is another. The latter confirms the close relationship that existed between the currencies, depending on the relationships between the different markets. If tradesmen in Marseille needed zermabub sequins for their purchases in the Levant, the rate of Tunisian gold pieces immediately rose. When, on the other hand, business in Marseille slowed down, as happened in 1780–1, for example, the rate of the Tunisian piaster fell as did that of the zermabub sequin. The rate also varied according to general conditions not only in Tunis but also in other Mediterranean ports. In 1789, for example, the difficulties experienced in the major markets of Leghorn were felt by Jewish businessmen in Tunis. The level of business dropped, drafts drawn on Leghorn were less frequent, currency was in short supply, and the value of money increased.[15] The volatility of the exchange rate increased during the revolutionary and imperial period in France, when business was in an upheaval and the money supply irregular. The Tunisian piaster seems to have benefited from this instability. Until the end of the eighteenth century, generally speaking, a certain balance could

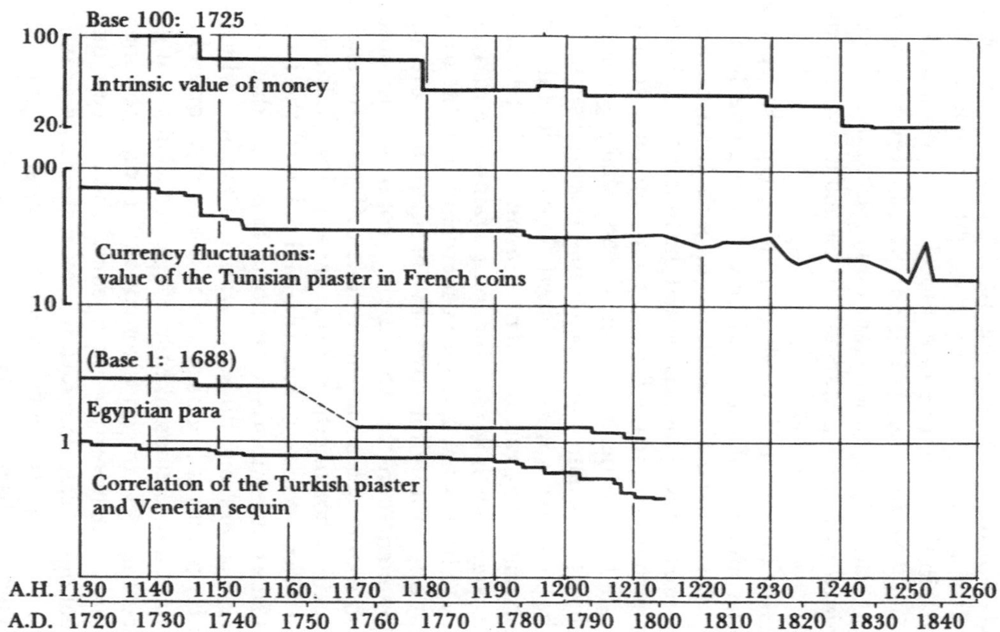

Fig. 7.1. The value of money.

be seen between the intrinsic value of the piaster and the rate of exchange. A drop in silver content or in weight was reflected – albeit with some delay – in the exchange rate, especially in relation to the French currency (Fig. 7.1). Between 1810 and 1820, however, despite the lowered content and weight under Hammūda Pāsha, the piaster nevertheless maintained its value. In Marseille or Genoa it was still worth 25–35 sous.

Once peace was restored, oscillations were both sharper and more directly determined by local conditions. On the one hand, the bey's increased expenses, and above all, the imports from Europe, required more and more money. This occasioned the monetary upheavals already observed, which in turn made for a greater confusion in exchange rates and aggravated the difficulties of an already shaky government. Thus in 1825, while the issuance of new money was equivalent to monetary inflation, the new pieces were produced slowly while the old ones continued to circulate. The rate of the new money could be maintained for a while but could not hold out for long against the disappearance of good money. This is what European merchants quickly understood. It was an ideal opportunity for currency speculation. "Foreigners, always more enlightened than the natives of a country," an observer commented, "no sooner see an advantageous difference in exchange rates than they begin exporting the old currency, and when foreign currency increases in price because of the reduced value of the local currency, speculators substitute imports for exports. It is a fact that now with four old Tunisian piasters, one buys five francs in Europe, which once back in the country procures five piasters for the proprietor and before long eight, and since transactions take place here in exchange for goods always based on local money, the government suffers an enormous loss as do the inhabitants, but never the Europeans, who are very quick in their business dealings to calculate differences in the value of money."[16]

No diagnosis could be more accurate. Subsequent events truly substantiated Filippi's observations.

On the other hand, the eagerness of foreign merchants to siphon off the country's products – be it oil or wool – made Tunisian money subject to sudden variations. For example, it was high when Tunisia had products to export, as in 1832 and 1842, and low when the situation changed. In the autumn of 1842, the abundance of the olive crop enormously increased the volume of exports and the need for currency. The piaster, whose rate in Marseille was only 74–80 centimes, immediately rose to 1 franc, then 1.25 and then to 1.50 in November. In a few weeks, the rate of the piaster had doubled.[17]

In all this, the Tunisian government increasingly became the prisoner of a market it could no longer control. Even its monetary policies lost all independence. No reform could be undertaken without the foreign consulates first being informed. In 1847, when the bey decided to open a bank, issue notes, and mint new money, the announcement of these measures provoked a meeting of foreign merchants and a protest by the French, who pointed out that notes with an imposed rate would suffer a 4 percent loss in the event of reimbursement. This amounted to a forced loan. It was a justified objection. Indeed, the Tunisian state was then being undermined from within by agents maneuvering to fleece the country. Inevitably, Tunisian finances were headed for disaster.[18]

Other means of exchange and communication

With regard to other instruments of commerce, I have already discussed elsewhere Tunisia's disadvantages in the areas of transportation and communication. Its lack of a merchant marine was a great handicap obliging it to turn to foreign shippers.[19] In Tunisia, a flat country with a dry climate, there was no impediment to the free circulation of goods within its borders. Nevertheless, there was no postal service, virtually no wheeled vehicles, and in the eighteenth century at least, European merchants were confined within the walls of the capital. In the nineteenth century, however, they settled in other port cities where foreign quarters slowly developed.

Language might have been another obstacle. The most common in the country, Arabic, was the least known by the tradesmen. Spanish and Italian Jews, the so-called *grāna*, may have spoken it, but not the French. Turkish, though spoken by new recruits from the Levant, was unknown in the rest of the country. The bey himself, a vassal of the sultan, understood not a word of this language. When he received a letter from the king of France in Turkish, he had it translated into "pidgin Moorish" and replied in the same jargon. This "pidgin Moorish" or "pidgin Frankish" or "bastard Italian" was one of the variants of the lingua franca in use around the entire circumference of the Mediterranean. It was spoken both in commercial circles and in the court of the bey. Through such contacts, the vocabulary of this lingua franca contaminated Tunisian Arabic. Conversely, the names of products of Tunisian fabrication passed into the language of commerce. In short, between traders, there was always a way to make oneself understood, if necessary through the intermediary of those dragomans, go-betweens, and interpreters attached to the consulate of foreign countries and to business houses – all obscure agents of an initial acculturation.

From the cycle of grain to the cycle of oil

"A vast storehouse of all kinds of grain"

Let us analyze the effect of these exchanges and how they were organized. Grain was the primary commodity of eighteenth-century trade. It nurtured the myth of Africa as the land of fertility and the granary of wheat. "It is quite fitting that the well-deserved title of Garden of Barbary is bestowed on the Kingdom of Tunis... It is a vast storehouse of all kinds of grain."[20]

The word grain in the eighteenth century covered many different varieties of cereals and pulse: in the first place, wheat and barley, then escayolle, large and small millet, maize, chickpeas, large peas, square peas, pointed peas, fava beans, canary grain, long grain, yellow grain, and so on. In addition to these raw grains, semolina, couscous, *mhamos*, and "dough meat" or biscuit were also staple items for export. To determine the importance of these grain commodities in the volume of business, let us first calculate the number of shipments made under the different flags.

More than half the French merchant marine carried grain, with France receiving 59 percent of the cargo. That France was the biggest customer is made even clearer if one adds the ships of the Compagnie d'Afrique, whose exclusive function was the purchase of grain. Between 1706 and 1742, the company loaded 542 ships with wheat in its trading post at Cape Nègre. This post was then destroyed by the Tunisian army and the transportation of grain from that part of the coast was permanently halted. Italy was in second place among importers of foodstuffs using French ships (Table 7.3).

At the end of the century, the French yielded their primacy in shipping to other flags, especially the Italians along with a few Maltese, and less frequently, Ottoman and Tunisian vessels. Grain continued to be the predominant cargo. Approximately 80 percent of the vessels transported grain; three out of four of the ships were bound for Italy. If we look at the ships from Tunisia arriving at the port of Leghorn between 1794 and 1798, of 185 vessels, 168, or 86 percent, carried grain in their cargo. It should be noted, however, that Tunisian exports to Leghorn were more varied than those to Marseille. On ships bound for Leghorn, grain was one item in a cargo that also included leather, wax, and raw and processed wool. Cargo destined for Marseille was more homogeneous, with grain constituting its largest component.

Since Tunisia in the eighteenth century was primarily a grain-exporting country, this immediately raises the question, What was the volume of grain exported? If we separate the exported grains into three categories

Table 7.3. *Transportation of grain under the French flag in the eighteenth century*

	Number of French ships			Direction		
	Total	Grain cargo	%	France	Italy	Other
1716–20	267	172	64.4	86	70	16
1721–25	213	93	43.77	36	38	19
1726–30	170	86	50	54	20	12
1731–35	163	126	77.4	79	41	6
1736–40	107	59	55.1	41	16	2
1741–45	64	46	72	29	15	2
1746–50	80	36	45	16	16	4
1751–55	218	130	59.6	43	66	21
1756–60	70	18	25.7	11	0	7
1761–65	113	30	17.7	16	1	3
1766–70	270	115	42.6	90	16	9
1771–75	586	461	78.6	265	117	79
1776–78	108	57	52.8	45	4	8
1781–85	178	95	53.3	80	13	2
1786–90	245	118	48.2	71	25	22
1791–93	113	56	49.6	34	3	19

– wheat, which was the most expensive in a category by itself, then barley and other secondary cereal products, and finally all the legumes and pulse – we can then plot three curves that can measure the annual variations in exports (Fig. 7.2).

Once again, we observe great volatility. There is no average level. The divergence between good and bad years is sharp. For the century as a whole, however, three phases emerge. In the first, which lasted until 1740, exports were relatively regular and similar in volume for all three groups of commodities. During the next period, from 1740 to 1768, the quantities traded were very low, and the curves hit bottom. The last third of the eighteenth century was marked by a general increase in exports. The level at the beginning of the century was surpassed in all the commodities; the volume received by each of the ports was higher as well.

The curves also show the concordance between the three groups of commodities. When cereals were plentiful, they all flowed into the market; when they were scarce, they all receded at the same time. In an average period, from 1740 to 1769, pulse, however, continued to appear among exports after the other cereals had disappeared from the market.

The oil cycle

The recession of grain. Until the first years of the French Revolution, Tunisia continued to serve, in good years and bad, as one of Europe's

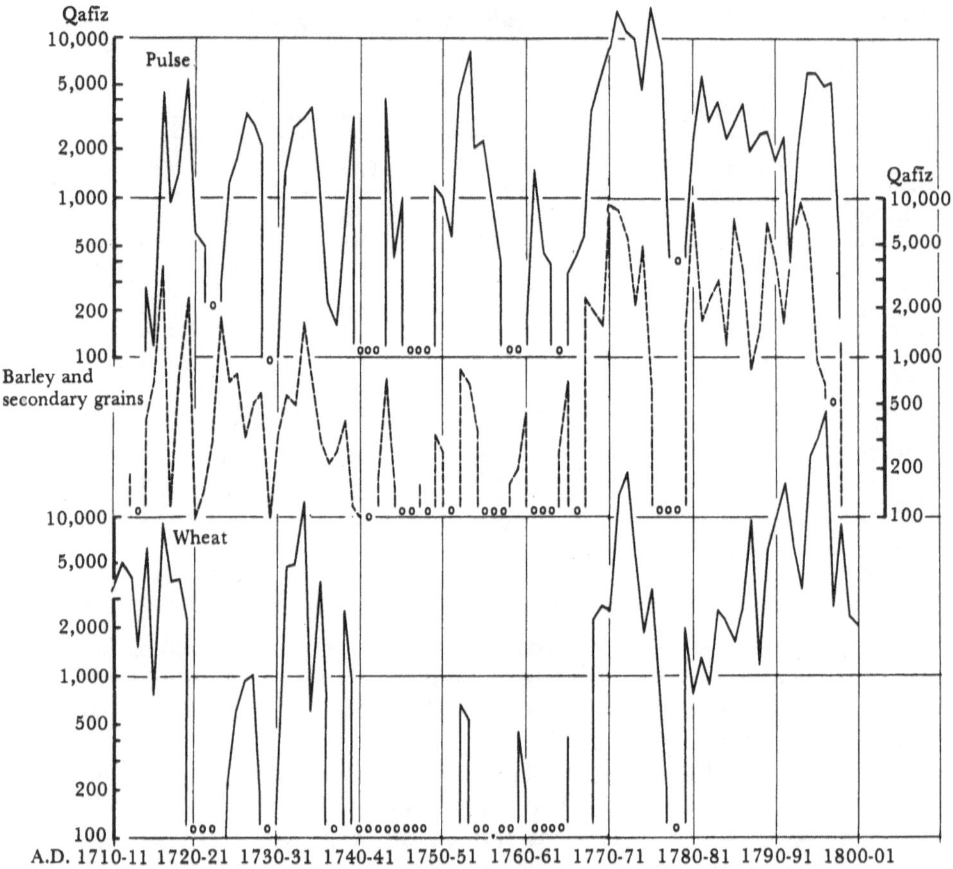

Fig. 7.2. Volume of pulse, barley, and wheat exported (in yearly harvests).

granaries. The nineteenth century presents an entirely different picture. Even after the turmoil in maritime trade created by the Napoleonic Wars, supply lines were not reestablished. The number of ships carrying grain to Marseille diminished to less than 10 percent of arrivals; the quantities transported became negligible. Tunisia shipped less wheat than escayolle. In Leghorn, a similar change took place (Table 7.4). What happened in both ports was a change in the provenance of grain imports. Ships now arrived in convoys from the Black Sea ports of Taganrog and Odessa. The global volume of French and Italian wheat imports was probably no lower than it had been in the eighteenth century, but the trade circuit had shifted.

Weather contributed to Tunisia's elimination from the grain market. From 1815 to 1820 the country suffered a series of mediocre to down-

Table 7.4. *Number of ships arriving in Marseille and Leghorn from Tunisia*

	Marseille		Leghorn	
	Total	Loaded with grain	Total	Loaded with grain
1800–09	262	56	—	—
1810–19	206	35	—	—
1820–29	555	22	214	21
1830–39	529	18	252	40
1840–49	574	65	169	23
Total	2,126	196	635	84

Table 7.5. *Volume and value of grain exports*

	1824	1826
Volume wheat	85,123 hl	276,110 hl
Volume barley	13,502 hl	71,230 hl
Volume fava beans		83,620 hl
Combined value	910,307 francs	4,313,180 francs
Total value of exports	5,876,160 francs	8,431,720 francs
Value of grain (%)	15.5	51.0

right bad harvests. Between 1818 and 1822, Tunisia, an exporter of grain, became an importer. "Contrary to normal conditions," we read in a document from Tunis in 1821, "this country so blessed by nature with its fertile soil, was obliged this year to obtain its needs from abroad. The devastation of last year's harvest by extreme heat and drought resulted in a widespread famine that could only be remedied by paying heavily for grains and other basic foods from outside the country."[21]

Once again, from 1827 to 1830, harvests were meager or deficient. In 1830 Tunisia imported grain, and during the following decade conditions remained unfavorable to grain production. During the first half of the nineteenth century, Tunisia's legendary fertility became an occasional occurrence. There seem to have been only three truly bountiful years, 1824–6. During these years wheat once again appeared among exports to Genoa, Gibraltar, Morocco, and Spain. The volume and value can be measured and were quite considerable in 1826 (see Table 7.5). But this exception aside, circumstances converged to bring about the total eclipse of the Tunisian grain trade.

Advances in the oil trade. It is by rounding Cape Bon toward the East that we come upon Tunisia's new source of riches. This was not unknown

Table 7.6. *Percentage of ships carrying oil to Marseille and Leghorn*

Years	Marseille	Leghorn
1710–19	10.8	—
1720–29	20.0	—
1730–39	12.7	—
1740–49	9.0	—
1750–59	14.6	—
1760–69	15.6	—
1770–79	4.8	—
1780–89	35.6	—
1786–89	—	8.7
1790–99	26.4	—
1800–09	62.9	—
1810–19	65.5	—
1820–29	78.4	17.8
1830–39	65.4	21.8
1840–49	70.2	21.8

in the eighteenth century. Leghorn, Malta, Marseille, and Alexandria all imported olive oil from Tunisia. Nonetheless, at least in the western Mediterranean, it was not an important commodity in foreign trade. Although few ships carried oil to Marseille before the last quarter of the eighteenth century, the number increased perceptibly in the 1780s. During the first half of the nineteenth century, oil replaced grain: Two out of three ships heading from Tunisian ports to Marseille carried it in their cargo. With Leghorn, without becoming the principal item of trade, oil gained in importance (Table 7.6).

At the same time, the volume of exported oil shows a steady increase. At the beginning of the eighteenth century, there was only one good year for every four years of little or no exportation of oil: 1728 (nearly 10,000 hectoliters), 1734 (4,600 hectoliters), 1736 (7,500 hectoliters). After 1780, exports became regular and voluminous. The level of 10,000 hectoliters per year was surpassed in 1781 and that of 50,000 hectoliters in 1817. In 1827, a record year, Tunisia shipped more than 76,000 hectoliters of oil to Marseille (Fig. 7.3).

In value, oil attained first place in Tunisia's foreign trade. In 1817 it accounted for nearly the total value of exports carried by French freighters (3.3 out of 3.5 million francs), one-third of the total in 1824, and one-quarter in 1826. From a total of 17.5 million francs in 1834, oil accounted for more than 10 million.

This oil trade, the result of Marseille's developing soap industry, moved the center of gravity of Tunisia's economic activity. Whereas Tunis, the capital city, continued to attract imported goods, it was gradually sup-

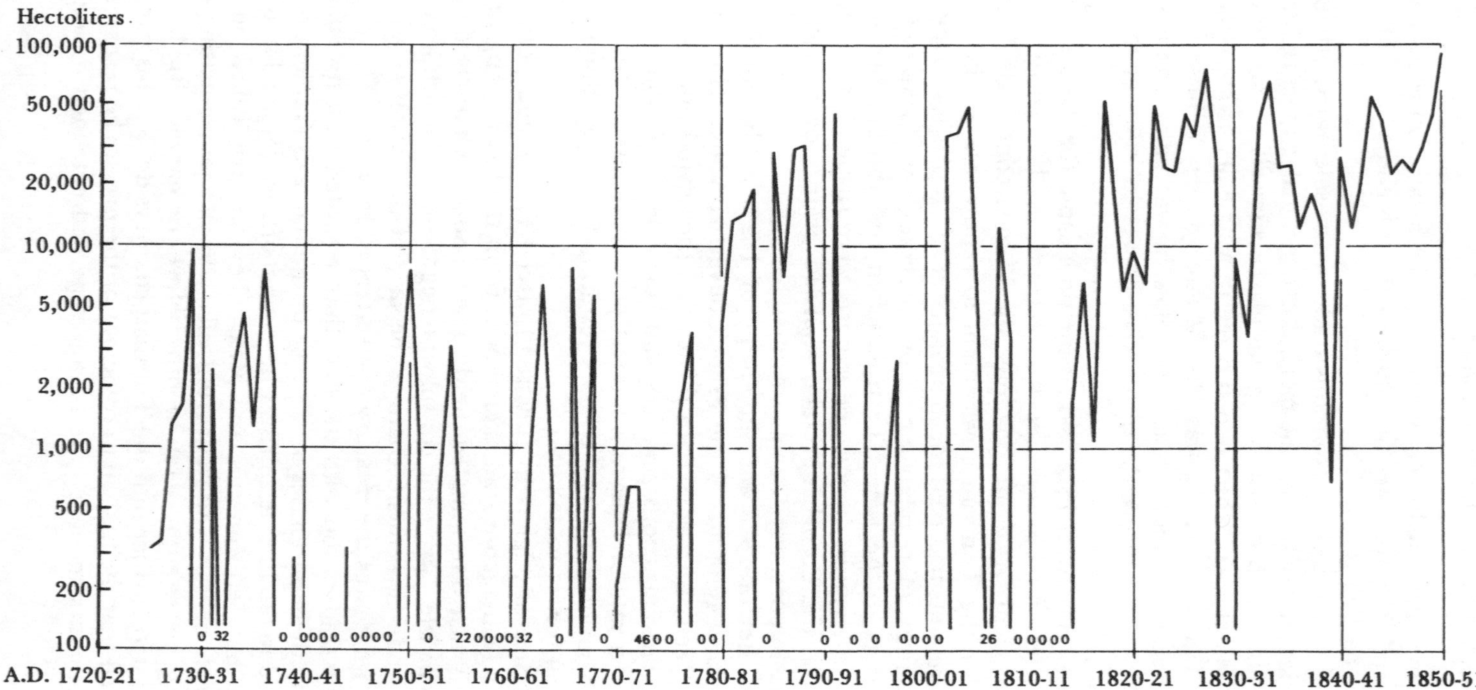

Fig. 7.3. Oil exports to Marseille (in yearly production).

planted in export trade by the two ports of the Sahel, Sousse and Monastir. The traffic moved steadily southward, to Mahdia and Sfax, and sometimes reached Jerba.

At first, the bey profited from this trade by the sale of export rights. Then he tried to monopolize the market, canceling all export rights and selling oil himself. But in so doing, he placed himself at the mercy of European merchants. When demand fell in Marseille, as happened in 1826, the Tunisian market was glutted and the bey deprived of his revenues. Because of his financial difficulties, he was led to sell the year's crop at a low price before the olives were harvested in order to obtain ready cash.[22]

The crisis erupted in 1828. When the time came for the delivery of the prepurchased oil to the French merchants, the harvest turned out to be insufficient. After negotiations, the French consul, de Lesseps, arranged for the Tunisian government to repurchase all the oil that French merchants had paid for in advance at seven piasters to the *mtār*, basing the price of reimbursement on the going rate in Marseille, of twelve piasters to the *mtār*. The transaction cost the bey two million piasters. Furthermore, because oil exports were suspended due to the poor harvest, the French were also awarded priority over other merchants once exports were again permitted.

In the winter of 1828 and the spring of 1829, the bey fulfilled his obligations and reimbursed the French buyers. But the crisis had cumulative effects. Burdened with this capital they could not invest, the French initiated usurious practices and began lending money against collateral at a rate of 1 percent interest per month. As for the bey, he made up from his subjects the losses resulting from the ruinous terms he had been forced to accept.

The capture of Algiers in July 1830 placed France in a position to secure an advantageous trade agreement from the bey on August 8 of that year. Article 6 terminated the diverse monopolies exercised by the bey. "This article," wrote the consul who negotiated it, "which is in itself an entire trade agreement, changes the face of the country's administration and deprives the treasury of its greatest resources."[23]

What the traders did with the bey, they repeated with his subjects. They made their purchases in advance of the harvests and lent money to be repaid in oil. Business firms whose main offices were in Tunis kept brokers in Sousse, Monastir, and Sfax. They, in turn, relied on local agents, "oil brokers," who went from village to village negotiating deals with olive growers eight to ten months before the harvest. Big business thus infiltrated further into the Tunisian countryside. For his part, the bey ordered that the first oil to come out of the presses be reserved for him, as reimbursement for the advances he had extended during the crisis of 1828. For a number of years, he maintained his special privilege while foreign traders were unable to determine when or whether the debt to him was finally repaid. In addition, in order to subvert the treaty of 1830, which deprived him of his monopoly, he demanded compulsory deliveries at prices he imposed, which were naturally disadvantageous to the peasants.

Out of this grew the new crisis of 1832. Since the bey had appropriated the bulk of the oil, the French merchants who had paid in advance were left with unfilled orders. Following new negotiations, the bey agreed to pay – at the price of oil in Europe, or 10 piasters to the *mtār* – the cost of the 15,000 *mtār* purchased by the French from the harvest of 1831 at 4 piasters to the *mtār*, resulting in a handsome profit of 900,000 piasters. But was it the bey who absorbed this loss? He agreed to indemnify the merchants in four installments but had every intention of compensating himself at the expense of his subjects. The shrewdest part of the bargain was the agreement obtained by the French consul for an even more advantageous arrangement: The bey would require his subjects to pay him in silver, not oil, thereby leaving the merchants free to trade as they liked. At the same time, the bey would relinquish his privileged purchase rights. The Tunisian peasant was thus reduced to selling his harvest in advance at figures well below the market price in order to have the cash required by the bey's treasury.

A further step in the takeover of the Tunisian economy by foreign interests occurred when the peasants were unable to repay their debts to European creditors. Lawsuits were instituted and property was seized. In the single month of November 1838, the French consulate received ninety-eight claims, many of which were requests for expropriations against debtors who had mortgaged as many as three successive harvests of olive oil. Twenty-five suits ended with the sale of the properties. Even the most important families were affected.[24] The idea that foreigners ought to be able to acquire land in Tunisia in order to prevent the default of harvests, compensate for the irregularities of trade, and deal with the decline of Tunisian money emerged at this time. As of 1836, despite the evident difficulties of directly exploiting the land, French merchants supported this notion, which was finally realized in the Fundamental Pact of 1857.

Contemporaries tell us that European capital was heavily invested in the olive oil trade.[25] But who were its beneficiaries? In the business ledgers that have been preserved, a few names recur more often than others: Paolo Gnecco, of Genoese origin, known to be the richest merchant in Tunis in the mid-nineteenth century;[26] Traverso, born in Liguria, married to a woman from Tunis; among the French were Arnaud, Vangaver, Hippolyte Rey, and Pierre Gay. Nor were these the only ones.

The bey's caids and agents also participated in the export of oil, either directly or under assumed names, such as Farhat, Muhammad, and Bakkar Jallūli, and Muhammad Ibn ʿAyād. Jews, whether native Tunisians or not, also made a place for themselves in this business.

Other export commodities such as wool and leather bound for Italy and France, and wax, foodstuffs, and livestock bound for Malta, also originated in the Tunisian countryside. In the nineteenth century, the practice of advance purchase soon contaminated other areas of commerce, especially wool, and produced the same effects of indebtedness and a deterioration in the terms of trade as occurred in the oil trade. The process that Marcel Emerit, and later Jean Ganiage,[27] analyzed and placed around the middle of the nineteenth century actually began earlier. These included the crisis in public finances and the alienation of the peasant who became a prisoner of usury, of the demands of the treasury, and of the need to sell his products in order to face new and heavier taxes levied in cash. Rather than the "extravagances"[28] of a bey concerned with establishing a standing army, it was the trade in rural products that set into motion destabilizing elements that brought Tunisia under the yoke of France.

8. A voracious tax system

Small-scale farming, a direct relationship between the peasant and his means of subsistence, an urban–rural relationship in which the town did not exploit the countryside's resources for its own benefit – these were the three salient features in the realm of production. The state in this system was the organism that appropriated the largest portion of the peasant's surplus production by means of an administration that encompassed the entire country and that each year placed the prince in contact with his subjects.

Fiscal organization in the eighteenth century

An imaginary frontier divided the country into two parts. Northern Tunisia, corresponding to the "summer campaign," and the southern part of the country, corresponding to the "winter campaign," alternately received the visit of the bey and his troops. The bey, or the *bey-de-camp* (the heir presumptive of the reigning sovereign), went in person to collect taxes. The summer campaign, with Béja as its destination, began at the end of June, after the harvests, and ended in August or September. The winter campaign ended at Tozeur, starting at the close of November, when olives and dates were ready for picking, and lasted longer. The bey did not return to his capital until February or March. On the local level, the sheikhs elected by their tribesmen and appointed by the bey, and the caids, selected directly by the bey, took charge of the assessment and collection of the taxes. Sheikhs and caids bearing the bey's revenues converged on his camp in an encounter that also renewed pledges of allegiance from the tribes. On the part of the bey, who was obliged to present gifts of food, textiles, and expensive garments to the notables he received, this was a manifestation of power and prestige.

On the local level, except in the Aʿrādh and Cape Bon, the caid served as the permanent representative of the bey to his subjects. Governor and receiver of tax money, he also had police and judiciary powers. Since he lived among the subjects he administered, he had every opportunity to extract payments in excess of the amount expected by the bey. But he had "to pluck the fowl without making it squawk," as a contemporary wittily remarked.[1] The surveillance of the sheikhs curtailed the freedom of the caids, and the population could complain directly to the bey. Each nomination for the office of caid was an occasion for the bey to receive gifts in kind and in cash from the new appointee. In Ibn Abi Dhiaf's chronicles, examples of the dismissals of caids resulting from the complaints of the people are numerous, as are the cases of extortion.[2]

Beginning with the reign of Hammūda Pāsha, a change in the regional administration radically altered relations between the central government and the countryside. The office of caid was henceforth sold to the highest bidder. As a result, wealth won out over competence. This practice of *ittifāq* forced the bey to close his eyes to the abuses of his governors. It also encouraged the caids to extort from the population under their jurisdiction sums larger than those they had paid the bey for their investiture. *Ittifāq* ushered in a period of excess and arbitrary rule the seriousness of which was unanimously condemned by contemporary observers.[3]

Tax stability of the eighteenth century

One major category of taxes was levied in kind. These varied with the region and with the crop. The most common was the *ʿashūr*, a tithe on cereals and pulse. In spite of its title (*ʿashūr* = one-tenth), its rate was not uniform. It varied along two axes, status and geographic region. The *raʿiyas* (the mass of ordinary subjects) paid a higher rate than descendants of the Prophet and army personnel. According to a regulation of 1742–3, for each unit of plowland, in the region of Tunis and the district of Kelibia, a farmer owed one Tunisian *qafīz* of wheat and one and a half of barley if he was a *raʿiya*; the privileged paid half as much in wheat and one *qafīz* in barley. In the canton of Riyāh, ordinary subjects paid one *qafīz* of barley and half a *qafīz* of wheat.[4] In the case of livestock, skins and fleeces served as substitutes for the tithe.

Effective collection of the tithe would have required rigorous control of the areas under cultivation. In fact, this occurred only in regions near the capital and in those that were heavily settled. Other regions simply evaded the tithe.

Taxes in kind specific to each group or region supplemented the *ʿashūr*. From the north, in the districts of Mateur, Bizerte, Béja, Téboursouk, and in Cape Bon, the bey received jars of butter, two to three thousand from all of these regions combined, as well as fodder and honey. In the south, villages and towns furnished woolen cloth and dates, and nomads provided livestock and raw wool. All had to furnish what was needed to maintain the bey's forces during their annual tax collection campaign.

In addition, the bey bought from his subjects raw or manufactured products, in fixed quantities and at fixed prices that bore no relationship to the fluctuations of the market. What this really meant was a tax in kind, disguised as a purchase. Another beylical practice, the *mushtara*, also amounted to a forced levy of local products, since the bey made his purchases before the harvest and at a price he himself determined. There were some years in which, according to the eighteenth-century Tunisian chronicler Hammūda Ibn ʿAbdalaziz, the price set by the bey was not even one-sixth of the market price. This is how grain and oil became items of authoritarian and preferential purchase made by the agents of the bey.[5]

A second major category was taxes paid in cash. A list of these is provided by the earliest remaining ledgers of revenues and expenditures. The same group of taxes was imposed throughout the country, in the south as well as in the north: *majba, hawā, zakkāt, ʿidīya, brādaʿ, ʿāda, dhīffa*. For each of these, there is a problem of identification. What, for instance, was the *majba*? When the bey levied a new head tax of thirty-six piasters on adult males in 1856, it was euphemistically presented as a *ʿiyāna*, a temporary tax to support the bey's treasury. But everywhere it was called *majba*. In spite of the protest of contemporaries that, according to canon law, only non-Muslims could be subjected to a head tax, the *majba* of 1856 was not entirely new, but was rather the reinvention of an old tax. Furthermore, one need not look far to trace it. The very edict that ordered the census of 1856 so as to determine the assessment of the new tax mentions the *majba* among taxes that had been abolished.[6] But was the original *majba* a head tax, and if so, what was its basis? These are difficult questions, for this text of 1856 refers to it without defining it, as is the case in earlier eighteenth-century documents. As for the enormous series of ledgers containing state revenues and expenditures, the amounts received for the *majba* are listed but the basis for its assessment is not given.

There is no doubt that a tax on individuals was levied on the bey's subjects in the eighteenth and nineteenth centuries. In 1856 they objected to the institution of a new *majba* on the grounds that Muslims were not liable to a head tax. In truth, it was not the first time that Muslims were subjected to this humiliating tax, nor was Tunisia the only Muslim country that imposed it. In neighboring Algeria before the French conquest, as in the Fayyum or in medieval Sicily, healthy adult male Muslims had to pay a personal tax in silver.[7]

Other contributions paid in cash are equally obscure. The *dhīffa* covered the cost of hospitality and a gift for the appointment of the caid or the sheikhs. The *brāda*ʿ (literally, the harnesses) was a levy on draft animals. The *ʿāda* was a "customary" contribution paid to the bey, the caid, and the sheikhs. The *ʿidīya* were revenues exacted on the occasion of religious holidays, and finally the *zakkāt* was a canonical contribution levied to provide assistance to the faithful. But it is impossible to determine what a tax like the *hawā* meant or what the method of apportionment and the rate of each of these taxes were.

Furthermore, the products of certain regions were liable to taxes in cash. Such was the case with the *qanūn* on trees, which affected the olive trees in the Sahel as well as a few other towns and villages, and the date palms in the region of Gabès and the oases. This payment seems to have exempted the inhabitants from the head tax. In Monastir, the Aʿrād, or wherever the *qanūn* was levied, men did not pay the *majba*.[8] Farmed taxes were also received in the form of cash. Throughout the land, payments in skins and fleeces, to which herders were subject, flowed into the hands of leather tax farmers, generally recruited during the eighteenth century from among Livornese Jews. In each town or community of any size, certain revenues were farmed out every year. In Tunis the taxes on olive groves and coal, and in Tebourba on cloth fulling, customs, fishing, silk, silver thread, and minting were farmed out. The same was true in Téboursouk for taxes on coal, tobacco, drums, and the marketplace, and in Jerba for the head tax on the Jews, customs, rights over markets and taxes on donkeys and horses.

Last but not least, even crime generated income for the state treasury. In Tunisia in the eighteenth and nineteenth centuries, killings occurred daily, with husbands murdering their wives, sons their fathers, and brothers each other. These crimes filled the bey's ledgers. Blood money, the compensation owed to the family of the victim, went instead to the bey, who, on these grounds, collected sizable sums from the entire country – 500 piasters for each man murdered and half as much for each woman. Fines in cash or in animals – camels from the Hamāma, otherwise horses – also provided a steady income for the Tunisian state.

Leaving aside these last two sources of revenue, which varied from year to year, what remains are the usual taxes paid by the totality of tribes and villages. Of these, the *majba* was the heaviest. In 1742–3, in the Jarīd, of the 2,197 dinārs paid in taxes by the village of Deggache, 1,947 went into the *majba*; 1,817 out of 1,947 in Zrqān; 1,707 out of 1,837 for the Awlād Mājid, etc. The same year, the Awlād Sindāssin of the Jlāss tribe paid 12,269 dinars in taxes, of which 10,886 went toward the head tax; the Awlād Idīr of the same tribe paid 9,110 to the *majba* and 11,137 as their total tax expenditure.[9]

What is surprising is that the fiscal system underwent no change in the eighteenth century. Neither the list of taxes nor their respective yields nor the share assessed to each division of the country were modified in any way. It was an inequitable apportionment that placed a greater burden on the south, particularly the Jarīd, and this uneven taxation did not correspond to the relative prosperity of the regions. If we compare such regions that were economically homogeneous, the Jarīd was taxed twice as heavily as Ifriqīya (excluding Kairouan), the country's granary, or the Sahel, its major olive oil producer. Nefta paid more taxes than the fertile region of Béja, and the relatively unfertile oases of Nafzāwah paid almost as much as Béja. This system of distribution had ancient roots. The fiscal organization of the eighteenth-century Husaynites had been inherited. It was already in use in the seventeenth century at the time of the Muradites. One would probably have to go back to Othman Dey, who was elected in 1593 and died in 1610, to recover the origin of the rules establishing the respective rights and duties of Tunisia's central power and subjects.[10]

Whatever its origin, we see here a fiscal system, a sharing of costs, that did not change from the seventeenth century to the end of the eighteenth. The irregularities of certain revenues – fines or blood money, for example – and the delays in payments by one group or another modified the total of the treasury's annual income. The amounts due, however, did not change, and the assessments of date and olive trees, or the population census, were not brought up to date. This inertia was not specific to Tunisia. In Ottoman Egypt, the general census was taken between 1527 and 1576; it was not completed in Upper Egypt until 1608. Although it was not revised, it served until the nineteenth century as the basis for the tax system and the administration.[11] Fiscally at least, Egypt and Tunisia share the same chronology.

To limit ourselves to Tunisia, the heaviest tax burden, the poll tax, remained stable. This indicates that since the value of money had depreciated, the fiscal debt placed on each group – provided the population remained unchanged – had also decreased. If the population increased, then Tunisians at the end of the century were less heavily taxed than the subjects of the first Husaynites.

Payments of taxes in kind, on the other hand, varied with the harvests. The sharp fluctuations in revenues from the tithe (illustrated in Figs. 6.6 and 6.7) indicate the close relationship between the finances of the state and the prosperity of the countryside. During a period of more intensive cultivation, the income of the state increased even though the rate for each taxpayer remained the same.

Tunisian peasants were thus fortunate not to suffer any increase in taxes during the eighteenth century. Better still, Ali Bey (1759–82), having ended the arbitrary practice of *mushtara*, made it possible for a portion of the surplus to enter the market and thereby reduced the amounted appropriated by the state.[12]

The nineteenth century: a ruinous tax system

This inertia, on the whole favorable to the Tunisian peasant, continued until the beginning of the nineteenth century, which ushered in a period of numerous innovations. The Sahel was the first region to feel the impact of change. Ever since the survey of olive trees carried out during the reign of Othman Dey, olive growers paid a few nāsris for each tree. Once the *qanūn* was established, plantings subsequent to the seventeenth century escaped taxation entirely. "Thus the blessed olive tree multiplied in the Sahel," wrote Ibn Abi Dhiaf.[13] In 1819, realizing that the old tax no longer corresponded to the actual production of the Sahel, the bey decided to replace it with a tithe on the oil produced. The Sahelians resisted. The bey insisted on the legality of the tax by demonstrating that it conformed to Islamic law. The reform was imposed. Henceforth the inhabitants of the Sahel would have to pay one-tenth of the oil extracted from olives harvested as of October each year.

What were the effects of this new regulation? For the treasury, it meant greater sources of revenue than had been provided by the previous *qanūn*. However, as Figure 6.7 shows, the tithe on oil suffered from the same shortcomings as the tithe on grain. In years of penury, as in 1827, the bey's coffers were empty. In years when harvests were plentiful, market prices dropped, and the bey, an oil trader himself, reaped a lower profit from his reserves. As for his subjects, the impact of the new tax is illustrated by the example of Msaken, a town already familiar to us. From 1819 to 1838, its inhabitants paid as a tithe an average of 1,234 *mtārs* of oil a year, with a maximum of 9,031 in 1832 and a minimum of 47 *mtārs* the following year. The olive groves of Msaken contained 236,000 trees of which 200,000 were productive. Assuming, as is generally accepted, that the olive tree produces only every other year and that the average yield is a single *mtār* of oil per tree (these figures are deliberately on the low side), then annual production from the Msaken olive groves would have been at least 100,000 *mtārs*. A payment of 1,234 *mtārs* as a tithe was therefore well below a tenth of the production. According to the rules of the former *qanūn*, inhabitants of Msaken had to pay 3 piasters for every hundred trees.[14] In the seventeenth century, the groves contained 30,181 trees. The tax therefore came to 905 piasters. At the going price of 12 piasters per *mtār* on the eve of the tax reform, this figure would have been equivalent to 75 *mtārs* of oil – a ludicrous amount. The tithe of 1819 was thus considerably more onerous for the Sahelians than the previous tax, which had become symbolic. Still, it fell far short of the tenth of production that the bey expected to receive.

This was so, since when he applied the *ʿashūr* on olive oil, the bey was unaware of the number of olive trees involved, and the degree of government supervision of the oil presses was insufficient to prevent fraud. It did not take long for the government to become aware of this fact and in 1840 the tithe was replaced by another tax. In the interim, every effort was made to augment the revenues from the old taxes. Under the administration of Shākir Sāhib at-Tābiʿ, numerous regulations defined more clearly the rates for taxpayers in the Sahel and guaranteed recovery by the treasury of tax monies usurped by the caids. Old taxes were adjusted and conditions of collection spelled out. Each village had to pay in two installments – October and April – the *majba*, the royalties payable to the treasury, and the tax that replaced the furnishing of pack animals, to which was added a service charge. Religious groups and Turks were liable to the same rules as all other taxpayers. When payment of the tithe on grain was made, taxpayers were also obliged to pay in cash – proportionate to the amount of grain they brought for threshing – the services of the tax collector, the scribe, guards, measurers, and overseers. They also had to provide food and forage for the *mzarqīya*, the bey's agents, when they passed through the villages.

It is impossible to measure the extent to which the updating of the various taxes was effective. For the *majba* at least, this reform provided the occasion for a new census of the male population, prefiguring the survey undertaken twenty years later. But the state soon relinquished a large part of these taxes to concentrate all its attention on the main resource of the Sahel, the olive tree. In 1840 the tithe was abolished and along with it, to make the reform seem more equitable, all sorts of royalties including the personal tax, considered unfair because it was more burdensome to the poor than to the rich. To compensate for its loss, a new *qanūn* on olive trees was instituted. All the trees were counted, and producing trees were divided into three categories: the lowest was taxed at twelve nāsris per tree; the middle at a quarter of a piaster plus five nāsris; the highest, a quarter of a piaster plus eleven nāsris. Young trees were also counted but were not taxed until they bore fruit, at which time they were placed in the first category. Each grower had to add 2.5 percent to his tax bill for the collector. The tax fell due twice, with the first installment due in October. No olive grower, regardless of his condition or position, was exempt.[15]

As we have already seen, the assessments were carefully made and were kept up-to-date. Using the same theoretical figures used to calculate the effects of the first reform in Msaken, let us see what the second reform brought about.

In round figures, the inhabitants of Msaken declared that they owned 91,000 trees of the lowest categories, 107,000 of the middle, and 26,000 of the highest. The total tax bill came to 70,038 piasters for the year, excluding the supplementary 2.5 percent for the tax collector. At the time of the tithe system, assuming an average price of 12 piasters per *mtār*, the olive growers of Msaken paid on average the equivalent of 14,808 piasters a year. From 1840 on, they paid three times that amount and were required to pay the same amount every year whether the harvest was good or bad. Admittedly, they were released from other taxes. But these were probably not very significant. The bey, on the other hand, could count on regular and increased revenues that arrived in cash. However, to maintain his army and his court, and to make a profit on foreign markets, the bey needed oil. He did not buy it at the market rate. By 1819 he inaugurated the practice of *salam*, that is, acquiring part of the harvest at a fixed price, which protected him from fluctuations in the price of commodities. Consequently, from 1820 to 1840, the Sahel was the victim of a brutal offensive on the part of the state to modify the volume, nature, and distribution of taxes particular to that region. The Sahel served as a testing ground whose experience was extended to other sectors. Olive trees in other areas were subjected to the new tax, and in 1841 the *qanūn* on date palms in the oases replaced the old tribute that had fallen into disuse.[16] There too the bey gave up a large number of local taxes – about thirty in all – many of which went to his agents. Noting that these taxes hurt the poor for the benefit of the rich, the bey "with the intention of gladdening hearts and, with God's help, reforming the general state of affairs," decided to limit taxes to two sectors: trade and date growing. Like the olive trees, date palms were grouped under three headings. Supplementary sums were exacted for the work of the tax collectors, and recalcitrant taxpayers had to pay fines.

With regard to grain, the bey first tried to institute a reform of the tithe, one that according to Ibn Abi Dhiaf, who authored the proclamation sent throughout the kingdom, was aimed at achieving a more regular levy. The collectors would no longer be remunerated by the peasants but by the bey; the measuring device, the *waiba*, was standardized and had to be level. Ibn Abi Dhiaf himself testified that this reform remained a dead letter. The collectors continued their abuses and, with the complicity of the caids, arbitrarily exacted quantities of grain in excess of the canonical tithe. In 1829 the bey gave up his attempt to reform the *ʿashūr*, and under Ahmad Bey, in 1841, the full measure replaced the level one everywhere. In 1857 his successor made a new attempt to standardize the tithe and to exact it from remote regions that had managed to evade it in the past. We do not know whether these regulations were any more effective than the preceding ones.

Olives, dates, and cereals, the three basic products, were thus subject to fiscal pressure. In 1831 a 25 percent tax was decreed on products other than olives and cereals, and in 1850 a levy was imposed on the irrigated lands of the region of Sfax, which was subsequently extended to the gardens of Cape Bon.[17] That still left livestock. In 1845 owners of herds had to pay the state one-quarter of the purchase price of each animal. To these taxes on production and property were added consumer taxes. In 1838 the *mahsulāt* was levied – a toll on all produce brought to the markets of large urban centers – and in the same year, a tax on coffee houses was instituted. In 1840 the market toll was extended to smaller towns and rural markets. The price of salt, a state monopoly, was increased and fresh soap and tobacco also became monopolies of the state.[18]

Progressively, all sectors of rural activity were thus submerged in the rising tide of taxation. The bey's preference to farm out taxes – for example, the market tolls and the revenues from monopolies – provided him with immediate cash against the anticipated state revenues but it also encouraged every sort of abuse, prevented any control, and added to his subjects' fiscal burdens. It does not seem that the state reaped great profit from the system of tax farming, for contemporaries were unanimous in denouncing its inefficiency for the central treasury. When the new *majba*, the last tax in chronological order but the most important in economic and political terms, was finally instituted in 1856, the bey reestablished free trade in tobacco, salt, and untanned hides. He decided to pay a salary to his employees and to the sheikhs responsible for collecting taxes in order to prevent the extortions that had been victimizing taxpayers. He also abolished the old taxes inherited from the previous century, and the 25 percent royalty on the sale of animals. What he did retain was the tithe on cereals (but the level measure was restored) and, wherever it was still being levied, the tithe on olive oil. The tax on date palms and olive trees was also maintained. The new head tax amply compensated for those that had been abolished since every male subject who reached the age of puberty had to pay thirty-six piasters a year. Important exemptions were allowed for inhabitants born in Tunis, Kairouan, Sousse, Monastir, and Sfax, locales whose fiscal procedures were not altered. Religious lawyers, students, indigents, and invalids were also spared the head tax.[19]

Of these many taxes newly created or revamped since 1819, the *majba* was the more broadly based levy. No community was exempted and the poor paid as much as the rich. It was a humiliating tax and a heavy one. At first, it was evaded through fraud; the population of the tax ledgers slipped from year to year. That still left more than 220,000 taxpayers who paid about eight million piasters to the treasury. In 1864, when the rate of the *majba* doubled and the exemptions were reduced, public discontent reached its limit.

The revolt

Demographic and meteorologic calamities, the financial crisis and depreciation of money, the unleashing of fiscal reforms, and the abuses of collectors produced a cumulative effect and multiplied the hardships of the peasantry. Simultaneously, other government measures affected not only their economic well-being, but also their relations with the central power, and above all, the very structure of their society. Cases in point were the judicial reform of 1860, which replaced the local judges, the *qādis*, with tribunals, and the military draft imposed by Bey Ahmad. The last was badly received, less for the gaps it created in local society and economy than for its very principle. A selective recruitment took soldiers for a distant army, alien to the communal framework, whereas until then every man had been a potential soldier, capable of taking up arms to defend the interests of his own group.[20]

A silent resentment seethed through the countryside. Each new increase in fiscal pressure was met with collective resistance. In 1831 trouble broke out in the region of Mateur and Le Kef following the inauguration of a 25 percent tax on farm products. Inhabitants refused to pay either the old or the new taxes.[21] In 1833 an uprising in Kairouan was related to the oil crisis already mentioned earlier. The minister, Shākir Sāhib at-Tābiʿ, believed he could collect an exceptional levy from the inhabitants of the Sahel and Kairouan. However, the inhabitants of the holy city of Kairouan had been granted an exemption from taxes because of their support of the founder of the reigning dynasty in his struggle against his nephew Ali Pāsha. They therefore challenged the ruling, claiming that their prayers were enough help to the bey. The minister, in violation of the right of asylum, arrested people from Msaken who had taken refuge in a sanctuary in Kairouan. This was the signal for an uprising. It was suppressed and the minister imposed a fine of 500,000 piasters on the holy city and increased the collection fee as well as the humiliations to the town's notables and populace.[22]

In 1837 it was the area of Bizerte that revolted, and Shākir Sāhib at-Tābiʿ was once again called upon to restore order.[23] The Aʿrādh rebelled in 1819, 1840, and 1856. In 1840 the reform of the *mahsulāt* and the abuses resulting from its collection provoked the uprising. The bey himself appeared on the scene. His troops captured the leaders of the insurrection, five of whom were executed. The entire province was punished with a fine of 600,000 piasters. This tax was no less unpopular in the rest of the country. When, in that year, the bey planned his expedition to the south, uncertain of the fidelity of the tribes, he decided not to recruit horsemen from their midst. Instead of returning to the Bardo, his capital, by land, he did so in part by sea.

The following year a tribe from the environs of Béja rose up against its caid and demanded his deposition. The same region refused to pay the head tax in 1856. Trouble broke out, the situation remained tense, and the bey sent his brother, Muhammad Sadoq Bey, to put down the rebel tribes. In the Aʿrādh at the same time, the inauguration of the *majba* coincided with the presence and activity of a Libyan leader as rebellious against the authority in Istanbul as against the bey in Tunis. There too a punitive expedition was sent to quell the insurgents.[24]

During the 1860s social discontent gave rise to widespread individual banditry and collective raids. In 1864 it burst into a generalized rebellion that inflamed the entire country. It developed around two centers: the Sahel and the central and western tribes. Initially, the uprising was an antifiscal protest. The doubling of the *majba* provided the spark. A boycott of taxes was the rebels' first line of action. However, in terms of its demands and its organization, the rebellion of 1864 was also a defensive movement on the part of Tunisian peasants to safeguard a social order that had been undermined by the bey's administration. What the rebels demanded was a repeal of the new tax, the dismissal of the officials of the central government and specifically Prime Minister Khasnadar, and the abolition of other recent reforms. The insurgents challenged the constitution of 1861, the judicial reforms, and the abolition of slavery. They preferred the ancient order to these innovations.

The organization adopted by the insurgents was in every way faithful to tradition. It mobilized in one movement all the men of the village or tribe, notables as well as common people. With regard to the well-to-do, Ibn Abi Dhiaf wrote that they gave their support to the people only to protect their property. In fact, they did more than merely tolerate the rebellion. In Msaken, Ahmad Maqrūn was its leader. He was the brother of a general who remained loyalist. I have been able to ascertain that his family owned thousands of olive trees in the forest of Msaken. In Sfax, the *amīn* of trade was among the leaders of the movement. The leader Ali Ibn Gdāham was a man of the people, but Fraj Ibn Dhāhar was one of the largest landowners of the Riyāh tribe. Among the Jlāss, the leader was a man whose name, Ibn Abi Dhiaf tells us, was famous from generation to generation. Old religious groups and jurists also supported the revolt in large numbers. In Sfax, the heads of the two major *zāwiyas* were the ones who took charge of the insurrection. In Sousse, the keys to the city were taken from the bey's envoys and given to the *qādi* and the religious court. Clearly, there was no split between notables and the rich on one side and the poor on the other.[25]

During the rebellion, each community was responsible for its own justice and its own defense. Above the local units, an assembly of representatives from several tribes took shape in April 1864. It does not seem to have played a leading role; rather it symbolized the alliance of the insurgents and permitted some concerted action. But it did not constitute a general staff or a parallel government that could have replaced the bey. Indeed, at harvest time, the confederates dispersed and each returned to his own territory.

The rebellion had a leader, Ali Ibn Gdāham, who was named "the bey of the Arabs." He propagated the revolt and concluded alliances between the different factions, but did not organize the insurrection or serve as its commander-in-chief. The principle of the bey's authority was in fact not questioned. At first, the insurgents hoped that the bey would reappropriate the judiciary functions that the reforms transferred to the tribunals. The insurgents considered the bey well disposed to his subjects, but poorly advised and surrounded by untrustworthy courtiers, and their intention was to maintain him in power. But once they lost hope of deflecting his course of action, they fell back on two alternatives: Either the bey would be replaced by another prince, or they would seek arbitration from a higher authority – the Ottoman sultan.[26]

The narrow local framework within which the rebellion was conducted made its victory impossible. Another structure, the soffs, worked toward the same end. The rebellion, which started out as a general movement, began to come apart in the autumn of 1864. The disintegration followed the lines inherited from time immemorial and that were described at the beginning of this book. The first to lay down their arms were the groups belonging to the Husaynite soff. The government was then able to turn them against the other insurgents. This split was doubtless engineered by the agents of the bey. But the success of this maneuver proves the power of the bonds that held the leagues together.

Weak in its overall coordination, but vigorous in its local solidarity and its traditional system of alliances, the revolt of 1864 was both the defense and the expression of the most deep-rooted of social structures.

Conclusion

For a long time it was held, and not only by historians, that humanity had but a single history whose direction and rationality were progress. This progressive movement was conceived as a train whose forward cars – Great Britain, France, the countries of Western Europe and North America – pulled the others along, one by one. This image has more than one meaning. It suggests that the past of distant regions is the same as that of locomotive countries, that theoretical models of Western societies could be applied, mutadis mutandis, to non-European societies. Conversely, it also implies that countries currently underdeveloped – the rear cars – present us today with an image of what Europe was yesterday, and finally, that the discrepancy between developed and underdeveloped countries is one of delay, that it is only a matter of catching up. Backward countries have only to follow a path laid out by the advanced countries, as though the control exercised by the latter over the master switches of an economy that has become worldwide were unimportant; as though metaphors of economic sluggishness and acceleration, advanced, backward, or delayed countries, and so on, could disguise the relation of dependency that bound the one group to the other.

The preceding pages offer no remedy for underdevelopment. They merely illustrate two related facts. One cannot, with regard to the Maghreb, observe any repetition of European history. Categories that are valid for the interpretation of feudal or capitalist societies in Western Europe are inappropriate outside its frontiers. Other paradigms have to be sought. In precolonial Tunisia, an original social formation existed whose keystone was the agnatic organization of the society. This organization could, for the nomadic segment of the population, take on the vast dimensions of the tribe, or, in the case of settled populations, the more limited ones of the extended family. In either case, its principles and its implications were similar. It was primarily on consanguinity and kinship that the right to land was based. Pastoralists moving over great expanses and villagers tied to their tiny plots were equally in direct relationship with their means and instruments of production. Lineage, conceptualized in the form of a genealogical idiom in which each person was assigned his place, his allies, and his rivals, provided the framework within which economic life developed. Agricultural and manufactured production, and the circulation of goods and services, passed through the same channels of kinship and common residence.

The durability of this system can be explained, in the first instance, by the low level of technology. Tools, irrigation methods, and overall agrarian techniques allowed for no more than small-scale farming. Large holdings, which did exist, simply lacked the means of large-scale agriculture and could only reproduce small-plot farming. This kind of farming, on the other hand, was possible only within the context of joint ownership and reciprocal exchanges in which all the members of the local group participated. The other corollary of this organization was the limited division of labor, reduced in many cases to a sexual division of work that did not give rise to a clear separation between peasants and workers engaged in other activities than farming.

It was within the same framework that all aspects of social practice were organized, matrimonial exchanges, political alliances, and arbitrations in the event of conflict, ritual celebrations that punctuated the episodes in the life of the people – in short, all the actions that enabled the social order to preserve and perpetuate itself.

Although the division of labor was limited, regional specialization was not. For the most part, each group tried to be self-sufficient, but at the same time, each one favored a particular activity and filled the voids of its own production with exchanges of trade, barter, and services with other producer groups. A relationship of interdependence thus united date or olive growers and farmers, nomads and settled peoples, northern people and southern people. The social complex operated as a vast network through which people and products moved freely, rather than as a juxtaposition of closed cells.

Was it a harmonious society? Not at all. Tension was as necessary to it as peace. A society of abundance? Even less so. Life was frugal and doubtless also brief.

These societal forms did not result in vertical social differentiations but rather in cleavages and rivalries between analogous segments. In an earlier work, I characterized this kind of social formation as archaic, referring to the categories proposed by Marx for precapitalist societies. Such a qualification, however, could be misleading by implying that Tunisian society was in a kind of primitive, or even a natural, state. There is no natural society, and history allows for the reemergence of earlier social forms. Furthermore, this "archaic" quality could make us lose sight of the possibilities of change as well as of the dynamic relations that existed between the different social formations.

Changes there were. Some were voluntary and resulted from processes of diffusion, such as the adoption of new crops and new consumer goods. Other, involuntary, ones made the peasants victims rather than agents, as during the recurrent epidemics and food shortages at the end of the eighteenth and through the nineteenth centuries. Admittedly, all other things being equal, these disasters might have been remediable and the structures, through a self-regulating system, might have endured. However, radical changes intervened that, over a period of time, exerted a destructive influence. Crowning the entire structure was the state, with its agents, both civilian and military. Its function included public security, the defense of Islam, the administration of justice (which the bey could mete out himself, and which his provincial representatives, the caids, rendered locally), and finally, the levying of taxes, which was legitimized by the fulfillment of these obligations. What is remarkable is that the bey, unlike the sultan of Morocco, had no ideological power. The prosperity of his subjects was not regarded as linked with the fortunes of the prince.

But the state had acquired a legitimacy that was unquestioned, and in the eighteenth century the government adequately fulfilled its functions. In levying taxes, it was the organism par excellence for draining off directly, regularly, and systematically the surplus of agricultural production. But this taxation left intact the relations of inhabitants with each other and with their means of production. Nor was the distribution of roles changed. With regard to everything that concerned the life of the peasants, both tribes and smaller groups enjoyed considerable autonomy. There was no change in the administrative system, and there was even a slight decrease in taxes.

At the end of the eighteenth century all this changed. First, the venality of the office of caid, systematized under Hammūda Pāsha, allowed the caids to bleed the peasantry with impunity. Forced to close his eyes to the extortions of his caids, the bey relinquished to them the government of the provinces and a portion of the tax revenues as well. The second change, of much greater importance, affected the fiscal system. The stability of the eighteenth century was abruptly disturbed by the rash of innovations that extended the hold of the state over all production and all activity, and generalized the arbitrary exaction of taxes. All of these changes took place precisely when a series of natural calamities – climatic and epidemiologic – created a conjuncture unfavorable to such innovations.

It was therefore the state that endangered the functioning, or at least the prosperity, of Tunisian society. The state, however, was also subject to a variety of pressures. Internally, the state suffered a reduction of revenues as a result of demographic calamities and alternating years of scarcity. As of 1816 it also suffered the loss of profits from privateering and the tributes paid by certain European countries. Simultaneously, the infiltration of industrial products from Europe became irresistible, leading to the temptation to make quick profits from the sale of raw materials from the countryside. How else to keep profits high except to raise taxes and extend the list of taxable items? In short, an inequitable relationship developed between the various social formations, with the bey and his agents supporting this process. In the nineteenth century, before the colonial and overtly imperialistic period, the development of some countries already depended on the underdevelopment of others.

Tunisia and its 155,000 square kilometers of utilizable land did not amount to much. This was a small country with a small population. Can it be regarded as typical of underdeveloped countries? It certainly can for the rest of the Maghreb and perhaps also for other parts of the "Near" East where, during the first half of the nineteenth century, the same processes of dependency were being enacted.

Notes

1. Population

1 Ganiage (1964, 1966). The more pessimistic contemporaries estimated less than a million under the regency; the more fanciful went as high as two million.

2 Antinori (1867), p. 280. For the rest of the Sahel, chap. 3.

3 Lucas (1712), p. 137, found Sfax very lovely; Sieur Raynaud, in 1727, found it wealthy and active but did not like the inhabitants (A.N. Paris, Marine B 7 89, project of expedition to Tunis). For an opposing view, see Maqdish al-Sfaxi, 1321 A.H.

4 Leo Africanus, vol. II, p. 27. The annual fair is described by Seghir Ben Youssef (1900), p. 20, and Shaw (1743), p. 210.

5 "Tent people": the expression is translated from the Arabic. In Tunisia, it was the dwelling rather than mobility that differentiated nomads from settled people. The displacements of "nomads" were, for the most part, circumscribed within the space occupied by their tribe, the range incomparably smaller than that of Algerian Sahara dwellers, for example.

6 This restitution is based on fiscal archives (A.G.G.T., regs. 1–313 for the end of the seventeenth and eighteenth centuries), accounts of voyages, and other contemporary texts.

7 According to Brunschvig (1940), vol. I, pp. 299ff., the Hedil, Wārgha Ushtata, Awlād Yahya, etc., have not moved out of their lands since the Hafsid era. See also Idris (1959) and Marçais (1946). All the data that follow come from A.G.G.T., regs. 621–1027.

8 A.G.G.T., regs. 1640 (Msaken), 1660 (Gabès), 1663, and 1665 (El Alia).

2. Social organization

1 A.V. Tunisie, boxes 29–31.

2 There would seem to have been a commingling of the episode regarding Husayn Ibn Ali's struggle against Ali Pāsha in the eighteenth century with the one about the quarrels between two brothers in the Mouradite dynasty, Ali and Muhammad, around 1675–86. See Grandchamp (1933a), pp. 227–32, and El Kairouani (1845).

3 Despois (1955), pp. 158ff. The same method is used in Ganiage (1959), esp. p. 171 on the Hamāma.

4 Berque (1955), esp. pp. 86–7: the filiation of the Ait Lh'hsen is given as mythical, though not their expansion, which Berque would date around the eighteenth century. Do the sources used allow, in this particular case, for such a hypothesis? Berque makes a sharper observation elsewhere: "Where the indigenous tradition sees a heredity with geographic connections, and *modern research sees the complex result of past migrations*, one would be tempted to see merely a series of verbal mutations" (1953, p. 265; my emphasis).

5 A.V. Tunisie, box 30, Hamāma tribe, caidate of the Awlād Sellāma.

6 A.V. Tunisie, box 28, the Awlād Ridwān. The dates provided are those of the Hegira. I have made uniform the spelling of proper names, which varied from one folder to another.

7 Evans-Pritchard (1968).

8 Gellner (1969), p. 41. This is an English rendition of the French notion of *emboîtement des unités.*

9 A.V. Tunisie, box 28, Hamāma tribe, subdivision of the Awlād ʿAziz.

10 A.V. Tunisie, box 29, the Awlād Maʿāmar and Awlād Sellāma.

11 A.V. Tunisie, box 30, the Awlād Maʿāmar.

12 The word even appears in the Littré dictionary, with the following definition and references: "Kabylian, word meaning confederation, or party. There is always, in every tribe and even in each family, what are called two soffs, meaning two confederations, two hostile parties; what is even very common, two or three tribes join forces and form a soff against two or three other tribes (Jour. Off. April 23, 1872, p. 2,938, 3rd column). It is well known that not a tribe exists in which there are not two soffs, that is, two hostile parties (ibid., April 27, 1872, p. 3,023, 1st column)."

13 Seghir ben Youssef (1900).

14 Ibn ʿAbdalaziz (Hammūda) (1970).

15 Slama (1967).

16 According to Malikite law, the occupation of an uninhabited zone is taken as possession (Santillana, 1938).

17 See Evans-Pritchard (1968).

18 A.V. Tunisie, box 28, Riyāh and Blidet.

19 A.V. Tunisie, box 29.

20 Peyssonnel (1838), vol. 1, pp. 210, 213.

21 A.V. Tunisie, box 29, Mahādhba tribe.

22 A.V. Tunisie, box 29, Awlād Abu Ghānim.

23 A.V. Tunisie, boxes 29, 30. Caidate of Gafsa.

24 Abdesselem (1973), p. 333.

25 Cuisenier and Miquel (1965), p. 34.

26 Lapidus (1967); Raymond (1973); Chelhod, (1969).

27 Peters (1963); Fortes (1953); Lewis (1961); Sahlins (1961).

28 A.G.G.T., reg. 620.

29 A.C.C.M., L III 1331, Compagnie Royale d'Afrique, Tabarca, Journal (1783–93), entry of June 13, 1784.

30 A.V. Tunisie, box 13, 1857, Report . . . by Tissot.

31 Seghir ben Youssef (1900), p. 42; Ibn ʿAbdalaziz (Hammūda) (1970), pp. 55, 64; Ibn Abi Dhiaf, vol. II, p. 163.

32 A.G.G.T., file 586, box 54.

33 A.G.G.T., file 215, box 19: undated letter, probably from the beginning of the nineteenth century.

34 Peyssonnel (1838), vol. 1, p. 211.

35 A.C.C.M., L III 1331, Compagnie Royale d'Afrique, Tabarca, Journal (1783–93), entry of June 13, 1784.

36 Bardin (1939), pp. 118ff.; Boris (1951), p. 104; Maquart (1937), p. 267; Rondot (1955), p. 267–75; A.V. Tunisie, box 13, 1857, Report . . . by Tissot; box 28, Bargu tribe.

3. Structures of property

1 Desme de Chavigny (1911) makes this clearer than anyone else: "Attention was naturally drawn to Algeria ... Material for study can be found in unusual abundance among our neighbors to the west" (p. XII). In the west, the interpretation of this material was very different. See the excellent critical analysis made by Ageron (1968), vol. I, pp. 67ff.

2 On this problem, see Godelier (1970, 1973).

3 Saint Gervais (1736), p. 54, note a. Also, Peyssonnel (1838), vol. 1, p. 63; Anonymous (1703), p. 143; A.N. Paris, AE B 1 1131, Pignon to Maurepas, letter of December 3, 1727.

4 A.G.G.T., reg. 1, 1080 A. H.; reg. 34, 1151 A. H.; reg. 1029, 1215 A.H.

5 Pouyanne (1900); Desme de Chavigny (1911), pp. 51ff.; and Housset (1939), p. 5, refer to this paradox.

6 A.G.G.T., regs. 26, 32, 42, 238, etc. A.G.G.T., reg. 20, contains a copy of a deed of transfer from 1250 A.H. (1834) whose object is to demarcate an estate of the bey with a piece of common land occupied without title by the Awlād Sbaa "according to Arab custom." A.G.G.T., reg. 2/2249: demarcation of the estates of the bey situated in the canton of Téboursouk and in the lands of the Awlād ʿŪn. Housset (1939), p. 10.

7 See Berque (1955), p. 128: "Qualifications of origin and kinship are more essential here than boundaries, and, it may be said, even more than the compost heap itself. This little corner, almost empty of matter, is primarily meaningful as an illustration of civil law."

8 Archives de la Conservation foncière, Title 3, Ez Zaouem.

9 Archives ... Ghaba, report on the Frashīsh, 1902, report on the Sawāsi, 1909, Monchicourt report, 1910: "Each family, each branch of a family, has been allocated its own special area. That area is sufficiently large to allow for annual or biannual fallow plots. Joint ownership is the absolute, general rule and admits no exception." Boris (1951); Desme de Chavigny (1911).

10 A.G.G.T., reg. 2/2249: lands of Sherif Maruān. Also, lands of the bey: The state of joint ownership results here in a manner of acquiring land, the contract of planting or *mugharsa*, which gives half the land to the farmer who has cultivated it.

11 Barrault (1903); Goguyer (1885).

12 Archives de la Conservation foncière, title 17659, act 1; title 4, act 1; title 5501, acts 1 (1764) and 10 (1871); title 17659, plot of Cherak Khalfallah, act 3 (1853); title 3508.

13 Koran, sura 4.

14 This classic example is taken from Luciani (1890), pp. 370–1. See also Surdon (1935), pp. 92ff.

15 Maternal kinship in that case has rights that the Malikite rite does not recognize. This example comes from Archives de la Conservation foncière, title 5501, Henshīr Smeia, acts of 1764–1851.

16 Hanoteau and Letourneux (1873), vol. II, pp. 282–3.

17 Archives de la Conservation foncière, title 15452, Henshīr Bou Hejba, acts dated 1723, 1744, 1745, etc. See title 125058 for another example.

18 When French jurists invented the notion of an *ʿarsh* ruling, they named a practice that already existed but: (1) they made *mīlk* and *ʿarsh* contradictory categories; (2) they intepreted the second as a piece of land not owned outright but to which rights of usufruct were ceded; and (3) they assimilated *mīlk* into individual private property.

19 In notes to his reading of a work by Kovalevski, Marx gave this definition to the system of land holdings in precolonial Algeria: "It is Algeria that retains *the most important traces* – after India – of the archaic form of landed property. Tribal property and jointly owned family property was its most common form" (Godelier [1970], pp. 383–4; emphasis in the text). It is important to note that Marx substituted the word "property" for "usufruct," which Kovalevski used constantly.

20 The literature is unanimous on the apparent fertility of this region: Peyssonnel and Desfontaines (1838); Shaw (1743); Frank (1850). Geographers have not refuted these early descriptions.

21 The geographic origin is known for only 34.1 percent of the proprietors.

22 A.G.G.T., regs. 1663, 1665, 1095, 1106, 1107, 1109.

23 One nāsri or aspre equals one fifty-second of a Tunisian piaster.

24 My calculation was based on the idea of each proprietor having an equal share in the association.

25 El Aouani (1966).

26 The mosque of El Alia has been included in this group even though it does not have any vineyards.

27 Deglin and Poitrineau (1954).

28 A.G.G.T., regs. 1667, 1707.

29 The villages of Jara, Menzel, Chenini, Methouia, Oudref, Mathrech, Teboulbou, and El Hamma accounted for 187,741 date palms. The two principal poles are El Hamma, in the west, with nearly 30,000 date palms, and the three villages presented here (A.G.G.T., reg. 1660, 1257 A.H.).

30 See chap. 4, subsection entitled "Cash crops."

31 This represents the percentage of properties belonging to men or women, with the exclusion of *habous* and collective holdings.

32 There were twelve, to be precise: individual alone; individual plus individual; individual plus collective; individual plus joint ownership; individual plus *waqf*; individual plus anonymous; collective alone; collective plus joint ownership; collective plus *waqf*; joint ownership alone; joint plus *waqf*; *waqf* alone.

33 Goguyer (1895); Martel (1965), vol. I, p. 198.

34 This is related to other forms of alliance and solidarity discussed in chap. 2.

35A.G.G.T., regs. 659, 694.

36 A.V. Tunisie, box 28, villages and oasis of Gabès.

37 Despois (1955), p. 180, even says that nothing was known about Msaken until the eighteenth century. Msaken appears in the assessment of 1677–8, mentioned in chap. 4. Would the town have changed names over the years? A comparison of the place names indicated by Arab geographers with those of today indicates the frequency of such changes.

38 Pellissier (1853), p. 86; see also Antinori (1867).

39 A.G.G.T., regs. of the majba, 762 and 813, dated 1276 and 1277, A.H., respectively, thus a period during which tax evasion was already considerable. These assessments list 2,033 and 2,066 adult males in Msaken. See also regs. 729, 870, 925, and 950. Ganiage (1964), p. 183.

40 Despois (1955), p. 336.

41 A.G.G.T., reg. 1640.

42 So as not to repeat what has already been observed in the other villages, I have not separated here individual properties from inherited and jointly held properties.

43 Pellissier (1853), p. 86.

44 A.G.G.T., reg. 1701.

45 A.G.G.T., reg. 2434.

46 In the 1960s the area planted with olive trees had doubled in the region of Sousse, but the population had quadrupled. The opportunities offered by the civil service and service industries (banking, insurance, hotels, etc.) did not absorb the surplus, which accounts for the breaking up of properties. However, 84 percent of the land farmed in 1961–2 was done so directly. ("Secrétariat d'Etat au Plan et aux Finances, Structure agraire du Gouvernement de Sousse, 1961–1962." Mimeo.)

47 *Habous* archives might provide important information on this subject.

48 Valensi (1967).

49 See the agrarian lexicon in chap. 4.

50 Gallico (1935), p. 196.

51 A.G.G.T., regs. 2/2249, 1139–40 A.H.; 2250, 1172 A. H; 2077, 1200–10 A.H.; 2255, 1235 A.H.

52 Arch. A.E., *Mémoires et documents, Afrique*, 9, 1775, pp. 146ff., de Saizieu; Desfontaines, 1830, p. 211; Filippi, in Monchicourt (1924), pp. 150–1; MacGill (1811).

53 Thevenot (1727), p. 883; Peyssonnel and Desfontaines (1838), vol. I, p. 49; Ibn Abi Dhiaf.

54 A.G.G.T., titles 2, 3, 14, 16, 25, from which the figures in the text were taken.

55 A.G.G.T., act 31, 1263 A.H. (1846–7); and above all, the whole series of farms belonging to the bey, regs. 2064–2122, 2250–85.

56 In Zeys (1910); on the question of the *khammās*, see Rectenwald (1912). For a comparison with the rest of the Maghreb, see Berque (1938).

57 A.V. Tunisie, boxes 28–30; Masselot (1901).

4. Crops and techniques

1 Desfontaines's account of his travels, published by Dureau de la Malle in 1838, is well known. In it one finds a portion of the observations he made in the *Flora* (1798) that is not well known, as is also the case with another version of Desfontaines's travel account published in 1830 in *Nouvelles Annales des Voyages*, 2d ser., vol. 16, 17. The author collected his articles in a single work whose manuscript title is *Itinéraire dans les Royaumes de Tunis et d'Alger en 1783 et 1784*, and that he offered to the Museum of Natural History.

2 *Flora*, vol. I, p. 5.

3 *Flora* vol. I, p. 400; Frank (1850), p. 85; Kennedy (1846), pp. 14, 17. One finds numerous traces of this activity in the bey's ledgers at the A.G.G.T.: income from farms belonging to the bey and located in the suburbs of Tunis, purchase of burners and beakers for the preparation of flower extracts, cost of flowers, etc. It was a timeless activity: Adorno speaks of it in the fifteenth century (Brunschvig [1936], pp. 202–3).

4 Desfontaines (1830), pp. 206–7; Pagni (1829), pp. 18–19.

5 Plantet, vol. II, document 495, and vol. III, document 122.

6 A.G.G.T., regs. 54, 74, 83, 93, 125, 175, 209, 220, 243.

7 A.N. Paris, F 17 2657 B, Ducouret.

8 Few indications are given in the archives in the port records of Marseille, Leghorn, Malta, and the commercial correspondence preserved in the Arch. A.E.; MacGill (1811); Puckler-Muskau (1837), pp. 118–19.

9 Desfontaines, *Flora*, vol. II, p. 179, and Peyssonnel and Desfontaines (1838), vol. II, pp. 115, 297; Filippi, in Monchicourt (1924), p. 275; Pellissier (1853), p. 346; J. Valensi (1873), p. 7; A.V. Tunisie, box 28, Report on the land around Mahdia.

10 *Flora*, vol. I, pp. 325–6; Puckler-Muskau (1837), p. 113. This custom has continued.

11 Benhadji Serradj (1951); Dornier and Louis (1954); Dornier (1955); Marçais and Guiga (1925), pp. 399–400, who provide an important bibliography; Westermarck (1921), pp. 104–5.

12 *Flora*, vol. I, pp. 325–6; Shaw (1743), vol. I, pp. 335, 343. The same therapeutic use is described in Zerdoumi (1970).

13 A.V. Tunisie, box 29, study of the Tunisian Jarīd, and also the Aʿrādh: villages and oases; A.N. Paris, F 17 2657 B, p. 261; Pellissier (1853), p. 347; Coustillac (1951–2).

14 A.V. Tunisie, box 28. Tunisia exported flax to Italy and Malta. It is hard to know whether this was domestic flax or whether it came from Alexandria.

15 Peyssonnel and Desfontaines (1838), vol. I, p. 246; Desfontaines, *Flora*, vol. I, pp. 189–90; A.N. Paris, AE B III 300, African Concessions, Instructions for the director of the Compagnie d'Afrique, n.d. (first half of the eighteenth century).

16 Desfontaines, *Flora*, vol. I, p. 53, and Peysonnel and Desfontaines (1838), vol. II, p. 297; Filippi, in Monchicourt (1924); J. Valensi (1873), p. 7. To this list one would have to add other species useful for cosmetics or hygiene, and medicinal plants.

17 Anonymous (1713), p. 80.

18 Laugier de Tassy (1757), p. 159.

19 Desfontaines, *Flora*, vol. II, p. 376; Pellissier (1853); A.V. Tunisie, box 29, study of the Tunisian Jarīd.

20 Peysonnel and Desfontaines (1838), vol. I, pp. 44, 181. The same observations are found in Shaw (1743), who speaks of beautiful plantings. On the other hand, at the beginning of the protectorate, this forest was described as poorly kept up. It is possible that the decree of 1870 was precisely a result of the destruction of the grove in the north.

21 A.G.G.T., reg. 1.

22 Of the census of 1677–78 we have only global figures and no knowledge of the conditions under which it was conducted. Let us therefore not take these figures to be accurate. It is nonetheless true that Ibn Abi Dhiaf, on the Tunisian side, like French writers, noticed the extension of olive growing in the Sahel ever since the first *qanūn* of olive trees.

23 Peysonnel and Desfontaines (1838), vol. II, pp. 296–7.

24 *Flora*, vol. II, appendix: *Phoenix dactylifera*, pp. 438–55. Only a part of this description reappears in the work published by Dureau de la Malle.

25 Pagni (1829), pp. 149ff. This text has not aged.

26 A.G.G.T., regs. 1660, 1680, 1710, 1715.

27 Desfontaines (1830), p. 227.

28 On the oasis, see A.V. Tunisia, boxes 28–30; Faivre-Dupaigre (1957); Masselot (1901); Penet (1931). Long before them, Al-Bakri (eleventh century) gave a similar description.

29 Arab agronomists had made the same observations. Ibn al-Awwam (1866), vol. 2, p. 44, wrote: "The same kind of cultivation is needed for barley as for wheat, with the difference that barley will grow where wheat will not. So that barley will germinate and ripen in brackish soils."

30 The vocabulary was put together from

1. Inventories of the bey's lands. A.G.G.T., regs. 2/2249, 2077, 2255, which lists several thousand properties. Register 2/2249, with more than 1,500 descriptions of properties whose listings were made at two different times in the eighteenth century, presents the most coherent and homogeneous general view. Registers 2077 and 2255 complement it with regard to later dates.
2. Archives de la Conservation foncière, analysis of some deeds of the eighteenth and nineteenth centuries. This is too small a sample but it permits the verification of observations made on the preceding series.
3. Notarized deeds that go from the eighteenth to the nineteenth centuries: documents for rental of shops, leases of farms, shipping bills, etc. A.G.G.T., folder 18, box 63.

All of this, however, concerns only the north and the center of the country. This vocabulary can be compared with the one in Marçais and Guiga (1960–1), *henshīr*, p. 4,191; *hūsh*, p. 973, etc.

31 Berque (1938); also Le Coz (1964), vol. I, pp. 342–3. Completely different vocabulary is found in Lebanon: Latron (1936), pp. 11ff.

32 Dainville (1964), pp. 207–9: garden, "a place enclosed by walls or hedges"; orchard, "an enclosure planted with fruit trees."

33 Monchicourt (1916). On the word *henshīr* see Marçais and Guiga (1960–1), p. 4,191.

34 A.G.G.T., reg. 2/2249.

35 Berque (1955), p. 126.

36 Archives de la Conservation foncière, title 5501, act of 1720; A.G.G.T., reg. 2250, 1172 A.H. /1758–9.

37 This word does not have the same meaning in Morocco, where it refers to a strip of land adjoining a number of plots (Le Coz [1964], vol. I, p. 342).

38 Archives de la Conservation foncière, title 157, 1280 A.H. /1863.

39 Marçais and Guiga (1925), vol. I, p. 190; Bardin (1965).

40 Description of work cycle in Desfontaines (1830), pp. 328ff.; Shaw (1743); Frank (1850), p. 48.

41 A.C.C.M., L III 1331, Compagnie Royale d'Afrique, Tabarque, Journal. For France under the ancien régime, see Bloch (1952), vol. I, p. 27.

42 Bloch (1956), vol. II, p. XXVII. I have collected here

1. The results of a survey of the land conducted during the plowing season of 1966;
2. Information gathered at the Institute des Arts traditionnels populaires in Tunis whose director and collaborators I thank for their diligent and invaluable help;
3. The copious documentation collected since the establishment of a protectorate. Reference to it will be found in Marçais and Guiga (1925), vol. I, p. 187n, and in Haudricourt and Delamarre (1955). Added to these are certain indications provided by more recent works cited later;
4. A monograph by M. Guillon, inspector of primary education, and written under his direction by the students of Beni Hassen in 1954–5.

43 The principle of classification and the definitions given by Haudricourt and Delamarre were used here.

44 Peyssonnel and Desfontaines (1838), vol. II, pp. 266–7. In *Nouvelles Annales des Voyages*, vol. 16, p. 189, Walkenaer, who published Desfontaines's account, announced that he was giving to the journal notes "with excellent drawings of the plow, shovel, and scythe of these lands." Unfortunately, they were not published. A contemporary, but contradictory, eyewitness account appears in Poiret (1789), pp. 74–8, who stayed on the frontier between Algeria and Tunisia and described the swing plow as "a simple plowshare attached to a long piece of wood bent in the middle, ending in the yoke."

45 Haudricourt and Delamarre (1955); Bardin (1965), p. 34, with no further detail, indicates that this plow was used in mountain regions.

46 A.G.G.T., regs. of receipts and expenses, among others, nos. 224 (1196 A.H.) and 229-1 (1197A.H.).

47 Information provided by Capot Rey and Marçais (1953) and Laoust (1930) for the south of Algeria; Guin (1861) for Algeria; Bertholon and Chantre (1913) for the Chaouia; Boris (1951) for the Nafzāwah. Personal investigation for the rest.

48 Dresch (1949).

49 Despois (1953).

50 Desfontaines (1830), pp. 337ff; Frank (1850), p. 52; A.V. Tunisie, boxes 28–30.

51 Ibn ʿAbdalazīz (1970), p. 51.

52 Miquel (1968).

53 A.N. Paris, AE B1 1129, letters of December 15, 1716, and May 13, 1717; A.C.C.M., J 1418, consulate in Tunis, document of July 1, 1717.

54 Leo Africanus (1830 ed.), vol. I, p. 91; Marmol (1667), vol. I, p. 4. See calendars of Cordova and of Ibn al-Banna' in Renaud (1948).

55 Seghir Ben Youssef (1900), p. 445.

56 A.N. Paris, AE B 1 1128, letters of May 31 and June 16, 1714; A.C.C.M., L III 1331, Journal, document of August 2, 3, 1783; Arch. A.E. Tunisia, *Correspondance commerciale*, vol. 54, folio 310.

57 A.N. Paris, AE B 1 1140, bulletin of February 25, 1764. Seghir Ben Youssef speaks of the invasion of locusts in 1763 (p. 448); is this the same one described by de Saizieu?

58 Kunckel d'Herculais (1893 and 1905) wrote in two heavy volumes (1,576 pp. and 752 pp.) about the struggle against locusts in Algeria. He also provides some information about Tunisia. See also Arch. A.E., Tunisia, *Correspondance commerciale*, vol. 55, folio 252. Other invasions occurred in 1864, 1887, and 1889. In 1891 the whole of the Maghreb and Egypt were afflicted with them.

59 A.C.C.M., L III 4, Compagnie Auriol; Archives departmentales du Vaucluse, B 324 and 325, documents of May 8, 1836, June 11, 1836, etc.; A.N. Paris, AE B III 300, African Concessions, Memoirs, March 1737; A.N. Paris, AE B 1 1132, document of 1729; Gandolphe (1925).

60 MacGill (1811), p. 135, indicates an annual production of 480,000 *qafīz* in a good year. This figure is repeated by Davies in 1841 (published by Sebag [1959], p. 180), but MacGill spoke of both wheat and barley combined, whereas Davies gave the same estimate for each of the two grains. Billon in 1811 (Arch. A.E., Tunisia *Correspondance consulaire*, vol. 40) estimated the harvest of that year, for all grains at 500,000 *qafīz*, which brings us back to MacGill's estimate. But he added that production could go as high as 800,000 *qafīz* and – totally improbable – that each year 100,000 to 300,000 *qafīz* of wheat were exported, or a sizable part of the harvest. If we follow MacGill's figures, who estimated the population at 2,500,000 inhabitants, the available grains for each inhabitant would be 1 hectoliter per year or 0.27 liter a day – a very meagre ration.

61 Shaw (1743); Poiron (1925), p. 8; Desfontaines (1830), p. 331, and

(1838), vol. II, p. 47; Pellissier (1853); Arch. A.E. Tunisia, *Mémoires et documents, Afrique*, 1775, folio 153, and Tunisia, *Correspondance commerciale*, vol. 42, folio 125.

62 Plinius Secundus, ed. Littré, 1848, V, p. 212; XVII, 21; XVIII, 94.

63 A.G.G.T., regs. 2064ff.

64 Poncet (1962), pp. 497ff.

65 But can they be believed? On the basis of their declarations the peasants obtained a loan; it is possible that they blackened the picture.

66 This was indeed seen by Minangoin (1908). Calculating the cost of production (a plow, a yoke of oxen, forty days of work for one *māshia* of 10 hectares) he estimates that "the product of this *māshia*, were it only 3 quintals per hectare, would suffice [the peasant] to feed his family and his livestock and, if there is a surplus, he places it in storage for the following year or gets rid of it easily by barter or sale."

67 Grenville Temple (1835), vol. II, p. 108; Despois (1937).

68 A.G.G.T., regs. 969ff., census of people and holdings. The state of disorganization into which the country fell makes these statistics useless.

69 A.V. Tunisie, boxes 28–30. One also finds here information about the techniques and traditions of transhumance.

70 A.N. Paris, AE B III 305, 1775, de Saizieu; Arch. A.E., *Mémoires et documents, Afrique*, 9, same author, same date.

71 A.N. Paris, AE B 1 1141, document of December 15, 1766.

72 A.N. Paris, AE B 1 1128, document of March 11, 1715: death of sheep because of severe cold; A.C.C.M., L III 4, document of March 3, 1731: mortality of bovines; Archives Departementales Vaucluse, B 326, December 12, 1740: "extraordinary mortality" of bovines; A.G.G.T., box 81, file 978, letters of August 2, October 6 and 14, 1809; Arch. A.E. Tunisie, vol. 52, April 26, 1841: after the summer drought, excessive winter cold killed the oxen.

73 On these techniques see Puckler-Muskau (1837), p. 103; Shaw (1743), pp. 307–12.

74 Peyssonnel, in Monchicourt (1916); Shaw (1743), pp. 369–70. Confirmed by Borg (1955) and Messabie (1955).

75 The most systematic investigation of nonagricultural activities was made, once again, by the officials of native affairs (A.V. Tunisia, boxes 28–30). Indirect information was furnished by transport archives (manifestos of cargo, in particular, can include details on the geographic origin of products) and the ledgers of receipts and expenses of the A.G.G.T. Also in Lucas (1712) vol. II, p. 36; Shaw (1743), vol. I, pp. 374–6; Desfontaines (1839); Filippi in Monchicourt (1924), pp. 121–2; Grenville Temple (1835), vol. II; Benjamin II, published by Sebag (1959); Pellissier (1853); A.N. Paris, F 17 2957 B.

76 According to Poinssot and Revault (1950), vol. II, pp. 8, 15, other tribes, the Drīd, Jlāss, Awlād Abū Ghānim, also numbered among them tasteful and talented artists who were called upon with solemnity; feasts, songs, and dances accompanied the making of the *ktīfa*.

77 In the Jarīd there were 2,325 looms distributed among the families in 1897; Fleury (1897).

78 A.G.G.T., receipts and expenses.

79 It should also be noted that the domestic and feminine form of production was equally widespread in the towns. In Kairouan, for example, where women wove the rugs, 1,000 looms were distributed among 400 families at the end of the nineteenth century; Fleury (1897). This is still true today. It is also the case in Béja; Bonniard (1934), vol. I, p. 369.

80 This was equally true for industries involving luxury items: silks and brocades of gold and silver, in which the countryside did not participate.

81 MacGill (1811), p. 136; Ibn Abi Dhiaf in Valensi and Ben Smail (1971).

82 A.V. Tunisia, box 13, Memoir... by Vigneral, 1864.

83 Marx quoted by Kula (1970), p. 54.

84 Shaw (1743); Filippi, in Monchicourt (1924), p. 122; Ducouret; A.G.G.T., regs. 1855, 1858, 1860.

85 A.G.G.T., regs. 1855, 1858, 1860; regs. 125, 130, 163, etc.; Filippi, in Monchicourt (1924), p. 122; A.N. Paris, F 17 2957 B.

86 A.G.G.T., reg. 2435.

87 Nouschi (1961).

5. Rhythms and networks of daily life

1 Salt was extracted by evaporation in Tozeur, Nefta, El Guettar, south of Zarzis; on the east coast, where the Awlād Sidi al Hāni carried it to the north in exchange for wheat and barley; and it was also collected on Cape Bon.

2 Braudel (1967b), p. 134.

3 A.N. Paris, AE B 1 1129, 1130, 1134, 1139. Statistics are for the years 1717–23, 1734–39, and finally 1759. For the years preceding the Revolution, A.N. Paris, AE B 1. For the nineteenth century, Arch. A.E., Tunisia, *Correspondance commerciale*, vol. 46, folio 194, and vol. 54, folio 336.

4 Plantet, vol. II, document 779; vol. III, document 1771.

5 Jouin (1957), pp. 229–328. Regarding the Jews of Tunis, oral documentation has been used.

6 Braudel (1967b), pp. 192ff.; *E.I.*, 1st ed. "Kahwa," p. 671.

7 Brunschvig (1936), pp. 203–4.

8 Dan (1967), p. 236.

9 Ibn Abi Dinar al Qairawāni speaks of the custom that arose in Tunis in the middle of the seventeenth century to drink coffee in public places and smoke tobacco; quoted by Abdesselem (1973).

10 Pagni (1829), pp. 18–19; Arch. A.E., *Correspondance commerciale*, vol. 52, folio 88; also Puckler-Muskau (1837), vol. 2, pp. 151, 156.

11 A.G.G.T., regs. 2434, 2435: among the various taxes, one was recorded on coffee, 1252 A.H./1836–7.

12 Peyssonnel and Desfontaines (1838), vol. I, p. 170.

13 Seghir ben Youssef (1900), p. 441.

14 Balzac, *Les Illusions perdues*; A.G.G.T. regs. 114, 121, 1174 and 1175 A.H./1760–2.

15 A.N. Paris, F 17 2957 B: Ducouret, pp. 120, 155–6, and 223.

16 Sergent (1941); Brunet (1939).

17 At the beginning of the nineteenth century; Pananti (1817), p. 332; Shaler (1826), p. 85.

18 This slightly advances the dates proposed by Hemardinquer (1970), p. 287, n. 3. Arch. A.E., *Mémoires et Documents*, Morocco, vol. 2, 1719, 1777, folios 456 and 458. See also for 1805, *Mémoires et Documents*, Morocco, vol. 1, folio 247.

19 A.S. Venice, Savi alla mercanzia, B 767.

20 For Morocco, see Lempriere (1791), pp. 249–50; Ali Bey (1816), p. 34, whose analysis deserves to be quoted: "In Morocco there had long been a large consumption of coffee; it was drunk at all hours of the day, as in the Levant; but after the English presented tea to the sultans, they began offering it to members of their court, and soon the custom of that drink spread from one to another all the way to the lowest classes of society, so that proportionately, more tea is drunk today in Morocco than in England." An important contribution was made by Hemardinquer (1970), pp. 285ff.; more accessible than the studies made by Miège, noted in Hemardinquer, p. 286, n. 1.

21 Braudel (1967b).

22 Montagne (1953), pp. 104–5.

23 Shaw (1743), vol. II, p. 394; Peyssonel and Desfontaines (1838), vol. I, p. 221.

24 Rodinson, "Ghidha" in *E.I.*, new ed., pp. 1,081–97; Lumbroso (1860), p. 67; Poiret (1789), p. 38; Boris (1951); Gobert (1940), p. 42; and Peyssonnel and Desfontaines (1838), vol. I, p. 73.

25 Shaw (1743), vol. I, p. 385; Gobert (1940); Marçais and Guiga (1925), pp. 3326ff. On the water of Nisan, see Calendar of Ibn al Bannā' (thirteenth to fourteenth centuries) in Renaud (1948), p. 39: "The dough for bread made with this water rises without leavening." Idem, in Calendrier de Cordoue.

26 Cour, "Kuskusu," in *E.I.*, 1st ed; Gobert (1940), p. 6 (and 1955).

27 Anonymous, *Etat des royaumes de Barbarie, Tripoly, Tunis et Alger* (1703), p. 115.

28 Saint Gervais (1736).

29 Idris (1959), pp. 592, 631.

30 Shaw (1743), vol. II, p. 312; Burnet (1939).

31 Burnet (1939), p. 27; Gobert (1940); Desfontaines (1798), vol. II, p. 444.

32 Marmol (1667), p 452.

33 Peyssonnel and Desfontaines (1838), vol. I, pp. 69–70.

34 *C.T.*, 1955, no. 12.

35 Peyssonnel and Desfontaines (1838), vol. I, p. 209.

36 Desfontaines (1798), vol. I, p. 208, and II, pp. 248, 252–3, 367, 395; Peyssonnel and Desfontaines (1838), vol. II, pp. 49, 55. These "snack" foods were still very common when Burnet (1939) and Gobert (1940) made their studies. The number and content of meals had hardly changed during the colonial period, if one exempts the two innovations already mentioned, the use of coffee and tea by the lower classes.

37 Kennedy (1846), p. 25.

38 Regular purchase of cakes during the month of Ramadan. A.G.G.T., reg. 11ff. for receipts and expenses.

39 Ibn Abi Dhiaf, vol. III; Valensi and Ben Smail (1971).

40 Montaigne, *Essais*, book I, chap. LV, "Des senteurs." This sumptuous repast has passed into Italian literature in a story by Bandello that came from the same sources as Montaigne's, and of which Sebag published a French translation in 1971.

41 Documents of the eighteenth and nineteenth centuries are silent on these culinary rituals. For the seventeenth, however, El Kairouani (1845, pp. 487–92) confirms the age of these present-day rites. They were inventoried by Marty (1935) and Monchicourt (1910). Similar rituals are practiced in Rabat (Morocco) in the twentieth century; Jouin (1957).

42 El Kairouani (1845), p. 492; Payre (1942). Students have told me that in Hammamet, it is customary to serve a couscous with fresh almonds on the first of May; and in Ksar Hellal, couscous is made with saffron. For Morocco, see Westermarck (1926), vol. II, chap. XV.

43 Hanoteau and Letourneux (1872–3).

44 Shaw (1743), vol. I, p. 368.

45 Shaw (1743), vol. I, pp. X–XI. Also Pananti (1818), p. 274; Antinori (1867), p. 55.

46 Boris (1951), p. 173; Gobert (1940); Marçais and Guiga (1925), p. 186, n. 1, and p. 187, n. 7. For broader coverage, see the excellent study by Maunier (1924–5).

47 Peyssonnel and Desfontaines (1838), vol. I, p. 214.

48 Dan (1637), p. 250.

49 Bardin (1939), pp. 114ff.; Boris (1951), p. 148; Menouillard (1911). The same rituals have been observed from one end of the Maghreb to the other. For Morocco, see Westermarck (1921, 1926).

50 Dan (1637), p. 75; Desfontaines (1830), p. 199: "On the face of the houses one often see the image of a hand painted in red or black. It is a kind of charm against evil spirits." Shaw (1743), pp. 396–7.

51 Marçais and Guiga (1925), p. 196, n. 23.

52 Peyssonnel and Desfontaines (1838), vol. I, p. 224; Shaw (1743), p. 398; Dubouloz-Laffin(1946).

53 Examples in A.V. Tunisie, boxes 28–30.

54 Boris (1951), p. 35.

55 Benet (1957), p. 193.

6. Demographic calamities

1 These two points were developed more extensively in *Annales, Economies, Sociéties, Civilisations*, no. 6, 1969, and *Revue historique*, no. 494, 1970.

2 Miquel (1968), pp. 282ff., formulates a double hypothesis for the Ottoman world: (1) discrepancy between European demographic growth and the stagnation of the Ottoman empire; (2) delayed demographic growth – in the second half of the nineteenth century – in Islamic countries. This does not seem to me to be contradicted by the analysis of the Tunisian situation.

3 Ganiage (1964) published an age pyramid for the town of Soliman. The pyramid for Hammamet, outlined here, presents the same profile. It thus invites the same remarks as those made by Ganiage, which need not be repeated here. The pyramid in this book was constructed to confirm the analysis related to Cape Bon and to compare it to other regions.

4 A.G.G.T., reg. 894, for Porto Farina, Aousdja, Sidi Ali, Galaat el Andleuss, and El Alia; reg. 845 for the Waslatiya.

5 A.G.G.T., regs. 747, 767 (1276 A.H.); 853, 876 (1278 A.H.).

6 Seklani (1961). Starting from the ages of the population in the census I have tried to establish a table of mortality according to the methods of demographers (Pressat 1961; Seklani 1961, *Etude démographiques*, no. 25, United Nations). The result obtained a life expectancy lower than that of all currently underdeveloped countries.

7 Archives de la Conservation foncière, acts accompanying titles 5501, 28, 125.058.

8 Yacono (1954). I have already presented this hypothesis in Valensi (1969b). Here I differ with Ganiage (1966), who wrote: "Tunisia, which remained agricultural, saw an increase in its rural population, thanks to a soaring birthrate" (p. 868).

9 The following discussion on the possibility of a history of prices, as well as that concerning variations in cultivated areas, was published in a different form in *Revue historique* (1970).

10 A.G.G.T., regs. 1–400. Since it was impossible to calculate annual averages, the curves register all known prices for a single year.

11 On this crisis see A.N. Paris, AE B 1 1127; Grandchamp (1933a), vol. X.

12 A.N. Paris, AE B 1 1127, 1130; Marine B 7 289; Arch. A.E. *Mémoires et documents, Afrique*, vol. 9, folio 77.

13 A.N. Paris, AE B 1 1132, 1134, AE B III 300; col. F 2 A, Auriol Co., correspondence of Soret-Maurepas 1737; A.C.C.M. L III 4, Auriol Co., lettres from Fénix, 1735–47; A.C.C.M., L III 271, Cie Royale d'Afrique, L III 252; Archives départementales du Vaucluse, B 324, 325, 326, 327, Soret; and Gandolphe (1924, 1925, and 1926).

14 A.N. Paris, AE B 1 1142–5; 134 AP 1, file 2; AE B III, 285; A.C.C.M., L III, 273, 274, 285.

15 A.N. Paris, AE B 1149, 1150; A.C.C.M., L IX 699, 701; L III 253, 275, 1331; A.C.C.M., L 1901, Commerce de Barbarie, Tunis; Archivio di Stato, Venice, *V Savi alla mercanzia*, B 768; Desfeuilles (1956).

16 Arch. A.E. Tunis, *Correspondance consulaire*, vol. 38; Algiers, *Correspondance consulaire*, vol. 37; MacGill (1811).

17 See chap. 7.

18 A.G.G.T., regs. 2064–2122; 2250–85, and nos. 6, 10, 20, 55, 90, 287 of the series of revenues and expenditures. See Valensi (1970) for a presentation of the source and technique of making the curves.

19 A.G.G.T., regs. 6, 10, 20.

20 On deficit years in Europe, R. Romano (1956), and S. F. Romano (1958).

21 Indications in Valensi (1969a).

22 A.N. Paris, AE B 1 1145, letter of November 5, 1773.

23 Until 1824, the date of the end of information about the estates of this district.

24 A.C.C.M., L III 275, letter of December 28, 1784.

25 A.V. Tunisie, box 29, file on Zaghouan, Tebourba, etc.

26 Arch. A.E., Tunisia, *Correspondance commerciale*, vol. 43, folio 111, letter of December 31, 1817; vols. 44 and 45, for the following years.

27 Ibn Abi Dhiaf, vol. IV.

28 A.G.G.T., regs. 1–13 (temporary numbering); 1174 A.H. to 1247 A.H. for Andalusian villages. This series, in the process of assemblage during my research, should be completed as the classification of archives continues. For the other regions, registers of receipts and expenditures.

7. Advent of a trade economy

1 1677–8 (A.G.G.T., reg. 1).

2 A.G.G.T., registers of receipts and expenses; Cherif (1968a).

3 On the refusal of payments in gold pieces, A.C.C.M., L III 252, Compagnie Royale d'Afrique, Villet, May 10, 1741; Cherif (1968a), p. 48.

4 Braudel (1967a), vol. I, pp. 155, 450; Sayous (1929).

5 This passage is largely the result of studies by Farrugia de Candia (1934, 1935), and the documents he published.

6 Savary (1723).

7 Farrugia de Candia (1938); Marcel in Frank (1850), p. 219, gives two examples of these seventeenth-century coins.

8 A.N. Paris, AE B 1 1128, letter of July 16, 1714.

9 Leo Africanus (1830 ed.), vol. II, p. 50.

10 After Marcel in Frank (1850), p. 216, who published an illustration of a nāsri struck in 1761; not mentioned in Farrugia de Candia's inventory.

11 Marcel in Frank (1850), p. 219. According to the same author, p. 218, quarter sequins were also created; de Candia does not mention this.

12 Figure provided by Farrugia de Candia. Bonneville (1806), p. 205, gives a content of 406 or 408 for that date.

13 Mintings known from 1172 to 1181 A.H., from 1186 to 1191 A.H., then in 1193 and 1194 for fels; from 1173 to 1178 A.H., in 1180, 1182, 1189, 1190, and 1195 for *qāfsi*. Ibn Abi Dhiaf, vol. II, speaks of these innovations (but he mistakenly attributes the first minting of gold money to Bey Ali). More interesting though unverifiable, Ibn Abi Dhiaf states that gold powder came at that time from the Sudan in abundance and was not liable to any tax.

14 Shaw (1966), p. 168, for the Egyptian para; also Raymond (1973), vol. I, pp. 17ff.; for the Turkish piaster Svoronos (1956), p. 82, gives the relationship between this coin and the Venetian sequin on the basis of which I have calculated the index transcribed on the curve.

15 A.C.C.M., Fonds Roux, L IX 699.

16 Filippi, in Monchicourt (1924), pp. 154–5.

17 Arch. A.E. Tunisia, *Correspondance commerciale*.

18 I refer the reader to Ganiage (1959), and particularly to chaps. IV, pp. 177ff., and VI, pp. 287ff.

19 Valensi (1969b).

20 Arch. A.E. Mémoires et Documents, Afrique, 9, 1775, Memoir . . . by de Saizieu, folio 152.

21 Arch. A.E., Tunisia, *Correspondance commerciale*, vol. 44, folio 24, Malivoire.

22 On this entire question, Arch. A.E., Tunis, *Correspondance commerciale*, vols. 43–52; also Ibn Abi Dhiaf, vol. III, pp. 172ff.

23 Arch. A.E., Tunis, *Correspondance politique*, vol. I, folio 77.

24 Arch. A.E., *Correspondance commerciale*, vol. 52, folio 100ff.

25 Antinori (1867), p. 96; Pellissier (1853), pp. 361ff.

26 Ganiage (1955b). Tunisian archives made it possible to follow the activity of these merchants and other people, particularly regs. 276, 416, 1039.

27 Emerit (1949); Ganiage (1955b, 1959).

28 Ganiage (1959).

8. A voracious tax system

1 Frank (1850), p.66.

2 Ibn Abi Dhiaf, vol. II, p. 172, and vol. IV.

3 Ibn Abi Dhiaf, vol. III, pp. 15ff.; Pellissier (1853). See also French consular correspondence for that period.

4 A.G.G.T., reg. 34, 1155 A.H.; reg. 1029, 1214 A.H.

5 Ibn ʿAbdalaziz, MS p. 553, quoted by Kraiem (1973), vol. I, p. 278.

6 Ibn Abi Dhiaf, vol. IV, pp. 203–7; translation in Arch. A.E. Tunisia, *Correspondance politique*, vol. 16, folio 122 to 129.

7 *E.I.*, "Djizya." See also Dan (1637), pp. 91–3 (the semiannual campaigns went out to collect the tax or the *lism* from "the dawārs and the hovels of the Arabs"); Pagni (1829), who reported in seventeenth-century Tunisia (the Moors paid "so much per head" each year); El Kairouani (1845), p. 343; Ibn Abi Dhiaf, vol. III, p. 130.

8 A.G.G.T., reg. 39, 1156 A.H.

9 A.G.G.T., regs. 36, 39.

10 Fitoussi (1901), p. 23, quoting Al Wazīr As-Sarrādj. The dey apparently put together a collection of rules, entitled *Al Mizān*, which outlined the responsibilities of the government and the subjects. Also El Kairouani (1845), p. 343; Ibn Abi Dhiaf, vol. III, p. 130.

11 Shaw (1966), pp. 16–17.

12 Ibn ʿAbdelaziz, MS p. 553.

13 Ibn Abi Dhiaf, vol. III, pp. 130–1.

14 A.G.G.T., reg. 1.

15 A.G.G.T., reg. 1639, p. 1. On the subject of legislation during this period, the chronicle by Ibn Abi Dhiaf, who was both an observer and a participant, is invaluable: vols. III, IV; Ibn Abi d-Diaf (1971).

16 A.G.G.T., reg. 1660, p. 1., text of the *qanūn*.

17 Arch. A.E., Tunisia, *Correspondance politique*, vol. I, document of July 5, 1831, should be added to the information from Ibn Abi Dhiaf.

18 Arch. A.E., Tunisia, *Correspondance politique*, vol. 4, January 1840; *Correspondance commerciale*, vols. 52, 53.

19 Ibn Abi Dhiaf, vol. IV, pp. 203–7.

20 On these reforms, see Ganiage (1959). The draft provoked the same reaction in the East, and for the same reasons; Chevallier (1971), p. 114.

21 Arch. A.E., Tunisia, *Correspondance politique*, vol. 1, July 5, 1831.

22 Ibn Abi Dhiaf, vol. III, p. 186, and for subsequent events, the chronicles of the beys Ahmad and M'hamad.

23 Arch. A.E., Tunisia, *Correspondance commerciale*, vol. 51, June 1837.

24 Ibn Abi Dhiaf, vol. IV; Cherif (1968b); A. Martel (1965), vol. I, pp. 118ff.

25 In view of recent publications on the subject of the 1864 revolt (Ganiage [1959], chap. V; Slama [1967]), only the social aspects will be discussed here.

26 This expectation of the sultan's intervention was primarily an urban phenomenon, specifically observed in Sfax and Sousse; the countryside was won over only by contamination. Reference to the sultan also had a somewhat complex significance. The revolt had never intended to overthrow the traditional power, but in addition, there were the effects of an ostentatious deployment of European naval forces, maneuvers by the French and British consuls, and the French presence in Algeria. All thus raised the fear (and the central government did not fail to brandish this weapon) of the direct intervention of Christians. The hope was that help would come from the sultan, whose power and independence were evidently overestimated.

Bibliography and sources

List of abbreviations

A. G. G. T.	Archives générales du gouvernement tunisien
A. N. Paris	Archives nationales, Paris
A. V. Tunisie	Archives du ministère de la Guerre, Vincennes (documents referring to Tunisia)
Arch. A. E.	Archives du ministère des Affaires Etrangères, Paris
A. C. C. M.	Archives de la Chambre de commerce de Marseille
R. M. L.	Royal Malta Library
C. T	*Cahiers de Tunisie*
I. B. L. A.	*Institut des Belles Lettres Arabes*
R. A.	*Revue africaine*
R. T.	*Revue tunisienne*
E. I.	*Encyclopedia of Islam*

Manuscript sources

1. Tunis

A. Archives générales du gouvernement tunisien
Registers in Arabic. Most, although not all, are fiscal archives. The numbers follow the handwritten Arabic catalogue.

I. *Registers of receipts and expenses*; nos. 1–400.
X. *Registers of the majba*: nos. 620–1027.
XI. *Registers of the tithe*: nos. 1028–1111. This series includes thirteen registers that do not appear in the catalogue.
XII. *Registers of the qanūn of olive trees*: nos. 1639–42, 1660–73, 1698–1701, 1742 and 1743.
XIV. *Agricultural taxes*: nos. 1855–1931.
XIX. *Registers of the olive groves*: nos. 2060, 2061.
XXI. *Registers of the bey's properties*: nos. 2064–2122.
XL. *Registers of the tax-gathering expedition*: nos. 2376–98.
XLV. *Registers concerning the Sahel*: nos. 2433–53.
XCIX. *Supplementary registers concerning the bey's properties*: no. 2/2249.

Boxes and files. A French catalogue exists for these archives. The documents and correspondence preserved in these boxes are late and generally beyond the chronological limits of this study. The following boxes are relevant: box 63, notarial acts; box 66, sanitary commission; boxes 82, 93; box 216, state property; box 217, *ghāba.*

B. Archives de la Conservation foncière
Titles 4, 28, 45, 53, 87, 157, 545, 834, 1563, 2092, 2225, 2233, 2375, 3122, 3421, 3458, 3508, 5136, 5501, 5623, 6973, 6974, 7059, 8269, 9437, 9763, 10108, 10387, 10996, 11447, 14354, 15452, 17659, 18575, 125058.

C. Archives de l'administration de la Ghaba

D. Private archives of the Jallūli family

2. France

A. Marseille
Archives de la Chambre de commerce de Marseille:
C. 1842: *Monnaie, Banque. Etat des bâtiments venus du Levant et de Barbarie ayant importé des espèces étrangères d'or et d'argent.* 1732–1750.
I 6 : *Registres, Statistiques.*
J 1416–1423: *Consulat de Tunisie, Lettres des consuls.* 1690–1740.
J 1872–1873: *Compagnie d'Afrique.*
J 1874: *Commerce direct avec les Barbaresques.*
J 1894, 1900, 1901: *Commerce de Barbarie, Tunis, Affaires diverses.*
J 1902–1905: *Consulat de Tunis. Manifestes de chargement des navires dans les ports du royaume de Tunis,* 1730–1776 (1766, 1770, and 1771 not included in records).
J 1906: *Consulat de Tunis, Etat des draps reçus à Tunis.* 1750–1780.
J 1907: *Passage et séjour d'envoyés de Tunis.* 1681–1790.
L I 32–51: *Livre de recettes.*
L I 52–113: *Comptes de quarantaine.*
L I 306–314: *Comptes de quarantaine.*
L III 252: *Compagnie Royale d'Afrique: lettres des agents du Cap Nègre.* 1741.
L III 253: *Compagnie Royale d'Afrique: lettres des agents de la Compagnie à Tabarque.* 1783–1793.
L III 271–278, and 280: *Lettres des agents de la Compagnie à Tunis.*
L III 1328–1334: *Compagnie Royale d'Afrique, Tabarque.*
L III 1335–1337: *Compagnie Royale d'Afrique, Cap Nègre.*
L III 1338–1339: *Compagnie Royale d'Afrique, Bizerte.*
L III 1340: *Comptes des agents de la Compagnie à Tunis.*
L IV 23: *Agence d'Afrique: Lettres des agents à Tunis.*
L IV 139: *Agence d'Afrique. Tabarque. Etat de caisse.*
L IV 140: *Agence d'Afrique, Tunis. Affaires diverses.*
L XI 699, 700 and 701: *Fonds Roux frères. Correspondants en Barbarie.*

B. Paris
1. Archives nationales:
AE B 1 1127–1154, Tunis, vols. 3 (1701) to 31 (1792).
AE B III 300–322 and 385. Compagnie d'Afrique.
Marine B 7 68, 71, 73, 75, 79, 85, 89, 93, 103, 105, 108, 112, etc., up to 202: *Commerce de Levant et Barbarie. 1700-1755. Départs*; B 7 276, 289, 295, 311, 321, 322, 340, 345, 357, etc., up to 534: *Levant et Barbarie, 1699-1789. Reçues.*
F 17 2957 B: Mission en Afrique du Colonel Ducouret.

2. Archives du ministère de la Guerre, Vincennes. Documents referring to Tunisia:

Box 13: *Renseignements fournis sur la Tunisie avant l'expédition de 1881.*

Boxes 28, 29, and 30: *Reconnaissance et rapports sur les villes, villages et tribus de la Tunisie, 1878 à 1888.*

3. Archives du ministère des Affaires Étrangères:

Algiers: *Correspondance commerciale*, vols. 32 (1793–5) to 47 (1824–9).

Morocco: *Correspondance consulaire et commerciale*, vols. 20 (1790–7) to 32 (1843–8).

Mémoires et documents, Morocco, 1, 2.

Mémoires et documents, Afrique, 5, 9.

Tunisia: *Correspondance politique*, vols. 1–22; *Correspondance consulaire et commerciale.*

C. Miscellaneous

Archives départementales du Vaucluse, B 426.

3. Port archives

A. Archivio di Stato, Leghorn

Governatori, Correspondenza con i consoli toscani in Africa.

Governatori, Affari staccati

Sanità maritima, arrivi di navi, protocolli e repertori, regs. 696 (1785–6) to 744 (1850).

Governatori, Affari generali e carteggio di sanità.

B. Archivio di Stato, Venice

V *Savi alla mercanzia*, B 767, 768, and 769.

C. Royal Malta Library, Valetta

1. Archives of the University: First division: Tempore ordino, call numbers 207, 218, 256, 306, 313–24, 334–37; second division: Tempore britannorum, call numbers 361–4, 365–75, 376–83, 388–96.
2. Archives of the Order of Malta, call numbers 6527–33.

Published archives

Grandchamp, P. (1928–38). *La France en Tunisie, au XVIIe siècle:* Vol. VI (*1651–1660*); VII (*1661–1688*); VIII (*1681–1700*); X (*de 1701 à l'avènement de la dynastie hassinite*). Tunis.

Plantet, E. (1893–9). *Correspondance des beys de Tunis et des consuls de France avec la cour, 1577–1830*, 3 vols. Paris.

Catalogues of archives and bibliographies

Ashbee, H. S. 1889. *A Bibliography of Tunisia.* London.

Bono, S. 1969. "Fonti e documenti italiani per la storia della Tunisia." *Quaderni dell'Istituto Italiano di Cultura di Tunisia* 1: 1–21.

Ministère de la Guerre. 1931. *L'Afrique française du Nord. Bibliographie militaire des ouvrages français ou traduits en français et des articles des principales revues françaises relatifs à l'Algérie, à la Tunisie et au Maroc de 1830 à 1926*, 4 vols. Paris.

Pearson, J. D. 1958. *Index Islamicus 1906–1955. Catalogue of articles on Islamic subjects in periodicals and other collective publications. Supplement 1956–1960; 1966–1970; 1971–1972.* Cambridge.

Riggio, A. 1933. *Bibliographia summaria dell'Oriente e dell'Africa.* Tunis.

Bibliography

Abdesselem, A. 1973. *Les historiens tunisiens des XVIIe, XVIIIe et XIXe siècles.* Tunis.

Ageron, Ch.-R. 1968. *Les Algériens musulmans et la France*, 2 vols. Paris.

Ali Bey, Domingo Badia y Leblich. 1817. *Travels of Ali Bey in Morocco, Tripoli, Cyprus, Egypt, Arabia, Syria and Turkey*, 2 vols. Philadelphia.

Anonymous

1703. *Etat des royaumes de Barbarie, Tripoly, Tunis et Alger.* Rouen.

1713. *Histoire des dernières révolutions du Royaume de Tunis et des mouvements du royaume d'Alger.* Paris.

1757. *Histoire des Etats barbaresques qui exercent la piraterie.* Paris.

1765. *Le voyageur françois, ou la connaissance de l'ancien et du nouveau monde*, vol. 1. Paris.

1785. *Voyages dans les Etats barbaresques de Maroc, Alger, Tunis et Tripoly ou lettres d'un des captifs qui viennent d'être rachetés par MM. les chanoines de la Sainte-Trinité.* Paris.

Antinori, O. 1867. *Lettere sulla Tunisia.* Florence.

Attya, H. 1957. "L'organisation de l'oasis." *C.T.* 5, nos. 17–18: 39–44.

Austruy, J. 1961. *L'Islam face au développement économique.* Paris.

Bardin, P. 1939. "Les Jebalia de la région de Gafsa. Etude des populations berbères des massifs montagneux à l'est de Gafsa." *R.T.*, n.s. 37: 87–126.

1965. *La vie d'un douar. Essai sur la vie rurale dans les grandes plaines de la Haute Medjerda, Tunisie.* Paris-La Haye.

Barkan, O. L. 1958. "Essai sur les données statistiques des registres de recensement dans l'Empire ottoman au XVe et XVIe siècles." *Journal of Economic and Social History of the Orient* I, no. 1: 9–36.

Barrault, A. 1903. *De l'organisation de la propriété foncière en Tunisie.* Paris.

Barthes, G. 1923. *Les impôts arabes en Tunisie (impôts directs).* Algiers.

Benet, F. 1957. "Explosive markets: the Berber Highlands." In Polanyi, ed. (1957).

Benhadji Serradj. 1951. "Quelques usages féminins et populaires à Tlemcen." *I.B.L.A.* 5, 55: 279–92.

Berge, S. 1909. *Répertoire de législation tunisienne.*

Bernard, A. 1921. *Enquête sur l'habitation rurale des indigènes de Tunisie, 1911.* Tunis.

1925. "La charrue en Afrique." *Compte Rendu du Congrès du Caire*, vol. III, pp. 283–93.

Bernard, P. 1925. *Les anciens impôts d'Afrique du Nord.* Paris.

Bernard and Comelin de la Motte, R.P. 1721. *Voyage pour la rédemption des captifs aux royaumes d'Alger et de Tunis.* Paris.

Berque, J. 1938. *Etudes d'histoire rurale maghrébine.* Tangier-Fez.

1953. "Qu'est-ce qu'une 'tribu' nord-africaine." In *Eventail de l'histoire vivante. Mélanges Lucien Febvre*, Paris. Vol. 1, pp. 261–71.

1955. *Structures sociales du Haut-Atlas.* Paris.

Bertholon and Chantre. 1913. *Recherches anthropologiques dans la Berbérie orientale: Tripolitaine, Tunisie, Algérie*, 2 vols. Lyon.

Bessis, A. 1912. *Essai sur la loi foncière tunisienne.* Tunis.
Bessis, A., Marthelot, P., Montety, H. De, Pauphilet, D. 1956. *Le territoire des Ouled Ali Ben Aoun.* Paris.
Birot, C. 1947. *Etude comparée des régimes fonciers tunisiens et marocains.* Tunis.
Birot, P., and Dresch, J. 1953. *La Méditerranée et le Moyen-Orient.* Paris.
Blaquiere, O. 1813. *Letters from the Mediterranean.* 2 vols. London.
Bloch, M. 1952, 1956. *Les caractères originaux de l'histoire rurale française,* 2d ed. 2 vols. Paris.
Boeuf, F. 1923. Les blés de Tunisie. Variétés. Aptitudes agricoles et industrielles. Report given at the Semaine nationale du Blé, Paris, January.
Bonneville, A. 1849. *Nouvelle encyclopédie monétaire.* Paris.
Bonneville, P.-F. 1806. *Traité des monnaies.* Paris.
Bonniard, F. 1934. *La Tunisie du Nord. Le Tell septentrional.* 2 vols. Paris.
Bono, S. 1964. *I corsari barbareschi.* Turin.
Borg, A. 1955a. "La tente dans la région de Kairouan." *Cahiers des Arts et Techniques de l'Afrique du Nord,* 4: 49–60.
1955b. "La tente nomade dans la région de Gafsa." *Cahiers des Arts et Techniques de l'Afrique du Nord* 4: 61–75.
Boris, G. 1951. *Documents linguistiques et ethnographiques sur une région du Sud tunisien (Nefzaoua).* Paris.
1958. *Lexique du parler arabe des Marazig.* Paris.
Boukhari. 1959. *Livres de l'ensemencement... et de la mousâquat.* Algiers.
Bourdieu, P. 1958. *Sociologie de l'Algérie.* Paris. (English translation: *The Algerians,* Boston, 1962.)
1972. *Esquisse d'une théorie de la pratique.* Paris-Geneva.
Bousquet, G. H. 1953. "Subsiste-t-il des traces de droit coutumier dans le Sud tunisien ?" *Travaux de l'Institut de Recherches sahariennes* 10: 193–8.
1957. "Notes sur les survivances du droit coutumier berbère en Tunisie." *Hespéris,* 40: 248–9.
Brancato, F. 1945. "Il commercio dei grani nel'700 in Sicilia." *Archivio Storico Italiano,* pp. 25ff.
Braudel, F. 1950. "Pour une économie historique." *Revue économique* 1: 37–44.
1958. "Histoire et sciences sociales. La longue durée." *Annales, Economies, Sociétés, Civilisations* 13: 725–53.
1967a. *La Méditerranée et le monde méditerranéen à l'époque de Philippe II,* 2d ed.; 2 vols. Paris.
1967b. *Civilisation matérielle et capitalisme,* vol. 1. Paris.
Braudel, F., and Romano, R. 1951. *Navires et marchandises à l'entrée du port du Livourne, 1547–1611.* Paris.
Brown, L. C. 1976. *The Tunisia of Ahmad Bey.* Princeton, N.J.
Bruce. 1790–1. *Voyage en Nubie et Abyssinie,* 5 vols. Translated into French by Castera. Paris.
Brunhes, J. 1902. *L'irrigation, ses conditions géographiques, ses modes et son organisation dans la péninsule Ibérique et dans l'Afrique du Nord.* Paris.
Brunschwig, H. 1962a. "Histoire, passé et frustration en Afrique Noire." *Annales, Economies, Sociétés, Civilisations,* 17: 873–84.
1962b. "La troque et la traite." *Cahiers d'Etudes africaines,* pp. 344–5.
Brunschvig, R. 1936. *Deux récits de voyage inédits en Afrique du Nord au XVe siècle,* publication de l'Institut d'Etudes orientales, 7. Paris.
1937. "Sur les mesures de capacité au commencement du 17e siècle." *Annales de l'Institut d'Etudes orientales d'Alger,* pp. 74–88.

1940. *La Berbérie orientale sous les Hafsides des origines à la fin du 15e siècle*, 2 vols. Paris.
Bulliet, R.-W. 1969. "Le chameau et la roue au Moyen-Orient." *Annales, Economies, Sociétés, Civilisations* 24: 1,092ff.
Burnet, E. 1939. *Enquête sur l'alimentation en Tunisie*. Tunis. Reprinted from *Archives de l'Institut Pasteur de Tunis* 27.
Burnet, E., and Viscontini. 1938. "Le pain et les céréales dans l'alimentation tunisienne." *Archives de l'Institut Pasteur de Tunis* 28.
Bussi, E. 1952. "Per la storia dei rapporti colla reggenza barbaresca." *Studi economici e giuridici dell'università di Cagliari*.
Capitaine XXX. 1844. *Une promenade à Tunis en 1844*. Paris.
Capot Rey, R. 1956. "Greniers domestiques et greniers fortifiés au Sahara: le cas du Gourara." *Travaux de l'Institut de Recherches sahariennes*, (Algiers) XIV: 139–58.
Capot Rey, R., and Marçais, P. 1953. "La charrue au Sahara." *Travaux de l'Institut de Recherches sahariennes* (Algiers) IX: 39–69.
Carette, E. 1884. *Etude des routes suivies par les Arabes dans la partie méridionale de l'Algérie et dans la régence de Tunis*, Exploration scientifique de l'Algérie, Vol. 1. Paris.
Caroni, P. F. 1916–17. *Relation du court voyage d'un antiquaire amateur surpris par les corsaires, conduit en Barbarie et heureusement rapatrié*. Translated into French by M. Conor and P. Carrigou-Grandchamp. Tunis.
Carriere, C. 1973. *Négociants marseillais*, 2 vols. Marseille.
Castelnuovo, Dott. cav. G. 1865. *Osservazione medico fisiche sul clima et sugli abitanti di Tunisie e d'altre parte di Africa*. Milan.
Cattenoz, H. G. 1954. *Table de concordance des ères chrétienne et hégirienne*. Rabat.
Chelhod, J. 1969. "La structure dualiste de la société bédouine." *L'Homme* 9, no. 2: 89–112.
1971. *Le droit dans la société bédouine*. Paris.
Chenel, M. 1912. *La Medjba, impôt de capitation tunisien*. Tunis.
Cherif, M.-H. 1968a. "Introduction de la piastre espagnole ('ryal') dans la régence de Tunis au début du XVIIe siècle." *C.T.* 16, nos. 61–4: 45–55.
1968b. "Les mouvements paysans au XIXe siècle en Tunisie." Unpublished mimeograph.
1970. "Expansion européenne et difficultés tunisiennes." *Annales, Economies, Sociétés, Civilisations* 25: 714–45.
1973. "L'Etat tunisien et les campagnes au XVIIIe siècle." *Publication des Cahiers de la Méditerranée*, special ser., no. 1: 9–22.
Chevalier, H. 1902. "Les charrues d'Afrique," *Memoires et Travaux de la Société des Ingénieurs civils de France, bulletin de février*, 237–42.
Chevallier, D. 1968. "Les cadres sociaux de l'économie agraire dans le Proche-Orient au début du XIXe siècle: le cas du Mont Liban." *Revue historique* 239: 87–100.
1971. *La société du Mont Liban à l'époque de la révolution industrielle en Europe*. Paris.
Cipolla, Carlo M. 1956. *Money, Prices and Civilization in the Mediterranean World – Fifth to Seventeenth Century*. Princeton, N.J.
Coustillac, L. 1951–2. "Note sur la teinture végétale à Oudref." *Cahiers des Arts et Techniques de l'Afrique du Nord* 1: 24–40.
1954. "Note sur la rénovation des tissus traditionnels de la région de Gabès." *Cahiers des Arts et Techniques de l'Afrique du Nord* 3: 64–73.

1958. "Note sur la teinture végétale dans le Sud tunisien." *C.T.* 23–4: 353–63.

Cubisol, C. 1867. *Notices abrégées sur la régence de Tunis.* Paris.

Cuisenier, J. and Miquel, A. 1965. "La terminologie arabe de la parenté, Analyse sémantique et analyse componentielle." *L'Homme* 5, no. 3: 17ff.

Dainville, P. de. 1964. *Le langage des géographes.* Paris.

Dan, P. 1637. *Histoire de Barbarie et de ses corsaires.* Paris.

Dapper. 1686. *Description de l'Afrique.* Amsterdam.

Daumas, Capitaine P. 1857. *4 années à Tunis.* Algiers.

Davis, N., and Sebag, P. 1959. "Une description de Tunis au XIXe siècle." *C.T.* 6, nos. 21–2: 161–81.

Debbasch, Y. 1957. *La nation française en Tunisie.* Paris.

Deglin, C., and Poitrineau, A. 1954. "Un terroir de la zone côtière du Nord: El Aousdja." *C.T.* 2, nos. 7–8: 254–64.

Dermenghem, E. 1954. *Le culte des Saints dans l'Islam maghrébin.* Paris.

Desfeuilles, P. 1956. "Scandinaves et Barbaresques à la fin de l'Ancien Régime." *C.T.* 4, no. 15: 327–49.

Desfontaines, R. L. 1798. *Flora atlantica sive historia plantarum quoad in atlante agro tunetano et algerensi crescunt*, 3 vols. Paris.

1830. *Itinéraire dans les Royaumes de Tunis et d'Alger en 1783 et 1784*, Extracted from *Nouvelles Annales des Voyages*, 2d ser., vols. 16, 17. Paris (Bibliothèque du Museum).

Desme de Chavigny. 1911. *La terre collective de tribu en Algérie et Tunisie.* Tunis.

Despois, J. 1931. "Essai sur l'habitat rural du Sahel tunisien." *Annales de Géographie*, 259–74.

1937. "Rendements en grains du Byzacium, il y a 2 000 ans et aujourd'hui." *Mélanges E.F. Gautier.* Tours.

1942. "Régions naturelles et régions humaines en Tunisie." *Annales de Géographie*, 112–28.

1948. "Le destin de l'Afrique du Nord." *Revue de la Méditerranée*, Sept./Oct.

1953. "Les greniers fortifiés de l'Afrique du Nord." *C.T.* 1, no. 1: 38–160.

1955. *La Tunisie orientale, Sahel et Basse Steppe*, 2d ed. Paris.

1956. "La culture en terrasse dans l'Afrique du Nord." *Annales, Economies, Sociétés, Civilisations* 11: 42–50.

1959. "Le djebel Ousselat, les Ousseltiya et les Kooub." *C.T.* 7, no. 28: 407–27.

Dornier, P. 1955. "La politesse bédouine dans les campagnes du Nord de la Tunisie: le mariage." *I.B.L.A.* 8, no. 69: 92–126.

Dornier, P., and Louis, A. 1954. "La politesse bédouine dans les campagnes du Nord de la Tunisie: le mariage." *I.B.L.A.* 7, no. 67: 251–68.

Dournon, A. 1913. "Kitab tarikh qosantîna par el Hadj Ahmed el Mobârek." *R.A.* 57, no. 289: 265–305.

Doutté, E. 1909. *Magie et religion dans l'Afrique du Nord.* Algiers.

Dovring, F. 1961. "Peasantry, land use, and change. A review article." *Comparative Studies in Society and History* 4: 364–74.

Dresch, J. 1949. "Dans le Grand Atlas calcaire." *Bulletin de l'Association des Géographes français* 200–1: 56–63.

Dubouloz-Laffin, M.-L. 1946. *Le Bou-Mergoud. Folklore tunisien, croyances et coutumes populaires de Sfax et de sa région.* Paris.

Dubout, F. 1938. *Le habous dans le droit musulman et la législation nord-africaine.* Algiers.

Durkheim, E. 1893. *De la division du travail social: étude sur l'organisation des sociétés supérieures*. Paris.

Dusgate. 1932. *Notice sur les monnaies, poids et mesures de Tunisie*. Paris.

El Aiachi and Moula Hamed. 1846. *Voyages dans le Sud de l'Algérie et des états barbaresques*. Translated by Berbrugger from a seventeenth-century text. Paris.

El Aouani, M. 1966. "Structure agraire dans un village côtier du Nord de la Tunisie: Galaat el Andleuss." *Revue tunisienne des Sciences sociales* 2, no. 3: 71–108.

El Bekri, Abu Obeid. 1965. *Description de l'Afrique septentrionale*. Translated from an eleventh-century text by MacGucklin de Slane. Paris.

El Kairouani (Mohammed ben Ali el Rami). 1845. *Histoire de l'Afrique*. Translated from a seventeenth-century text by Pellissier and Remusat. Exploration scientifique de l'Algérie, vol. 7. Paris.

Emerit, M. 1949. "La crise des finances tunisiennes et les origines du protectorat." *R.A.* 93, nos. 420–1: 248–76.

Ennasiri Esslaoui, A. 1906 and 1907. "Kitab Elistiqsâ, chronique de la dynastie alaouie du Maroc." Translated by E. Fumey. *Archives marocaines* 9, 10.

Es-Snoussi, T. 1935. *Concordance du droit musulman avec le droit tunisien en matière "Habous."* Tunis.

Evans-Pritchard, E. E. 1968. *Les Nuer, description des modes de vie et des institutions politiques d'un peuple nilote*. First published in English, 1940. Paris.

1969. *Anthropologie sociale*. Paris.

Ezziani, A. 1886. *Le Maroc de 1631 à 1812*. Translated by O. Houdas. Paris.

Fagnan, E. 1900. *L'Afrique septentrionale au XIIe siècle de notre ère, description extraite du "Kitab el Istibçar."* Constantine.

1924. *Extraits inédits relatifs au Maghreb*. Algiers.

Faivre-Dupaigre, J.-P. 1957. "L'irrigation traditionnelle dans l'oasis de Gabès." *C.T.* 5, nos. 17–18: 23–38.

Farrugia De Candia, J. 1934. "Monnaies husseinites. Monnaies frappées de l'année 1196 à l'année 1262 Hég. (1782 à 1846)." *R.T.* n.s. 17: 73–92.

1935. "Monnaies husseinites. Monnaies frappées de l'année 1117 à l'année 1196 Hég. (1705 à 1782). *R.T.* n.s. 21: 15–36.

1938. "Monnaies hafsides du musée du Bardo." *R.T.* n.s. 35: 231–88.

Faye, R. P., J.-B. De La. 1703. *Etat des royaumes de Barbarie, Tripoly, Tunis et Alger*. Rouen.

Ferchiou, S. 1968. "Différenciation sexuelle de l'alimentation du Djérid (Sud tunisien)." *L'Homme* 8, no. 2: 64–86.

Ferraud, L. C. 1927. *Annales tripolitaines*. Tunis.

Fitoussi, E. 1901. *L'Etat tunisien. Son origine, son développement et son organisation actuelle 1525–1901*. Tunis.

Fitoussi, E., and Benazet, A. 1931. *L'Etat tunisien et le protectorat français. Histoire et organisation (1525 à 1881) et (1881 à 1931)*, 2 vols. Tunis.

Flaux, A. De. 1865. *La régence de Tunis au XIXe siècle*. Paris.

Fleury, V. 1895a. *La natterie, la vannerie de feuille de palmier et la sparterie en Tunisie*. Paris.

1895b. *Les tapis de Kairouan et l'industrie de la teinture en Tunisie*. Paris.

1897. "Les industries indigènes en Tunisie. "*Revue des Sciences pures et appliquées*, 174ff.

1900. *Les industries indigènes de la Tunisie*. Paris.

Fortes, M. 1953. "The structure of unilineal descent groups." *American Anthropologist* 55: 17–41.

Fortes, M. and Evans-Pritchard, E. E. 1940. *African Political Systems*. Oxford.

François, A. 1867. *Tunis et la régence sous Mohamed es Sadok Bey*. Paris.

Frank, Dr. L. 1850. *Tunis. L'univers pittoresque*. Edited by J. J. Marcel. Paris.

Gallico, A. 1935. *Tunisi e i consoli sardi, 1816–1834*. Bologna.

Gandolphe, M. 1918. "Notes inédites sur la Tunisie en 1786 et sur son épidémie de peste en 1785. Extraits du journal du père Vicherat." *R.T.* 25, no. 125: 210–21.

1924, 1925, 1926. "Lettres sur l'histoire politique de la Tunisie de 1728 à 1740." *R. T.* 30, nos. 162–3; 209–30; 31, no. 164: 287–303; 32, no. 165: 352–64; no. 166: 457–83.

Ganiage, J. 1955a. "La crise des finances tunisiennes et l'ascension des juifs en Tunisie, 1860–1880." *R.A.* 99, nos. 444–5: 153–73.

1955b. "Les Européens en Tunisie au milieu du XIXe siècle (1840–1870)." *C.T.* 3, no. 11: 388–421.

1957. "Etude démographique sur les Européens de Tunisie au milieu du XIXe siècle." *C.T.* 5, nos. 19–20: 167–202.

1959. *Les origines du protectorat français en Tunisie. 1861–1881*. Paris.

1960. *La population européene de Tunis au milieu de XIXe siècle*. Paris.

1964. "La population de la Tunisie vers 1860. Essai d'évaluation d'après les registres fiscaux." In *Etudes maghrébines. Mélanges Charles-André Julien*. Paris; reprinted in *Population* 5 (1966): 857–86.

Gaudiani, D., and Thiaucourt, P. 1910. *La Tunisie, législation, gouvernement, administration*.

Gellner, E. 1969. *Saints of the Atlas*. London.

George, P. 1952. *La Ville*. Paris.

Ghaloussi, B. 1960. "Archives du Sahel au XIXe siècle." *C.T.* 7, no. 31: 97–108.

Gibb, H. A. R., and Bowen, H. 1950–7. *Islamic Society and the West in the XVIIIth century*, 2 vols. London.

Girard, P. S. 1812. "Mémoire sur l'agriculture, l'industrie et le commerce de l'Egypte." In *Description de l'Egypte, Etat moderne*, vol. 2. Paris.

Gobert, E. G. 1940. *Usages et rites alimentaires des Tunisiens*, reprinted from *Archives de l'Institut Pasteur de Tunis* 29 (Sept.–Dec.) Tunis.

1955. "Les références historiques des nourritures tunisiennes." *C.T.* 3, no. 12: 501–42.

Godefroi and Comelin De La Motte. 1703. *Royaume de Barbarie, Tripoly, Tunis et Alger*. Rouen.

Godelier, M. 1970. *Sur les sociétés précapitalistes, textes choisis de Marx, Engels, Lénine*. Paris.

1973. *Horizons, trajets marxistes en anthropologie*. Paris.

Godin de Souhesme, G. De. 1875. *Tunisie, histoire, moeurs, gouvernement, administration*. Paris.

Goguyer, A. 1885. *Choix splendide de preceptes . . . ou Petit manuel de dro[illegible] immobilier tunisien*. Paris, Tunis.

1895. "La mejba (impôt de capitation) d'après le chroni[illegible]eur Abou[illegible]diaf." *R.T.* 2: 471–84.

Golvin, L. 1957. *Le Magrib central à l'époque des Zirides*. Paris.

Goy, J., and Le Roy Ladurie, E. 1972. *Les fluctuations du produit de[illegible]îme*. Paris-La Haye.

Graf–De La Salle. 1944, 1946. "Contribution à l'étude du folklore tun[illegible]" *R.A.* 89: 67–82, and 90: 99–117.

Grandchamp, P. 1933a. *La France en Tunisie de 1701 à l'avènemen[illegible] la [illegible]ie Hassinite (1705)*, X. Tunis.

1933b. *Le royaume de Sardaigne et la régence de Tunis. Les incidents de 1830, 1832–1833, 1843–1844*. Tunis.

1935. *Documents relatifs à la révolution de 1864 en Tunisie*, 2 vols. Tunis.

Grenville Temple, T. 1835. *Excursions in Algiers and Tunis*, 2 vols. London.

Gsell, S. 1920–8. *Histoire ancienne de l'Afrique du Nord*, 8 vols. Paris.

Guin. 1861. "De la charrue arabe." *R.A.*, no. 28: 430–4.

Hanoteau, A., and Letourneux, A. 1872–3. *La Kabylie et les coutumes kabyles*, 3 vols. Paris.

Harris, D. R. 1969. "Agricultural systems, ecosystems and the origins of agriculture," in Ucko and Dimbleby, eds., *The Domestication and Exploitation of Plants and Animals*. London.

Haudricourt, A. C., and Hedin, L. 1943. *L'homme et les plantes cultivées*. Paris.

Haudricourt, A. J., and Delamarre, M. 1955. *L'homme et la charrue à travers le monde*. Paris.

Hebenstreit. 1830. "Voyage à Alger, Tunis et Tripoli . . . 1732." *Nouvelles Annales des voyages*, vol. II. Translated into French by M. Eyries. Paris.

Hemardinquer, J.-J. 1970. *Pour une histoire de l'alimentation*. Paris.

Horta y Prado, C. De. 1903. *Tradato de metrologia universal*. Barcelona.

Housset. 1939. *Le statut des terres collectives et la fixation au sol des indigènes en Tunisie*. Paris.

Ibn ʿAbdalaziz Hammūda. 1970. *Kitāb al-bāshī*, vol. 1. From an eighteenth-century text. Tunis.

Ibn Abi Dhiaf. 1963–5. *Ithāf ahl az-zamān*, 7 vols. From a nineteenth-century text. Tunis.

1971. *Ithāf ahl az-zamān bi ahbār mulūk Tūnis*, chap. VI. Edited by A. Abdesselem. Tunis.

Ibn El Awwam. 1864. *Livre d'agriculture*, 3 vols. Translated by Clément-Mullet. Paris.

Idris, H.-R. 1959. *La Berbérie orientale sous les Zirides, Xe-XIIe siècles*, 2 vols. Paris.

Jouin, J. 1957. "Valeur symbolique des aliments et rites alimentaires à Rabat." *Hespéris* 44: 299–328.

Juillet Saint Lager, M. 1874. *La régence de Tunis*. Algiers.

Julien, Ch.–A. 1931. *Histoire de l'Afrique du Nord. Tunisie-Algérie-Maroc*. Paris. (*History of North Africa*. London, 1969.)

Kraiem, M. 1973. *La Tunisie précoloniale*, 2 vols. Tunis.

Kula, W. 1969. "Il sottosviluppo economico in una prospettiva storica." *Annali della fondazione Einaudi* III: 23–26.

1970. *Théorie économique du système féodal. Pour un modèle de l'économie polonaise. 16e-18e siècles*. Paris-La Haye.

Kunckel D'Herculais. 1893, 1905. *Invasions des acridiens vulgo sauterelles en Algérie*, 2 vols. Algiers.

Lacheraf, M. 1965. *L'Algérie, nation et société*. Paris.

La Faye. 1703. *Etat des royaumes de Barbarie*. Rouen.

Lane-Poole, S. 1875–90. *Catalogue of Oriental Coins in the British Museum*, 4 vols. London.

Laoust, E. 1920. *Mots et choses berbères*. Paris.

1930. "Au sujet de la charrue berbère." *Hespéris* 10: 37–47.

Lapidus, I. M. 1967. *Muslim Cities in the Later Middle Ages*. Cambridge, Mass.

Latron, A. 1936. *La vie rurale en Syrie et au Liban*. Beirut.

Laugier De Tassy. 1757. *Histoire des Etats barbaresques qui exercent la piraterie*, 2 vols. Paris.

Lavoix, H. 1891. *Catalogue des monnaies musulmanes de la Bibliothèque nationale*, vol. 2. Paris.

Le Coz, J. 1964. *Le Rharb. Fellahs et colons, étude de géographie régionale*, 2 vols. Rabat.

Lempriere, W. 1791. *A Tour from Gibraltar to Tangier, Sallee, Mogadore, and Santa Cruz*. London.

Leo Africanus, J. 1956. *Description de l'Afrique*. New ed. transl. from Italian by A. Épaulard. 2 vols. Paris.

Lescure, P. 1900. *Du double régime foncier tunisien: droit musulman et propriété foncière*. Tunis.

Le Tourneau, R. 1949. *Fès avant le protectorat*. Casablanca.

Lewis, I. M. 1961. "Force and fission in Northern Somali Lineage structure." *American Anthropologist* 63, no. 1: 94–112.

Littré, É. 1874–75. *Dictionnaire de la langue française*, 4 vols. Paris.

Lucas, P. 1712. *Voyage dans la Grèce, l'Asie mineure, la Macédoine et l'Afrique*, 2 vols. Paris.

Luciani, J.-D. 1890. *Traité des successions musulmanes*. Paris.

Lumbroso, Dr. A. 1860. *Lettres médico-statistiques sur la régence de Tunis*. Marseille.

MacGill, T. 1811. *An Account of Tunis*. London.

Malle, Dureau de la. 1838. *Peyssonnel et Desfontaines, voyages dans les régences de Tunis et d'Alger*, 2 vols. Paris.

Maltzan, Heinrich Freiherr Von. 1869. *Sittenbilder ans Tunis und Algerien*. Leipzig.

1870. *Reize in den Regenschaften Tunis und Tripoli*. Leipzig.

Mantran, R. 1955. "Une relation inédite d'un voyage en Tunisie au milieu du XIXe siècle." *C.T.* 3, no. 11: 475–80.

1959. "L'évolution des relations entre la Tunisie et l'Empire ottoman du XVIe au XIXe siècle." *C.T.* 7, nos. 26–7: 319–33.

1962. *Istanbul dans la seconde moitié du XVIIe siècle. Essai d'histoire institutionnelle, économique et sociale*. Paris.

Mantran, R. and Sauvaget, Jean. 1951. *Règlements fiscaux ottomans: les provinces syriennes*. Paris.

Maqdish al-Sfaxi. 1321 A.H./1903. *Nuzhat al-anzâr fî lagâib at-tawârîkh wa le-akbhâr*, lithographic ed. Eighteenth-century text. Tunis.

Maquart, Capitaine. 1937. "Etude sur la tribu des Haouaîa (territoire de Médenine)." *R.T.* 30: 253–97.

Marçais, G. 1913. *Les Arabes en Berbérie du XIe au XVe siècle*. Constantine-Paris.

1946. *La Berbérie musulmane et l'Orient au Moyen Age*. Paris.

1957. "Réflexions sur la structure de la vie familiale chez les indigènes de l'Afrique du Nord." *Mémorial A. Basset*. Paris.

Marçais, W., and Guiga, A. 1925, 1960–1. *Textes arabes de Takrouna*, book I, *Textes, transcription et traduction annotée*, 1925; book II, *Glossaire, Contribution à l'étude du vocabulaire arabe*, 1960–1, 8 vols.

Marcel, J.-J. 1844. *Tableau général des monnaies ayant cours en Algérie*.

Marmol. 1667. *L'Afrique*, 3 vols. Paris.

Martel, A. 1965. *Les confins saharo-tripolitains de la Tunisie (1881–1911)*, 2 vols. Paris.

Martel, Ch. 1955. "La transhumance et la tente chez les Zlass (Tunisie)." *Cahiers des Arts et Techniques d'Afrique du Nord* 4: 46–8.

Marty, P. 1935. "L'année liturgique musulmane à Tunis." *Revue des Etudes islamiques* I.

Marx, K. 1953–60. *Le capital*, 8 vols. Paris.

1964. *Pre-capitalist economic formations*. Introduction by Eric Hobsbawn. London.

1967. *Fondements de la critique de l'économie politique*, vol. I. Paris.
Masselot, F. 1901. "Les dattiers des oasis du Djérid." *Bulletin de la Direction de l'Agriculture et du Commerce de la régence de Tunis*, no. 119: 114–61.
Masson, P. 1903. *Histoire des établissements et du commerce français dans l'Afrique barbaresque (1590–1793) Algérie, Tunisie, Tripolitaine, Maroc*. Paris.
Maunier, R. 1924–5. "Recherches sur les échanges rituels en Afrique du Nord", *L'Année sociologique*, new ser. 2: 11–97.
Mélanges, Lucien Febvre. 1953. *Eventail de l'Histoire vivante*, 2 vols. Paris.
Menouillard, H. 1905. "Une noce à Zarzis." *R.T.* 12, no. 49: 3–8.
1910. "Pratiques pour solliciter la pluie." *R.T.* 17, no. 82: 102.
1911. "Moeurs indigènes. Comment se fait un mariage à Gafsa." *R.T.* 18, no. 85: 480–7.
1911. "L'année agricole chez les indigènes du Sud tunisien." *R.T.* 18, no. 85: 428–33.
Mercier, E. 1899. *La propriété indigène au Maghreb d'après les juristes musulmans*. Constantine.
Messabie, G. 1955. "La tente et la vie nomade dans le Nefzaoua." *Cahiers des Arts et Techniques d'Afrique du Nord* 4: 76–9.
Miege, J.-L. 1961. *Le Maroc et l'Europe (1830–1894)*, 4 vols. Paris.
Milliot, L. 1911. *L'association agricole chez les musulmans du Maghreb*. Paris.
1930. *Les terres collectives*. Paris.
Milliot, L., Rectenwald, G., and Benet, H. 1933. *Répertoire alphabétique de jurisprudence, de doctrine et de législation algérienne, tunisienne et musulmane*. Algiers-Paris.
Miquel, A. 1968. *L'Islam et sa civilisation*. Paris.
Monchicourt, C. 1905. "La Tunisie et l'Europe. Quelques documents relatifs aux XVIe, XVIIe et XVIIIe siècles." *R.T.* 12: 516–30.
1910. "La fête de l'Achoura." *R.T.* 17: 276–301.
1913. *La région du Haut-Tell en Tunisie*. Paris.
1916. "Le voyageur Peyssonnel de Kairouan au Kef et à Dougga. Août 1724." *R. T.* 23: 266–77.
1924. *Fragments historiques et statistiques sur la régence de Tunis . . . par le Comte de Filippi*. Paris.
1929. *Documents historiques sur la Tunisie*. Paris.
Montagne, R. 1930. *Les Berbères et le Makhzen dans le Sud du Maroc*. Paris.
1931. *La vie sociale et la vie politique des Berbères*. Paris.
1953. *Révolution au Maroc*. Paris.
Montels, Y. 1889. *Les biens de mainmorte (habbous) en Tunisie*. Tunis.
Murphy, R. F., and Kasdan, L. 1959. "The structure of parallel cousin marriage." *American Anthropologist* 61: 17–29.
Nallino, C. A. 1910. "Venezia e Sfax nel secolo XVIII secondo il cronista arabo Maqdîsh," in *Centanario della nascita di Michele Amari*, vol. 2. Palermo.
Nouschi, A. 1961. *Enquête sur le niveau de vie des populations rurales constantinoises de la conquête à 1919. Essai d'histoire économique et sociale*. Paris.
Pagni, G. 1829. *Lettera di Giovanni Pagni, medico ed archeologico Pisano a Francesco Radi in ragguaglio di quanto egli vidde, ed opero in Tunisia*. Florence.
Pananti, F. 1818. *Avventure e osservazioni di Filippo Pananti sopra le coste di Berberia*, 2 vols. Florence.
Paris, R. 1957. *Histoire du commerce de Marseille*, book V: *De 1660 à 1789. Le Levant*. Paris.
Pauphilet, D. 1953. "La disposition des terres collectives chez les Ouled Chehida." *C. T.* 1, nos. 3–4: 207–28.

1954. "Les procédés de dépiquage en Tunisie." *C. T.* 2, no. 5: 108–12.
1955. "Observations sur le niveau alimentaire de la population tunisienne." C. T. 3, no. 12: 615–26.
Pauphilet, D., and Uzan, Dr. M. 1955. "Aperçus d'ensemble sur le problème alimentaire en Tunisie." *C. T.* 3, no. 12: 627–32.
Payre, G. 1942. "Une fête de printemps au Djérid." *R. T.* n. s., 49–51: 171–8.
Pellissier. 1853. *Description de la régence de Tunis.* Exploration scientifique de l'Algérie, vol. 16. Paris.
Penet, P. 1913. *L'hydraulique agricole dans la Tunisie méridionale.* Tunis.
1931. "L'utilisation des eaux dans les oasis", *Compte Rendu du Congrès agronomique du cinquantenaire*, vol. II. Tunis.
Peters, L. E. 1963. "Aspect of rank and status among muslims in a Lebanese village." In Pitt-Rivers, 159ff.
Peyssonnel and Desfontaines. 1838. *Voyages dans les régences de Tunis et d'Alger*, 2 vols. Paris.
Piollet, P. 1897. *Du régime de la propriété foncière en Tunisie.* Paris.
Pissaloux. 1955. "Production agricole et alimentation humaine en Tunisie." *C. T.* 3, no. 12: 543–614.
Pitt-Rivers, J. 1963. *Mediterranean Countrymen (Essays in the social anthropology of the Mediterranean).* Paris-La Haye.
Plinius Secundus, Gaius (Pliny "the Elder"). 1848. *Historia Naturalis.* ed. Littré. Paris.
Poinssot, L., and Revault, J. 1937. *Tapis tunisiens*, I: *Kairouan.* Paris.
1950. *Tapis tunisiens*, II: *Tapis bédouins à haute laine*; III: *Tissus décorés de Gafsa.* Paris.
1957. *Tapis tunisiens*, IV: *Tissus décorés de Kairouan et du Sahel.* Paris.
Poiret, Abbé. 1789. *Voyage en Barbarie, ou lettres écrites de l'ancienne Numidie pendant les années de 1785 et 1786.* 2 vols. Paris.
Poiron, M. 1925. *Mémoires concernans l'état présent du royaume de Tunis.* Text from the eighteenth-century, ed. by Jean Serres. Paris.
Polanyi, K. 1968. *Primitive, Archaic and Modern Economies.* New York.
Polanyi, K., et al. 1957. *Trade and Market in the Early Empires.* New York.
Poncet, J. 1962. *La colonisation et l'agriculture européenne en Tunisie depuis 1881. Etude de géographie historique et économique.* Paris-La Haye.
Pouyanne, M. 1900. *La propriété foncière en Algérie.* Algiers.
Pressat, P. 1961. *L'analyse démographique.* Paris.
Propp, V. 1965. *Morphologie de conte.* Paris.
Prost, G. 1954. "Utilisation de la terre et production dans le Sud tunisien: Matmata et Ouderna." *C. T.* 2, no. 5: 28–66.
1954. "Habitat et habitation chez les Ouderna et les Matmata." *C. T.* 2, nos. 7–8: 239–53.
Puckler-Muskau, Fürst Von. 1836. *Semilasso in Africa, aus den papieren des Verstorbenen*, 2 vols. Stuttgart. Translated into French, 1837; into English, 1837 (edition consulted).
Rampal, A. 1907. "Une relation inédite du voyage en Barbarie du médecin naturaliste marseillais Peyssonnel." *Bulletin de Géographie historique et descriptive* 2.
Raymond, A. 1973. *Artisans et commerçants au Caire au XVIIIe siècle*, 2 vols. Damascus.
Rectenwald, G. 1912. *Le contrat de khamessat en Afrique du Nord.* Paris.
Renaud, P. J. 1948. *Le calendrier d'Ibn al Bannā' de Marrakech, 1256–1321 J.-C.* Paris.
Rodinson, M. 1965. Entry "Ghida." *E.I.*, 2d ed., pp. 1081–97.

Romano, R. 1956. *Commerce et prix du blé à Marseille au XVIIIe siècle*. Paris.
Romano, S.-F. 1958. "Dans la Sicile du XVIIIe siècle: pauvreté et disette." *Annales, Economies, Sociétés, Civilisations* 13, no. 2.
Rondot, P. 1953. "L'émigration ancienne des Mekna, 1800–1890." *C.T.* 1, no. 1: 18–37.
1955. "Assemblées traditionnelles dans les Nefza." *C.T.* 3, no. 10: 267–75.
Sahlins, M. D. 1961. "The segmentary lineage. An organisation of predatory expansion." *American Anthropologist* 63, no. 2: 322–45.
1968. *Tribesmen*. Englewood Cliffs, N.J.
1972. *Stone Age Economics*. Chicago-New York.
Saint Gervais De. 1736. *Mémoires historiques qui concernent le gouvernement de l'ancien et du nouveau royaume de Tunisie*. Paris.
Santillana, D. 1938. *Instituzioni di diritto musulmano malichita*, 2 vols. Rome.
Savary De Breves. 1628. *Relation des voyages faits . . . aux royaumes de Tunis et d'Alger*. Paris.
Savary des Brûlons, J. 1723. *Dictionnaire universel de commerce*. 3 vols. Paris.
Sayous, A.-E. 1929. *Le commerce des Européens à Tunis depuis le XIIe siècle jusqu'à la fin du XVIe siècle. Exposé et documents*. Paris.
Scemama, R. 1935. *Essai théorique et pratique sur le droit de chefâa en Tunisie*. Tunis.
1938. *La Tunisie agricole et rurale et l'oeuvre de la France*. Paris.
Scemla, A. 1935. *Le contrat d'enzel en droit tunisien*. Paris.
Schnerb, R. 1955. *Le XIXe siècle*. Paris.
Schwartz, M. 1924. *La dia ou prix du sang chez les indigènes de l'Afrique du Nord*. Algiers.
Sebag, P. 1959. "Les juifs de Tunisie au XIXe siècle, d'après J.-J. Benjamin II." *C. T.* 7, no. 28: 489–510.
1965. "La peste dans la régence de Tunis au XVIIe et XVIIIe siècle." *I. B. L. A.* 109: 35–48.
1971. "Une nouvelle de Bandello." *I.B.L.A.* 127: 35–62.
Seghir Ben Youssef, M. 1900. *Mechra el melki, chronique tunisienne, 1705–1771*. Translated by Serres and Lasram. Tunis.
Seklani, M. 1961. "La population de la Tunisie. Situation actuelle et évolution probable jusqu'en 1986." *Population*, 473–504.
Sergent, E. 1941. *Le théisme*, extracted from the *Archives de l'Institut Pasteur d'Alger*.
Shaler, W. 1826. *Sketches of Algiers, Political, Historical, and Civil*. Boston.
Shaw. 1743. *Voyage de M. Shaw M. D. dans plusieurs provinces de la Barbarie et du Levant*, 2 vols. Translated into French. La Haye.
Shaw, S. J. 1966. *Ottoman Egypt in the Age of the French Revolution*. Cambridge, Mass.
Slama, B. 1967. *L'insurrection de 1864 en Tunisie*. Tunis.
Smith, M. G. 1956. "Segmentary lineage systems." *Journal of the Royal Anthropology Institute* 86: 39–80.
Snoussi, M. 1896. *Lettres sur la mejba*. Tunis.
Solignac, M. 1952–3. "Installations hydrauliques de Kairouan et des steppes tunisiennes du VIIe au XIe siècles." *Annales de l'Institut d'Etudes orientales* X–XI. Algiers.
Stirling, P. 1963. "The domestic cycle and the distribution of power in Turkish villages." In Pitt-Rivers.
Stuhlmann, F. 1912. *Ein kulturgeschichtlicher Ausflug in den Aures*. Hamburg.
1914. *Die Mazighvölker*. Hamburg.
Surdon, G. 1939. *Précis élémentaire de droit musulman de l'école malékite d'occident*. Tangier-Fez.

Surin, R. 1948. *Les terres collectives en Afrique du Nord.* Tunis.

1949. "La réforme des terres collectives de Tunisie." *Bulletin économique et social de la Tunisie* (May-June).

Svoronos, N. 1956. *Le commerce de Salonique au XVIIIe siècle.* Paris.

Thévenot. 1727. *Voyages de M. de Thévenot au Levant,* 3d ed., book 2 (from a seventeenth-century text). Amsterdam.

Tollot. 1742. *Nouveau voyage en Levant en 1731.* Paris.

Tridon, A. 1913. *Le régime des habous: ce qu'il est, ce qu'il doit être.* Tunis.

Turquan, V. 1897. "Notes statistiques sur la Tunisie. Dans la France en Tunisie." *Revue générale des Sciences pures et appliquées,* 257ff.

Valensi, J. 1873. *Rapport statistique-économique sur la régence de Tunis.* Vienna.

Valensi, L. 1964. "Le djebel Ousselat au XVIIIe siècle." *C. T.* 12, nos. 47–8: 89–100.

1967. "Esclaves chrétiens et esclaves noirs à Tunis au XVIIIe siècle." *Annales, Economies, Sociétés, Civilisations* 22, no. 6: 1,267–88.

1968. "Le Maghreb précolonial: mode de production archaique ou mode de production féodal?" (in collaboration with R. Gallissot). *La Pensée* (December): 57–93.

1969a. "Islam et capitalisme: production et commerce des chéchias en Tunisie et en France aux XVIIIe et XIXe siècles." *Revue d'histoire moderne et contemporaine* XVII: 376–400.

1969b. *Le Maghreb avant la prise d'Alger (1790–1830).* Paris.

1969c. "Calamités démographiques en Tunisie et en Méditerranée orientale aux XVIIIe et XIXe siècles." *Annales, Economies, Sociétés, Civilisations* 24, no. 6: 1,540–62.

1970. "La conjoncture agraire en Tunisie aux XVIIIe et XIXe siècles." *Revue historique* 494: 321–36.

Valensi, L., and Ben Smail, M. 1971. "Le règne de Hammuda Pacha dans la chronique d'Ibn Abi d-Diaf." *C. T.* 19, nos. 73–4: 87–108.

Vidal-Naquet, P. 1964. "Histoire et idéologie. Karl Wittfogel et le concept de 'Mode de Production asiatique.' " *Annales, Economies, Sociétés, Civilisations* 19, no. 3: 531–48.

Vilar, P. 1956. Problems of the formation of capitalism." *Past and Present* 10: 15–38.

1962. *La Catalogne dans l'Espagne moderne. Recherches sur les fondements économiques des structures nationales,* 3 vols. Paris.

Violard, E. 1905a. *L'Extrême-Sud tunisien.* Tunis.

1905b. *Le contrôle civil de Béja.* Tunis.

1905c. *Le contrôle civil de Souk-el-Arba.* Tunis.

1906. *Enquête sur la Tunisie du Nord. 1902–1903.* Tunis.

Westermarck, E. 1921. *Les cérémonies du mariage au Maroc.* Paris.

1926. *Ritual and Belief in Morocco,* 2 vols. London.

Wittfogel, K. 1964. *Le despotisme oriental.* Paris.

Wolf, E. 1966. *Peasants.* Englewood Cliffs, N.J.

Worms, Dr. 1846. *Recherches sur la constitution de la propriété territoriale dans les pays musulmans.* Paris.

Yacono, X. 1954. "Peut-on évaluer la population de l'Algérie vers 1830." *R. A.* 98, nos. 440–1: 277–307.

Yaqubi. 1937. *Les pays.* Translated by Wiet. Cairo.

Zaccone. 1875. *Notices sur la régence de Tunis.* Paris.

Zerdoumi, N. 1970. *Enfants d'hier. L'éducation de l'enfant en milieu traditionnel algérien*. Paris.
Zeys, P. 1910. *Code annoté de la Tunisie*. Paris.
Zohary, D. 1969. "The progenitors of wheat and barley in relation to domestication and agricultural dispersal in the old world." In Ucko and Dimbleby, eds., *The Domestication and Exploitation of Plants and Animals*. London.

Index

www.ingramcontent.com/pod-product-compliance
Lightning Source LLC
LaVergne TN
LVHW090312210926
848480LV00001B/217
9780521109017